The Electronic Library

The Electronic Library

Fourth edition of *Computers for libraries*

Jennifer Rowley

Head, School of Management and Social Sciences
Edge Hill University College

Library Association Publishing

London

© Jennifer Rowley 1980, 1984, 1993, 1998

Published by
Library Association Publishing
7 Ridgmount Street
London WC1E 7AE

Library Association Publishing is wholly owned by The Library Association.

First published as *Computers for libraries* by Clive Bingley 1980
Second edition Library Association Publishing Ltd 1985
Third edition Library Association Publishing Ltd 1993
This fourth edition as *The electronic library*, 1998

British Library Cataloguing in Publication Data

A catalogue record for this book is available from the British Library.

ISBN 1-85604-149-2

Typeset from author's disk in 10/12pt Castle and Transitional 521 by Library Association Publishing.
Printed and made in Great Britain by Bookcraft (Bath) Ltd, Midsomer Norton, Somerset.

Contents

Acknowledgments

I am grateful to all of those who have made some contribution to the creation of this work. Since this book is a review of current practice, I have drawn widely on other literature and contacts with others in the library and information world. I am particularly grateful to all of the publishers, database producers, systems suppliers and authors who have permitted me to use extracts from their works. These are acknowledged individually as they appear.

The past few years have given me the opportunity to exchange academic and professional debates with many people across a wide discipline base. I have at various times felt myself to be a member of many teams. It is difficult to identify, from amongst these, anyone for special mention, because it might appear that I value others less. Undoubtedly the most significant recent impact on my life as an academic came from my colleagues and friends at the Crewe and Alsager Faculty, Manchester Metropolitan University, primarily in the Department of Business and Management Studies. I wrote the last edition of this book when I had just moved to a new post at Crewe and Alsager, in the expectation that it would be the last. Events overtook all of us, and now it seems like only the beginning.

Preface to the fourth edition

I have spent the intervening years, since the previous edition of this book was published in 1992, less intimately involved than previously with the minutiae of the operation of information systems, and specifically those systems that might be regarded as components in an electronic library. I have instead focused more on the environment in which such systems operate. This contextual understanding has become increasingly important. Not only do information professionals and many other groups need to understand the implications of the information society for the community and organizations in which they live and work, but they, more immediately, need to understand their customers. The final years of the twentieth century have been characterized by a customer and contract culture in which organizations understand that to survive and succeed they need to understand their customers and the benefits that they seek, or can be persuaded to seek, from specific goods or services. Libraries have always acknowledged the imperative of customer service, and have taken initiatives in customer care seriously. In addition, they have been concerned about whether their stock and services meet customer needs. This culture of customer orientation, tightly coupled with their underlying information orientation, is one of the most valuable contributions that library professionals can make to an expanded information profession. Effective customer service depends, not only on the service exchange, but also, most significantly, on the systems that underpin service delivery. This book is concerned with the functions, technicalities and management of those systems. Effective library and information service delivery is dependent upon systems and people, and upon the integration of these two key resources.

The preface to the third edition of this book emphasized the increasing importance of library networking, and the associated shift in emphasis from collection management and development to access-based policies which are concerned with the availability of a document or information. This edition has adopted a new title in recognition of, perhaps, a further phase in the development of the impact of information technology on libraries. The roles of all information providers are being re-evaluated and re-shaped in the advent of opportunities offered by information technology, and specifically the widespread networking that is characterized by the Internet. The walls around the network of libraries have crumbled. Until recently, information technology has been used primarily to facilitate the way in which we have for centuries, as individuals, organizations and societies, processed information. The age when such technologies challenge the way in which we live, the transactions that we perform, the knowledge creation process and the way in which knowledge is evaluated for the public domain, is just beginning to dawn. A significant area which illustrates the issues in a more concrete context is journal publishing. This is particularly significant since journals have for many centuries been a major source of primary information and comprise a significant knowledge base for subsequent 'generations'.

The systems and concepts presented in this book are a strange mixture of the futuristic and the traditional. This reflects the way in which information technology is being experienced in libraries and other information environments. It is easy to postulate the seamless electronic world of the future, but all of our experience of information management, and perhaps more specifically of bibliographic control, teaches that information creation and processing defies such order. The real challenge lies in identifying the steps – and there will be many – that individual organizations in the information industry must and can take to create effective electronic libraries that provide appropriate access to information, coupled with the preservation of cultural heritage, in a world in which information is stored and retrieved in a variety of different formats.

Reviewers of this title have noted that *Computers for libraries* was too broad a brief to contain within one text. The preface to the third edition emphasizes the role of this text in identifying key issues, and in offering a structure which forms a basis for further study. Whilst it would appear that this approach has always been welcomed by readers, the major advances of the past few years have made such an approach increasingly difficult, but at the same time increasingly important. Given the shifting boundaries between the roles of the different organizations in the information marketplace – illustrated perhaps by the complexity of providing answers to the questions 'What is an online search service?' or 'What is a publisher?' – structure has become more difficult to discern. This book then, offers, through its chapters and models, one such structure. This structure reflects the way in which I understand the information marketplace and the library and information professional's role in that market-place. The bibliographies at the ends of chapters provide either further details or other people's perspectives. I hope that together they will help the reader towards a better understanding of the environment in which they operate, and the systems that can be employed to achieve an effective electronic library.

Two further points are necessary on references to other sources. Although I have drawn upon a variety of the references listed at the end of chapters, the style of this text is not that of a formal literature review. In addition to other published literature the content of the text is significantly informed by a wide range of other information sources. In general, it would impair readability to cite specific concepts. On those occasions where specific sources are used or quotations are included, references are indicated in the text, and full citations are listed at the end of each chapter. Many of the topics in this book could be further explored through the use of electronic information resources, such as electronic journals and newsletters, and most importantly through access to the web sites of a number of the organizations cited in this text. Web and Internet site addresses are not included in this text; they are too volatile to merit inclusion in a text of this nature. On the other hand this text includes numerous references to the main brand names in the information industry; these are much more stable than web site addresses. Readers wishing to collect the latest news on developments associated with these brands can quickly locate the current web site of the appropriate organization by submitting these brand names as search terms to an Internet search engine. This is my solution to a hybrid information environment. I hope that it is acceptable to my readers.

The book is divided into three parts: Part 1 is a brief introduction to computer systems; Part 2 examines a number of applications in the area of information retrieval; whilst Part 3 offers an overview of library management systems and related aspects of document delivery. Part 1 introduces the platforms on which applications are mounted. Parts 2 and 3 are concerned with those applications themselves. The terms that are used to describe these applications have evolved significantly over the past few years, and the relationship between systems designed to fulfil the different functions has become yet more blurred. There is some validity in the argument that a more integrated treatment should have been attempted.

Whilst there are a number of models at various points in the text that illustrate the links between the different systems, all documents need a structure and the one presented here serves my purposes as well as any other, whilst at the same time reflecting the way in which the literature is divided. I hope that it makes this text accessible to the reader. Perhaps the next edition of this book will need to be more revolutionary, if books such as this (in printed or electronic form) still have a place in the information society of the future.

Professor Jennifer Rowley

Part 1

Introduction to information technology

1

Introducing the electronic library

LEARNING OUTCOMES

This chapter examines the basis of the concept of the electronic library. By briefly reviewing key developments in the evolution of the electronic library over the past 20 years, and placing these in the context of the Library and Information Commission's Vision for 2020, it seeks to contextualize today's systems in a broader scenario. At the end of this chapter you will:

- be aware of the ways in which the electronic library may be understood
- have an awareness of systems in the electronic library
- be familiar with the major trends in the development of information systems in libraries over the past 20 years
- be able to reflect on the relationship between today's systems and future visions
- appreciate that future visions imply changed marketplace roles for all stake-holders
- be aware of the wider social and political implications of electronic information processing.

1.1 The electronic library

'The term "electronic library" means many things to many people and in any study of the literature the reader must be aware of the myriad interpretations which are applied to it, as the terminology has not yet settled' (Day et al. 1996). Such a quotation suggests that the use of the title *The electronic library* should be approached with caution. On the other hand, the earlier title of this text *Computers for libraries* now sounds outdated with regard to both the terms that it uses ('computers' and 'libraries') and the way in which those terms are juxtaposed. The literature abounds in terms that might have provided inspiration: library without walls, networked library, desktop library, logical library, virtual library, information nerve centre, information management centre (Corrall, 1995), and digital library. The term 'electronic library' is widely used and best fits the concepts that will be covered in this book. But what does it mean? This is a topic that has been well debated in the literature. For example, Oppenheim (1997) describes it as 'an organized and managed collection of information in a variety of media (text, still image, moving image, sound, or combinations thereof), but all in digital form'. The collection is organized and managed for the benefit of an actual or potential user population, and in particular is structured for easy access to its contents. Typically, such an electronic library will include a number of search or navigation aids that will both operate within that particular library and allow access to other collections of information connected by networks worldwide. Trolley (1995) defines an electronic library as 'the common vision of librarians, publishers, technology experts and researchers of access to all information anywhere, anytime.' This concept of universality of access is shared by many writers, but it also raises the issue of the distinction between an electronic library and a virtual library. For example, Collier et al. (1993) see an electronic library as a physically identifiable library but with no print, and which is part of a virtual library. Beckman (1993) argues that the difference between the electronic and virtual library is that the electronic library can still maintain a physical presence, whereas the virtual library, since it is perceived as transparent, will have transparent physical facilities and transparent librarians. Poulter (1993), for example, regards the Internet as a virtual library, although it might be argued that it does not meet some of the other criteria for a library such as a defined user population and sufficiently sophisticated search aids. Others might argue that the real electronic library is not a library at all, but a data warehouse.

This book is not about electronic libraries in the full digital form in the sense of the definitions that we have briefly introduced above. There are two reasons for this. First, and perhaps most concretely, it is concerned with the path *towards* the electronic library; since it is grounded in current practice, it is constrained by current systems and libraries. Secondly, I remain unconvinced that optimum access to information and documents for all of the different segments of library customers, or more broadly, information users, will be offered through completely digital collections in the foreseeable future. Significant archival collections remain in print and other forms, and electronic information has been associated with significant increases in the quantity of print on paper. My vision is of a multimedia library which reflects the different forms and formats that its community find convenient for communication and storage. Not all information or documents will be in digital form, and not all will be available for access over digital networks. The real challenge will not differ much from that which libraries face today: to manage a multimedia collection for their community or customers. On the other hand, the options and tools available to support this process are undoubtedly likely to undergo further significant change.

Reflection   Make a checklist which illustrates how you understand the concept of an electronic library

1.2   Systems in the electronic library

Library management systems focus on ordering and acquisitions, cataloguing, online public access catalogues, circulation control, serial control, management information, interlibrary loans and community information. Standardization, increased efficiency, networking and enhanced services have resulted from the introduction of computer systems. Computer systems were first seen as particularly appropriate in those organizations or networks where the number of library management transactions was large. The first systems were based on mainframe and minicomputers. Later, the increasing availability of microcomputer software and hardware extended the use of library management systems to all sizes and categories of libraries. Library management systems can be viewed as the systems that manage access to documents in a library collection, or in a more limited way, documents that can be temporarily drawn into library collections through, for instance, interlibrary loans. The central concern is to maintain the library collection, and to monitor the whereabouts of documents so that library staff and customers are aware of the availability and status of the documents in the collection. Increasingly OPACs (online public access catalogues) have improved their search facilities to include many of the features originally only encountered in information retrieval applications, so that, provided that the catalogue records provide sufficient information, they also provide rudimentary information retrieval, which identifies the information held within the documents. In addition, many OPACs act as windows on a wider collection of resources than is available within one library, including Internet resources and the collections in other libraries.

Information retrieval applications were traditionally designed to provide access to information, as distinct from documents. In many instances they give access to information in documents. Originally, this was achieved through bibliographic databases, which included records for articles in journals and other documents. More recently, information retrieval applications have provided access to information embedded in electronic documents. Currently this is most effectively achieved with primarily text-based documents, but most systems also include some facilities for access to multimedia documents, and access to information and objects within multimedia documents (such as pictures and video clips) will become more important as the number of multimedia documents increases.

Information retrieval applications include document management systems, online search services, the Internet and CD-ROM. Current-awareness services and printed indexes are other examples of special-purpose information retrieval systems. Document management systems may be created to manage the corporate document collection within an organization; the document management system may store the documents in electronic form and provide appropriate retrieval mechanisms so that individual documents, or sets of documents on specific topics, can be retrieved. In some systems, the documents may be held in microfiche or print form, and only the index is in electronic form. The Internet is a worldwide network of telecommunications networks, which provides access to a number of computers, or servers. Search engines support retrieval in this undefined and enormous bank of information. Some of the computers or servers are those of the online search services which provide access to selected and evaluated databases as a commercial concern. Another way of accessing some of the same databases, and also others that are not available over the international network, is to acquire the database on CD-ROM. Organizations, and specifically libraries, may then choose to network these CD-ROMs. The CD-ROM is supplied with search or information retrieval software, so that it is possible to locate specific information within the database.

With the advent of the electronic library, the distinction between library management systems and information retrieval systems is gradually being eroded. This has commenced with improvements in the information retrieval facilities available in OPACs, but needs to progress much further. Ultimately the way in which information or documents are retrieved should be dependent upon the needs of the anticipated client group, and not on the accident of its type of publication (e.g. journal, book or directory), or its form of publication (e.g. print or electronic) or its location (e.g. in a local or remote database). In such an environment, it will also be necessary to reflect on the nature of access. The concept of loan is something of an anachronism, but copy and ownership (which appears to be the only viable alternative at present) may not be the optimum solution either. Once many of these issues have been resolved there will be no distinction between library management systems and information retrieval systems, but in the meantime they are likely to continue to coexist, with overlapping but largely complementary functions.

Table 1.1 *Systems in the electronic library*

	Local Resources	External Resources
Documents	Library management systems Document management systems	Document delivery
Information	CD-ROM	Online hosts The Internet

Reflection Table 1.1 offers a simplified picture of systems in a library. Do you know of any examples of applications which suggest that the Internet might also be placed elsehwere in the table from where it has been placed?

When the first edition of this book was written, the norm was to treat library management systems and information retrieval as two very distinct fields. I argued then, and believe that it is even more the case today, that common technology underlies both types of systems, and that similar developments feature simultaneously in the different categories of systems.

Reflection   What is a document? Why is this concept important in library management systems?

1.3   Developments in the past 20 years

These are exciting and changing times. Sometimes when the network is down, or e-mail communication does not satisfactorily transmit attached files, progress can seem annoying slow, but the reality is that the pace of change in the possibilities that technological developments have offered information managers is a challenge even to the most enthusiastic change agent. Figure 1.1 gives an example of electronic information use in 1998.

This and the previous three editions of *Computers for libraries* map the relationship between information technology and libraries (see Table 1.2). In the context, for example, of library management systems (in those days called library housekeeping systems), the first edition reveals a series of separate systems supporting the separate functions of, say, acquisitions, cataloguing and circulation control, reminiscent of the file-based approach of early transaction systems. Actual case study systems described in that edition were primarily developed by library cooperatives, often working within regional or national boundaries. Computer-based systems were a novelty and a target for eager professional visitors. By the third edition, the range of modules and functions supported had expanded significantly, the functions within each module were much more sophisticated and online operation with workstations throughout the library system was the norm. Systems were marketed by organizations that specialized in the design and implementation of library management systems and had considerable expertise in the area. Many libraries were installing their second or third-generation system, and library managers were becoming much more discriminating in system specification and selection.

In 1980 (Rowley 1980) it was necessary to justify a book on computers and to answer the question 'Why use a computer?' The answer then was framed in terms of:

- the need to handle more information and a greater level of activity
- the need for greater efficiency
- opportunities for offering new or enhanced services
- opportunities for cooperation and centralization in the creation and exploitation of shared data.

Sitting at his desk in his office, Joe has just returned from a meeting with his manager, the Research Manager, who has asked him to investigate the state of the art of non-destructive testing of aluminium tubes, and to prepare a report which his manager can use to investigate the practices at a new subsidiary, with a view to offering advice for continuing improvement of the product. Joe turns on his computer, and commences his search by scanning the catalogue of the nearest significant university library to which the company holds corporate membership. Joe keys in the search term 'non-destructive testing' and uses the Boolean logic operator AND to narrow the search to include just aluminium. A search output window reveals that the search set for this search is empty. Joe deletes 'aluminium' from the search statement and tries again. This time he identifies three books, whose bibliographic details are revealed in a further window. Joe decides that each of these would be useful, and selects the interlibrary loan option to order these books for borrowing. They will arrive some time tomorrow. In the meantime, Joe performs an online search of Metals Index 1988 – date, by linking up to the online host Dialog, through its World Wide Web interface. The company is registered with DIALOG as a user, and as Joe is frequently involved in preparing reports on specific topics, he is an experienced searcher, and knows the best search strategies and understands the terminology of metallurgy. He keys in the terms 'non-destructive', 'aluminium and tubes', and 'testing', linking all of these with a Boolean AND. This search retrieves around 100 hits. Joe does not wish to read so many articles and reports, so he scans the bibliographic citations of the retrieved documents. The most recent items are at the top of the list. He marks for further consultation any items that are from within the last two years, in English, and appear otherwise relevant; when necessary he opens a further window and reads the abstract of an article; this produces a set of 22 items. Some of these are available electronically in full text, whilst others he needs to order through the special document delivery service that is offered by the online host. Joe downloads onto his local network server, for later consultation, the full text of those documents that might be useful, and places a few document delivery orders, indicating that he would prefer delivery by fax, so that the documents will arrive by later that day. He considers whether it would be worthwhile to conduct the search on another database, but decides that he has sufficient information to be working on for the moment. His entire search has taken less than half an hour. Having scanned a number of citations and abstracts, he now has a sense of some of the important issues and debates on his topic. He opens his word-processing package and makes a few notes on the proposed structure of the report that he will work on tomorrow, when most of the documents that he wants to consult will have arrived. He makes a cup of coffee, replies to some e-mails and returns to some experimental work in which he is involved. When he does come to write the report, he writes with the aid of a word-processing package which allows much flexibility in the formatting of the report, and supports editing and corrections. Bibliographic citations and a few quotations can be imported from the downloaded documents. He sends an electronic draft to his manager, who makes a few annotations that can easily be incorporated into a final version of the report.

Fig. 1.1   *Information processing in 1998*

We are now operating in an environment in which innovative use of information technology in organizations in general has led to the creation of new products, improved service and dramatically reduced costs.

These types of information use can be described as strategic, and are generally managed by strategic information systems. Strategic information systems allow the business to achieve competitive advantage. Such systems differ from traditional IT systems in that their focus is on treating information on a strategic resource. Specifically strategic information systems are:

- outward-looking with a focus on the service to customers
- offering real benefit to the customers
- capable of changing the marketplace's perception of the organization.

Not surprisingly these dimensions feature in the changes that are evident between the third edition and this edition. Let us revisit the developments between the first and third editions, and summarize the changes that are reflected in the current edition:

Table 1.2   *Computers for Libraries contents lists*

First edition	Third edition
Introduction	Introduction
Planning and designing the computerized library system	Computers
Computers	Systems
Information structure and software	Information structure and software
Databases	Databases
Information storage retrieval systems and the computer	Managing information systems
Current awareness services	External online hosts
Retrospective searching	Optical discs
Printed indexes	Text information management systems
Library housekeeping operations and the computer	Other information retrieval topics
Acquisitions, ordering and cataloguing systems	Functions of library management systems
Circulation control and document delivery systems	Overview of the market for library management systems
Serials control	Networks
159pp.	305pp.

Embedded communications and information technology

This is seen as the main means for recording and managing transactions with users and suppliers. In addition, a significant proportion of the documents and information supplied to users are in electronic form.

Systems management

Systems development has focused on migration from one system to another; new systems are almost always upgrades to offer enhanced functionality; systems suppliers need to be able to deliver trouble-free upgrade and migration. Also, systems are less frequently acquired as turnkey packages including hardware and software, but are acquired as system components that need to be integrated into an operational system.

Integration

Integration of components of systems, such as in a library management system, is taken for granted. Through open systems (see below) the focus for integration has turned more to integration with other systems. So, for example, a university will seek to use common student records for library access, access to information technology resources, and contact with students concerning results and financial transactions.

Technology

Advances in technology continue. Multimedia documents can only be stored and transmitted with technologies that offer increased storage capacity and increased communication bandwidth. Perhaps, since no workstation is standalone any more, the major trends in technology can be encapsulated through an examination of the changes in the now not so humble PC. In the last five years, new chips with different processing technology offer increased and faster processing capacity. To accommodate multimedia operation PCs have sound cards, speakers, CD-ROM drives and video cards. To accommodate communication, sophisticated high-speed modems are standard.

Open systems

The Internet is the ultimate open system; this would not have been achieved without the range of open systems standards that are now well established and widely recognized. Having achieved a platform in which many systems can communicate with each other, and users can benefit from relatively cheap international communication and file exchange, applications are emerging in which the need for security, personal data protection and controlled access to information is more pressing. Open systems now offer a very important avenue through which organizations can communicate with their customers.

User-friendly interfaces

The widespread penetration of GUI (graphical user interface) based interfaces, the use of multimedia interfaces and the implementation of other public access interfaces have been essential prerequisites to wider public use of information systems. Public access systems demand self-explanatory interfaces.

....

Reflection   Examine and compare the interfaces of two systems available to you. Are there any special facilities that support, separately, both novice and expert users?

....

1.4 Future visions

Section 1.3 has been systems focused, because it has taken as its inspiration earlier editions of this text, which have shared this systems-based perspective. Placing these systems developments in a wider context, and examining the cumulative effect on information processing, it can be seen that the past 20 years have witnessed:

- more information, communicated from
- a greater range of sources, through
- a wider range of channels, many of which have
- faster response and turnaround times.

The competitiveness and effectiveness of individuals, organizations and societies is increasingly dependent on their information-processing and knowledge-creation capacity, which means that there is a greater focus on individual, organizational and societal competencies in relation to communication, information processing and knowledge creation.

Information management is concerned with the facilitation of this information processing through, in the widest sense of the term, the creation and evolution of systems. These systems have been concerned with imposing a structure that deals with selection, time, hierarchy and sequence. These systems are under continual review. It is not a case of one process or medium of information processing being substituted for another, but rather of a diversification of systems, processes and technologies. In addition, progress and development paths are distinct for different disciplines, individuals, organizations and communities. Information managers need to be able to create systems that evolve effectively in a rapidly changing environment. If they succeed in this challenge, the Library and Information Commission's Vision for 2020 (see Figure 1.2) will become a reality. There are, however, a number of challenges that will need to be tackled, and issues that will need resolution, in working towards this vision. These are issues concerned with the structure of the information marketplace, and a range of societal issues associated with access to, and ownership of, information. These are explored in the next two sections.

- Governments, companies and individuals will put a top priority on information.
- The UK will be an information/knowledge based society with the UK acting a knowledge powerhouse and hub of the global information economy.
- In the global information economy the UK will be a world leader in connectivity, standards, content development, management and mediation skills.
- Industry and commerce will be more knowledge intensive learning organizations.
- There will be an information economy which empowers citizens through a network of information/knowledge centers acting as flagships of access in their community.
- There will be a digital library collection coordinated nationally/internationally embracing the world's knowledge and creativity in which the UK's heritage of intellectual property will be globally available in digital form.
- Value added content and universal connectivity will ensure that every individual will have unfettered access to global information/knowledge.
- Individuals will need a range of literacies to enable them to maximize their potential individually and collectively.

Fig. 1.2   *Library and Information Commission's Vision for 2020*

....

Reflection   With reference to Figure 1.2, what literacies do you suppose individuals might need in order to enable them to maximize their potential individually and collectively in an information age?

....

1.5 Changing marketplace roles

In the same way that business or marketing systems exist in a wider environment, so the contexts in which information management occurs can be placed in a wider environment. Here we draw a parallel between the information environment and a marketing or business environment. Whilst sociological, technological and political forces are important in the information environment, those factors which transcend national and international boundaries and are arguably the most important in determining access to information, with all of the associated social and political ramifications, are those of the marketplace. Indeed, in recent years, most governments in developed countries have recognized the need to put in place infrastructures that ensure that not only are their industries competitive in a global marketplace, but also their public sector organizations are exposed to marketplace pressures. Thus, marketplace issues play a significant role in determining access to information and the role that information professionals play in facilitating such access. What is the electronic information marketplace? Schwuchow (1995) warns that: 'the very definition of the information sector is in flux. It is indeed very difficult to define this sector of economic activity because of the dramatic development in the technologies and all of the recent mergers in the entertainment, telecommunications and information industries.'

Nevertheless, it is important that information professionals seek to understand the key characteristics of this marketplace, however elusive and changing its boundaries might be. Key issues are the nature of electronic information as a product, the identification of market segments and the stakeholders who will shape the industry, coupled with issues such as price and technological distribution. The opportunities offered by enhanced electronic information and communication systems have affected the way in which businesses operate and are impacting on both internal communication and communication with suppliers and customers. For example, marketing with IT is beginning to establish itself with the emergence of multimedia kiosks, database marketing and commerce over the Internet (Rowley 1995; Rowley 1996). The application of such systems also fuels the drive towards an information society. All parties in the information industry, as shown in Table 1.3, are on the front line of such changes. Whilst in other organizations effective information management may be a means to an end, or an internal product that supports staff in achieving organizational objectives, the primary product of most of the players in the information industry is information management, either in the form of a service, such as information management consultancy or library service, or as a product which provides packaged information, such as a database or a printed directory.

Table 1.3 lists some of the key stakeholders in the traditional publishing process, and describes their roles in terms that are applicable in both a print-based and an electronic environment, with the environment influencing both the way in which the product is created, as in, for example, electronic refereeing or editing, and the nature of the final product, as, for example, with a multimedia encyclopaedia. In some contexts some of these roles may be merged, or one organization may adopt more than one role. Many of the stakeholder categories can be split into other subcategories. Thus in the redistributor's role we might also include national document delivery centres, cooperative interlibrary loan services, commercial document delivery services, offprints and reprints, and current-awareness service suppliers. Each category of stakeholders hides a whole sector of organizations which will be concerned to stay in business and to develop their existing competencies, product and service range and customer base to secure a position in the developing marketplace. There is already some competition for the roles of publisher and distributor from organizations such as Microsoft and some of the PTTs.

Table 1.3 *Stakeholder roles in the electronic information marketplace*

Role	Example
Producers of intellectual content	Authors, illustrators, multimedia creation teams.
Controllers of intellectual content, with reference to quality standards and suitability	Editors, referees, reviewers
Publishers establish a corporate brand image and act as an interface between producers of intellectual content and distributors	Publishers, printers, database producers
Distributors ensure that the document/ information reaches the potential customers and engage in appropriate promotion	Library supply agents, booksellers, Web sites, online search services, Videotex services, Audiotex services, distributors of CD-ROM
Archivers maintain archival copy for later retrieval	Libraries, private collectors
Redistributors make documents or information available to others	Libraries, educational institutions copying for students, information consultants
Users	Corporate and individual users

Reflection List some of the roles that an academic librarian fulfils today. How might these be fulfilled in a world that was consistent with the Vision for 2020 in Figure 1.2?

1.6 Challenges for the information society

Information systems are changing society. The ultimate scenario of the virtual society, where all communication is electronic, and processes such as teleworking, telelearning, and teleconferencing, or even videoconferencing, substitute for actual person-to-person contact, must have significant implications for the way in which human beings satisfy their need for interaction with one another. Furthermore, in such a society the traditions that have evolved over centuries concerning the conventions surrounding meetings with other people, the serendipity associated with new social contacts and the use of non-verbal communication, will all be challenged. Most of us will be relieved to recognize that this new era will not emerge overnight. Currently, information and information systems, and the associated communication, are gradually increasing their impact on our society and the values that we espouse. The key issues are:

Globalization

Improved telecommunications allow people to form their own communities irrespective of geographical location. This supports the formation of groups of people with similar interests, politics or objectives. At this level there is the potential for the development of the global village. One other consequence of the global village is that improved communication changes people's horizons and expectations of life styles. This is likely to impact on the other aspect of globalization: the global economy. There are a number of characteristics of the global economy that are likely to be in a state of evolution. These include:

- the regional differentiation of the global economy
- the segmentation of the global economy
- sources of competitiveness in a global economy.

Changing employment patterns

Initially, information technology was seen as challenging the established order in the workplace, and as a means of eliminating clerical tasks. It was therefore anticipated that the introduction of information technology would herald unemployment and less jobs. This has probably happened to some extent, but the overall picture is not as simple as this. One consequence of the information age has been to open up global competition, and to speed the pace of change. Workers need to adapt to this change. There is increased focus on flexible working patterns, and a variety of different contractual arrangements between employees and employers. Those who expect to find another job need to take responsibility for keeping their skills up-to-date. These changes are creating new categories, including networkers, flexitimers and the unemployed.

The network enterprise

The nature of corporations is subject to change. Shifts towards flexible production have been witnessed, and interfirm working, with associated corporate strategic alliances, has had a significant impact on marketplaces, employment and national economies. Information technology has increased organizations' capacity to form business networks and networked enterprises.

Information rich, information poor – or who pays for information?

There is a fear that, as the value of information becomes more widely recognized, and access to it becomes more straightforward, whole sections of society will be disenfranchised. This may take us back to the original concept of a public library, or in this case the electronic public library!

Intellectual property and copyright issues

These are not unrelated to marketplace issues. Quality information, whether it be text, statistics or multimedia, costs time, effort and money to create. Producers seek to recoup their investment. Yet it is difficult to enforce appropriate copyright protection with electronic documents. It is too easy to copy or download sections of databases.

Security and data protection

Some data – including, for example, financial transactions, national security and commercially sensitive data – needs to be kept secure. In addition, we may all rightly be sensitive about the data about us that is stored in a variety of different databases. Data protection safeguards the privacy of the individual.

Standards

This is an issue with which the computer industry has wrestled long and hard. Essentially, if a major player can achieve competitive advantage it can make its standards for a new technology the de facto standard for the industry. On the other hand, all players recognize the need for standards. This type of market/power struggle in relation to standards is likely to recur with each new advance in technology and may well act as a hindrance to the creation of a fully networked, intercommunicating community.

Archiving and bibliographical control

Libraries have long been concerned to maintain an archival record of information. Electronic documents pose many problems for the maintenance of an archival record. Electronic documents may be dynamic and changing documents, and the creation of a number of different versions is relatively easy. Which version should form the archive document? Clearly is it is difficult to decide what constitutes a document; it is also difficult to maintain bibliographical control over these documents. Other questions include:

- What data should be archived?
- Which storage media should be used?
- How long will the database last without deterioration?
- How can individuals access archived databases?

If these issues can be satisfactorily addressed, then the scenario in Figure 1.2 may be the reality in 2020. Technologically this model is already possible, although there are no implementations that draw together all of the components of this experience. Before this scenario can become an experience shared by whole communities, it is necessary that more attention be paid to the issues outlined in this section. Indeed, the way in which these issues are addressed may determine the boundaries, nature, culture and values of the emergent virtual communities. As the past 25 years have shown, this will take time, and as we grope towards one mirage, so alternative visions will evolve, and our projections for the future will prove to have been partially realized. It is just as well that the process is sufficiently interesting that it is not necessary to reach the end of the journey!

Reflection   Discuss the issues associated with the archiving of:

- a collection of print-based newspapers
- a collection of electronic newspapers
- a video of a television programme
- company information such as that displayed on company Websites.

Summary   There are a number of different interpretations that can be applied to the term, the 'electronic library', but this book is really about the path towards the electronic library. The electronic library features two main categories of systems: library management systems, and information retrieval systems such as document management systems, online search services, CD-ROM and the Internet. There have been many developments in these systems over the past 20 years, and such systems can now be regarded as integral to the operation of organizations. The Library and Information Commissions Vision for 2020 summarizes directions for future development. Development will lead to changes in the roles of many of the stakeholders in the information marketplace. Progress towards the information society will, however, be influenced by the way in which issues such as globalization, standards, intellectual property rights, security and bibliographic control are tackled.

REVIEW QUESTIONS

1   What do you understand by the term electronic library?
2   What are the main systems in an electronic library?

3   Make a checklist of the main developments which have con-
     tributed towards the evolution of the electronic library in the
     last 20 years.
4   What are the key aspects of the Library and Information
     Commission's Vision for 2020?
5   What are the main stakeholder roles in the electronic informa-
     tion marketplace?
6   What are the key issues that need to be managed in the infor-
     mation society?

....

IMPLEMENTATION CASE STUDY: DE MONTFORT UNIVERSITY

Definition of the electronic library

When we at De Montfort University conceived the ELINOR project for our new campus at Milton Keynes in 1991, we came up with the definition of 'a teaching and
learning environment for higher education in which information is held primarily in
electronic form'.

That was the first electronic library project in Britain and we were very much
engaged in speculative research. It was a working definition which needed to be
flexible and not too precise as we were dealing with many variables across all the relevant areas of technology, publishing, copyright, information management and user
issues. Our caution was justified. Although our vision and strategy has been
absolutely borne out by developments in e:Lib and other initiatives worldwide, many
practicalities could not have been predicted. Six years on we have learned a great
deal, and the Internet and World Wide Web have developed out of all recognition.
From our first project ELINOR, which was concerned with document image processing approaches, we have worked with pictorial imaging and retrieval (ELISE 1) SGML
(ELSA) PDF (Phoenix). In ELISE 11 we are looking at video, audio and multimedia
packages in the electronic library context. We have learned about and stimulated
developments in licensing of electronic products, in user aspects and interfaces, and
made progress in standards, particularly Z39.50 for images.

It helps in reaching a definition to agree that the electronic library is not about
library automation. It is not just the Internet, because everyone agrees the Internet
is anarchic. It is not datasets of secondary data. All of these are relevant aspects or
components, but the necessary and sufficient characteristic of the electronic library
must be that it consists of primary material primarily in electronic form. In 1995 we
enhanced our definition to take account of research and produced the following: 'a
managed environment of multimedia materials in digital form, designed for the benefit of its user population, structured to facilitate access to its contents and equipped
with aids to navigation of the global network.'

We did not expect our definition to last for long, but for now it appears to be holding up well.

The electronic library and the virtual library

As De Montfort University we have just completed an extension to our 1970s-built Kimberlin Library. It is 4000m2 in area and consists of 600 networked reader places, with no accommodation for books. A digital library facility based on an IBM SP2 supercomputer is being developed to deliver electronic products to the new extension and to the other campuses of the distributed university. In one way one could argue this is a true electronic library, but on the other hand it could be some time yet before the majority of information is delivered to students in electronic form. Certainly we are some way off spending more on electronic information than on printed products.

In a university context it is clear to me that space for information and study will always be important, even if a substantial new market for home or workplace-based distance learning develops. The library as a conducive space for learning is important to students even if it is full of computers, not books. The electronic library therefore is a library, which satisfies our definition above, but is associated with a physical space to which people can go for services delivered in electronic form.

The virtual library, however, implies no sense of physical location, whether for the end-user or the source. The user can access the information from anywhere and the information can be held anywhere. There is a sense of randomness in that it is irrelevant to the user where the information is held.

For me, therefore, the virtual library is location-independent, accessed and delivered over networks, while an electronic library can be visited in person. The virtual library can, of course, be offered by the electronic library but not the other way round.

Whether this differentiation is important to any but a purist is debatable. I expect most people will continue to use the terms indiscriminately.

The vision

Well, it depends. The pharmaceutical library of 2005 will be a rather different thing from the suburban branch library, but to take an example let us consider the library of a medium-sized new university of about 10,000 students deriving its income 80% from teaching and 20% from research. The following scenario is quite feasible:

1 All university courseware, support materials, videos, simulation and key reading are held in the electronic library.
2 University programmes are delivered primarily through student-centred, resource-based methods.
3 The library is a member of the National Digital Library consortium and through it the Global Digital Library.
4 Staff is composed of multi-skilled learning support people comprising information, IT and academic expertise.
5 Information access/study time per student is 70% electronic, 30% print.
6 Library space is 70% networked study space, 30% book stock.

7   Expenditure is 70% electronic, 30% print.
8   Usage is regulated by user smartcards giving access to both free-at-point-of-use services and chargeable services.
9   All study bedrooms are networked.
10 All services are accessible from home, workplace and public libraries.

Mel Collier
De Montfort University

....

References

Beckman, M. and Pearson, E. M. (1993) 'Understanding the needs of users: the timeliness factor', in Helal, A. H. and Weiss, J.(eds.), *Opportunity 2000: understanding the needs of users in an electronic library*, 15th International Essen Symposium, Essen, University Library, 307–21.

Collier, M. W., Ramsden, A. and Wu, Z. (1993) 'The electronic library: virtually a reality?', in Helal, A. H. and Weiss, J.(eds.), *Opportunity 2000: understanding the needs of users in an electronic library*, 15th International Essen Symposium, Essen, University Library, 136–46.

Corrall, S. (1995) 'Academic libraries in the information society', *New library world*, **96**, 35–42.

Day, J. et al. (1996) 'Higher education, teaching, learning and the electronic library: a review of the literature for the IMPEL2 project: monitoring organisational and cultural change', *The new review of academic librarianship*, **2**, 131–204.

Oppenheim, C. (1997) 'Editorial', *International journal of electronic library research*, **1** (1), 1–2.

Lord Phillips of Ellesmere (1997) 'Information society: agenda for action in the UK', *Journal of information science*, **23** (1), 1–8.

Poulter, A. (1993) 'The virtual library: virtually a reality?', *Aslib information*, 1993, 159–60.

Risher, C. 'Libraries, copyright and the electronic environment', *The electronic library*, **14** (5), 449–52.

Rowley, J. (1980) *Computers for libraries*, London, Bingley, 1980.

Rowley, J. (1995) 'Multimedia kiosks in retailing', *International journal of retail and distribution management*, **23** (5), 32–40.

Rowley, J. (1996) 'Retailing and shopping on the Internet', *Internet research: networking applications and policy*, **6** (1), 81–91.

Sack, J. R. (1986) 'Open systems for open minds: building the libraries without walls', *College and research libraries*, **47** (6), 535–44.

Schwuchow, W. (1995) 'Measuring the information market(s): a personal experience', *Journal of information science*, **21** (2), 123–32.

Sheppard, E. and East, H. (1995) 'Access to wide area networked bibliographic databases: end-users behaviour and perceptions', in *Online information 95: 19th International Online Information Meeting Proceedings, London, December 1995*, 109–25, Learned Information

Trolley, J. (1995) 'Planning the electronic library', *Bulletin of the American Society for Information Science*, **21**, 17–20.

Webb, T. D. (1995) 'The frozen library: a model for twenty first century libraries', *The electronic library*, **13** (1), 21–6.

Bibliography

Arnold, S. E. (1990) 'Marketing electronic information: theory, practice and challenges 1980–1990', *Annual review of information science and technology*, **25**, 87–144.

Baldwin, C. (1996) 'Superjournals deliver the goods', *Library Association record*, **1** (2), 37–8.

Barker, P. (1994) 'Electronic libraries: visions of the future', *The electronic library*, **12** (4), 221–29.

Barker, P. (1996) 'Living books and dynamic electronic libraries', *The electronic library*, **14** (6), 491–501.

Batt, C. (1997) *Information technology in public libraries*, London, Library Association Publishing.

Benn, T. (1994) 'Information and democracy', *The electronic library*, **13** (1), 57–62.

Bloch, R. H. and Hesse, C. (1993) *Future libraries*, Berkeley, University of California.

Bradley, P. (1997) 'The information mix: Internet, online or CD-ROM', *Managing information*, **4** (9), 35–7.

Castells, M. (1996) *The rise of the network society*, Oxford, Blackwell.

Cornish, G. (1997) *Copyright: interpreting the law for library, archive and information services*, London, Library Association Publishing.

Cornish, G. P. (1997) 'Copyright, libraries and the electronic information environment: discussions and developments in the United States', *IFLA journal*, **23** (4), 280–3.

Cox, J. (1997) 'Publishers, publishing and the Internet: how journal publishing will survive and prosper in the electronic age', *The electronic library*, **15** (2), 125–31.

Eisenschitz, T. and Turner, P. (1997) 'Rights and responsibilities in the digital age: problems with stronger copyright in an information society', *Journal of information science*, **23** (3), 209–24.

King, H. (1995) 'Walls round the electronic library', *The electronic library*, 11 (3), 165–74.

Martin, W. J. (1995) *The global information society*, Aldershot, Aslib/Gower.

Malinconico, S. M. and Worth, J. C. (1996) 'Electronic libraries: how soon?', *Program*, 30 (2), 133–48

Miido, H. (1997) 'The librarian and he library user: what the future holds', *The electronic library*, 15 (1), 15–22.

Myhill, M. (1997) 'The electronic library and the former Soviet Union and Mongolia', *Program*, 31 (1), 23–32.

Norman, S. (1997) 'Copyright and fair use in the electronic age', *IFLA journal*, 23 (4), 295–8.

2

Hardware

....

LEARNING OUTCOMES

Computer systems comprise five components:

- hardware – the physical components of computers that you can see
- software – the programs which are placed into the hardware to tell it how to solve a particular problem or execute a task
- networks, which link computers together so that they can communicate with each other
- databases – the form in which data is held in systems
- people, who use and design the systems.

This chapter focuses on the basic hardware configuration of a computer and its components. At the end of this chapter you will:

- understand the role of the basic components of a computer
- appreciate the importance of the central processing unit or processor in determining the processor of the system
- be aware of external storage devices
- be aware of the range of data input devices and the context in which each is appropriate
- be aware of the range of output devices and printers
- be aware of the different processing modes.
....

2.1 Introduction

In order to understand the systems that are described later in this book, it is necessary to be acquainted with the basic hardware or physical components of computer systems. This chapter offers a brief overview of the main components of such systems. It starts by examining the basic configuration of a computer system, and then goes on to examine its components in greater detail. The basic configuration as described below is equally applicable to all types of computer system, whether we are considering mainframe, minicomputer or microcomputer systems. The differences between these types of system are summarized in the following chapter. The current chapter concludes with a brief review of processing modes.

2.2 The basic computer configuration

A computer system accepts data as input, processes that data and provides data as output. During the processing the data must be stored. The processing is controlled by a sequence of instructions – the program – which is stored in the computer. The basic components of a computer system are therefore input devices, processor, backing storage devices and output devices. These fit together as illustrated in Figure 2.1.

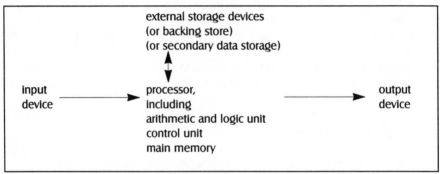

Fig. 2.1 *Basic computer configuration*

The functions of the components of a computer system

The various components of a computer system each have unique contributions to make. These can be summarized as follows:

Input devices accept data, convert data into machine-readable form and transmit data to the processor unit. The **processor** comprises the control unit, the arithmetic and logic unit and the main memory. Their functions are:

1   **The control unit** decodes and executes program instructions, and controls and coordinates data movements within the processor, and between the processor and other components of the computer system.
2   **The arithmetic and logic unit** carries out arithmetic operations and performs logical operations.
3   **The main memory** stores programs during their execution, stores data that are being used by the current program, and stores the operating system which controls the operation of the computer system.

4   **The secondary or backing memory** maintains a permanent record of data and programs, maintains a store for the program and data being processed if the main memory cannot accommodate the data and program, and acts as an input/output device when the input/output is in machine-readable form.

5   **Output devices** accept data from the processor, and convert data into the required output format.

Today a computer is rarely one machine, but a group of interlinked machines that are used to execute certain tasks. In a networked environment a user may have access to a number of different processors, printers and other peripherals. Even in a standalone configuration, where there is only one processor, users may choose to attach a different range of peripherals, including, for example a CD-ROM drive or two different types of printer. The particular combination of hardware that a user has access to is known as the computer configuration. Smaller systems are often purchased as a package. Figure 2.2 shows a typical specification for a multi-media PC. Note that this includes CD-ROM drive, sound card, graphics card and internal modem.

Next we explore some of the devices that fit into each of these categories and discuss some of the criteria to consider in the selection of the various components. Different devices and configurations are appropriate in different types of applications and this to some extent accounts for the range of options available.

```
Intel Pentium II P300 Processor
Intel 440FX chipset
Form Factor Motherboard
64 Mb EDO RAM
24 x CD-ROMs
5.25 GB hard disk drive
3.5 inch/1.44Mb floppy disk drive
Exabyte Eagle Nest (IDE)
16-bit sound card
512k Pipeline burst
8 Mb graphics card
56k internal modem
PS2 keyboard and mouse
Mini tower case
Windows 95
12 months' warranty (3 years available on-site)
```

Fig. 2.2   *An example of a specification for a PC workstation*

2.3 The processor

The processor varies from one system to another, although all processors comprise three components: the main memory, the arithmetic and logic unit and the control unit. The role of each of these will now be explored.

The **main memory**, otherwise known as the immediate access memory, or direct access memory, stores the operating system. It also stores data and programs whilst they are in use. Main memory is based upon silicon chips, which use large scale integration techniques (LSI). A chip is a small square of semi-conducting material which holds hundreds of thousands of electronic circuits. Each bit on the chip is held on an individual two-state cell which can therefore hold either a zero or a one. Cells can be individually written to and read from. The term VLSI, for very large-scale integration, is used to describe chips that hold more than one million bits.

Memory is divided into separate storage locations, each of which has an address and holds a number of bits of information.

Each cell is a two-state device capable of holding a one or a zero. It is therefore necessary to use a group of cells to store symbols such as numbers or letters. The different combinations of values in the cells in a group will thus be used to represent different symbols. Chapter 4 considers the codes that are used to allow symbols to be stored.

There are three types of memory chip: RAM, ROM and PROM. RAM or random access memory chips are used to write programs and data to for temporary storage. New data can overwrite existing data. Data is held as temporary electrical states in the chips. The contents of RAM disappear when the machine is switched off, and therefore RAM is described as volatile. Each computer has different amounts of RAM. RAM is important in determining the power of the processor. Typical amounts of RAM required for applications have increased over the years, as more sophisticated software has been written which requires greater quantities of RAM to run effectively.

Some computers also use read-only memory or **ROM**. ROM stores data permanently, and the data recorded on ROM at the time of manufacture cannot be changed. ROM is sometimes used for the storage of commonly used programs and the operating system, so that they need not be loaded from secondary storage.

PROMs are programmable read-only memories. They are nonvolatile, but the user can alter the items in them if required, using a PROM burner. An **EPROM** is an erasable PROM, i.e. the bit patterns on the PROM can be erased.

In addition to RAM, computers may use virtual storage. If the RAM is too small to store a large program, parts of the program can be stored in virtual storage and brought into the main store when required. The virtual storage is usually in the form of a backing store such as a magnetic disk.

Reflection   Explain the difference between ROM and RAM.

The **arithmetic and logic unit** (ALU) carries out logical and arithmetical operations. For example, it may be necessary to execute some calculations to total library fines, or (in a retrieval system) to retrieve all records with a publication date after 1.6.1997. The ALU consists of a number of storage locations called registers, which are used for storing data before, during and after the execution of a program instruction involving an arithmetical or logical operation.

The **control unit** (CU) is the nerve centre of the computer. It exercises control over the operation of the system. It decodes and executes program instructions one by one, and controls and coordinates data movements within the processor and between the processor and other components of the computer system.

The processor works very much faster than a peripheral device such as a printer. The control unit ensures that the processor can send a print message to the printer, continue working whilst the printer is printing, and then send additional data to be printed when the printer has finished its first task.

Improvements in processor design are central to the development of more powerful computers. Work has focused on increasing the speed of operation of the processor so that programs can be executed more quickly, and also on making larger amounts of RAM available to the processor so that larger and more complex programs can be held in the processor during execution, thus eliminating the need to call programs from secondary storage during processing. Other developments include parallel processing, which allows tasks to be carried out in parallel rather than in sequence, and reduced instruction set chips (RISC).

2.4 External storage devices

As indicated above, the processor has volatile memory. It is also relatively expensive. It is necessary to have a more permanent and cheaper means of storing data in machine-readable form. This is provided by secondary, external or backing storage devices. Data and programs are held in backing store until they are needed; then they are moved into the main store. There are currently only three main types of external storage media: magnetic tape, magnetic disk and optical disc. Some of the criteria for the selection of such storage devices are:

- cost in terms of Mb of data stored
- total storage capacity
- the permanency of the data storage medium
- the physical nature of the storage medium
- functional features such as ease of erasure or availability of direct access

- speed of data retrieval, e.g. access time and data transfer rate (from store to computer)
- methods of file organization available
- the robustness of the medium during handling and processing.
- portability between systems.

Reflection   Why is portability sometimes important for an external storage device?

Magnetic tape

Magnetic tape was once widely used as a storage medium, but it is gradually being replaced by magnetic disk. On magnetic tape data are stored as rows of magnetizable spots. The tape is a plastic tape that has been coated with ferrous oxide. In order to read or write onto magnetic tape it is necessary to pass the tape across read/write heads. These heads change or sense the magnetization of the spots, and data may be written, read, erased or overwritten. Data, once written, remains on the tape indefinitely, and can be read any number of times. Tape is wound from one spool to another during reading or writing, with the aid of a tape drive.

Access to data stored on tape is sequential. In a **sequential-access device** data can only be retrieved by searching through the complete device. Clearly, a tape can only be searched by scanning through the tape and winding the tape through the read/write heads. Tapes are good in batch-mode operation where sequential access is acceptable. Typical applications include the accumulation of transactions, the printing of bills, and the sorting and processing of edited records.

Tapes have two main advantages: they are cheap and they are portable. This has made them appropriate as a back-up or security medium. Copies of data held on other storage media may be dumped onto tape and stored for security.

Magnetic disk

A magnetic disk has a magnetizable surface on which data can be stored in concentric rings known as tracks. Data are stored as a pattern of magnetizable spots. Tracks are divided into sectors or blocks. The pattern of tracks and sectors is determined by the disk drive manufacturer and the program controlling the movement of the disk head. The combination of a track number and a sector number is called an **address**. Read/write heads pass over the disk as it rotates in the disk drive and are able to locate individual addresses. Thus disks are **direct-access** storage devices.

Disk packs are written to, or read from, using peripheral devices called disk drives. The drives are permanently linked to the computer's processor, but disk packs are usually exchangeable or removable. Most disk packs on large systems are exchangeable – in other words they can be removed from the disk drive. Those packs that are fixed tend to have a larger capacity. Once loaded the drive causes the disks to spin continuously at a very fast speed. The drive has read/write heads, usually one head per surface, which are mounted on movable access arms. The heads do not touch the disk, but float on the cushion of air created by the rotation of the disc. The alternative is to use a sealed disk unit, known as a Winchester or hard disk. This has been used widely in microcomputer systems.

Floppy disks are widely used with microcomputer systems. Most disks are now 3.5 inches in diameter. Floppy disks have varying storage capacities. A 3.5-inch high-density disk has a capacity of 1.44 MB.

Optical discs

In optical storage systems a focused laser beam is used to create a hole or pit on a disc so that the two states hole(pit) and no hole (land) may be used to store a zero or a one. Pits and lands have different light-reflective properties which are detected by the laser when reading the disc. Spots are much smaller than those written to magnetic disk, and so recording densities are higher. There is no physical contact between the disc and the reading head. Optical media are therefore more robust than magnetic media for long-term storage of information.

Optical discs are read by an optical disc drive. This drive may be linked to a standalone machine or a local workstation, or be accessible over a network. In standalone configurations, drives were originally separate from the workstation. Increasingly workstations are becoming available which integrate the CD-ROM drive. Often it is necessary to provide access to multiple discs, This can be achieved by the use of:

- daisy-chained drives, where a series of single drives are linked together
- stacked systems of towers, where several drives are housed in one unit
- jukebox systems, which function in a similar way to a record jukebox.

Multidrive jukeboxes, which allow more than one disc to be read by users at the same time, are particularly flexible. See Chapter 10 for additional details concerning the networking of CD-ROMs.

There are three main categories of optical disc:

Read-only optical discs

In this case the publisher encodes the data on the disc and the end-user receives a read-only disc that is placed in a player in order to read data, text, audio or video information that has been recorded on the disc. These discs are a publishing medium and are finding wide application. There are a number of different kinds of read-only discs which have found various applications. Videodiscs were developed for the distribution of pre-recorded video. Hybrid videodiscs store a number of different types of information on one disc, including text, data and high-quality video; lack of standardization and the high cost of hardware has restricted their adoption. Compact discs (CDs) are very popular consumer products in the audio playback market. CD-ROM (Compact Disc–Read-Only Memory) is a direct adaptation of the CD system for publishing and data-processing applications. CD-ROM is also used as a distribution medium for software suites, where the software suite would require many floppy disks if it were distributed in this format. Increasing numbers of CD-ROMs are multimedia (we shall return to the concept of multimedia later). More recent developments have attempted to offer standards to accommodate multimedia information on a compact disc. Compact Disc Interactive (CD-I) and CD-ROM Extended Architecture (CD-ROM XA) are such standards. Digital Video Interactive (DVI) is a powerful compression and decompression system for digital video and audio. DVI allows more than 60 minutes of full-screen, full-motion video to be stored on a CD-ROM.

Video CD and Digital Video CD (DVD) are means of storing full-length videos of films. DVD discs, for example, store at least 4.7 Gb of data, with the potential for double-sided discs that would double this capacity. Applications are likely to be primarily in the entertainment sector, and DVD may replace videotapes and VCRs for viewing movies. DVDs could also store the complete backfiles of large bibliographic databases such as ERIC and MEDLINE on a single disc.

Recordable optical discs – (WORM and CD-R)

Write Once Read Many (WORM) discs are used for in-house archiving of data that organizations may wish to store and consult, but not amend. WORM users record their own data onto disc, and the disc may then be read as often as desired. In libraries, for example, WORM discs have been used for the archiving of newspapers. Also publishers may develop image databases on WORM, and then distribute them on CD-ROM.

A more recent entrant to the market is CD-Recordable, a technology that is sufficiently inexpensive to be available to small niche market software developers, multimedia producers and for organizational publication. CD-R as compared to CD pressing makes the creation of a CD-ROM disc accessible. CD-R is a secure and easy-to-store archive medium.

CD-E

Data can be recorded, read, erased and re-recorded on CD-E, so that they can be used in applications where magnetic disks are currently in use. CD-E uses a quaternary phase change alloy as the recording medium. The system operates on the principle of changing the phase of the recording material between a highly reflective crystalline state and a low-reflection amorphous state. This is a relatively new product.

Reflection   In what types of applications could optical discs replace magnetic disks?

2.5 Input devices, media and data capture methods

Input and output devices, together with backing memory, are known as **peripherals**. Input devices bring data to the processor for processing, while output devices present the results of such processing to users. Peripherals are slower in operation than the processor. In order to make maximum use of the processor, the relatively slow-speed peripherals are interfaced with the processor through buffer stores. Buffer stores hold input (and output) data until the processor or output device is ready to handle the data.

Input devices are the means whereby both data and programs enter the system, and are generally responsible for converting data into machine-readable format. People work with letters, numbers and words. Data is stored in the computer as binary digits. Input devices bridge this gap and act as translators or an interface. There are a number of different input devices. The most suitable device for any given application will depend upon the nature of the data to be input into the system. The data may be characters, numbers, graphics, video or voice, and the quantity of data may vary considerably. The specific method used depends upon the computer configuration installed, and to some extent the nature of the operations to be performed. For example, when recording loans transactions in a library, online access is important, but the quantity of data to be input is relatively limited. Other operations, such as database creation, may involve the input of significant quantities of data.

Some input devices enter data straight into a computer system, whereas others may enter data onto an intermediate medium. For example, some hand-held devices allow the user to store data initially onto disk. That disk may then be inserted in a disk drive in a computer system, and the data read from the disk drive into the computer's central processing unit. The appropriate selection of input method can have a significant impact on the accuracy, speed and effectiveness of data entry. Some common input devices are:

Keyboard

The keyboard is the most common data entry device. Keyboards can be in the standard QWERTY layout, or can be tailored to specific applications. Keyboards are often used in conjunction with a screen on which the data are entered are displayed. Keyboards are used for:

- entry of data from a source document, such as an invoice
- interactive use whereby a user, for example, inputs commands or search terms in order to interrogate a database
- entry of text data as in word processing
- the creation of images and graphics
- the use of graphics
- entry into a database.

Keyboards are widely used because they are a flexible method of data entry and can be used in most applications. They do have limitations, however. Keyboarding is a slow form of data entry and is prone to error. It may be costly.

Reflection   What are the limitations of keyboards as data entry devices?

Magnetic ink character recognition

Magnetic ink character recognition (MICR) is a means of deciphering characters printed in an ink containing magnetizable material. Before reading, the document is passed under a device that creates a magnetic field; these magnetizations are then detected by the reader. The characters must be in a special typeface. MICR is widely used on cheques, and the typeface used by the British banking system is E13B. Another international standard format is CMC7. MICR is particularly useful for turn-around documents which are machine-produced and machine-readable, yet readable by people. In banking, cheques are printed using MICR with ink containing magnetizable material. Thus the encoding of serial number, bank, branch and customer account number takes place before transactions take place, and thus avoids delay in processing. When a cheque is passed for payment, the amount is encoded using a MICR cheque encoder. Thus only one field of data is post-encoded after the transaction has taken place.

   MICR is fast and cheap in operation for high-volume activities and has low error rates. MICR is not more widely used because the equipment is expensive to purchase, and the type fonts are not easy to read. MICR is successful in banking because standards have been agreed by all interested parties, error rates are low and forgery is difficult because it is difficult to alter MICR characters without mutilating them.

Optical character readers

Optical character recognition (OCR) is similar in concept to MICR, and has likewise found early application in turn-around documents such as electricity and gas billing systems. Characters in a special font are printed on a document, and the reader scans the document for reflected light patterns, then translates those patterns into a pattern of electrical signals which are passed to the computer store. OCR-A and OCR-B are examples of standard fonts. Characters that cannot be recognized are rejected.

The real potential of OCR has begun to be realized as equipment has become available that will recognize a wider range of fonts and even handwriting. In general, the more standard and better-quality the original, the better will be the machine-readable copy produced by optical scanning. Error rates may still be regarded as unacceptable in some applications, but OCR has great potential for text entry and the creation of electronic documents. OCR is much cheaper than keyboard entry, and can be fast.

Microfilm may be used as a computer input medium, if the data are encoded in an appropriate OCR or other type font.

Bar code readers

Bar codes are widely used in retail outlets and libraries. Each bar code represents a number. The bar code is a pattern of thick and thin bars divided by thick and thin spaces. Only the relative separations and thicknesses of the bars are important. Bar codes can be printed in different sizes and colours. The bar code is read either by passing a light-pen over it or by passing the bar code over a flatbed scanner. Bar codes are suitable for data input when all that is necessary is to identify an item, and the data input simply comprises a code. The reading of the bar code records a transaction, and information is fed back to a computer database. Bar code systems are easy to operate and have very low error rates. Since the readers are linked to a computer system, it is easy to change details and control transactions; for example, prices may be changed centrally, or borrower loan periods may be adjusted. Also transactions update the database and indirectly provide management information.

Optical mark readers

Optical mark readers (OMR) are similar to OCR readers except that the reader recognizes marks in appropriately positioned boxes rather than characters. Typically a printed document is prepared which offers the user a number of alternatives. The mark-sensed document is divided into columns, each of which has ten digits printed in it. The user makes a mark in those boxes that correspond to a given alternative, and the document is then passed through an optical mark reader, which scans the boxes and determines where marks have been made. OMR is used in surveys and multiple-choice examinations, time-sheets and order forms, and the UK National Lottery. OMR works well for standard applications where selection from a few alternatives is possible. In such circumstances it is easy to use, fast and relatively error free.

....

Reflection   Identify some applications of optical mark readers. Explain why
this technology is attractive in these applications.
....

Image scanners

When a page of text already exists, perhaps also including drawings and photographs, it can be directly input into a computer using a scanner.

When scanning text it compares each character to a known shape or pattern
so that the appropriate code for that character can be entered into the computer.
This is effectively a more sophisticated OCR system.

When scanning graphics, it converts the pattern of light and dark images on a
page into a series of dots called picture elements or pixels. These can then be
stored as binary digits in a computer's memory and in backing store, and retrieved
as required. This is the basis of image processing technology. The key problem is
that images occupy a lot of memory. Thus developments in this field have moved
ahead apace as optical storage devices have become more widely available.
Scanners now have a wide variety of different applications, including the scanning
of photographs and logos into databases and documents.

Scanners are available in hand-held and desktop versions.

A digitizer is a device which allows an image to be scanned and converts that
image into digital data for computer storage.

A digitizing tablet incorporates a special stylus which allows the user to draw
or trace images so that they can be converted into computer-readable form.
Digitizing tablets are used in CAD and CAM.

Other input media

1   **Voice or speech data entry** involves the reception of speech via a microphone,
the conversion of that data into electronic signals, and its final conversion
into electronic form. Words when spoken are recognized by a matching technique, whereby the computer compares the speech pattern with the stored
speech pattern. The closest match is displayed. If it is incorrect the word
must be re-spoken. The computer is only able to recognize sounds for which
it has stored data, and people must therefore pronounce the word in the same
way as in the reference data so that the word can be successfully recognized.
Voice data entry is attractive, not only because it frees the user from the need
to use the keyboard, but also because the operator has both hands free and
can move. Data input is also potentially quicker and cheaper than via other
methods. However, voice systems are still under development, and there are
still difficulties in designing systems that adequately recognize accents and
dialects.

2   **A mouse** is a small device with a ball underneath and one or two selection
buttons on the top, which moves the cursor or pointer across the screen.

Once the pointer has been appropriately positioned, an item or option may be selected by clicking on the mouse. The standard mouse is normally moved on a flat surface beside the screen. A number of variations on the basic mouse have been developed, particularly for use with portable computers. Here, typically, the mouse is held in the hand and the ball rotated with the fingers, or it is integral to the keyboard in the form of a rotating ball and two buttons. A mouse is a necessary adjunct to the GUS (graphical user interface). A mouse is usually used in conjunction with a keyboard.

3   **Graphics tablets** work in a similar way to light-pens except that the movement is made by an electric pen onto a specially prepared flat tablet in front of the screen.

4   **Touch-sensitive screens** allow the user to select an item from a screen display by touching it with a finger. The touch breaks the network of horizontal and vertical infra-red beams and thus the touch can be detected. Such screens were tested in early OPAC applications, and have more recently become popular in various public access environments such as multimedia kiosks (we return to multimedia kiosks later in this chapter).

5   **Joysticks, trackerballs etc.** are widely used in computer games to move the sensor around the screen.

6   **Magnetic cards or badges** are in the form of plastic cards the size of a credit card. Data are encoded in a magnetic strip. These are used as credit cards in point-of-sale systems for credit sales and in ATM systems that allow customers to execute banking transactions such as checking their balance or drawing cash. Since they are easy to copy, substitutes have been developed in the form of smart cards, in which the information is encoded within a microchip built into the structure of the card. Smart cards can also hold account balances and historical transaction data. These cards are increasingly being used as a means of identification.

7   **Magnetic tapes and disks** and **optical discs** may be regarded as input and output media in that data can be recorded on these media and then transferred to a different computer system. The data that they handle are already in machine-readable form, and they are therefore different from other input media.

8   **Telephone input**. Many banking systems today allow data to be input directly into computer systems via a touch tone telephone. In response to audio instructions the customer enters account number, password and details of the transaction.

A number of criteria may be applied in the selection of a specific input or output medium:

1   **The nature of the data** to be input or output, including whether it may already be in a font readable by OCR, whether it is text or graphics, and

whether the user is interrogating an existing database or creating the database. Is colour necessary in output? What quality of output presentation is appropriate?

2   The speed and volume of the data to be input or output.
3   Environment in which the data entry or output is being performed. Is the environment public and noisy or private and quiet? Will concentration be difficult? Will a noisy printer intrude on other people? Are there are special security considerations that affect input and output media?
4   Cost, and in particular the balance between initial set-up costs and operating costs.
5   The error tolerance of the application. How critical are errors?
6   Compatibility with other hardware, operating systems and software.
7   Frequency of data input and output.
8   Turn-around speed or acceptable response time.

Reflection   Apply the criteria given above in order to evaluate the suitability of a mouse for an application with which you are familiar, such as an office application, or the use of an information retrieval system.

2.6 Output devices

Output devices are the means by which computer systems communicate with people. The convenience of use of these devices and the quality of their results has a significant impact on the effectiveness of computer systems. Output devices accept data from the processor and convert them into the required output format. In other words, output devices translate the data in the processor into a format that is suitable for people to use.

Printed output is likely to be required when large quantities of data need to be read or processed. Screens are good for interrogating the system, and for identifying facts such as prices and quantities, or whether a transaction has been completed.

Printers

Printed output is important for permanent records and there are applications in which a printed copy is the requirement for statutory reasons. Also printed output is portable and hopefully easy to read. Printed output is likely to persist for some time. One of the ironies of computer systems is that they have managed to generate so much paper. Neither paper costs nor the environmental effect of paper use in association with computer systems should be overlooked.

There are a number of different kinds of printers. The key characteristics of printers that should be considered are:

- the speed
- the quality of output
- the range of type fonts available
- the graphics capabilities
- whether colour is available
- noise levels
- the ability to produce multiple copies
- the cost of purchase
- the cost of operation.

Choosing a printer is usually a matter of matching a budget to the other considerations.

There are two categories of printer: impact printers, where characters are formed by the device striking a ribbon, and non-impact printers. Impact printers have a tendency to be noisy but can produce multiple copies simultaneously, whilst non-impact printers are quiet but restricted to single copies at a time (though they can still be fast).

Printers can also be categorized in accordance with the amount printed by a single command: line printers print a line at a time; serial printers print a character at a time; and page printers print a page at a time. Inkjet and bubblejet printers are one example of serial printers. Inkjet printers have tiny spray nozzles which spray ink onto the page at the appropriate place. Laser printers are page printers. The image to be printed is digitized and used to modulate a laser beam, which scans across a photoconducting drum, building up an electrostatic image which is then transferred to paper using a carbon toner.

Computer output microform

Computer output microform (COM) is a further means of outputting large quantities of data. Microform is not a direct computer output medium. A computer may assemble and edit the information and then either write it onto magnetic tape or display it directly onto a monitor. Where tape is used, the tape is fed into a COM recorder or transcriber, which displays the output into a monitor. The output is photographed onto microfilm. COM is then produced from the tape, in an offline process. COM can be either microfilm or microfiche. COM is cheaper and faster to produce than print and is easy and cheap to store. COM can also store diagrams, graphs and colour, and multiple copies may be easily generated. The only disadvantage is that a reader is necessary in order to access the microform. Retrieval requires that the films be indexed in some way. COM has been used in library catalogues and indexes, and in spare-parts catalogues.

Monitors

A monitor is a component of a workstation. Monitors are a common output device because they produce fast and virtually costless output of information. The screen displays everything that is entered at the keyboard as well as messages from the computer system. Some computers such as notebook computers come with built-in screens but most screens are separate components.

The standard monitor is a cathode ray tube (CRT). Electrons are fired at the screen and light up tiny dots of phosphor, which then glow for a short period of time. Each point is called a picture element or **pixel**. The quality of the screen display, or its resolution depends on the number of pixels on the screen. Colour monitors comprise three electronic guns and three different phosphors which glow red, green and blue. Since the phosphors only glow momentarily, the rate at which the gun refires the same signal is a further characteristic of the screen. This is known as the **refresh rate** and is usually measured in Hz (hertz) or cycles per second. A low refresh rate leads to screen flicker.

Monitors normally have **graphics boards**, which support the display of graphics (i.e. non-text) images. Super VGA is standard. The physical size of screen varies from the usual 12 or 14-inch screen upwards.

Flat-screen technology is used in portable computers. These use liquid crystal displays and gas plasma displays.

Reflection   What are the limitations of monitors as output devices?

Voice output

Audio response terminals are available which present output to the user in the form of speech. These units either store pre-recorded phrases spoken by a human voice or use a voice simulator. Queries or transactions may be input to the processor via a touch screen or keyboard. When the program is ready to respond, the device selects the appropriate words and relays a message to the user, possibly over a telephone line. Such systems can be useful in transaction processing remotely where there is a low volume of output.

Multimedia kiosks

Multimedia kiosks are workstations which are specifically designed for public access. They may be standalone or networked through to a larger computer system. The description multimedia implies that they present information in a variety of different media, including, for example, text, sound, graphics, images and video. In a number of environments where it is useful to offer public access to a database, a kiosk format with the workstation just displaying a screen to the user, is robust and attractive. This screen is often a touch screen. Some kiosks also have keypads and card readers. Multimedia kiosks are an attractive and interesting means of presenting information, and are beginning to find wide application in advertising, retailing, banking, education and training, the provision of information and advice, and public access to community information and online catalogues. Library systems suppliers are integrating kiosks (sometimes multimedia) with touch-sensitive screens into public access and self-service kiosks. Such kiosks may also have printing, coin/card operation, access controls (e.g. via a borrower badge reader) and messaging facilities. The displayed multimedia information might include audio, documents, photographs, objects, newspapers, maps and video. Although such screens usually use menus, some screens also use onscreen keyboards to allow more flexible dialogues, as in, for example, the entry of search terms. Some kiosks also have keyboards and integrated numerical keypads. Self-issue terminals may use a light-pen or flatbed scanner. This can also be used to scan in images into the database. Such self-service terminals free staff from routine transactions to allow them to engage more fully in customer services such as advice and information provision.

Virtual reality

The ultimate input/output experience is virtual reality where the user experiences the virtual library or the virtual office. In the virtual library, there are no books and the total experience is electronic. The reality being experienced by the user is simulated or virtual. Simulations of various degrees of sophistication have been under development for, for instance, pilot training for many years. There are now moves to create more virtual reality experiences for the consumer marketplace. Games use virtual reality techniques. We might also encounter virtual libraries, virtual education and virtual holidays. The question is which experiences are worth having in the virtual state? Simulation and training are clearly beneficial, but to what extent are simulated pleasure and leisure experiences appropriate?

To experience virtual reality requires a visual display. This can be achieved by:

- the user wearing eyephones and datagloves
- wall-sized projections of images, including animation that allows clients to see what happens of they move left or right or approach the images
- for users who prefer to look at (rather than be in) virtual reality, displays using animation on a standard screen or even a palmtop computer.

The necessary animation is challenging graphics designers. Creation of images is time-consuming and specialized, but as the software for creating and rotating, cutting and pasting images becomes more sophisticated, virtual reality is becoming less expensive to create. There is also further work to be done in sound input and output, and other sensations such as tilting, vibration and smell. Shared virtual reality experiences, possibly with two or more users at remote sites, are another possibility.

2.7 Processing modes

Computer systems can operate in a variety of different modes. In many systems one mode will be appropriate for one function, and another mode for another. When selecting a mode of operation, the response time required for different functions, together with the cost of achieving that response time, must be considered.

Batch processing

Most early mainframe systems operated in batch-processing mode. Batch processing is now generally performed in the 'background' with any online activities performed by the system taking priority. In batch processing, data are entered and processed as a batch job, and this is performed by the computer when it is not fully occupied on some other activity. Once the job is completed, the results will be printed out, or updated files will be available for interrogation. Batch processing remains appropriate in applications where large volumes of data are to be processed, turn-around times are fairly long, processing efficiency can be achieved by batch processing, or a suite of programs has to process one set of data. Batch processing is used to sort, merge and update files, and for applications requiring regular runs such as payrolls, printing library overdue notices, invoicing and printing orders.

Reflection   List some jobs that would be suitable for batch processing in an application known to you. What characteristics do these jobs have in common?

Online processing

Online processing offers the opportunity to communicate or converse with the computer and to receive immediate or almost immediate response. Online processing is the technique of processing data by computer by means of terminals connected to, and controlled by, a central processor. The fast response time is the major advantage of online systems. Thus with an online system it is possible to formulate and submit a request for information and to receive a prompt response. A library circulation control database, where transactions are recorded in online mode, gives the user the opportunity to view any earlier transactions. Communication with the computer for online processing requires the availability of a workstation, and appropriate telecommunication links to the main processor. Such a system offers the following advantages:

- centralization and integration of separate files, functions and decisions
- more up-to-date databases
- the routing information to those who require it
- quicker modifications and reading of information and more efficient inputting
- availability of computer facilities to more sites, and more cheaply
- reduction in paperwork.

Real-time systems are online systems which respond extremely quickly. They are used, for example, in controlling chemical processes, routing work through a factory, and controlling traffic flow with traffic lights. In a sense, the microprocessors in, for example, domestic appliances perform in real-time mode. The term 'real-time' refers to systems where files are updated with transaction data immediately the event ocurs to which they relate.

Multi-tasking

This means that users can access a library database whilst, for example, a spread-sheet program is calculating or a desktop publishing program is re-formatting a screen. MIS reports may be generated in the background whilst a user works on another application. Several different modules, such as cataloguing, searching and circulation, may be live concurrently, so that the user can move quickly between these tasks.

Remote job entry or remote batch processing

This is a technique whereby batch processing is conducted on data that are input at a remote terminal in offline mode. The data are then transmitted in bulk to the central processor.

Multi-programming

This is an arrangement where one or more programs are held in the processor simultaneously. When the processor is unable to work on one of them owing to slow peripheral activity (e.g. because it is waiting for a user at a workstation to respond), it can switch to another program, and then later back to the first. Multi-programming is used in most large computer systems, but it does require a sophisticated operating system which will support multi-programming. One function of such an operating system will be to conduct work scheduling – i.e. work out which job has processing priority at any given moment in time.

Timesharing

A timesharing system is one where a number of users at remote points have access to a central computer virtually simultaneously via workstations linked by communication lines to the computer. Each workstation is allocated a very short 'time slice', during which it has exclusive use of the processor. A large number of workstations can be serviced in around one second.

Distributed processing and client–server systems

Computer systems increasingly involve distributed processing. A distributed system is one in which there are several distinct but interacting processors and/or data stores at the same or different geographical locations. Thus a distributed system involves a number of processors and a network to link those processors.

The objective is to process as many tasks as possible at the processor closest to the user activity, and to pass larger jobs or hold larger files in some other processor. In this way users have more control over their own data. The workstation or local processor may be an intelligent terminal, a microcomputer or a minicomputer. Typically, the local processor may be engaged in: program checking and compilation; file editing; file handling; local interrogation of files; local bulk printing; small jobs; and local jobs. There are a number of different types of distributed systems. Such systems may be classified on the basis of the scale of the equipment, the network configuration and the application of remote intelligence.

As workstations in distributed processing systems have become more sophisticated, distributed processing systems have been seen as **client–server systems.** The server is a larger workstation or a mainframe which hosts the central resource, including, for example, a database and more sophisticated peripherals. Clients are PCs or workstations that are connected to the server via a network. Clients both run processes on their own, but also call on the server for central resources. Applications that were originally written for mainframes are now being rewritten for client–server architectures. Many of the applications which run over the Internet run in client–server mode, including a range of library management systems and online retrieval systems. An effective client–server configuration reduces the amount of data that needs to be exchanged between the workstation and the server, and thereby makes communication faster and more efficient.

Summary   This chapter has introduced some basic concepts concerning the hardware in computer systems. The basic computer configuration comprises the central processing unit, input devices, output devices and storage devices. The central processing unit comprises an arithmetic and logic unit, a control unit and the main memory. This is important in determining the power of the computer. External storage devices provide a more permanent means of storing data. Input devices and data capture methods are used to input data into systems. Output devices such as printers and monitors allow information to be output from the system. Newer technologies such as multimedia kiosks and virtual reality integrate input and output. The chapter concludes with a brief overview of computer processing modes, including specifically client–server configurations.

REVIEW QUESTIONS

1   What is the function of main memory in a computer system?
2   What criteria should be applied when selecting a keyboard?
3   List three different applications of bar code readers.
4   Using the criteria suggested at the end of section 2.5, explain why:
    • a bar code reader is a good data input device in a super-market
    • image scanning is an appropriate input device for generating an electronic archive of office documents.
5   What criteria would you apply when choosing a printer?
6   Why is a stable, high-resolution image important in a VDU monitor?
7   What is RAM?
8   What is the difference between a CD-ROM and a WORM disc? What implications does this have for the respective use of the two devices?
9   Describe some applications for multimedia kiosks.
10 What are the advantages of client–server configurations?

Bibliography

Anderson, R. G. (1990) *Data processing (Vol. 1: Principles and practice; Vol. 2: Information systems and technology)*, London, Pitman.
Bingham, J. (1989) *Data processing*, Basingstoke, Macmillan.

Burton, P. F. and Petrie, J. H. (1991) *Information management technology: a librarian's guide*, London, Chapman and Hall.

Curtis, G. (1989) *Business information systems: analysis, design and practice*, Wokingham, Addison-Wesley.

Clifton, H. D. and Sutcliffe, A. G. (1994) *Business information systems*, New York/London, Prentice Hall.

French, C. S. (1992) *Computer studies*, London, DP Publications.

French, C. S. (1990) *Oliver and Chapman's data processing and information technology*, London, DP Publications.

Lester, G. (1992) *Business information systems, vol. 1: Hardware and programming*, London, Pitman.

West, B. (ed.) (1994) *Basic computing principles*, Oxford, Blackwell.

West, C. and Lording, R. (1989) *Information technology applications*, Oxford, Heinemann Newnes.

Zokorczy, P. and Heap, N. (1995) *Information technology: an introduction*, London, Pitman.

3
Systems and networks

LEARNING OUTCOMES

Computers function as interlinked systems. The potential for computers to revolutionize business and society hinges to a large extent on the communication facilities between computers. This chapter examines the different types of computers and features of the networks that are used to link such computers into a system. When you have read this chapter you will:

- understand the terms mainframe, minicomputer and microcomputer
- be aware of the importance of the data transmission features of networks
- be aware of the different features that characterize data communication systems
- appreciate the basic features of a local-area network
- know how wide area networks are used
- be aware of other data communication systems such as value-added networks, facsimile transmission, videotex, electronic funds transfer and electronic data interchange.

3.1 Introduction

Chapter 2 has considered the components of a computer system, viewing the basic configuration of a computer in terms of a standalone model, or one computer working alone. Most computers are part of a system or network and it is appropriate to proceed by considering the computer system as a linked network of a number of computers or processors. This chapter starts with a brief review of the different types of computer and their role, and then proceeds to examine telecommunications networks, or the links between the computers, in more detail. A review of the basics of data transmission, such as the speed of data transmission, duplex and half-duplex, timing modes, multiplexing, modems and network switching, is followed by a consideration of some of the characteristics of data communication systems. This includes network architectures and protocols, and network topologies. The chapter concludes with a brief review of local-area networks and wide-area networks, and other network applications such as videotex, value-added networks, facsimile transmission, electronic funds transfer and electronic data interchange.

3.2 Mainframes, minicomputers and microcomputers

The history of computers can be described in terms of the generations of computers. The first three generations can be clearly identified in terms of the basic electronic units that provide the arithmetic and logic power. These are, respectively:

1st generation	electronic valves
2nd generation	transistors
3rd generation	integrated circuit.

The transition between one generation and the next brought benefits in terms of:

- reduced size
- increased reliability
- reduced power demand
- increased working speed
- reduced purchasing and running costs.

Concurrently with the developments in the basic processing units, the peripherals have improved, yielding, in particular, faster input and output, and larger amounts of storage.

Manufacturers have sought to identify new models as belonging to the fourth and fifth-generation of computers. However, there is no widely accepted concept of a fourth or a fifth-generation computer. Some would argue that fourth-generation computers are those based on VLSI. Fifth-generation computers may be those with a more fully developed artificial intelligence interface. However, there has as yet been no quantum leap from third-generation computers which it is generally agreed justifies the identification of a new generation.

Some years ago it was possible to distinguish three categories of computer on the basis of the power or capacity of the processor chip. The most powerful machines were described as mainframes, intermediate machines as minicomputers, and small machines as microcomputers. As all machines, but especially microcomputers and minicomputers, have been improved with enhanced processor power, the dividing line between, say, a super-microcomputer and a small minicomputer has become increasingly difficult to draw. In particular, when examining the computer system that is appropriate for any given application, it is now frequently appropriate to design a system consisting of a series of linked processing units. Some processing may be conducted at individual workstations, other processing at processor nodes communicating with a group of workstations, and other processing at a different node, or a central mainframe. The design of the system needs to take into account which databases need to be stored where, and where different kinds of processing can most effectively be conducted. If we also remember that any large computer system, or even a standalone microcomputer, can be linked via telecommunications networks to other computers – possibly on the other side of the world – it becomes apparent that it is difficult to identify the boundaries of a computer system. We return to the networks and their features later in this chapter. First, although distinctions are difficult to draw, it is helpful to describe further the typical characteristics of mainframes, minicomputers and microcomputers.

Mainframes

Mainframes are the largest type of computer, and may be the central hub of a system accessible from distributed minicomputers or microcomputers. They work at the rate of millions of instructions per second or more, and have gigabytes or terabytes of memory in their backing stores. Mainframes are capable of supporting high-volume processing, and typically are used to hold large databases and powerful software. They are likely to support a wide range of different applications. In a local authority, for example, they may support systems that deal with local taxation, personnel and payroll, accounts and sales, as well as specialist systems such as library management systems. Mainframe computers are used by the online search services to mount and make available large numbers of large databases. In order to support such a range of applications effectively, mainframe computers will have a wide range of peripherals, some of which will be special-purpose, such as plotters, and others of which, such as line printers, will serve many purposes. Mainframe systems are complex hardware configurations, supporting numerous and large applications, and as such require a significant number of staff to manage the system. Mainframe systems are timesharing, multiprogramming systems.

Supercomputers are massive mainframes which process billions of instructions per second and can deal with 10,000 or more workstations. Supercomputers are used by government departments and major research centres, particularly in defence and space for large 'number-crunching' applications, such as are necessary in aircraft design, space vehicle design and nuclear research.

Most existing computers perform their operations one after another. **Parallel processors** use an array of processors operating in parallel to speed up operations. Hundreds of thousands of separate processors may operate in parallel. For example, each processor may evaluate a different part of a complex equation independently, and the results can then be brought together for the final examination. There is debate concerning the best architecture for such systems. Two fundamentally different approaches have been explored:

- SIMD (single instruction multiple data), where the processor consists of lots of processors each handling a single instruction
- MIMD (multiple instruction multiple data), where each component handles a number of instructions.

Parallel processing machines are available, and they are beginning to impact on the mainstream of computing.

Minicomputers

Minicomputer-based systems have medium-sized processors. Minicomputers are used by educational institutions, estate agents, libraries and retailing organizations to support operations such as invoicing, accounting routines, stock control and payroll. Minicomputers can be used 'standalone' to support a specific application such as a library management system. In this application the advent of minicomputers permitted library managers much closer control of their own computing requirements and systems. Such systems were described as **turnkey systems**, because a packaged solution to specific applications that included both hardware and software was often marketed to user organizations. Minicomputers can also be used as major remote terminals or 'front-end' processors to mainframe computers, or can be linked together to provide the equivalent of a mainframe processing facility.

Microcomputers

Microcomputers, or **personal computers** are small computers consisting of a processor on a single silicon chip, mounted on one circuit board together with memory chips (ROM and RAM chips). Interfaces permit the connection of printers, disk drives, tape streamers, CD-ROM drives, mice, light-pens and other peripherals. Initially, most microcomputer systems were standalone systems. Most microcomputers are now used as part of a network. The simplest microcomputer networks comprise anything from two or three to 100 microcomputers, linked together and communicating with a file server which controls the network. The file server itself may be a more powerful microcomputer. In other applications, such a network may be linked to a central processor that is either a minicomputer or a mainframe computer, or alternatively individual microcomputers may be linked to the minicomputer or mainframe. Linking microcomputers together in a network offers the opportunity to share data and databases, software and peripherals, such as more expensive and better-quality printers.

Portable microcomputers are light and compact computers which will run off either the mains or a rechargeable battery allowing several hours' mobile use. Depending on their size they can be categorized as laptop, notebook or palmtop. With an appropriate network card they can communicate over a network, from a base in the office or the home. Some users use a portable computer whilst in transit and then attach the portable to an office workstation. The office workstation offers a larger keyboard and better screen display, for input and output to the portable processor and storage.

Reflection   Do you have access to any computer networks? If so, what type
of machine do you use to access them and what type of
machine acts as the file server?

Table 3.1 summarizes some of the typical characteristics of mainframe, minicomputer and microcomputer systems.

Table 3.1 *Characteristics of mainframe, minicomputer and microcomputer
systems*

Feature	Mainframe	Mini	Micro
Physical size	Large	Small, e.g. 3 or 4 m would contain a large configuration	Smaller still, e.g. A4 size upwards
Computing power	Depends upon the nature of the application, but generally mainframes are the most powerful, followed by minis and then micros		
Processor	Multiple chips	Multiple chips	Single chips
Peripherals	Larger range	Smaller, slower and less sophisticated, but quite good	Cheaper and still less sophisticated, but often still adequate
Software	A wide range of utility and applications software, depending on machine	Also a good range of utility and applications software	A good range of certain types of software, but tends not to be as specialized as on large machines
Operating	Needs some full-time, trained and experienced operators	Simpler, but extent of supervision required depends on size of installation	No problems, although manager/user is likely to need basic familiarity with maintenance of system, etc.
Number of users	Multi-user	Multi-user	Single user (unless networked)
Environment and location	Special suites with air-conditioning; false floors to cover cables	Ordinary office, etc., with some screening to reduce noise from peripherals, etc., and simple air-conditioning with large installations	Ordinary home or office
Maintenance	Contracts, with weekly checks	Contracts with monthly or less frequent checks because less use and less equipment	Contracts usually with call-out
Availability	Manufacturer only	Manufacturers, system packages (for types of application), system houses (for particular users)	Same outlets as minis, but also retailers and business equipment agents
Price	£100,000–£2m+	£10,000–£50,000+	£500–£5000

3.3 Information communication and networks

The combination of computer technology and telecommunication links is a necessary prerequisite for an advanced information society. Originally, telecommunications involved the transmission of information, whilst computers were dedicated to the processing of information. Now data communication systems linked to computers have made it possible to process information and transmit data to any location instantaneously. In addition, the combination of computers and telecommunications has improved the technology of both contributing areas, and offered new means of communication and data storage, such as electronic mail, electronic journals and videotex. The use of telecommunications in conjunction with computers offers an important opportunity to affect the way in which information is handled, stored, processed and communicated.

All telecommunications systems have some essential components:

- a **transmitter** to send information
- a **receiver** to accept it
- a **transmission medium** through which the message travels
- **signals and codes** which represent the message
- **network controls** to ensure that the message gets to its destination.

Computer networks have a variety of transmitters, receivers, transmission media, signals, codes and network controls.

The most basic computers are standalone computers with integral VDUs, such as standalone microcomputers. As soon as we move to a larger computer which supports a number of terminals, a terminal network becomes necessary and telecommunications links must be used to connect the terminals to the computer. Similarly, a group of microcomputers that are to communicate with one another or share a printer must be linked together by a network. A network is also necessary to link a terminal to a distant computer. Various different kinds of networks are used in different circumstances. The factors that determine the most appropriate network for any given application are:

- volume of traffic and required capacity
- speed required
- fidelity required
- acceptable cost.

Organizations may use different elements of the telecommunications networks for different purposes. Some examples might include:

- a local-area network linking the workstations within a building to support access to transaction processing systems such as a library management system

- national and international wide-area networks for access to e-mail, document delivery, news bulletins and databases
- national data and voice networks to access videotex services
- national and international voice networks for telephone calls
- broadcast services to receive teletext.

The remainder of this chapter reviews some characteristics of telecommunication networks.

3.4   Data transmission and communication

Data transmission is the movement of information using some form of representation appropriate to the transmission medium. This might include electrical signals, optical signals, or electromagnetic waves.

Data communication includes data transmission, but is wider in that it is also concerned with:

- physical transmission circuits and networks
- the hardware and software which support data communication
- procedures for detecting and recovering from errors
- standards for interfacing user equipment to the network or medium
- rules and protocols to control the exchange of information.

This section considers some of the characteristics of data transmission, whilst the following section considers the features of the data communication system.

Speed of data transmission

The speed of data transmission along a telecommunications line is an important characteristic of a telecommunications link. The speed of data transmission is measured in baud, and is referred to as the **baud rate**. Baud rate equals the number of signal elements transmitted each second. The term 'baud' is named after Henri Baud, the originator of an early communications code. The baud rate is usually the same as the number of bits of information transmitted each second, because the signal element is usually one bit. Thus, for example, a 2400-baud line transmits a maximum of 2400 bits in a second. Voice grade lines such as telephone lines can transmit data at 600 or 1200 bits per second (bps). Faster modems allow transmission at up to 4800 bps on these lines. On broad-band lines speeds of 50,000 bps are achievable.

The speed of transmission depends on the bandwidth of the channel. The bandwidth is measured in Hertz, or cycles per second. Relatively low speeds are acceptable for voice mail and other messaging systems, but higher speeds are necessary if the volume of data to be transmitted is higher, as in file transfer or in the transmission of multimedia data. Without high transmission speeds large volumes of data will use all of the network capacity for an extended period of time, and jam the network for other users.

Full and half-duplex

Full and half-duplex refers to the way in which data are sent between computers. In full duplex the characters typed are passed along the telephone lines as a modulating tone on one frequency and returned on a different frequency, before being channelled to the screen. Therefore what is on the screen is what actually arrived at the remote computer, which may or may not be what was typed. Half-duplex channels will permit data to be passed along the line in both directions, but not in both directions at the same time.

If the remote computer is expecting full duplex and the terminal is set for half-duplex, the character will appear on the screen twice, once directly from the keyboard, and again as the remote computer echoes it back.

Many networks that do not actually require data to be transmitted both ways at the same time nevertheless use full-duplex data channels because the turn-around time of the channel would lead to unacceptably long response times from the computer. This is a particular problem with systems that need to be compatible with satellite communication channels, which involve relatively long transmission delays and therefore cannot be turned around quickly; this means that most will use full-duplex techniques.

Simplex systems use transmission in one direction only. When digital information is being sent in a switched network, synchronization must be maintained so that the receiver collects the stream of bits as it was transmitted.

Timing modes

It is necessary for the data receiver to be able to split the stream of bits that it receives into groups of bits of information so that they can be translated into data. There are two means of achieving this, described as timing modes: **asynchronous** and **synchronous transmission.**

Asynchronous transmission is simpler for systems where information has to be passed over long communication links. Asynchronous transmission demands that the receiving end has some method of detecting the start of each character to ensure that no pulses are lost. This is achieved by surrounding each character by a start code and one or more stop codes, namely:

- start code character 1
- stop code character 2.

Both start codes and stop codes are represented as one bit of data each. Thus, with asynchronous data transmission a character that might be represented as an 8-bit code (see Chapter 4) will be transmitted with 10 or 11 bits. Thus, for example, 300 baud is approximately equal to 30 characters per second and 1200 baud is approximately equal to 120 characters per second.

Some asynchronous systems employ start–stop at the beginning and end of blocks, rather than characters. A block is a group of bits that is treated as a logical unit of data.

Synchronous timing leads to faster data transmission, but relies upon accurate counting and timing of the bits that are transmitted. Synchronous transmission is achieved by synchronizing the internal clocks of the receiving and sending equipment. For example, the first eight bits transmitted are recognized as the first character, the next eight bits as the second character. Clearly, this relies upon accurate timing and the data being transmitted at a fixed rate. One faulty bit would result in the complete message being garbled. Clearly, this timing mode is not sufficiently robust for long public telecommunications networks, where noise is not an uncommon occurrence. Synchronous timing is, however, attractive for in-house networks, where large volumes of data have to be communicated rapidly. Equipment for synchronous transmission is more expensive than that for asynchronous transmission.

Multiplexing and transmission modes

Multiplexing is the use of a single telecommunications link to transmit a number of signals. Simple multiplexing provides a transparent connection between remote terminals and the computer ports to which those terminals are attached. Multiplexers are normally required at both ends of a 'shared' telephone line. There are two types of multiplexing: frequency division multiplexing (FDM), and time division multiplexing (TDM). FDM involves a number of parallel messages from different terminals travelling at different frequencies. These different frequencies allow the receiver to distinguish between the messages. TDM interleaves bits or characters from different terminals. TDM is more popular than FDM in today's systems. More efficient use of channels can be achieved with statistical TDM or statistical multiplexers (STDM). An STDM is an intelligent device that is capable of judging each terminal's instantaneous requirements for line capacity and allocating line time accordingly. Multiplexers are often integral with concentrators and modems.

Multiplexing was originally introduced to enable more efficient use of communications channels, but it has become an important component in wide-area networks.

Concentrators help to enable full utilization of high-speed data lines. There is a significant discrepancy between line speed and the operator's keying speed, even in low-speed networks. This discrepancy results in blank spaces in the succession of bits. A concentrator acts as a buffer by gathering bits from each terminal or group of terminals and holding them in its buffer until there are sufficient bits to justify forward transmission.

Modems

The term 'modem' is a contraction of modulator/demodulator. The process of modulation/demodulation involves the conversion of digital signals, typically from a computer terminal, into a form suitable for transmission over analogue systems. For example, a modulator is used to turn digital computer code into the analogue form required by many public-service telephone networks (PSTNs). A demodulator at the other end reconverts from analogue to digital. Modems are devices that are placed at either end of an analogue link to allow digital data to be communicated. Acoustic couplers perform a similar function, but differ from modems in that they are not permanently wired to the telecommunications network. Their main limitation is that the transmission speeds at which they operate are relatively slow, but they can be connected to any telephone, and therefore have some special applications in the field.

There are three basic types of analogue modulation: amplitude, frequency and phase. Amplitude, frequency and phase modulation are merely different ways of using sound waves to represent zeros and ones. Digital modulation is called pulse modulation, and one common form of pulse modulation is known as pulse code modulation (PCM). In PCM data are transmitted as a train of discrete, coded pulses.

Modems can be separate units, but today they are frequently built into PCs in the form of a modem board. Modems with different characteristics are available. For example, a modem may allow: full-duplex or half-duplex operation; synchronous or asynchronous transmission operation at different speeds, e.g. 14,400/9600/4800/1200 bps; operation over private circuits or the PSTN; and may support multiplexing. There are standards relating to the use of modems for transmissions at different speeds. For example, V22 applies for 1200 bps in full duplex, V32 for 9600 bps, and V32bis for 14,400 bps. When choosing a modem it is important to assess the uses to which it will be put and the networks with which it will be used.

Reflection   When will modems become obsolete?

Network switching

Messages can move from transmitter to receiver using either switched or non-switched techniques. There are three main switching techniques: circuit switching, message switching and packet switching.

Broadcasting from a single transmitter to many receivers which can 'tune in' the messages is the most common non-switched network. Another non-switched approach is where a workstation is directly linked to a central computer.

Reflection   Why is switching necessary in telecommunications networks?

Circuit switching is used in the traditional PSTNs. Here, the switch mechanism sets up a physical link from the transmitter to the receiver. In order to reach its destination a call may be routed through many exchanges (or network nodes). Early exchanges were manual; later, electromechanical devices connected calls at each node. Since the 1970s, fully computerized exchanges have been in operation. These both create the switched circuit links and perform various control functions such as setting up a call, initiating ringing or engaged tones, monitoring and recording charges. These are called stored program control (SPC) exchanges. British Telecom's System X is an SPC exchange.

Some large organizations have their own telephone exchanges, referred to as private automatic branch exchange (PABX) or private branch exchange (PBX). It is possible to have leased lines or dedicated lines on the PSTN.

Message switching systems overcome the problem of engaged lines by allowing messages to be sent to, and temporarily stored at, the switching centre. The messages are then delivered by a call from the switching centre to the called party.

Packet switching is a type of message switching which involves the switching and transmission of data in discrete quantities called packets. In contrast to a circuit-switched system (such as the public telephone network), no permanently allocated end-to-end transmission paths are required for the duration of a particular call. Each packet contains within itself both the data and the necessary information for routing it through the network.

Packet-switching exchanges or nodes are all computerized. They interpret the control information that is included in each packet. Packets are stored in the main store of each node for a short time before being forwarded to the next node or receiver. Although the original message is fragmented into packets which may arrive at different times, the packet-switching system ensures that they all arrive at their destination accurately, and that they are re-assembled correctly. There are two kinds of packet switching: the datagram method and the virtual circuit technique. In the datagram method each packet is individually addressed, and datagrams may pass through different routes on the network. In the virtual circuit technique, all packets are routed down the virtual circuit.

Packet Switch Stream (PSS) is British Telecom's national packet-switching network. Tariffs are based on usage and transmission speeds, regardless of distance. PSS provides access to the International Packet Switched Service (IPSS), for international data transmission.

Packet switching makes more efficient use of networks than circuit switching, because messages can be interleaved to remove gaps. Also, synchronization is handled by the network nodes. However, packet switching requires more computing resources at each node.

In some of the most recent exchanges, both the exchange and the switching network are computerized. This type of exchange is described as **digital switching**, and in such exchanges all signals, including speech, are in digital form. Most telecommunications organizations plan to convert the present analogue signal transmission networks to all-digital networks. Conversion is, however, gradual, on account of the scale and cost of the task, and may take between 20 to 30 years.

....

Reflection   Explain, in your own words, the difference between circuit switching and packet switching.

....

3.5   The data communication system

This section examines three important features of networks: transmission media, network architectures and protocols standards, and network topologies.

Transmission media

The telecommunications networks that are used for data transmission may comprise one or more of the following physical transmission media:

1   **Twisted copper wires or cable**, such as in normal telephone lines. Twisted pair cable is a little cheaper than coaxial cable, but is vulnerable to noise. It is still widely used and is satisfactory with low data transmission rates.

2   **Coaxial cable**, which has many insulated wires in the same cable, has a greater capacity than twisted pair cable, and may be used to carry different services in different frequency bands. Thus a single cable can be used to carry data, voice and video. Coaxial cable is used as the transmission medium for local and international data communications.

3   **Fibre optics** is based on hair-thin glass fibres through which light waves representing electrical impulses are transmitted. The light comes from a light source, such as a laser, and is red or infra-red. A large number of parallel fibres are contained in a strong waterproof cable. Light is passed into and taken from the fibres by a device known as a transducer, which converts electrical pulses into light, and vice versa. Fibre optics have a number of advantages over twisted copper wires or coaxial cable. These are:

   • high bandwidth, of several hundred megabits per second

- low attenuation, or little loss of signal; light can travel up to 5 km without the need for a repeater to re-amplify the light intensity
- no interference from external electrical and electronic equipment
- high reliability
- economy, because glass is cheap compared with copper.

Fibre optics can be used within computers as the bus for high speed communications as well as for longer-distance communication between computers.

4   **Microwaves.** A microwave link is an ultra-high-frequency (UHF) radio transmission between two line-of-sight points. These points house radio transmitters and receivers (transceivers) known as repeaters. These points are usually on hills to give the maximum line-of-sight distance. Microwaves have a high frequency and a large bandwidth, and hence are capable of transmitting without distortion.

5   **Communications satellites,** which are used for telephone and television transmission. Communications satellites remove the requirement for line-of-sight positions. In particular, because of the line-of-sight requirement, microwaves cannot be used for transoceanic communication. To overcome this problem, repeaters are installed in satellites. The satellite repeater receives radio transmissions for each earth station, amplifies the message and retransmits it. The message is picked up from the satellite by earth stations, which are often dish aerials.

6   **Standard electrical mains wiring,** through which control signals can be sent by a computer to switch devices (e.g. light switches) on and off.

The various transmission media vary in physical form, speed, capacity (i.e. the rate at which data can be transmitted without error), fidelity of transmission, and cost. In practice an international data communication network uses a combination of the above media. Data may pass through twisted copper wires or coaxial cable from the workstation, into a fibre-optic cable and then into a microwave network, before being transmitted to satellite by a radio station. The satellite might then retransmit the message to the receiving station. The message may then be passed through a further series of microwave, fibre-optic, and coaxial networks before reaching its destination.

When selecting a transmission medium for any given application, it is important to look for high capacity and good fidelity, coupled with cost-effectiveness. The capacity of a channel is determined by its bandwidth. Different types of information (e.g. voice, colour television broadcast) require different volumes of information to be sent. The bandwidth of the channel therefore determines the types of applications that can be handled by a network.

Network architectures and protocol standards

Computer networks are concerned with linking together various pieces of computer equipment and systems. The potential effectiveness of information technology depends heavily upon the effectiveness of the telecommunication networks. One important aim in a network is to provide end-to-end compatibility so that any terminal or system can be linked to any other. In order to consider networks further it is useful to examine network architecture. A network architecture consists of a systematic definition of:

- the topology of the way in which units are distributed through the network
- the control and flow of information through the network
- the protocols and standards for data encoding and transmission.

Architecture from one manufacturer has tended to be incompatible with architecture from another manufacturer. The mutually determined set of formats and procedures governing the exchange of information between systems is referred to as the **protocol**. Protocols are concerned, for instance, with error detection methods, recovery after errors, transmission speeds, data format and message initiation, transfer and termination. Individual manufacturers have had their own protocol. For example, IBM developed their Systems Network Architecture (SNA). Other suppliers wishing to link to IBM equipment had to develop SNA-compatible facilities. National and international standards have since been framed in an attempt to resolve this situation. The International Standards Organization's Open Systems Interconnection (OSI) recommendation consists of seven layers and synthesizes recommendations concerning the user's view of the system (levels 5 to 7) and the telecommunications controls (levels 1 to 4), as shown in Table 3.2. The ISO model has been important in facilitating communication about standardization between different network manufacturers and users. The International Telegraph and Telephone Consultative Committee (known as CCITT) has set important standards in this field, with its X25 protocol, for example, covering levels 1 to 3 for packet-switched open systems interconnected networks. This standard covers the actual mechanics of passing a packet from one node to another, the way in which the packets are assembled and broken down, the setting up of the link between the nodes, and the method of linking the terminal to the host computer.

A further outcome of OSI which is of particular relevance to libraries has been the establishment of the interlibrary loans (ILL) protocols based on the work of the National Library of Canada, and the search and retrieve (SR) protocol. Z39.50 and SR are discussed more fully in Chapter 4.

Table 3.2 *The ISO levels of open system interconnection*

Group	OSI level	Control function	Type of activity at this level
User	7	Application	Initiates and carries out application tasks with information as perceived by the user, such as file transfer, message handling and terminal emulation
	6	Presentation	Presents information to the user in an appropriate application form, perhaps by converting the control characters used by different types of terminals, using DCA-DIA and X-400 protocols
	5	Session	Sets up, maintains and terminates the logical connections and interaction for data transfers as seen by the user
Transport	4	Transport	Manages data transfers between network nodes, including addressing flow control
	3	Network	Routes messages and carries out other detailed network management controls (X.25 standard fits into this level)
	2	Data link	Controls transmission of message signals and formats across links between terminals and networks
	1	Physical	Handles electrical, mechanical and other physical interconnections; factors such as the transmission medium, voltage levels and number of pins in the plug are defined

Network topologies

One aspect of a network architecture is its topology. The network topology is the way in which the communications links connect the equipment. Figure 3.1 shows some of the common network topologies. In practice, many networks are composite networks which interlink networks with different topologies and protocols. The interface between the networks is provided by a gateway switch.

Star networks have a single network node at the centre, which is attached directly to a number of subscriber workstations. Workstations can not communicate directly with one another, and must communicate through the central node. This topology is appropriate when workstations need to access a central database. It is, however, vulnerable to failure of either the central processor or transmission.

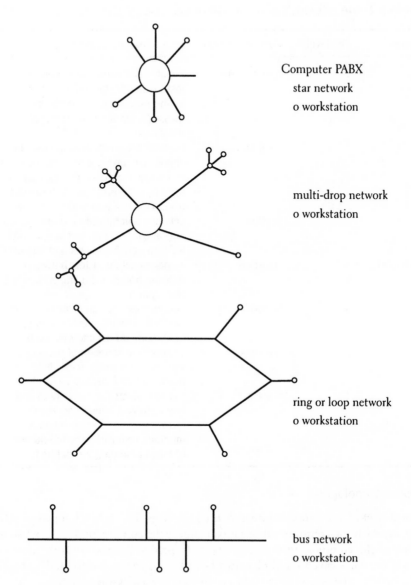

Computer PABX
star network
o workstation

multi-drop network
o workstation

ring or loop network
o workstation

bus network
o workstation

Fig. 3.1 *Network topologies*

Ring or loop networks are those in which all nodes are linked together on an equal basis. Data is input via any node, and communicated through the network. The appropariate node accepts the data.

Multi-drop networks have many workstations hanging off links to a central node. Multiplexing is used to allow many workstations to share the same channel. This topology reduces the line costs by using a single branched circuit to connect all nodes. It is suitable for connecting workstations to a host computer or server. Nodes cannot communicate directly with one another.

A **bus network** is a single end-to-end cable from which connections to the peripherals are made. All workstations are in direct contact with one another. The topology is suitable for local-area networks because nodes can be plugged in and out at will.

Within a network such as a local-area network, it is necessary to ensure error-free transmission of data. In local-area networks there are three systems for providing the individual station's access to the network or access protocols: token passing, empty slot, carrier sense multiple access/collision detection (CSMA/CD). In the first two of these, a station on the network is either given a token (on a regular basis) giving it authority to transmit, or it waits until an empty slot passes, and fills it with a package of data. CSMA/CD relies on all stations listening to the network and transmitting when it is quiet. When they transmit they continue to listen, and if they hear a collision (two or more stations transmitting simultaneously), they stop transmitting and try again a short moment later.

Reflection   What do you understand by the term network topology? What is the difference between network architecture and network topology?

3.6 Some network applications

This section briefly explores some of the different types of network applications.

Local-area networks (LANs)

A local-area network (LAN) is a data communications network used to link together a number of computers, terminals, printers and backing storage devices over a limited geographical area, typically of up to 10 square kilometres. The limited area means that high-speed data transmission can be achieved. The primary objective is to share computing resources, such as processors, disk storage, printers and communications gateways to other networks, amongst a group of users. The links are made by direct cables in the form of twisted wire cable, coaxial cable or fibre-optic cable. Each device that is linked to the LAN is called a node. A network interface card has to be slotted into a microcomputer so that it can be connected to a LAN. A network operating system is required to control the operation of the LAN. A bridge, or a router, may be used to connect two different LANs so that a node on one LAN can communicate with a node on another LAN. A hard-wired gateway connects, for example, a LAN with a mainframe computer.

The shared resources on a LAN are controlled by processors known as file servers. Special software is available for controlling LANs. Often an organization may have more than one LAN. These LANs can be connected together using a bridge or router.

The physical layout of a LAN is called its topology. The possible topologies (shown in Figure 3.1) are star, ring and bus.

Some typical applications of LAN's are:

- file transfer and access
- word processing
- electronic message handling
- personal filing and information handling with database software
- graphical information creation
- remote database access
- digital voice transmission and storage.

Wide-area networks (WANs)

Wide-area networks (WANs) use telecommunications links to allow computers to communicate with one another irrespective of their location. Star, ring and bus topologies may be used. LANs and WANs may be connected into one all-embracing network. The Internet is a series of linked wide-area networks. (Chapter 8 discusses the Internet and information retrieval in more detail.)

Reflection   What are the differences between LANs and WANs?

Electronic funds transfer (EFT)

EFT systems allow computer users to transfer money from their accounts into another account electronically. Employees may be paid, supplier's invoices met, and payment in retail outlets handled, through EFT. Clearing banks deal with several million transactions per working day, many of which involve the preparation and handling of paper documents. EFT allows details of financial transactions to be represented by electronic or magnetic means instead of on paper documents. In addition, accounts are updated concurrently in computer storage. EFT may be achieved through a magnetized credit or debit card, which can be inserted at a point-of-sale terminal in a retail outlet, or in the home via viewdata, using a domestic television. EFT in the home is often described as home banking. EFT is also an important component of business-to-business electronic ordering systems.

Value-added networks (VANs)

An organization which offers communications services to the public at large is described as a common carrier or a postal, telegraph and telecommunications authority (PTT). When an organization leases lines from a common carrier and then adds on computerized enhancements to the service, this is described as a VAN. Common enhancements include better error detection, faster response times, and handling of incompatibilities between different kinds of equipment. These enhancements simplify the exchange of electronic data between users of the service. A user merely plugs into an interface, and the network resolves any incompatibilities in protocols.

Facsimile transmission (fax)

A fax machine looks like a small photocopier. The document to be communicated is placed on the machine and the recipient's fax number is keyed in. The document is then scanned and converted into digital form. After transmission, the original document is reassembled at the other end as an exact copy, or facsimile. Text, charts, handwritten documents and drawings can all be transmitted. Fax is a document delivery option. Using a fax board inside a microcomputer allows computer-generated text and graphics to be faxed without a hard copy being made initially. The CCITT has developed various standards for fax transmission which specify details such as:

- the direction of scanning
- the size and number of scan lines
- data compression techniques
- the speed with which a machine transmits a typical A4 page of text.

The main disadvantage of fax is its slowness of conversion. An A4 sheet takes from 40 seconds to several minutes to convert, because there is a large amount of data when the page is recorded as an image.

Videotex

Videotex applies to a range of electronic systems that use a modified television set or other terminal to present textual and graphic information directly to end-users. Videotex systems which also use telephone lines or other channels of communication to provide a two-way link are known as interactive videotex (or sometimes simply videotex) or viewdata systems. Broadcast systems are known as teletext.

The first teletext system to be introduced was Ceefax, which was introduced by the British Broadcasting Corporation in 1973. Ceefax offers a number of pages of information to the general public on current affairs, sport, weather forecasts, financial data, traffic reports and television programmes.

The first videotex service was Prestel, introduced by the UK Post Office in 1979. Prestel was initially introduced as a public service, but it is now mostly used for business purposes, and is widely used in the travel industry. Many countries have developed national videotex systems, including:

- Telidon in Canada
- Captain in Japan
- Bildschirmtext in Germany.

The French system, known as Minitel, has been particularly successful. This is mainly because the French government, through its PTT, has supplied free videotex terminals to the users of the service, and has provided the French telephone directory as a videotex service.

Electronic mail (e-mail)

E-mail allows messages to be sent over a telecommunications network from one computer to another without any use of paper. An e-mail system may be a local system that delivers messages around one site using a LAN, or a national or international system using the PTT's telecommunications network. The chief advantage of e-mail as compared with the telephone is that messages may be sent and received by the computer whether or not the recipient is available. The recipient may read the message at his/her convenience.

Video and teleconferencing

Telephone conferencing may be of interest in many contexts. This facility is available on many private exchanges, and via the public network. Teleconferencing involves linking more than two parties in a single call. A teleconference may be combined with a video (television) conference link, so that participants can see each other and view presentations. At present the cost of videoconferencing is high, but with the wider introduction of digital wide-band networks and computerized exchanges into the public telecommunications network, corporate applications are growing, and this technology could potentially change the way in which we communicate.

Electronic data interchange (EDI)

EDI is becoming more widely used as a means of placing orders for goods. EDI allows a purchaser's computer to communicate directly with the supplier's computer over a telecommunications link, so that the goods can be ordered direct.

(For further details concerning document ordering and electronic document delivery see Chapter 15.)

Summary   Most computers operate as part of a system or network. Computer systems may encompass mainframe computers, minicomputers and microcomputers. These processing units must be linked together by network or telecommunications links. There are a number of characteristics of networks that affect their operation. These include:

- speed of data transmission
- whether data is sent full or half-duplex
- timing modes
- the use of multiplexing
- the need for modems
- network switching techniques.

It is important to examine the data communication system, the transmission medium, network architectures and protocol standards, and the topology. Local-area networks and wide-area networks are important means of communication within and between organizations. Electronic funds transfer (EFT), value-added networks (VANs), facsimile transmission, video and teleconferencing, e-mail and electronic data interchange all contribute to the effective communication of information.

REVIEW QUESTIONS

1   Draw up a table that summarizes the differences between mainframes, minicomputers and microcomputers.
2   What are the essential components of all telecommunications systems.
3   Explain the meaning of the following terms:

- baud rate
- full duplex
- synchronous transmission
- multiplexing
- modulation
- packet switching.

4   Why is the OSI standard important?

5   Draw the different types of network topology. Give some examples of when individual topologies might be appropriate.
6   Explain the meaning of the following terms in the context of a local-area network:

- node
- bridge
- router
- gateway.

7   What is the difference between videotex and teletext?
8   Why is electronic data interchange likely to have a significant effect on business operations?

Bibliography

Note: A number of the books listed at the end of Chapter 2 offer a basic introduction to the topics covered in this chapter.

Breeding, M. (ed.) (1992) *Library LANs: case studies in practice and application*, London, Meckler.
Devargas, M. (1992) *Local area networks*, Oxford, Blackwells.
Harries, S. (1993) *Networking and telecommunications for information systems*, London, Library Association.
Hodson, P. (1992) *Local area networks*, London, DP Publications.
Marks, K. and Nielsen, S. (1991) *Local area networks in libraries*, London, Meckler.
National Computing Centre (1992) *Handbook of data communications*, Oxford, Blackwells.
Pastine, M and Kacena, C. (1994) 'Library automation, networking and other online and new technology costs in academic libraries', *Library trends*, **42**, 524–36.
Robinson, L. (1995) *Installing a local area network*, London, Aslib.
Zuck, G. and Flanders, B. (eds.) (1992) *Wide area networks in libraries: technology, applications and trends*, Westport/London, Meckler.

4

Information structure and software

LEARNING OUTCOMES

This chapter covers two related topics: the means of representing data in computers, and software and programming languages. Software is the instructions which tell the computer hardware which tasks to execute. At the end of this chapter you will:

- understand how data is represented in computers
- be aware of the nature of programming languages
- understand the difference between different categories of programming languages
- be aware of the stages in program development and the importance of structured programming
- appreciate the role of an operating system
- be aware of the roles of some key types of applications software
- have considered some of the issues associated with the selection of applications software
- be aware of some of the key issues associated with human computer interface design.

4.1 Introduction

Any business or library system must be represented in the computer as:

- the information to be processed
- instructions on how the information is to be processed.

Both the information or data and the instructions must be coded in a form that the computer can store, interpret and act upon. This will involve coding both instructions and data into a machine-readable form. Often the coding also involves structuring the information or data in some way in order to make it easier to handle within the computer system. This chapter starts by examining the basic coding of data and information for storage within a computer system, and progresses to the coding of instructions in programs and software. Software is the programs or instructions used by computers which instruct the hardware in the details of the task to be performed. Software conveys the human instructions that are necessary for computers to complete a task.

An introduction to programming languages is followed by a review of some important types of applications software and a discussion of some of the features that need to be considered in the selection of applications software. Finally, some features of human computer interface design are explored.

4.2　Representing data in a computer

The simplest unit of data which the computer can handle is a single binary digit, called a bit. A bit is either a zero or one. Since each cell is a two-state device, it is necessary to use a group of cells to hold a symbol. All data in a computer are held in groups of bits. The bit is stored in the computer electronically, magnetically or optically, and transmitted along telecommunication lines as aural, electrical, magnetic or optical signals. For example, an electrical pulse represents a one and the absence of a pulse a zero.

A group of 8 bits makes up a byte. The storage capacity of computer systems (including memory, tapes and disks) is usually quoted in bytes. Because numbers are large, figures are given in kilobytes (Kb) or megabytes (Mb). In this computing context, kilo = 2^{10} = 1024, and mega = 2^{20} = 1,048,576. One byte is often used to store one character. This is because characters are stored as codes which comprise a number of bits; 7- or 8-bit codes are common.

Thus a floppy disk that can store 1.44 Mb will store: 1,048,576 × 1.44 = 1,509,949 characters. A computer with 32 Mb of RAM can hold in its memory: 32 × 1,048,576 = 33,554,432 characters.

There has been considerable standardization in alphanumeric code systems. Two important codes for representing characters are the American Standard Code for Information Interchange (ASCII) and the Extended Binary Coded Decimal Interchange Code (EBCDIC). ASCII is a 7-bit or 8-bit code. Table 4.1 shows some examples of characters in ASCII 7-bit code format and the EBCDIC code. The ASCII 7-bit code provides for 128 different characters (27 = 128). There is also an 8-bit ASCII code. An 8-bit code permits 256 (28) different characters to be represented.

Table 4.1 *Some examples of ASCII and EDCDIC codes*

Letter	ASCII	EBCDIC
A	1000001	11000001
B	1000010	11000010
C	1000011	11000011
D	1000100	11000100
E	1000101	11000101

Many different types of data may be held in a byte of information. One byte of storage might store:

- one or more characters
- an instruction to the processor
- the address of some other item of data
- the address of an instruction
- an integer
- a floating point number.

A **word** is a group of bits representing a number in binary form, a computer instruction or one or more characters. The various computer models have different numbers of bits per word. A word may be split into groups of bits, so that, for example, a 24-bit word can be split into three bytes. The longer the word, the more powerful the instruction that it can hold.

Parity bits are additional bits, added to each character in the computer's store, to allow the computer to carry out a rudimentary check on the accuracy of the data representation. When a symbol is first written to a storage location, the parity bit for that location is set to either a zero or a one. Under odd parity:

- if the number of data bits in the character which are set to '1' is an odd number (1,3,5,7), then the parity bit is set to '0'
- if the number of data bits in the character which are set to '1' is an even number (0,2,4,6,8), then the parity bit is set to '1'.

Objects, such as graphs, pictures, and sound and video clips, are stored as image files. Scanned images of documents, which include page layout, may also be stored as image files. There are a number of different image file formats. One is the bitmap file (.bmp), in which the picture is broken down into a number of different small squares and a value is recorded for each of those squares. For black-and-white reproduction it is only necessary to record black or white, but for colour reproduction it is necessary to record the colour of the square as well.

....

Reflection How many characters might 512 Kb of cache memory be able to store?

....

4.3 Software – some definitions

Computers are general-purpose machines that could potentially perform a whole range of tasks, from recording issues of books, manipulating management statistics, keeping a record of expenditure, to maintaining personnel records. In order for a computer to perform the specific tasks required of it at specific times, it is necessary to provide instructions to the computer. These instructions, which indicate which tasks are to be performed, are known as programs or software. Programs or software specify, for instance, how information should be stored, and how it should be formatted and sorted, and manipulated to meet output requirements.

Program instructions are held in main memory and passed one at a time to the control unit. Here they are decoded, so that the control unit can set up the circuits and units appropriate for obeying the instruction. Computers obey instructions at a rate of millions per second and it is common to indicate a computer's internal speed in mips (millions of instructions per second). It is, however, important to recognize that the same calculation can take a differing number of mips depending on both the processor and the programming language in which it is encoded.

A software package is a set of programs designed to perform a specific function or set of functions. Usually a package incorporates several programs and it often covers a wide number of different functions. Many packages are available in the marketplace.

4.4 Programming languages

All software is written in a programming language. A programming language is a means of representing actions to be performed by the computer. The programming language is a series of codes that can be interpreted by the computer as instructions concerning the handling of data. Since data are held as electrical pulses, the programming language is a device for coding instructions concerning the passage of electrical pulses through the machine so that the pattern of pulses at a certain point in time can be reinterpreted into a form that makes sense to the user.

There is a variety of different programming languages, each of which has been designed to facilitate the coding of a specific kind of application. There are basically three kinds of programming language:

- machine code, which computers understand but people do not (without help)
- high-level languages, which people understand but computers do not (without help)
- assembly code, which lies somewhere between machine code and high-level languages.

Machine code

Machine code is the most fundamental of programming languages. Machine code is a binary coding of instructions in the same format as the instructions will be held in the computer. Thus a program in machine code is merely an organized sequence of zeros and ones. Both an operation and a store location address may therefore be held as a string of zeros and ones.

Programs written in machine code are specific to a given computer model or series of models, because the way in which the zeros and ones in a piece of code are interpreted will depend upon the internal circuitry of the computer. This means that:

1   Programs written in machine code are not portable between different machines.
2   To program in machine code a programmer must have an intimate knowledge of the workings of that particular computer.
3   Programs are generally longer than equivalent programs written in a high-level language.
4   Machine code is difficult for people to read and write.
5   Machine code is quick in computer operation and makes economical use of computer processing power.

Assembly-code or low-level languages

Assembly-code languages use mnemonic literal sequences to designate machine codes and reference storage locations. Thus, using a similar example to that cited above,

if INC represents an operation, such as 'add 1 to',
and B represents a store location address,
then INCB will mean add 1 to the number stored at address B:
for example, make 6 into 7 at address B.

Assembly-code languages are therefore not directly interpretable by the computer. A program in assembly code (**source program**) must be translated into machine code (**object program**) before it can be run. Programs in assembly code language are translated into machine code by a language program known as an **assembler**.

Once translated, execution takes place through the object program. The source program is, however, retained to allow changes. Any updating of the program is made to the source program, which is then re-assembled to produce a new object program.

Although assembly code is more mnemonic than machine code, it is still specific to a group of machines.

Third-generation or high-level languages

Most applications programs are written in what are termed high-level or third-generation programming languages. 'High-level' refers to the fact that the languages are well removed from machine code in the way that they code instructions. There are quite a number of high-level programming languages, each individual language having been designed for a specific application area.

Each language codes operations in different ways, and any given language will tend to do those tasks more readily which are common in the application area for which it was intended. Programming languages are designed to be user-amenable, and relatively easy for a programmer to read and understand, although programs in some programming languages are easier to follow than others.

A program in a high-level language must be converted into machine code before it can be executed. This conversion can be performed with the aid of either a compiler or an interpreter. Thus:

Program in high- ————▶ compiler or ————▶ Program in
level language   interpreter   machine code

A compiler or interpreter converts high-level languages into machine code. Once the program is in machine code it will be stored on a storage medium, and can be called into the main store when it is necessary to execute it. Thus, once translated, it can be executed through the object program.

Table 4.2 *Some programming languages*

Programming language	Application area
Algol (ALGOrithmic Language)	Mathematical problems and science
BASIC, QBASIC, GW-BASIC, VBASIC (Beginners' All-purpose Symbolic Instruction Code)	Beginners
COBOL (Common Business Oriented Language)	Business, including many library systems
Fortran (FORmula TRANslator)	Mathematical problems and science
Pascal, Turbo Pascal	Beginners
PL/1 (Programming Language 1)	Commercial and scientific applications, text)
LISP (LISt Programming)	Artificial intelligence (including expert systems)
PROLOG (PROgramming in LOGic)	Artificial intelligence (including expert systems)
C and C++	Systems programming
MODULA3	Systems programming
Java	Graphical applications, Internet
VRML	Virtual reality applications

Although there could potentially be as many different programming languages as there are programmers, there is, fortunately, a fair degree of standardization with respect to programming languages. Table 4.2 lists some of the best-established languages, together with the application areas for which they were designed. Some languages are available in a variety of different versions. Naturally, a language that has been in use for 20 or so years will have undergone revision, and there will be both older and newer versions in use; the newer versions will offer additional features and may be easier to use. In addition, some languages such as BASIC or COBOL may be available in different versions or dialects. Clearly, it is important to have the compiler available for the version of the language that will be in use.

Programs written in high-level languages are:

- shorter than those written in low-level languages (typically, one statement in a high-level language may expand into several machine-language instructions)
- easier to use, and therefore less prone to error and easier to maintain (programmer training is less arduous)
- machine-independent, which leads to good portability between machines and enables parts of the program to be re-used in different applications.

On the other hand, because the programs do not permit a programmer to accommodate the peculiarities of the computer on which the program will be executed, object programs produced by a compiler will not be as economic in terms of core store used and execution time as a machine-code or assembly-code program.

Fourth-generation languages

Although many current systems are written in high-level languages, there are three problems associated with such languages:

- high costs of software production
- the need to produce systems quickly
- the need for systems to meet user requirements.

Fourth-generation languages attempt to overcome the problems of high-level languages. There is no agreed definition of what constitutes a fourth-generation language, although a major distinction that can be made between fourth-generation languages and previous languages is that the latter are **procedural languages**. In programs written in procedural languages, the programmer uses the language to instruct the computer step-by-step in exactly how to execute a given task. Fourth-generation languages are essentially non-procedural or **declarative languages**. programs in these languages tell the machine *what* it has to do and the language works out *how* to do it. Most fourth-generation languages are centred around database applications, and may aid in the specification of input and output screens, reports, record contents, menus and interfaces, and as such include data-description, report-writing and screen-painting facilities. The languages are designed for fast-application development, and many are intended for use by the knowledgeable end-user. Fourth-generation languages have brought a measure of systems design to the end-user, but they are slow in execution and need powerful processors.

Table 4.3 *The generations of programming languages*

Generation	Typical languages	Capabilities
First	Machine code	Machine-oriented; language specific to a processor type
Second	Assembly languages	Easier to read than machine code, though still machine-oriented and specific
Third	High-level languages	Procedurally-oriented, task-oriented; easier programming and easier to read; portable programs
Fourth	Fourth-generation languages (4GLs)	Fast application development; sometimes end-user oriented
Fifth	Object-oriented languages	End-user oriented; facilitate graphical applications; network and Internet-applicable; platform-independent

Object-oriented programming languages

A number of object-oriented languages have been developed. For organizational applications C++ is important, but probably the most significant language is Java, which is currently revolutionizing the capability of the Internet and the World Wide Web. Java is a fully functional standalone object-oriented language that can be used to write applications unrelated to the Internet, but its architectural neutrality (which means that it can run on any hardware platform or OS) and its security features make it very attractive for use in the Internet environment. The Java interpreter, which is used to interpret Java code, is now available in most Web browsers. This means that executable code, often in the form of Java applets, can be downloaded over the Internet. Such applets can be used to create dynamic web pages. Examples include a ticker tape across a page, which shows the latest news stories, and a weather map coupled to a meteorological database; when you run your cursor over a city, the temperature, humidity and wind speed appear at the top of the screen.

Reflection   What is the key difference between an object-oriented programming language and a fourth-generation programming language?

4.5   Programming

A computer program is generally created by a programmer using a systems analyst's specification of the task to be completed. Before commencing to write the detailed program instructions, the programmer will write either a program design or a structured representation of what is to be programmed. Programs are frequently highly complex, containing many instructions.

Programs development is usually performed by a team. The process starts with the user's request for systems enhancement or, in a software house, an evident market need. Systems analysts examine and codify what the new system should do and draw up a program specification. The program specification acts a as reference document during development and through the operational life of the program. It contains a specification of:

- the context of the program, including its main functions
- input to the program
- output from the program
- master files read and updated by the program
- processing conducted by the program
- controls in the program
- details of testing of the program.

Next the programmers design the programs by identifying the logical sequence of operations. A program flowchart may be used to assist in the identification of all of the actions necessary for the job to be done. Then the programs are coded, compiled and tested, before being implemented and, where appropriate marketed.

Programs need to be understandable, because they often require changes during their lifecycle, and it is important that other programmers can appreciate the original programmer's intent. In order to make programs easier to understand and modify, the concept of structured programming was introduced. Structured programs consist of a number of modules. These modules are groups of related instructions or statements. The objective is that these modules should, as far as possible, be independent of one another.

Reflection   Give some examples of situations in which a program
                   specification might be useful.

Object-oriented programming

Object-oriented programming (OOP) has demanded the development of specific object-oriented (OO) systems analysis and design methodologies. These methodologies are relatively new, but will probably become increasingly important. In a sense, object-oriented programming is an extension of structured programming.

The fundamental motivation of OOP is to facilitate development by creating software components that can be re-used. The basic approach is to create objects, to group them in class hierarchies, and to define their properties and methods. OOP languages contain features such as inheritance, encapsulation and polymorphism which make them particularly suitable for interface development. They allow easy construction of screen objects by the use of existing code, they are less error-prone, and the programmer does not need to be familiar with the fine detail of how the code works. In visual, direct-manipulation environments this allows the developer to concentrate on the design of the interfaces.

It may be helpful to more explicitly define some of the terms that have been used above:

1   **Objects** are a combination of entities with methods (see below). Thus an object includes both an entity and the processes to which it might be subject. An object might be a form, table, report or control, such as a button on the screen that can be manipulated as a unit.
2   **Classes** are categories to which objects belong. Lower-level classes are specializations of higher-level classes, so that, for instance, a proforma order is a type or specialization of a general order.
3   **Attributes** are data items which describe the object.
4   **Operations** are actions which create, change or delete the object's attributes.
5   **Methods** (sometimes called **services**) are procedures, algorithms or calculations which carry out the activity inside objects. Methods are the processing part of objects, and are specified in structured English or pseudo-code.
6   **Messages** are communicated by objects. Messages may contain data to be processed by the object or requests for services.

The concepts of inheritance, encapsulation and polymorphism are also important in understanding object-oriented methods:

1   **Inheritance.** Lower-level classes inherit properties (such as attributes, operations and methods) from higher-level classes; this facilitates the re-use of more general higher-level objects by specialization, which creates a new class by addition of further detail. So, for example, a code could be written for a NEXT button. The OK button can then be simply written by defining the OK button as an instance of the button class of objects, in which case it inherits all of the properties of the button class. The code for a button only needs to be written once. If at a later stage the developer decides to change some characteristic of the buttons such as their default colours, this could be achieved for all buttons by changing the properties of the button class definition.
2   **Encapsulation** is the concept that objects should hide their internal contents from other systems components to improve maintainability. The encapsu-

lated parts of objects are hidden to insulate them from the effects of modifications to higher-level objects.

3   **Polymorphism** refers to the ability to define general procedures such as PRINT without the need to define specific parameters. The same command is interpreted differently according to the context and the recipient of the command. Thus, although the detailed operations associated with printing, say, a chart, a spreadsheet or a text file are very different, in Windows applications all of these can be achieved by choosing the PRINT icon or option.

The virtue of OO methods is that the specification becomes the implementation. Analysis and design proceed by gradual addition of detail to the objects. The system is modelled as a collection of objects connected by message-passing channels. Objects pass messages to each other to request a service, such as the updating of an object's attributes, or to request a report. More detail is added to objects until the specification becomes sufficiently detailed to be programmed in an object-oriented language.

4.6   Software packages

A software package is a suite of programs that are packaged together because they perform a specific function. The concept of a software package sits more comfortably in a commercial environment, where software is packaged and sold. In-house suites of software programs may be under continuing evolution, and it may be difficult to identify the boundaries of such a suite.

There are three different types of software package:

* operating systems
* utility software
* applications software.

Operating systems (OS)

The operating system is one type of software package. It is a set of master programs which supervises the progress and use of all other programs, and controls input and output to peripherals and the compilation of programs. (In mainframe systems this is provided by the manufacturer.) It is designed to control the activities of the computer configuration as a whole. In a sense, the operating system is the set of programs that 'tells the computer how to work' and sets up an environment in which the computer can start to understand and execute other, more applications-oriented programs. The operating system may vary depending on the function of the computer. For example, if the computer is to be connected via a telephone line to another computer, the OS will need to encompass software to organize that link. The user of the system can communicate with the OS through a set of OS commands, which are commands from a special language. Typically, such commands may instruct the computer to display a directory of files, copy files from one directory to another, send files for printing, list files on the screen, etc. The functions of the operating system can be grouped into:

- communications with the operator
- input/output control
- communications software
- program management.

The move towards connectivity and standardization of platforms in recent years has led to the domination of two operating systems: UNIX and Windows (in various versions). Solaris, from Sun Microsystems, is also in evidence. Earlier generations of mainframe and minicomputers relied upon proprietary operating systems, which would only run on a specific manufacturer's series of machines. In the microcomputer field, MS-DOS and PC DOS (sometimes referred to as DOS) have been established standards for many years, and in different ways underpin Windows-based systems.

Utility software

Utility software is made available by computer equipment manufacturers or software houses in order that certain basic functions may be performed; these functions are common to many applications. It is sometimes difficult to differentiate an OS function from a utility function, and indeed some operating systems include utility functions. Utility programs include, for example:

- sorting – assembling records into sequence
- merging – merging two files
- file copying – copying a file held on one medium to another
- file handling and processing – showing files in alphabetical or other orders, renaming files, displaying files
- dumping and re-starting routines – for storing data during a long processing run, to ensure that data is not lost during a breakdown
- editing routines – converting output data to the format required for visual or printed output
- diagnostic or de-bugging routines and file recovery
- antivirus software – detecting viruses and disinfecting disks.

....

Reflection   Summarize the difference between an operating system and
                   utility software.
....

Applications software

Applications programs are programs written individually to operate specific tailor-made procedures and systems, such as sales ledger systems, wages systems, stock inventory systems, library circulation control systems, word-processing systems, etc. Some applications programs are available in the commercial marketplace as packages or software packages. where there are a number of requirements that are common to different users. Some common types of software packages of interest to information managers are listed below.

When an applications software package is required, the options are:

- to acquire a pre-written, off-the-shelf software package
- to acquire a turnkey package incorporating both hardware and software
- to write in-house programs
- to commission the writing of programs
- to participate in a cooperative venture that offers access to software and/or hardware and/or databases.

In many instances it is sensible to choose a commercially available package, since it is too costly to write a local software package or to commission someone to do this, even though a tailor-made package designed specifically for a given application is most likely to fit all the requirements of that application.

The advantages of using packages are:

1   They are economical, because the investment cost for the initial creation and later maintenance of the package is spread over several users.
2   The package comes as a well-tested set of programs, and the supplier has a sufficient number of clients to justify adequate maintenance arrangements.
3   The software producer is likely to be a specialist in that kind of software, and should therefore produce a better-quality product with valuable features whose importance might not occur to the new user.
4   Packages have good documentation, including a detailed system specification, identification of hardware requirements, input, output and file specifications, systems timing and user manuals.
5   Packages are available at short notice, and the system can therefore be implemented more quickly.
6   Support and advice services should be available from the package supplier.
7   Packages incorporate expertise that is difficult to acquire and not otherwise available to the organization.
8   Packages can be evaluated in a user situation and compared with others.

Reflection   Think of an example from your experience where the availability
of a software package at short notice has been a particularly
attractive characteristic of the package.

Disadvantages of packages are:

1   The package will probably not fit the user's present system or requirements
exactly. Its acceptability depends on how easily the package or the requirements can be modified so that a satisfactory compromise can be achieved.
2   The user depends on the expertise and reliability of the software supplier,
both for the initial package and for subsequent maintenance and support.
The quality of support may change over the lifetime of the system.
3   The package program may be less efficient than a tailor-made package in
terms of computer running time and processor utilization.

Even when a software package is implemented, it is important to remember that
there is still a need for trained, experienced staff who are fully familiar with the
package, and that it remains necessary to acknowledge the importance of a systematic approach to systems investigation and implementation as discussed in
Chapter 6.

There are a number of different kinds of software packages. We shall confine
ourselves to some general-purpose applications software packages.

Office software

General-purpose office software includes word-processing, spreadsheet, graphics,
desktop publishing, database and communications software. Database and communications software are mentioned briefly later. We shall first identify the functions of word-processing, spreadsheet and graphics software. General business
software has wide application in all organizations, and is likely to be used in
libraries alongside specialist products for handling library and information functions.

Word-processing software

This is designed to support the creation of text-based documents, their storage,
later retrieval, modification and possible re-use. Typical applications are standard
letters, reports, forms, lists and manuals. Word-processing software must support
the manipulation of text, including, for example, the alignment of margins, the
deletion and insertion of words, lines and paragraphs, the creation of back-up
files, underlining, different typefaces, and general document design and layout.

Spell-checkers, thesauri and a sophisticated range of document design features are common in today's packages.

Spreadsheet software

This supports the storage and manipulation of numerical data. A spreadsheet may be used to store financial and production data, and can be used to assess the existing situation or to plan for the future. A spreadsheet is a large table which contains a number of cells arranged in rows and columns. Numbers, text and formulae can be entered into the spreadsheet cells. The software allows the user to rearrange the data and perform mathematical operations on the data. Increasingly, spreadsheet packages offer facilities for graphical presentation of the data.

Graphics software

Graphics software for use in business supports the creation of graphs, histograms, pie charts and other graphical analyses of data. The data may then be used in documents and for other communication processes such as in presentations.

Desktop publishing software

This is useful in publishing applications, such as in the preparation of in-house magazines, advertising material, brochures, pamphlets and overhead projector slides. Desktop publishing packages allow the user to create documents, including text and graphics, or to import documents from, for example, a word-processing package. The desktop publisher enables the user to set up the page and other design for a document, so that it can be set up ready for printing in-house or despatch to an external printer. Many word-processing packages now offer some 'desktop publishing' features.

Presentation packages

These support the creation of audiovisual aids to enliven presentations, such as report briefings or marketing presentations. These packages are becoming more popular for the creation of sets of slides and auto-running slide shows.

Office suites and integrated software packages

These typically cover a number of business software functions, such as word-processing, database, spreadsheet and graphics in a single package. The chief attractions of an integrated package are the ease with which documents containing text, numbers and graphics may be created, and the common interface across all application areas. The main drawback of such packages has traditionally been that all of their components are not necessarily as good as the software that is available for the separate functions. But many current packages offer a powerful suite of high-quality applications with common interface features that support ease of use. In addition, such packages offer straightforward transfer of data between, say, word-processing and spreadsheet functions.

Reflection   Which of the above types of software are available on a computer to which you have access?

Database software and database management systems

Database software supports the creation of databases and files. Typically, data are held in the form of records which are composed of fields. The strength of a database lies in the ability to select records according to specified criteria, and then to print or display the data in various orders and formats. The next chapter explores databases and record formats in more detail, especially as they apply to library and information applications.

There is a range of general-purpose database software available. Some of the cheaper microcomputer-based systems might be described as flat-file systems: they handle only one file at a time. More sophisticated database software will take the form of a database management system (DBMS). A DBMS has the potential to relate two or more databases to one another so that it is possible, for example, to examine data from more than one database simultaneously – in, say, printing an invoice. A DBMS would, for example, support the creation of two related databases, one of which contained the details of suppliers, while the other contained the full specification of the items that might be ordered. If data is used from both databases simultaneously, then details of the items required may appear together with the name and address of the supplier on, say, an order form.

DBMSs can be regarded as systems development tools. Many incorporate a fourth-generation language which allows users to develop their own system. Some library management systems have been built with a DBMS.

Communication software

Communication software may be used not only within an organization across a local-area network but also to talk to external computers. Internal electronic mail software is likely to be used within an organization where there are many networked users. Other communications software can assist in access to external computers, such as those accessible through the Internet. When a communications package is part of a suite of software which also encompasses a database package, the database package can be used to reformat, store and retrieve downloaded data.

4.7 Criteria for choosing applications software

The strategies associated with the selection and implementation of software and hardware are considered in Chapter 6, which deals with systems analysis and design, and issues associated with the implementation of systems. Here the key factors to consider when examining software, and choosing one application package in preference to another, are rehearsed in general terms. Specifically, it is important to apply these criteria in such a way that they are used to identify a match between what the package offers and the requirements of the system. Clearly there are additional specific factors that must be considered when choosing any specific kind of package, such as a library management system or a document management system, which are determined by the functions that the system needs to fulfil.

General points

First, there are a number of general features of any software package that need to be ascertained and taken into account.

Other people's experiences

A well-tested package that is established in the marketplace, and where several applications similar to that being considered are available for examination, is generally to be preferred. Such a package is less likely to have bugs and should have adequate support. Other people's experiences are useful in indicating the potential and problems of a software package, and they may also offer help and advice in tailoring and implementing the package.

Cost

Clearly, cost is a primary consideration in the purchase of any software package. For example, software packages for database management range in price from £100 to over £50,000. Obviously, more expensive packages offer a wider range of features and facilities, but the application under consideration may only merit a more limited expenditure. Comparisons of prices of packages must be made. These may be made difficult by the fact that some software is sold separately, whilst other software is sold as part of a turnkey package which also includes hardware. Also, it is important to recognize that the price of a package is only a small element in the overall cost of installing a system. In addition to hardware costs, there will be database creation, system installation and implementation costs that will significantly outstrip the price of the package.

Originator

The reputation of the systems house responsible for writing a software package is important to consider. Experience with other packages from the same originator may be useful in assessing a new package. Some software houses are well established and have long-established packages in the marketplace, whereas others are less stable. An established software house is more likely to be able to offer continuing support.

Supplier

Sometimes the supplier is the same as the originator, but especially with business software for microcomputers, the supplier may be an agent. Agencies may specialize in certain types of software and/or may be selling complete systems. Obviously the supplier is an intermediary between the user and the originator, and may hinder direct communication between user and originator, although the better suppliers and originators will have worked out their respective responsibilities so that the customer is offered satisfactory support.

Technical points

In addition to general points, there are a number of technical features of software packages that it is necessary to ascertain, both when choosing between packages and when assessing whether any specific package is suitable for a given application.

Language

The programming language in which the software is written may be a high-level language or assembler, or often a combination of both. It is important that the language used permits the application to be run efficiently (in terms of machine time and storage requirements).

Operating system

The package must be suitable for running under an operating system that will run on the hardware being used.

Hardware

The software needs to be available in a version that will run on the hardware available. Alternatively, even if software is being chosen before hardware, it may nevertheless be important to choose software that will run on a machine for which a lot of other software is available, so that additional software can be selected at a later date.

Ease of use

Ease of use of software is clearly important. Many of the factors that might be considered are related to the quality of the human–computer interface. Factors to be considered include dialogue design and screen display design. This theme is developed further in the next section. Clearly, support in the form of documentation and help systems will influence ease of use.

Support

Support in the use of software is important if the user is to exploit the features of the software to its utmost. In general, more support should be expected with more expensive packages, where the task of implementation is likely to be more daunting. Clearly, there is a significant difference in style and quantity of documentation required between, say, a simple one-function microcomputer system and a multi-function, multi-user mainframe system. Documentation is, nevertheless, important in all circumstances. Support may take various forms:

Documentation

This includes both printed documentation and online documentation and help systems. Ideally, different kinds of documentation should be available for different kinds of users. At the very least, documentation should include an introductory exploration of basic features, a full account of all features, and an online help system. Additional tutorial support which introduces the new user may also be available, either on disk or in printed form or via a telephone or e-mail help line. In a sophisticated package, help systems and tutorial support will be available in several different versions, and the user, or the system, may choose the level of assistance in accordance with the user's level of experience with the system.

Advice in setting up

In addition to tutorial support, some assistance in implementing a software package is to be expected. With larger systems in particular, the contract for the purchase of the software will include a number of hours' assistance provided by suppliers in order to help establish databases, input forms, report forms and other activities.

Training

This may be available from the system supplier, or from training centres licensed by the system supplier. Other agencies, such as educational establishments, may also offer some introductory training in the use of some packages. With larger systems, most suppliers will offer both on-site and off-site training. Both types of training may be suitable for different groups of staff. It is important to recognize that proper training can save much time in trial-and-error experimentation and learning.

Maintenance

Maintenance of a software package involves two areas of activity:

* removing any bugs or errors that might become evident in the software as it is used for a greater variety of applications
* improving the software so that it incorporates new facilities and concepts as fashions and requirements change.

Both types of maintenance are important. Many of the established software suppliers offer maintenance contracts at a percentage of the cost of the original package. Minor upgrades are made available to users with maintenance contracts. Substantial changes to software, new versions and new modules, will often be made available to existing users at preferential rates.

User clubs

Many of the larger, and some of the smaller, well-established software packages have user clubs, or user groups, which assist in the use of software. User clubs are groups of users of software packages that have two main functions:

* to share expertise and experience in the application of the package between different users
* to discuss and present a concerted front to software suppliers concerning problems and desirable improvements and developments.

Reflection   Why is the reliability of the software supplier an important consideration in the selection of a software package?

4.8 Human computer interface design

Interface design in all information systems is central to the effective use of the system. The designer's objective is to create an interface which supports the full spectrum of potential users with the full range of potential tasks that the user may seek to perform with the system. Good interface design leads to:

*   increased user acceptance of the system
*   increased frequency of use of the system
*   lower operator error rates
*   decreased operator training time
*   increased speed of performance.

In general human computer interface.(HCI) design has become more important in the last 10 to 15 years, as the number and range of users has expanded. Early users of computer systems were often programmers or designers, and could thus be classified as expert users, whereas nowadays most users are discretionary users.

There is no unified theory or explanatory framework of HCI. Nevertheless, a number of sets of general dialogue design guidelines are generally acknowledged. Shneiderman (1987) suggests eight rules:

1   Dialogues should be consistent.
2   Systems should allow users short-cuts through some parts of familiar dialogue.
3   Dialogues should offer informative feedback.
4   Sequences of dialogues should be organized into logical groups.
5   Systems should offer simple error handling.
6   Systems should allow actions to be reversed.
7   Systems should allow experienced users to feel as though they, rather than the system, are in control.
8   Systems should aim to reduce short-term memory load. In other words, users should not be expected to remember too much.

It is important to remember that the physical devices through which interaction can be achieved – i.e. the input and output devices – impose important restrictions on the nature of the interaction, and the development of new physical devices offers new opportunities for different styles of interaction. The number of interactional devices is continuing to expand, and each of these is finding a niche in the market. The objective of any development in this area is to create input and output devices that maximize the advantages of human physical and cognitive characteristics, and so promote efficient, reliable and possibly even pleasurable interaction with the system.

Dialogue components and styles

Much of the consideration of HCI design has focused on the style of the interaction, with the screen as the central output device. There are a number of different dialogue design styles. Several of these may be used in any one system, possibly to cater for different functions or different groups of users. Furthermore, the categories are not exclusive or mutually dependent. Voice systems will eventually become a form of natural language interface, and icons are a different way of presenting menus. The designer must consider which combination of interface styles to use, and how to apply the components of that style in the design of an effective interface. These must be considered in the context of the user and the task that the user wishes to perform with the system.

Command languages

Command languages are one of the oldest and most widely used dialogue styles. In dialogues based on commands, the user enters instructions in the form of commands. The computer recognizes these commands and takes appropriate action. For example, if the user types in PRINT 1-2, the computer responds with a prompt to indicate that the command has been carried out or a message stating why the command can not be executed. The command language for a given system is a features of the software under which the system runs. There are command languages associated with operating systems, and with applications software. The online search services make extensive use of command-based interfaces, and many early text retrieval systems were primarily command-based.

The command language must include commands for all of the functions that the user might choose to perform, and therefore, since different systems perform different functions, it is inevitable that command languages will differ between systems. Some attempts have been made to adopt standard command languages for systems that perform similar functions, and one result of this is the Common Command Language used by some of the online search services. However, standardization is difficult, and an inherent feature of command-based dialogues is the need for users to become familiar with the command language used. An intermediate option which is widely used, and is suitable for users with some familiarity with the system, is the use of commands in menus, so that the menus prompt users in their use of commands. This is not, however, effective for new users because they can only guess what the commands displayed on the menus mean.

Command languages are potentially the most powerful interface, but this brings the penalty of difficulty of learning. The user must learn not only the actual commands but also their syntax, including the order in which commands much be written. The placing and choice of separators such as spaces, commas, semicolons and colons is often crucial as to whether a system will accept and execute a command. For example, to display the author inverted file around the author J. Keen on DIALOG, the searcher needs to know that the correct syntax of the search statement is 'AU=KEEN,J'.

The main advantages of command languages are the economy of screen space, the direct addressing of objects and functions by name, and the flexibility of system function which a combination of commands can provide.

Menu-based interfaces

Menus present users with a number of alternatives, or else a menu on the screen, and asks them to select one option in order to proceed. The menu options are usually either displayed as commands, which is particularly appropriate for more experienced users, or as short explanatory pieces of text. Pictures or icons may also be used to represent the menu options. The appropriate option is selected by keying in a code (often a number or letter) for that option, or by pointing to the required option with a mouse or other pointing device. Menus are generally recognized to be a sound approach for the occasional or novice user. Additional help is rarely necessary, and little data entry is required of the user. The system designer has restricted the total set of options, and thus the novice user is less liable to make mistakes. Equally, users not familiar with the terminology of the interface can be assisted, since the menus restrict the choice set. If menus are appropriately structured, and the items selected carefully, menus can be quick and easy to use, often requiring only one or two key presses or mouse clicks to complete a selection. Also, since any input must be one of the options offered, menu-based systems are easy to program.

Menus can be frustrating and confining to more experienced users. Menu-based interfaces must be closely defined with the user in mind. This involves careful consideration of the menu structure, key presses required and menu bypass techniques. For example, expert users should have the option of accessing a specific screen or making a selection without necessarily passing through all previous menu selections.

Where there are many possible commands and displaying them all might be difficult, then menus are sometimes organized hierarchically in tree-like structures. In other words, a menu might not only contain commands, but also routes to other menus. For example, a FORMAT command in a word-processing package, when selected from a menu, might display a further menu which listed the options of items for formatting, such as characters or paragraphs.

Although menus can be very useful in retrieval, they do have some limitations:

1   They are not suitable for inputting data such as numbers or text.
2   A lot of information is presented on the screen, and this information takes time to read.

3   Only a limited number of options may be presented on one screen, and in order to offer a large number of options it is necessary to design a hierarchy of menus.

4   Once a hierarchy of menus and sub-menus is included, it is important to give the user the menus to keep track of where they are, and to be able to trace a path through the hierarchy.

Today's interfaces use a number of different types of menu, often in combination. Commonly encountered menu types include:

1   **Single option menus**, often used to request a confirmation of a response offered by a user.

2   **Pop-up menus**, which pop-up or appear, often in the centre of the screen, and request a response or a selection.

3   **Pull down menus** are often attached to a main menu across the top of the screen. When a user clicks on a menu option on the main menu bar, a further menu appears, showing a number of options.

4   **Step-down menus** are a series of menus. So, for example, a user may click on an option on the main menu bar at the top of a screen to display a pull-down menu. Options on this menu that will lead to the display of further menus may be indicated, for example, with three dots, e.g. 'Field...'. Clicking on these options leads to a further menu. This is known as a step-down menu. Such a menu can be particularly helpful when there is a series of actions to perform, since they can remind the user of the sequence in which these actions must be completed.

5   **Main menu bars** appear at the top or bottom of the screen, and remain on the screen whilst the user performs other functions and displays other menus. They may have pull-down menus attached as indicated above, or they may simply display some common menu options such as 'help', 'save' and 'exit'.

....

Reflection   Examine the range of different types of menus used in a software package to which you have access. Explain the benefits of the different types for the specific application.

....

Function keys

Function keys are a hardware equivalent of menus, with options allocated to special keys on the keyboard. Function keys might cover options such as 'copy', 'insert', 'delete', 'help', 'display record', and 'call menu'.

Hard-coded function keys have an operation permanently allocated to a particular key, and are located accordingly. With **soft-coded** keys the command call is allocated to the function key by the application program. Most keyboards have 10 to 12 function keys, so the number of options that can be covered by these keys is extremely limited.

Question-and-answer dialogues

The user of a question-and-answer dialogue is guided through the interaction by questions or prompts on the screen. The user responds to these by entering data through the keyboard. Often questions may require only a simple 'yes' or 'no' response, but on other occasions users may be required to supply some data, such as a code, a password, their name, or other textual data. Usually, however, one-word responses are expected. On receiving the user's response, the computer will evaluate it and act accordingly. This may involve the display of data, additional questions or the execution of a task such as saving a file. The prompt information can easily be tailored to the requirements of the user, and this dialogue style may therefore suit novice and casual users. The main drawback of this dialogue mode is that, since an input data item must be validated at each step before continuing with the dialogue, the interaction can be slow. Question-and-answer dialogue is widely used in a simple form in GUI interfaces, where a question might be posed in a dialogue box and the user is expected to respond by clicking the 'yes' or 'no' button.

Form-filling dialogues

In a form-filling dialogue the user works with a screen-based image of a form. The screen form will have labels, and space into which data are to be entered. It should be possible to move a cursor to any appropriate position on the form for the entering of data. Labels will normally be protected from amendment or overwriting, and some users may be able to amend only certain fields, so that others are protected. Form filling is a useful dialogue for inputting records and blocks of data. In searching it is used in query-by-example interfaces. All data input should be validated and errors reported to the user. Form filling, because it may involve large amounts of data entry, can take a lot of time and can be a source of frustration and errors. In form-filling dialogues the user has little control over the dialogue, but the approach has the advantage that the user rarely needs to remember commands or their syntax.

Graphical user interfaces (GUIs) and direct manipulation

The idea of **direct manipulation** is that the user's actions should directly affect what happens on the screen, in the sense that there is a feeling of physically manipulating objects on the screen. Typically, direct manipulation systems have icons representing objects which can be moved around the screen and manipulated by controlling a cursor with a mouse. One might, for example, move a file by clicking on an icon representing the file and dragging it to a new location.

A **graphical user interface (GUI)** is not the same as a direct manipulation interface. Strictly speaking. it means an interface that uses bitmapped displays rather than character displays. Often the two terms are used interchangeably, although it is possible to have a GUI which does not use direct manipulation, and some of the more straightforward public-access interfaces based primarily on touch screens are GUIs without direct manipulation.

Direct manipulation interfaces, led by Microsoft Windows, have become very widespread. Shneiderman (1982) identifies the following positive features of direct manipulation systems:

1   Novices can learn basic functionality quickly (so they can get started easily and learn more functionality as they work).
2   Experienced users can work extremely rapidly to carry out a wide range of tasks.
3   Users can see immediately whether or not their actions are moving towards their goals, and take corrective action if necessary.
4   Users experience less anxiety because the system is comprehensible and actions are reversible.
5   Users gain confidence and mastery because they initiate an action and can predict system responses.

GUIs are regarded as particularly useful when the user population is expected to contain a high proportion of novices, or alternatively where the user population contains a mixture of novices and more experienced users.

The tools available for interface design in Windows and other GUI-based environments are determined by the standard components of the GUI interface. These components are used to design the software in its native state and in the design of any interfaces in applications based on the software. The standard GUI components are windows, dialogue boxes, menus and commands, buttons and check boxes, and icons. (Menus and commands have been dealt with earlier in this chapter.)

Windows

A window is a rectangular area on the screen in which an application or document can be viewed. Most windows can be opened, closed, moved and sized. Several windows can be opened simultaneously, and most windows can either be reduced to an icon or enlarged to fill the entire desktop. Sometimes windows are displayed within other windows. There are two types of windows: tiled and overlapping. Tiled windows are where the screen is divided up in a regular manner into subscreens with no overlap. Overlapping windows can be nested on top of one another. Windows have a number of uses. Screen areas can be separated for error messages, control menus, working area and help.

Dialogue boxes

A dialogue box is a special window that appears temporarily to request information. Many dialogue boxes contain options that you select to tell the software to execute a command. A dialogue box requests information from the user. For example, the users may need to select certain options, type some text or specify settings.

Buttons and check boxes

Buttons and check boxes are similar in that you click on them to select an option or to choose a command.

There are two types of buttons: command buttons and option buttons. Command buttons allow you to choose a command, such as 'save' or 'help'. They appear as images of keys. Command buttons displayed with '...', such as 'set-up', will display a further dialogue box when clicked. Option buttons are usually shown as small circles. When clicked and selected, the circle is filled with a smaller filled-in circle.

Check boxes are shown as small boxes. When selected the box is filled with an X, and clicking on the box turns the option on or off. Often a series of check boxes may be shown in the dialogue box to allow the user to select a number of options or settings.

Icons

Icons are graphical representations of various elements in a GUI, such as disk drives, applications, embedded and linked objects and documents. An icon can be chosen by double clicking on it. For example, the main window in Windows shows the main applications that are included in Windows, such as File Manager, Control Panel, Print Manager, Clipboard Viewer, MS-DOS Prompt, Windows Set-up, PIF Editor, and Read Me. Group icons represent other groups of icons.

Natural-language dialogues

Natural-language interfaces are those that allow users to communicate in their native language, such as English. The system needs to be able both to interpret inputs in natural language from the user, and to act upon them, and preferably also to generate natural-language statements in response to user input. In order to achieve such a dialogue, the system must include both English understanding and generation capabilities. In general, natural-language interfaces cannot yet be designed so that they can interpret every request correctly, but they can be used effectively in more structured environments where the set of all terminology, usage, phraseology and the common requests are known. Thus some information retrieval systems have been designed where the user searches by inputting a natural-language phrase. The system then has algorithms for breaking down that phrase into component search terms, performing a search and providing feedback to the users on the set of retrieved documents.

There are still a number of difficulties in generating interfaces that can deal with natural language. These include:

1   **Ambiguity**. Humans can afford to be ambiguous because we use different forms of communication such as actions, body language and pronoun antecedent relationships to assist in communication.
2   **Multiple meanings**. Words have multiple meanings depending upon their position in the sentence or the context of the communication.
3   **Imprecision**. There are many words used in natural language, such as 'average', 'lots', 'few' and 'many', which are imprecise, and difficult for the system to interpret into a specific number or range of numbers.

Natural-language interfaces are generally regarded as being helpful to naïve users because they can approach the system with no knowledge of the system, the contents of the database or the retrieval strategies that the system will employ. More experienced users may find natural-language interfaces frustrating in that they may wish to specify the range of retrieval facilities that are used in a search. For example, they may wish to specify whether truncation is used in a search. Users often need support in framing their hypothesis or questions as a query statement, even with natural-language interfaces.

Voice-based dialogues

All of the dialogues considered so far are concerned with screen-based communication with the aid of keyboards, mice, touch screens and similar devices. There are many circumstances in which a voice-based dialogue would be most convenient for the user. Such dialogues would be attractive to the occasional user inputting only 'yes' and 'no' and other one-word answers, and also to the user inputting large quantities of textual data. Voice-based dialogues might be voice-to-voice (i.e. the computer and the user talk to each other) or screen-to-voice (i.e. the computer talks, the user operates keyboard).

With voice-to-voice dialogues, communication may be remote from a workstation, through a telephone receiver and telecommunications link. All of these modes may have their applications, and the dialogue modes outlined above (e.g. menu, command, form filling) might be employed in a voice-based dialogue.

Although there are some applications of such systems, they have limited application, and further development is to be expected.

Multimedia interfaces

Multimedia interfaces present interesting challenges to the interface designer with regard to how best to incorporate sound, video, stills, graphics, text, numbers and animation. Multimedia interfaces can be viewed as having two components:

- the navigational interface, which exhibits many of the characteristics of a GUI interface such as buttons and windows
- the graphics elements that contribute to the appearance of the application, including backgrounds, textures, colours, the way that the type is displayed on the screen, and how the stills, graphics and videos are displayed.

These components need to be integrated so that, for example, the complementary colours of the design may be used to match a still, or the lighting of a sequence of video may be designed to match the look and feel of the rest of the job production.

There are a number of unanswered questions as to how people might use multimedia interfaces. This may depend on the nature of the application for which the multimedia are being used; application areas embrace entertainment, marketing, information provision and education.

Combining user-interface design styles

A system must be designed to:

- encompass all of the tasks that need to be accomplished with the system
- be used by different types of users.

Some information retrieval systems, such as CD-ROM and online information retrieval from external search services, may in some applications be effectively standalone in that the only tasks to be performed by users are retrieval-oriented tasks. Other information retrieval systems, most notably OPACs, may be part of a larger system. A consistent interface design approach must be adopted across all of the components of the system. A library management system, for example, needs to support the routine operations associated with the issue and return of books, as well as data inputting in relation to catalogue and borrower records, and information retrieval in the OPAC.

GUIs make wide use of a variety of different interface styles, and demonstrate that it is possible to combine different interface styles. However, it is important to make use of an appropriate interface design methodology to ensure that the interface style matches the range of users and the tasks that they are likely to want to perform.

Table 4.4 summarizes some of the advantages and disadvantages of different interface design styles.

Table 4.4 *Interface design styles*

Style	Advantages	Disadvantages
Menus	Easy to learn; easy to use; easy to program; suitable for novice users in access to system options	Slow to use in large systems; limited choice per menu; transmission overhead; can be irritating to experienced users
Icons	Very easy to learn; easy to use; language-independent; relatively easy to program; suitable for novice users in system access and command interfaces	Not economic in use of screen space; need some text back-up; require graphics hardware; needs icon-builder software
Question-and-answer	Easy to use; easy to learn; easy to program	Unsophisticated; slow to use
Form-filling	Quick to use; easy to use; easy to learn; suitable for all user types, data enter, display and retrieval interfaces	Form only suitable for data entry
Command languages	Quick to use; sophisticated; Suitable for expert users with complicated requirements	Difficult to learn; difficult for novices to use; difficult to program
Natural-language	Natural communication; no learning required; suitable for novice users in a restricted problem domain	Difficult to program; needs knowledge base; verbose input; can be ambiguous
Multimedia	Easy and interesting to use; attracts attention; supports learning and understanding in a multidimensional mode	Needs optical-disc-type storage capacities and high-bandwidth communication channels; relatively expensive to create good-quality databases and interfaces

Reflection   Use Table 4.4 to compare two interfaces that are easily available to you.

Colour in interface design

A basic use of colour is in the colour of the background and the text on the screen. Many applications also make extensive use of colour in status bars, menus and other areas of the screen. Colour can be an effective mechanism for communicating alerts, drawing attention and defining relationships. In a number of database systems, colour is used to draw attention to specific parts of records. In general colour can be used to:

- draw attention to warnings
- improve legibility and reduce eyestrain
- highlight different parts of the screen display, such as status bars and menus
- group elements in menus or status bars together, so that, for instance, an instruction is associated with the number of its function key.

Nevertheless, colour must be used with care and with an understanding of how potential users see colour differences and obtain information from colours. Colour used inappropriately can be distracting, confusing or objectionable.

Z39.50 and SR

Z39.50 and SR are standards for information retrieval. Z39.50 is a national US protocol developed by ANSI (American National Standards Institute), whilst SR, or ISO 10162/3 Search and Retrieve, is the international standard emanating from the International Standards Organisation. Z39.50 and SR are compatible, but Z39.50 is more frequently used because it has greater functionality.

Z39.50 is an application layer protocol which supports the construction of distributed information retrieval applications (see the OSI model in Chapter 3, in which the applications layer is the top layer, or the layer that processes the data). The implementation of the Z39.50 standard allows users of different software products to communicate with each other and to exchange data. Most significantly, the local familiar interface can be made available for searching other remote databases. This means that a user, can for instance, search a remote OPAC mounted under a different library management system through the interface available in the local library.

Z39.50 functions in a client–server environment (see Chapter 2). In this context the client is known as the origin and the server as the target. At the client end, a request from the user application is translated into Z39.50 by the origin and sent to the target. At the server end, the target translates the request into a form understandable by the database application, which processes the request, locates the required information and returns it to the target, which then, in turn, passes it back to the origin. The reciprocal translation process accommodates returning information.

Many, but not all, systems suppliers offer Z39.50 clients and/or servers. Z39.50 is used in a number of library management systems, OCLCs FirstSearch service (document delivery and interlibrary loan) and in the online search services offered by Mead Data Central and DIALOG; SilverPlatter have embedded it in their Electronic Reference Library. Whilst Z39.50 allows the use of a local search interface, this does not mean that all search facilities normally offered by that interface are available. Since the remote database application performs the search, the user is restricted to the facilities of that system. There are also some restrictions imposed by the protocol itself. For example, the protocol does not cover relevance ranking.

Summary   The chapter started by explaining the way in which data are represented in a computer. Programming languages by which instructions can be issued to a computer include machine code, assembly language, high-level languages, fourth-generation languages and object-oriented languages. Program development needs to take account of the principles of structured programming. Operating systems are responsible for managing the basic operation of the computer. Applications software packages have been designed to cater for a range of different applications such as database management, word-processing and graphics. A package is often a more cost-effective solution than the development of in-house software to support specific database applications, such as the management of the transactions in a library. Human computer interface design is an important feature of software packages, and can have a significant effect on the effectiveness of the system. Dialogue styles include graphical user interfaces, multimedia interfaces, menus, commands, form-filling, question-and-answer and natural-language dialogue. Z39.50 and SR make an important in the development of greater standardization in interface design.

REVIEW QUESTIONS

1   Give some examples of the types of data that one byte of storage might store.
2   Explain the difference between machine code and a high-level programming language.
3   What are the central functions of an operating system?

4 Why should an organization always consider using existing applications software packages before designing a special-purpose package?

5 What is utility software, and what functions does it perform?

6 Describe the different types of office software.

7 What forms of support are there in the use of applications software?

8 What are the different forms of components in interface design?

9 Distinguish between direct manipulation and GUI interfaces.

10 What are the special features of multimedia interface design?

11 Explain the significance of the Z39.50 protocol.

References

Shneiderman, B. (1982) 'The future of interaction systems and the emergence of direct manipulation', *Behaviour and information technology*, 1, 237–56.

Shneiderman, B. (1987) *Designing the user interface: strategies for effective human–computer interaction*, Reading, MA, Addison-Wesley.

Bibliography

Note: Most of the books listed at the end of Chapter 2 offer a brief introduction to the topics covered in this chapter.

Booth, P. A. (1989) *An introduction to human–computer interaction*, Hove, Erlbaum.

Dempsey, L. (1994) 'Distributed library and information systems: the significance of Z39.50', *Managing information*, 1 (6), 41–2.

Hobart, J. (1995) 'Principles of good GUI design', *UNIX review*, 37–46.

Large, A. (1981) 'The user interface to CD-ROM databases', *Journal of librarianship and information science*, 23 (4), 203–17.

McGraw, C. L. (1992) *Designing and evaluating user interfaces for knowledge based systems*, New York/London, Ellis Horwood.

Mohan L. and Byrne, J. (1995) 'Designing intuitive icons and toolbars', *UNIX review*, 49–54.

Powell, J. E. (1991) *Designing user interfaces*, San Marcos, CA, Microtrend.

Preece, J. et al. (1994) *Human computer interaction*, Wokingham, Addison-Wesley.

Rowley, J. and Slack, F. (1998) *Public access interface design*, Aldershot, Gower.

Russell, R. (ed.) (1996) 'Z39.50 and SR', *LITC report*, 7.

Shackel, B. (1997) 'Human–computer interaction: whence and whither', *Journal of the American Society for Information Science*, 48 (11), 970–86.

Shaw, D. (1991) 'The human–computer interface for information retrieval', *Annual review of information science and technology*, **26**, 155–95 (ed. M. E. Williams).

Temple, Barker and Sloane Inc. (1990) 'The benefits of the graphical user interface', *Multi-media review*, 10–17.

Vickery, B. and Vickery, A. (1993) 'On-line search interface design', *Journal of documentation*, **49** (2), 103–187.

5

Databases

LEARNING OUTCOMES

Using the term database generically, databases are the way in which data is stored in computers. Such databases may be:

- a collection of data about the operations of an organization, which thereby allows the control of those operations
- a collection of publicly available data held on a host computer or server that is accessible via a telecommunications network or on CD-ROM.

At the end of this chapter you will:

- be aware of the concepts of records and fields
- appreciate the different types of databases that might be important to information managers
- understand the nature of the MARC record format for bibliographic databases
- understand the difference between physical and logical database structures
- be aware of the need for database structures.

5.1 Introduction

Library and information managers have always compiled files of information, in the form of catalogues and lists of borrowers. Early computer-based systems in many businesses held master files, typically containing data relating to payroll, sales, purchase and inventory. Such applications comprise a series of related and similarly formatted records. External databases may be accessed through the online search services, or acquired on CD-ROM. The information manager may download sections of these databases, with appropriate licensing arrangements, to integrate into local databases. Since databases are central to the way in which data is stored and retrieved, it is important for the information manager to be aware of the types of database that are available, any standard record formats that are likely to be encountered, and approaches to database structure.

This chapter, then, offers some basic definitions in the area of databases and goes on to examine the types of database. Standard record formats are then considered, and the final section explains some fundamental ideas about database structure.

5.2 Basic definitions

A file is a collection of similar records, with relationships defined between those records. A database system may comprise a number of linked files. We consider this further in Section 5.5, which looks at database structures. To commence our discussion we shall focus on the individual database or file.

A **record** is the information contained in a database relating to one document or item. For example, in a cataloguing database a record may contain all of the information relating to one book. In a source database, a record may contain the contents of a directory entry, or an article in a journal. In a inventory database, the record may contain all of the information pertaining to the stock level of a specific item. Records are composed of a number of fields. The types of fields used, their length, and the number of fields in a record, must be chosen in accordance with a specific application. Figure 5.1 lists the types of fields to be found in a file in an inventory control system, and the fields that are found in a bibliographic record are shown in Figure 5.2.

There are two types of field: fixed length and variable length. A **fixed-length field** is one which contains the same number of characters in each record. Since field lengths are predictable, it is not necessary to signal to the computer where each field begins and ends. Fixed-length fields are economical to store, and records using fixed-length fields are quick and easy to code. However, fixed-length fields may not adequately accommodate variable-length data. Fixed-length fields

---

Item No
Balance
Re-order level
Danger level
Selling price
Item description
Location
Quantity available
Item vendor code
Item vendor
Order unit
Number/unit
Last cost
Unit selling price
Value of current stock at last cost

Fig. 5.1 *Some typical fields in a master inventory file*

```
USMARC record

001 $a94-790547
005 $a19950106130304.3
008 950106s1994####dcun#######m#########eng##
040 $aDLC $cDLC $dDLC
050 00$aZ695.615
082 10$a025.3 $212
111 2$aSeminar on Cataloging Digital Documents $d(1994 : $cUniversity of Virginia
        Library and Library of Congress)
245 10$aProceedings of the Seminar on Cataloging Digital Documents, October 12-
        14, 1994 $h{computer file}
        /$cUniversity of Virginia Library, Charlottesville, and the Library of
        Congress.
256 $aComputer data and program.
260 $a{Washington, D.C. :$bLibrary of Congress,$c1994}.
538 $aAccess: Internet. Address:
        http://lcweb.loc.gov/catdir/semdigdocs/seminar.html.
500 $aTitle from title screen.
500 $a"Sponsor: Sarah Thomas, director for cataloging, Library of Congress"--Home
        page.
520 #$aText, graphics, and audio files, including a summary of the seminar by Sarah
        Thomas, color photographs of the presenters and various events, texts of the
        presentations, notes taken by Library of Congress staff, records of the panel
        discussion, an action plan, and a list of participants.
650 #0$aCataloging of computer files $xCongresses $xDatabases.
700 1# $aThomas, Sarah.
710 2#$aUniversity of Virginia. $bLibrary.
710 2#$aLibrary of Congress.
856 7$uhttp://lcweb.loc.gov/catdir/semdigdocs/seminar.html$2http
```

Fig. 5.2 *Fields in a bibliographic record (USMARC; see also section 5.4)*

are ideal for codes, such as ISBNs, reader codes, product codes, bank account numbers, dates and language codes, where the length of the information will be the same in each record. With variable-length data, variable-length fields are necessary. A **variable-length field** will consist of different lengths in different records. Here, the computer cannot recognize when one field ends and another starts, so it becomes necessary to flag the beginnings and ends of fields. The discussion of the MARC record format explores one way of achieving this. The databases discussed in this chapter use a mixture of fixed- and variable-length fields in order to accommodate the varying kinds of data. In addition, objects such as pictures and video clips may be stored as separate files linked to records that contain primarily fixed- or variable-length fields.

Reflection   Examine the fields in the bibliographic record in Figure 5.2. Why is each of them included? Which of these data items could be accommodated satisfactorily in a fixed-length field?

Within fields, individual data elements or units of information may be designated as **subfields**. Subfields need to be flagged so that they can be identified.

Records in a database can be retrieved by entering appropriate character strings, and asking the computer to locate those character strings. This will allow subsets of the database to be selected in accordance with some query criterion. Clearly, what can be retrieved depends on what is in the database, and the way in which the information has been structured. Typically, some parts of records can be searched and their contents used as **search keys**. There will usually be a reasonable range of types of search keys available, and different ways in which a database can be searched. Also, it is normally possible to select the fields in a record that are displayed in any given application and to format this display in a number of different ways.

5.3 Types of database

Databases may be stored on magnetic or optical media such as disks, and accessed either locally or remotely. This may include access to an organizations database covering transactions and financial records, or to other databases that might be accessed remotely. Some of these databases will hold publicly accessible information such as abstracting and indexing databases, full text of reports, encyclopaedias and directories, whilst other databases will be databases that are shared within an organization or group of organizations.

Reference and source databases

Databases that might be available to information users in the public arena, and which might be accessed either remotely via an online search service, or more locally on CD-ROM, can be categorized as either reference or source databases.

Reference databases refer or point the user to another source such as a document, an organization or an individual for additional information, or for the full text of a document. Examples include:

1 **Bibliographic databases**, which include citations or bibliographic references, and sometimes abstracts of literature. They tell the user what has been written, in what kind of source it can be located (e.g. journal title, conference proceedings) and, if they provide abstracts, will summarize the original document.
2 **Catalogue databases**, which show the stock of a given library or library network. Typically, such databases list which monographs, journal titles and other items the library has in stock, but do not give much information on the contents of these documents. Catalogue databases are a special type of bibliographic database, but since their orientation is rather different from that of the other bibliographic databases, they are worth identifying as a separate category.

3   **Referral databases**, which offer references to information or data such as the names and addresses of organizations, and other directory-type data.

Reflection   Examine the record on your local library catalogue. Which fields does it display for your viewing as a user?

Source databases contain the original source data, and are one type of electronic document. After successful consultation of a source database, the user should have the information that is required and should not need to seek information in an original source (as is the case with reference databases). Data are available in machine-readable form instead of, or as well as, printed form. Source databases can be grouped according to their content:

1   Numeric databases, which contain numerical data of various kinds, including statistics and survey data.
2   Full-text databases of newspaper items, technical specifications and software.
3   Text-numeric databases, which contain a mixture of textual and numeric data (such as company annual reports) and handbook data.
4   Multimedia databases, which include information stored in a mixture of different types of media, including, for example, sound, video, pictures, text and animation.

Bibliographic databases contain a series of linked bibliographic records, with each record typically containing some combination of the following components:

- document number
- title
- author
- source reference
- abstracts
- full text
- indexing words or phrases
- citation, or number of references
- organization originating the document, or author's address, or both
- language of the source document
- local information such as classification numbers, or location.

These components might be described as a document reference or citation, and each one will usually be shown by a different field. There is considerable variability between the record formats of bibliographic databases, so the above list is only an indication of typical components. The components listed above do not give the information or the text of the source document, but only point to where the information might be found. In many databases an abstract will also be included for each reference, and a good informative abstract may yield valuable direct information, even in a bibliographic database.

Some of the above components are more commonly used as **primary retrieval keys** (e.g. author name, title words, indexing words), whilst others may be more helpful as **secondary retrieval keys** (to limit, say, the set of records retrieved during a search on a subject indexing term). Typical secondary retrieval keys are: language, local information, journal title. The remaining elements of the record are merely displayed or printed for additional information to the user concerning the document, and may be useful in judging relevance or locating the source document.

Even though a number of the large bibliographic databases have been available in machine-readable form for more than 20 years, the basic elements in the database still have their roots in the printed product, which was often the abstracting or indexing tool with which they were associated. These databases were often originally constructed to aid in the more efficient generation of a printed abstracting or indexing service, and a print product often still accounts for a significant component of the database producer's revenue. One of the benefits of maintaining records in a machine-readable format was the opportunity to generate a series of different products for different marketplaces from the one set of records (see Figure 5.3). These products often include current-awareness services, online search services, licensing for downloading sections of databases, and printed abstracting and indexing services.

Source databases are electronic documents. Table 5.2 gives some examples. The contents of such databases may be as varied as the contents of the printed book, and may include text, numbers, tables, figures and graphics. Indeed, many such databases take advantage of the fact that they are not constrained by the same physical limitations as print, and are multimedia, embracing, in addition to text and numeric data, computer software, images, sound, maps and charts. These databases can be accessed online through the online search services, on CD-ROM or via videotex and teletext. CD-ROM is the medium that has supported the initial developments of the more ambitious multimedia databases, because there is no need to transmit images over external communications networks.

Multidisciplinary indexes
Science Citation Index
Social Science Citation Index
Arts and Humanities Citation Index
Available in the following formats: print, print cumulating, compact disc, compact disc with abstracts, magnetic tape, online, Intranet

CompuMath Citation Index
Available in the following formats: print, print cumulation, online, CD-ROM

Discipline-specific indexes on compact disc
Biochemistry and Biophysics Citation Index
Biotechnology Citation Index
Chemistry Citation Index
Neuroscience Citation Index
Material Science Citation Index

Indexes to the contents of books, proceedings and reviews
Index to Scientific Book Contents
Index to Scientific and Technical Proceedings
Index to Social Sciences and Humanities Proceedings
Index to Scientific Reviews

Custom services including
Research Alert
Medical Documentation Service
Contract Research
Science Watch

Chemical products including
Current Chemical Reactions (print)
Current Chemical Reactions In-House Database (magnetic tape, magnetic tape cumulation)
Index Chemicus (print and CD-ROM)
ChemPrep on CD-ROM

Magnetic tapes including
Current Contents Search
SciSearch
Social SciSearch
Arts and Humanities Search
Research Alert

Online databases including
Current Content Search
SciSearch

continued overleaf

Fig. 5.3 *Products extracted from a related group of databases from one producer: Institute for Scientific Information (ISI)*

Social SciSearch
Arts and Humanities Search
Computer and Mathematics Search
ISTP Search
ISTP&B Search

Current contents in various fields e.g. life sciences; agriculture; biology and environmental sciences
Print, diskette, CD-ROM, online, magnetic tape, Internet

Other products including
The Genuine Article (document delivery
ISI Document Solution
Request-a-Print (printed request cards)
Pro-Cite, and Reference Manager (bibliographic software packages)
Journal Citation Reports
Social SciSearch
Arts and Humanities Search
Research Alert

Fig. 5.3 *Continued*

Table 5.1 *Some bibliographic databases available through STN International*

Database	Producer	Content
ABI-INFORM	University Microfilms Inc.	Business and management
BIOSIS Previews	BIOSIS	Biosciences
CA	CAS (Chemical Abstracts)	Chemistry
COMPENDEX	Engineering Information Inc.	Engineering
DISSABS	University Microfilms Inc.	Bibliographic, focusing on dissertations in North America
EMBASE	Elsevier Science Publishers	Biomedicine and pharmaceuticals
EVENTLINE	Elsevier Science Publishers	Multidisciplinary conferences and events
INPADOC	European Patent Office	International patents
INSPEC	Institution of Electrical Engineers	Engineering, physics and electronics
JGRIP	The Japan Science and Technology Corporation	Multidisciplinary research from public research organizations in Japan
MEDLINE	US National Library of Medicine	Medicine
SCISEARCH	Institute for Scientific Information	Science and technology, bibliographic with citation references
WORLDCAT	OCLC Online Computer Library Center	Multidisciplinary, containing the merger catalogues of libraries around the world

Table 5.2 *Some source databases from Questel-Orbit*

Database	Producer	Content
EDOC	European Patent Office	Patent applications
FMARK	Institut National de la Propriété Industrielle	Trademarks from France
DUNS United Kingdom	Dun & Bradstreet	UK Company information
ASPO	Agence France-Presse	French and international sports newswires, reports, results, summaries and biographies
LOGOS	Documentation Française	Full text information about French politics, society and economy
PROMT	Information Access Company	Articles on products, markets and technologies
Who's Who in Technology	Gale Research Inc.	Detail of leaders of American technology
Gale Directory of Databases	Gale Research Inc.	Descriptions of databases available on CD-ROM, online and other formats
Chemical Economics Handbook	SRI International	Market research data for the chemical industry

Source databases are so varied in their nature and origins that it is difficult to make generalizations. Earlier in this chapter we divided source databases into numeric, full-text and text-numeric. We might also consider referral databases in this way. Although these can be categorized as reference databases in the sense that they offer a pointer to further information, they are often also source databases in that they might contain the full text of a directory that could be regarded as a source document. Source databases, then, may include the full text of journal articles, newsletters, newswires, dictionaries, directories and other source materials. Many (although not all) source databases have a print equivalent. Some source databases do not contain the complete contents of the print equivalent, but only offer selected coverage.

Title: Primary ovarian non-Hodgkin's lymphoma: Outcome after treatment with combination chemotherapy.

Author(s): Dimopoulos, M.A. {a,b,c}; Daliani, D. {d,e,f}; Pugh, W. {g,h}; Gershenson, D. {j,k,l}; Cabanillas, F. {m,n,o}; Sarris, A.H.

Corporate Source: {a} Section Lymphoma, Box 68, Univ. Texas M.D. Anderson Cancer Center, 1515 Holcombe Blvd., Houston, TX 77030, USA; {d} Dep. Exp. Clin.Oncol., Aarhus Univ. Hosp., Noriebrogade 44, DK-8000 Aarhus, Denmark; {g} Div. Neurosurgery, UCLA Med. Cent., Los Angeles, Ca 90024, USA; {j} H.H. McGuire VAMC, Dep. Radiol. (114), 1201 Broad Rock Blvd., Richmond, VA 23249, USA; {m} Dep. Otorhinolaryngology, Univ. Tamper Med. Sch., PO Box 607, FIN-33101 Tampere, Finland {b} http://www.utah.edu/lymphoma/~mmdimopoulos; {e} http://www.aarhushosp.ed./eco//~ddaliani; {h} http://www.uclamed.edu/neuro-surg/~wpugh; {k} http://www.hhmvami.edu/radiology/~dgershenson; {n} http://www.utampermededu/otorhm/~fcabanillas {c} mmdimopoulos@utmed. edu; {f} ddaliani@arhushosp.edu; {i} wpugh@uclamed.edu; {l} dgershenson@ hhmvamc.edu; {o} fcabanillas@utampermed.edu

Source: Gynecologic Oncology 64(3) [cited August 21, 1997], 1997. 446-450.
http://www.gynecology.com/

Document Type: Article: Research Article

ISSN: 0090-8258

Language: English (EN)

Abstract: Because the outcome of patients with primary ovarian non-Hodgkin's lymphoma (NHL) is controversial, we retrospectively analyzed experience with adults seen at the University of Texas M. D. Anderson Cancer Center from 1974 to 1993. Patients were included if at least one ovary was pathologically involved, and if combination chemotherapy was used that must have included doxorubicin for intermediate grade histologies. We identified 15 patients who constituted 0.5% of all untreated NHL and 1.5% of untreated ovarian neoplasms that presented to our institution during this time. One patient refused therapy, leaving 14 assessable for response. Nine patients had intermediate-grade, 5 had high grade, and none had low-grade NHL. One ovary was involved in 4 patients, and both in 10, in 7 of whom additional sites were involved, including supradiaphragmatic nodes in 2. Four patients had AAS I and 10 had AAS IV. Favorable (0 or 1) and unfavorable (gt 1) IPI scores were seen in 5 and 9 patients, respectively. The complete remission rate for all patents was 64%, and 5-year survival and FFS for all assessable patients were 57 and 46%, respectively. We conclude that the complete remission rate and FFS of patients with ovarian NHL treated with appropriate chemotherapy appear to be similar to that of patients with other nodal NHLs. Further work is required to determine prognostic factors in ovarian NHL.

Major Concepts: Oncology: Human Medicine, Medical Sciences; Pharmacology

Super Taxa: Hominidae: Primates, Mammalia, Vertebrata, Chordata , Animalia

Organisms: human (Hominidae): adult, female, patient

Taxa Notes: animals, chordates; humans; mammals; primates; vertebrates

Diseases: primary ovarian non-Hodgkin's lymphoma: blood and lymphatic disease, combination chemotherapy, endocrine disease/gonads, neoplastic diseases outcome, reproductive system disease/female; malarial infection

Chemicals & Biochemicals: bleomycin: antineoplastic-drug, combination therapy; cyclophosphamide; antineoplastic-drug, combination therapy; dexamethasone: antineoplastic-drug, combination therapy; doxorubicin: antineoplastic-drug, combination therapy; etoposide: antineoplastic-drug, combination therapy; methotrexate: antineoplastic-drug, combination therapy; prednisone: antineoplastic-drug, combination therapy; vincristine: antineoplastic-drug, combination therapy; Dithranol; Iron(II)

Fig. 5.4 *Some records from databases*

Registry Numbers: 9041-93-4:BUBOMYCIN; 1143-38-OQ:DITHRANOL; 15438-31-0
Methods & Equipment: radiotherapy: therapeutic method
Alternate Indexing: MeSH: Lymphoma, Non-Hodgkin's Ovarian Neoplasms
Notes: This journal has 16 issues per volume.
Record Type: Abstract

Title: Survival rates and their relationship to life-history traits in some common British birds.
Author(s): Dobson, A. {a}
Corporate Source: {a} Biology Dep., Univ. Rochester, Rochester, NY 14627, USA
Source: Current Ornithology, E Power, D.M.: Ed.7 1990, 115-146
Document Type: Book Chapter; Review
ISSN: 0742-390X
ISBN: 0-306-43307-9
Book Publisher: Plenum Press, New York, New York, USA; London, England, UK
Language: English (EN)
Major Concepts: Ecology: Environmental Science; Mathematical Biology; Models and Simulations; Computational Biology; Morphology; Physiology; Reproductive System: Reproduction; Systematics and Taxonomy
Super Taxa: Aves - Unspecified: Aves, Vertebrata, Chordata, Animalia
Organisms: bird (Aves); Aves (Vertebrata)
Taxa Notes: animals, birds; chordates; nonhuman vertebrates; vertebrates
Geopolitical Locations: UK: Europe, Palearctic region
Miscellaneous Descriptors: adult; banding data; body weight; britain; fecundity; haldane's mathematical model; lack's mathematical model; life-history trait; migratory strategy; population studies; survival rate

Fig. 5.4 *Continued*

5.4 Bibliographic record formats

All records in one file have a standard format. In order to facilitate exchange of records between different computer systems, there have been attempts to develop some standard record formats. Such formats were seen to be particularly beneficial in cataloguing applications, where a standard format which also embodies an agreement on the elements of a bibliographic record has been particularly attractive in allowing the exchange of cataloguing records. This exchange has minimized the need for local cataloguing. Accordingly, one of the fields in which a standard record format is best established is in the creation of cataloguing records. The work in this area has led to the MARC record format.

The MARC record format

The MARC record format uses a directory format to handle fixed- and variable-length fields. The character position at the start of each field is specified by a directory at the beginning of the record.

The MARC record format was designed by the Library of Congress and the British Library with the object of being able to communicate a bibliographic description in machine-readable form in such a way that records could be re-formatted for any conceivable purpose. Early trials around 1966, conducted by the Library of Congress, worked with the MARC I format; but this format was jettisoned in 1967 and superseded by MARC II, or MARC as it is usually called.

As more countries have exploited MARC, variations in practices have spawned deviations from the original format. The UNIMARC format was developed for international exchange of MARC records. National organizations creating MARC records have used national standards within the country and re-formatted records to UNIMARC for international exchange. Recently, however, a number of major suppliers of MARC records have agreed to use the USMARC format, so it is likely that this format will very rapidly become the international standard. Hence, the text that follows describes the USMARC format.

The MARC format includes up to 61 data elements, of which 25 are directly searchable. The format is compatible with the latest edition of the Anglo-American Cataloguing Rules and the most recent edition of the Dewey Decimal Classification, and can be expected to be modified in order to accommodate any new editions of these tools.

The MARC format comprises two sections: section 1, which gives information describing the bibliographic data; and section 2, which holds the bibliographic data themselves:

- record label
- directory
- control fields
- variable data fields.

The fields that comprise section 2, and thus hold the bibliographic data, are all variable-length fields, and hence it is necessary to signal the beginning and end of each field. So each field is preceded by a three-character tag and two numeric indicators, and ends with a special delimiter. Tags consist of three numerals within the range 000–945. The tags have a mnemonic structure in that they follow the order of a catalogue record, and the tags for added entries mirror those for main headings. The variable fields are grouped in blocks according to the first character of the tag:

1xx   Main entries
2xx   Titles and title paragraph (title, edition, imprint)
3xx   Physical description, etc.
4xx   Series statement
5xx   Notes
6xx   Subject access fields
7xx   Added entries other than subject or series
8xx   Series added entries
9xx   Local data.

Tags for specific fields are created by entering digits in the final two places. So, for example, the following tags apply:

100   Personal author main entry heading
110   Corporate name main entry heading
240   Uniform title
245   Title and statement of responsibility
250   Edition and statement of edition author, editor, etc.
260   Imprint.

Furthermore, a personal author's name generally has '00' in the second and third positions, so that, for example:

100 is used for a main entry personal author heading
600 is used for a personal author subject heading
700 is used for a personal author added entry heading.

Each of the main fields also has two field indicators; these are single-digit numerals which follow the tag, and are unique to the field to which they are assigned. Indicators are used to distinguish between different types of information entered in the same field, to provide for title added entries, to indicate the number of characters to be dropped in filing titles and to show whether information such as edition and imprint relates to a part or the whole of a multipart work. For instance, in the field for main entry corporate author heading, the following indicators are used in conjunction with the 110 tag:

110.00   Inverted corporate heading
110.10   Government heading
110.20   Direct order corporate heading

Many fields in a catalogue record contain smaller distinct units, known as subfields. Typical subfields in the imprint area are place of publication, publisher and date of publication. All subfields are preceded by a subfield code, which consists of a single symbol (e.g. '£') and a single letter. The imprint might be coded as '260.00 £a London £b Pitman £c 1996'.

Subfield codes are defined in the context of the field in which they are used, but similar codes are used in parallel situations. For example, the subfield codes for a person's name are constant, regardless of whether he/she is main (or additional) author or subject.

Having completed the variable data fields, we can return to section 1. The control fields are the only part of section 1 that is input by the cataloguer. These contain data such as the record control number (e.g. ISBN), the language of the text, the intellectual level code, the country of publication code, and the control access to the main record.

Each record starts with a label and a directory, both of which are supplied by the program. The label contains information about the record, such as, for example, its length and status (new, changed, etc.), type and class. The directory is a finding list which lists, for every tag, the tag, the number of characters in the field, and the starting character position within the record.

The structure of the MARC record is deliberately complicated to enable maximum flexibility. Almost any element can be used as an access point, and each element can be of any length. This complexity was designed in an age when printed or microfilm catalogues were the norm. The MARC record format has made a major contribution to standardization and networking, but some would feel that the time has come for it to be reassessed. A different format may be more appropriate in an OPAC-dominated environment. A record showing the MARC format appears in Figure 5.2 (page 103).

....
Reflection   What is the role of each of the items of coding in the MARC
                  record format?
....

The Common Communications Format (CCF)

There are many formats for bibliographic records. The bibliographic descriptions carried by these formats differ widely depending on their source. Abstracting and indexing services use different rules of bibliographic description from those followed in library cataloguing. The MARC format, which is used as an exchange format by major libraries, assumes the ISBN to be the standard. On the other hand, most (but not all) abstracting and indexing services acknowledge the UNISIST reference manual, which prescribes its own content designators for the bibliographic descriptions of various types of material. These two major formats define, organize and identify data elements in different ways and rely upon different sets of codes. Thus it has been difficult or virtually impossible to mix bibliographic records from different sources in a single file. The Common Communications Format (CCF) was therefore designed with the aim of facilitating the communication of bibliographic data among the sectors of the information community. In common with MARC, the Common Communications Format constitutes a specific implementation of ISO 2709. The CCF:

*   specifies a small number of mandatory data elements which are recognized to be essential in order to identify an item
*   provides mandatory elements that are sufficiently flexible to accommodate varying descriptive practices
*   provides a number of optional elements

- permits the originating agency to include non-standard elements which are considered useful within its system
- provides a mechanism for linking records and segments of records without imposing on the originating agency any uniform practice regarding the treatment of related groups of records or data elements.

In the Common Communications Format, each record comprises four parts:

- record label
- directory
- data fields
- record separator.

Other bibliographic record formats in non-cataloguing applications

In addition to applications in which standard formations are used, there are a range of other applications that use non-standard formats. Essentially there are two different categories of systems which may be encountered: publicly available databases, and local systems supported by software packages.

For the large public databases, there has been little pressure to accept a standard format, and each database producer has in general chosen a record format to suit the particular database. Even one database may emerge in different record formats according to the on line search service through which it is made available. Individual decisions are made concerning the fields to be included and the subject indexing made available. Yet another variable factor is the presence of fulltext, and more recently multimedia databases, which demand a somewhat different record format from bibliographic records if the information is to be appropriately displayed.

The record formats to be encountered in local systems which are supported by software packages are many and various. Most of these software packages offer cataloguing systems which will work in a MARC record format, or which produce records which are compatible with the MARC record format. Others do not offer such an option. Virtually all software packages offer the purchaser the opportunity to develop a record format to suit a specific application. Thus in local systems there may well be great variability in record format, as designs are implemented within the parameters set by the various software packages.

Metadata

Metadata is data about data. Bibliographic records are a type of metadata. However, Metadata is increasingly being used in the more specialized context of data which refer to digital resources available across a network. Metadata also differs from bibliographic or cataloguing data in that the location information is held within the record in such a way as to allow direct document delivery from appropriate applications software, or in other words the records may contain detailed access information and network addresses. In addition, bibliographic records are designed for users to use, both when judging relevance and making decisions about whether they wish to locate the original resource, and as a unique identifier of the resource so that a user can request the resource or document in a form that makes sense to the recipient of that request. These roles remain significant. Internet search engines (see Chapter 8) use metadata in the indexing processes that they employ to index Internet resources. Metadata needs to be able to describe remote locations and document versions. It also needs to accommodate the lack of stability of the Internet, redundant data, different perspectives on the granularity (what is a document or a resource?) of the Internet, and variable locations on a variety of different networks.

5.5   Database structures

The crudest way to search a database is to go through it record by record, looking for the appropriate data element. For large files, given the present state of the art, this is slow, and alternative methods of locating specific records have been developed.

The online search services, and other applications that use document management systems, have always used the inverted file approach described below. This is useful for searching complex text-based databases, where the searcher does not know the form in which the search key may have been entered in the database, and has essentially to guess the most appropriate form.

Transaction-processing systems, such as library management systems, travel bookings information systems, and sales and marketing information systems, may also use this approach to locate individual records within a database, but these also need a mechanism for linking a series of distinct databases together so that information can be drawn from more than one database for display on the screen or printing at one time. This requirement in transaction-processing systems has led to the development of strategies for optimizing database design. We describe some of the approaches to this below.

One-way linked lists

One-way linked lists are a simple way to locate a specific record. They are introduced here to provide a basis for discussion of inverted files later. One-way linked lists use a key field – for example, the author field – to locate a specific record. Records may be arranged in order according to the key field, but this can be inconvenient in a field which is subject to change. More often, records are stored in a different order and a system of pointers is used to represent the arrangement.

Processing is achieved by following these pointers. Figure 5.5 offers a diagram of this.

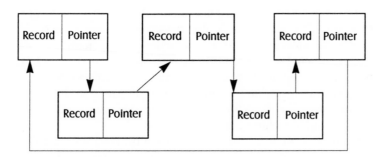

Fig.5.5 *A one-way linked list*

This approach is based upon a single key, and is not satisfactory if the search needs to be conducted on some other record element. So, for example, where the key field is the author field, the pointers will not support searching on the title or subject fields. Many systems are required to support searching on more than one key, and so multi-indexed systems have been developed which use a number of indexes to point to records in the main field. Many of these systems use inverted files.

Inverted files

The inverted file is similar to an index. In the inverted file approach there may be two or three separate files. Here, in the interests of communicating the basic concept, we will describe the two-file approach. This uses two files: the text or print file, and the inverse or index file.

The **text file** contains the actual records. The **index file** provides access to these records. The index file contains a record for each of the indexed terms from all of the records in the database, arranged in alphabetical order. Each term is accompanied by information on its frequency of occurrence in the database, the file in which it is to be located, the record in which it is entered, and possibly further location information such as the paragraph (or field) within which it is located. When a new record is added to the database, it is necessary to update the index file.

These files are used together in the database search. If a user is interested in performing a search on the word 'hedges', for instance, he/she will enter the term at the keyboard, and the system will seek the term in the index file. If the term is not present in the index file, the system responds by indicating that there are no postings for that term. If the term is found, the user will be told how many postings, or occurrences, of the term there are in the database. To display the records, the text file location is used to locate records in the text file.

If three files are used, there is an intermediate file which allows search terms input at the keyboard to be checked quickly and the number of postings displayed on the screen. This is particularly useful with a complex search, which may involve using the index file records for a number of search terms.

The above description is intended to offer a simple introduction to the basic concept of an inverted file. In practice, file structures may be more complicated. For example, if it is possible to search terms in proximity to other terms (e.g. terms within two words of each other), the index file must contain information about word positions within a field for each term.

Inverted files are often created for a number of fields within a record. However, not all fields are usually indexed, because each index takes disk storage space; indexes are created for those fields that are commonly searched. Inverted files are often created for author names, title words, subject indexing terms and author-title acronyms.

The retrieval strategy described above hinges upon being able to retrieve specific records and subsequently identify fields within these records. Long full-text records need to be split into paragraphs, and those paragraphs must be assigned identifiers before indexing can commence. Alternatively, the positions of individual words in the file can be used as identifiers.

Authority files, in the form of lists of author headings or subject headings, or thesauri, are used with some databases. Here there must be a link between the index file or the term file and the authority list, so that approved terms and their relationships can be displayed.

Reflection   Are authority files necessary in the creation of indexes to text based documents?

The development of database structures

In the early days of computing, business and library systems worked with a series of individual master files, covering, for example, in the case of libraries, borrowers and books in stock, or in the case of many businesses, payroll, sales, and inventory. When organizations used computers for distinct applications and not all of the operations that might have been were computerized, this worked satisfactorily. However, it soon became apparent that programmes for, say, circulation control in a library needed to access two or more different files, and it was appropriate to start to examine the relationships between these files. This led to the introduction of the concept of a database, and the software to manage such databases, known as database management systems. It then became necessary to examine the optimum way to structure data, or to develop data models to support specific applications. More formally:

1   **A database** is a generalized integrated collection of data together with its description, which is managed in such a way that it can fulfil the differing needs of its users.
2   **A database management system** (DBMS) is a system that generates, runs and maintains databases, and as such the system must include all of the software needed for this purpose.
3   **A data model** specifies the rules according to which data are structured, and also the associated operations that are permitted. It may also be viewed as a technique for the formal description of data, data relationships and usage constraints.

Database features

One of the central purposes of a database is that the data in the database should be used for a variety of different applications. For this to be achieved it is important for a database to have the following features:

1   It must be substantially non-redundant, i.e. have minimal (or preferably no) duplication of identical data. Duplication of data leads to difficulty in ensuring data consistency, especially during updating, and wastes storage space.
2   It must be program-independent (a concept known as data independence) so that the data can be moved or restructured without the need to make alterations to the programs.
3   It must be usable by all of the programs.
4   It must include all of the necessary data interrelationships, to support the variety of different uses to which the data might be put.
5   It must have a common approach to the retrieval, insertion and amendment of data.

....
Reflection   Why is duplication of data likely to lead to inconsistencies in the data records? (Think about the update process.)
....

Logical and physical data

In the database approach, although the database will probably be stored physically as a set of files, users and applications do not need to know anything about the physical data storage. Stored with the actual data is a description of the database, which enables the DBMS to retrieve information from the database, and to store new data in appropriate places in the database, establishing relationships with other data if relevant. The applications do not directly access the database; instead they pass the requests to the DBMS to retrieve or store data. In essence, then, the DBMS is data-oriented. This shift towards data orientation has placed much more importance on data modelling and database design, with the physical storage of the data being handled by the DBMS rather than the applications system designer.

Reflection   Explain the difference between logical and physical database structures.

Logical database structures

Where access is required to a series of linked files, as in a library management system, it is necessary to have some guidelines for allocating data to specific files within the database system, and defining the optimum links or keys between files. There are three main structural types of databases and associated DBMS: hierarchical, network and relational.

Hierarchical databases

Hierarchical databases are structured in a branching tree-type arrangement. Each data item is located within a higher-level data item. Thus, if the database contained information relating to company employees, this might be organized into factories, departments and then employees at the different levels. This method allows for the rapid retrieval of data provided that the higher-level details, such as the employees' department, are known. If these details are not known, a hierarchical structure can be difficult to search. For each catalogued book, there will be information relating to each copy of the book and each reservation at the first level in the hierarchy. For each copy of the book, there will be loan information and also information about the person to whom the book is lent, which will include loan-status information. For each reservation, there will be information about the person who has made the reservation, again including loan-status information. In this model data will be accessed via 'catalogued book'. To find data on a particular person, for example, it is necessary to scan through the database, since there is no direct access by person.

Network databases

The network approach is based on explicit links or pointers between related entities. The best-known network model is the Codasyl model. Codasyl stands for Committee on Data Systems Languages, which is the body responsible for conceiving this model. In the network model there is a more direct link between the data items at the various levels than in the hierarchical model, through the use of pointers linking data at different levels. A network approach requires a large number of links between data items, which occupy a significant amount of storage space.

Relational databases

These use a type of database structure which has been widely adopted in database systems. In relational systems, information is held in a set of relations or tables. Rows in the tables are equivalent to records, and columns in the tables are equivalent to fields. The data in the various relations are linked through a series of keys. Figure 5.7 shows a simple example of a relation known as catalogued–book. In this relation the ISBN is the primary key and may be used in other relations to identify a specific book. For example, if we maintain the relation order–book, the ISBN acts as a link to the order–book relation. If we wish to complete an order form with details from the order file, data for each book can be extracted from the catalogue file and printed on the order slips and printed alongside data from the order file.

Relational databases are designed using a data-analysis technique called 'normalization'. Normalization is used to break the data into tables so that the fields in each table are dependent only on the key field and not linked to any other key. Relationships are represented by replication of data items. Normalization ensures that insertions, deletions and amendments may then be made to the data without undesirable consequences.

Catalogued–book relation occurrences

ISBN	Title	Author	Year
0-82112-462-3	Organic chemistry	A.J. Brown	1989
0-84131-460-7	Alchemy	R.M. Major	1987
0-69213-517-8	Expert systems	S. Estelle	1988
0-93112-462-1	Computer science	S. Estelle	1989
0-71143-526-6	Bibliography	J. Johns	1991

Order–book relation occurrences

Order no	ISBN	Quantity ordered
678	0-82112-462-3	1
678	0-84131-460-7	4
678	0-69213-517-8	20
679	0-93112-462-1	2
680	0-82112-462-3	3
681	0-71143-526-6	2

Fig. 5.7 *Two simple relations*

Multimedia database structures

Multimedia databases present new challenges for database structure. Multimedia DBMS are being designed to manage such databases. As pictures, animation, sound, text and data tables have very different storage needs, MM-DBMS seek to use a range of technologies, such as relational technology for tables, text databases for documents, and image storage devices for graphics and animation. A central problem is the handling of non-text items such as drawings and moving images. In time-varying media, access by frame is provided by DVI standards. For more sophisticated access the images have to be indexed with keywords in a similar manner to text-based documents.

Object-oriented database structures

Object-oriented DBMS (OO-DBMS) provide facilities for storing items created by object-oriented programs. Since an object is a complex collection of data items, which are defined as being related to other objects, OO-DBMS need to provide facilities for large objects that are organized in hierarchies in accordance with their relationships with other objects. These structures have something in common with the hierarchical model. OO-DBMS technology is still developmental. It is unlikely that OO-DBMS will replace relational technology for standard business applications because they do not offer the same advantages in data management. However, when data items are complex and heterogeneous as in multimedia databases, OO-DBMS may prove an interesting possibility.

Summary   Data in computers is stored in files, which comprise a series of records that may be subdivided into fields. A group of such files, or an individual file supporting a specific application, can be described as a database. There are a number of different types of database, including bibliographic and source databases. Reference databases include bibliographic databases and catalogue databases. The record structure affects the way in which data can subsequently be retrieved. The MARC record format and the CCF record format are special record formats that may be encountered in bibliographic databases. In other applications a variety of different record formats may be encountered. In order that data can be retrieved, databases must be structured and indexed appropriately. Inverted files are widely used in database management systems. Database management systems use one of three different approaches to the logical structuring of databases: hierarchical, network and

relational. Multimedia and object-oriented databases are
important in some special applications.

REVIEW QUESTIONS

1   Explain the difference between a record structure based on variable length fields and one based on fixed-length fields.
2   List the different types of bibliographic databases
3   Why is the MARC record format important?
4   Describe briefly:
   • a one-way linked list
   • an inverted file.
5   What are the main logical database structures? What are the
advantages and disadvantages of each?

Bibliography

MARC record format

Anderson, D. (1989) *Standard practices in the preparation of bibliographic records*,
(UBCIM Occasional Papers 13),London, IFLA UBCIM.

BEDIS (1990) *Report of the Working Party of the UK Book Trade Electronic Date
Interchange Standards Committee*, London, Whitaker.

Bierbaum, E. G. (1990) 'MARC in museums: applicability of the revised visual
materials format', *Information technology and libraries*, 295–9.

Bourne, R. (1992) 'UKMARC – a format for the 21st century', *New library world*,
93 (1101), 4–8.

Gredley, E. and Hopkinson, A. (1990) *Exchanging bibliographic data: MARC and
other international formats*, Ottawa/London, Canadian Library Association/
Library Association.

Holt, B. P. et al. (ed.) (1987) *UNIMARC manual*, London, IFLA UBCIM.

McCallum, S. H. and Roberts, W. D. (eds.) (1989) *UNIMARC in theory and practice: papers from the UNIMARC Workshop, Sydney, Australia, August 1988*,
London, IFLA

Plessard, M.-F. (1990) 'The Universal Bibliographic Control and International
MARC Programme', *International cataloguing and bibliographic control*, 35–7.

Sweeney, R. (1991) 'Survey of the use of UKMARC 1991: selected results', *New
library world*, 92 (1097), 5–9.

Other record formats and database structures

Ashford, J. A. and Willet, P. (1989) *Text retrieval and document databases*, Bromley,
Chartwell Bratt.

Dierickx, H. (1983) 'The UNISIST reference manuals and UNIBID standardisation for development', *Program*, 17 (2), 68–85.

Dierickx, H. and Hopkinson, A. (1981) *Reference manual for machine-readable bibliographic descriptions*, Paris, Unesco/General Information Programme and UNISIST.

Flynn, R. (1987) *An introduction to information science*, New York, Dekker.

Kemp., A. (1990) *Knowledge based systems*, London, Aslib.

Oxborrow, E. A. (1991) *Databases and database systems: concepts and issues*, Bromley, Chartwell Bratt.

6

Designing and managing information systems

LEARNING OUTCOMES

This chapter explores issues associated with the installation and maintenance of information systems. Effective planning of information systems is central to their efficient operation. At the end of this chapter you will be able to:

- recognize the stages in the systems lifecycle
- be familiar with the five stages of systems development
- understand the nature of a systems requirements specification
- be aware of the main steps in the implementation phase
- be aware of the need to consider ergonomic characteristics, and workstation and workplace design
- be aware of the role of the systems developer
- appreciate the role of information systems methodologies and CASE tools
- be aware of the concept of strategic information systems planning
- appreciate the special issues associated with the design of public access and multimedia systems and products
- have considered some of the issues associated with the day-to-day management of information systems.

6.1 Introduction

Information systems must be managed effectively if they are to give useful service. This chapter examines some of the key issues and approaches associated with the management of information systems. The emphasis is upon the stages associated with the implementation of a new computer system, since this will certainly be a major project. However, there is also a need to manage the system on a day-to-day basis. Specifically, this chapter starts by exploring the system lifecycle. The systems development project is then considered, as a basis for systematically analysing systems requirements, and designing and implementing a new system. The concept of an information systems methodology is introduced, and a section on strategic information systems planning emphasizes the need for systems planning to be fully integrated into the strategic planning process of the organization. The special issues associated with public access and multimedia systems and products are briefly introduced. A final section briefly highlights some of the basic issues of day-to-day systems management such as maintenance and user support.

6.2 The system life-cycle

A system can be seen as having a life-cycle that passes through a number of standard phases. In each of these phases, different management activities are required. Figure 6.1 shows the basic phases. First, an **analysis** should be conducted in order to establish systems requirements and options available in systems design. Next, during systems design a specific system will be developed to match the application. **Implementation** leads into **operating evolution** during which the system fulfils its objectives and is modified from time to time to reflect minor changes in requirements. Eventually the system becomes less effective than it was initially, either due to mechanical or other faults, or because the system environment has changed and the system is not able to evolve to meet the changes in the environment. Decay may also be allowed to progress when a new system is being planned. The final stage of the system's life cycle is its replacement. The duration of each of these stages will vary from one system to another. Indeed, whilst it is hoped that the operating evolution phase will always be the longest and should last a few years, some of the other stages, such as analysis, may last only a few hours, or may take several months or even years. The life of computer systems is relatively short. Changes in both the environment and the technology contribute to the decay and replacement of computer systems.

Analysis → Design → Implementation → Operating evolution → Decay→ Replacement

---

Fig. 6.1 *The system life cycle*

....

Reflection   Draw the life cycle of a computer system known to you, showing the length of each phase.

....

6.3 Systems development

Systems development embraces both project based developments and evolutionary change. With early systems, incompatibilities between different generations of hardware and software usually meant that systems replacement was viewed as a major project, and methodologies developed that were essentially project based. This is the approach that is described in this section. The project-based approach remains an important element in systems development, as organizations implement the latest generation of systems. The open-systems approach and greater use of standards means that it might be realistic to look forward to evolutionary systems development, in which systems are replaced and upgraded incrementally. Even if this becomes the dominant scenario, there will still be occasions when a systems upgrade will be sufficiently significant to merit being managed as a distinct project. Again, even in evolution, many of the steps described below may be applicable, although possibly they may be executed on a smaller scale.

For projects associated with the introduction or replacement of a computer system that are significant projects, a formal study will usually be undertaken to investigate the nature and potential of any new system. Changes in information systems are likely to affect work patterns, and sometimes affect the nature of the public service offered by the organization to its customers. Thus careful management of any computerization programme is of vital importance. An organized systems development project will contribute to a successful system implementation.

Often the information manager is not engaged in designing a system, but rather in selecting the most appropriate system or software package. Increasingly, the information manager is not managing an initial computerization project, but a project to upgrade an existing computer-based system. To summarize, a systems analysis and design project may be used:

- in the replacement of a manual system with a computer-based system
- in a changeover or migration from one computer system to another computer-based system
- in modifications, upgrades and extensions to existing computer-based systems.

The methodology may be used:

- to aid in the choice and implementation of a commercially available system
- to aid in the design and implementation of a new, specifically tailored system.

Information managers are often concerned with the first of these two situations. In this context the focus is on systems requirements specification and systems implementation. Although systems development methodologies vary, the following five main stages are commonly featured:

- definition of objectives
- definition of systems requirements
- design
- implementation
- evaluation.

The role of each of these stages is summarized in Figure 6.2.

---

1   **Definition of objectives**
     Terms of reference developed; initial needs analysis as a study proposal leads to fea-
     sibility study, including evaluation of options and analysis of existing systems.
2   **Definition of systems requirements**
     Specification of systems requirements.
3   **Design phase**
     Logical systems model; physical systems model; choice and ordering of hardware
     and software configuration.
4   **Implementation phase**
     Planning and preparation; education and training; database creation; system instal-
     lation; switch-over.
5   **Evaluation phase**
     Initial evaluation, ongoing monitoring, maintenance and evolution.

Fig. 6.2 *Summary of the stages in systems development*

None of these stages is self-contained or rigidly delimited. The design and implementation stages in particular will reconsider issues that have been studied during the earlier two stages. Back-tracking is likely, with, for instance, some re-working of objectives at the design stage. The first two stages – definition of objectives and definition of systems requirements – can be grouped together as systems analysis.

A strategy for a systems development project aids in communication within a team and offers a framework for the newcomer to such projects. Clearly defined stages help in the allocation of tasks and the setting of deadlines. A plan facili-tates the evaluation of progress, and makes for easier management control.

Plainly, if the first three stages lead to a conclusion that a ready-made package or system, including both hardware and software, is the most desirable option, then there will be no need for detailed design. Nevertheless, even here design is necessary, although it may be addressed chiefly to fitting an off-the-peg system to a specific organization's requirements. Equally, whether a new system is designed from the beginning or an established system is taken and adapted, careful imple-mentation and evaluation remain important.

It is important to remember that many organizations may conduct several sys-tems projects, or parts thereof, at different points in time, and in relation to dif-ferent areas of activity. Obviously, a relatively all-embracing analysis of the organization's operations helps the entire range of operations to be viewed as a whole, and increases the likelihood of the various subsystems which perform dif-ferent functions being compatible with one another. Under all circumstances, the choice, design and implementation of a system are time-consuming, and time must be allocated for these activities, even if the system being implemented is relatively modest.

Definition of objectives

A suggestion that a new system might solve problems and offer opportunities for new developments is not a sufficient basis for launching into a systemization project. The first step must be to engage in discussions to define the objectives of any new system. This phase is valuable, not only in evolving guidelines and requirements which will be invaluable later in the project, but also in commencing the communication process and ensuring that all points of view are considered from the very beginning, and that early agreement and support for changes is achieved. It is clearly important at this stage to establish the various project committees, to start discussions with trade unions, and to involve all interested parties. This phase should review established practices and procedures, and attempt to identify where, when, why and how a change in system might be helpful. An initial needs analysis should be conducted, in cooperation with those staff whose activities are likely to be affected by any changes, and should culminate in a written specification of the terms of reference for more detailed work, in the form of a study proposal.

If the study proposal is accepted by management, more detailed investigation of the existing system or problem area will take the form of a **feasibility study**. The purpose of the feasibility study is to establish the systems options that are available, and to define the resources needed to complete the detailed investigations which might follow. The outcome of the feasibility study will be a feasibility study report. This report typically embraces:

- a general description of the present system
- any problems with the existing system
- possible solutions
- order-of-magnitude costs of possible solutions
- benefits of new systems
- work required before a system can be chosen
- an approximate implementation schedule for the new system
- impact on space, staff and other issues.

The next step is to start to gather information on how to achieve the objectives identified during the first phase. This stage is essentially about information gathering, from both internal and external sources. The information collected should facilitate a decision about the type of system that is available to meet the requirements of the organization. Possible conclusions are:

- that an organization-specific system needs to be developed
- that cooperative system development with another organization is the most attractive option
- that a standard applications package should be selected.

This stage is unlikely to lead directly to the selection of a specific system, although if there are very special requirements, there may only be one system which is satisfactory. Normally, general directions and a group of possible systems will be identified for further consideration. It is important to collect as much information as possible from as many sources as possible, and to build up well-organized files of information for all committee members and other interested parties to consult.

Clearly, software houses and other suppliers of systems are important at this stage. Also, directories that review systems and various other special sources may provide valuable assistance. Workshops offered by professional associations, educational institutions, exhibitions and conferences are all valuable. If at all possible, other managers with experience with computerized systems should be visited, telephoned and generally consulted whenever the opportunity arises.

Reflection   Do you know of any information sources which provide information that might assist in the selection of a library management system?

A reputable system vendor will be prepared to put potential customers in contact with other users. At some stage during the collection of information, when it becomes reasonably clear what is likely to be available, it would be wise to evolve, from the objectives identified in the first phase, a preliminary checklist of features of systems that might be of particular interest. Various directories of software packages, systems and hardware include checklists, which can be used as a model for the evolution of a local checklist. The checklist will facilitate purposive sifting of the information gathered, and will support decision-making. Both hardware and software aspects should be considered.

In addition to gathering information concerning systems options, this phase may involve the development of a **logical system description** for the existing system. If the existing system is already well understood and well documented, or alternatively will be superseded by a new system which offers completely different functions from the old system, then it may be unnecessary to investigate the existing system further. If, however, the new system must perform many of the same processes as the old system, then an analysis of the existing system is a useful prerequisite to the in-depth study of user requirements which leads to the logical design of the new system. If a new system is to be designed, a feasibility study may involve assessing specific aspects of any potential system and possibly building small trial subsystems.

Definition of systems requirements (investigation and specification of requirements)

With more complete knowledge of the options available, and some insight into how the various solutions might be applied to meet the requirements in a specific application, it is necessary to go back and develop a full system specification. Typically, a definition phase should seek to answer questions such as:

- Which operations is the system to cover?
- Which databases need to be created?
- How are these databases to be created?
- What kind of records are to be in the databases?
- What information will be sought from the databases?
- How will the information sought from the databases be presented?
- Which are the vital features and which are merely desirable additions?
- Who will use the system regularly?
- What level of experience can be expected of users?

Systems specification

The objective of the analysis phase of a systems analysis and design exercise is the establishment of the requirements for the system that is to be acquired, developed and installed. The analysis and logical design of a system can be summarized in a system specification, or specification of operational requirements (O/R). The precise nature of a specification will depend upon how it is to be used. Typically, however, such a specification will include:

- background information about the organization
- details of the facilities to be provided by a computerized system, identifying which are mandatory and which desirable
- details of the environment in which the system will operate, including any standards, communication protocols, and health and safety regulations
- the size of the system in terms of the numbers of records and transactions to be handled, the number of workstations, and growth rates
- a timetable for implementation of the system
- mandatory questions to be answered by suppliers, such as size of hardware, electrical requirements, system support arrangements, costs etc.
- information concerning any special constraints such as timetabling problems
- information about terms or forms of contract and any acceptance tests.

The system requirements specification has three basic roles:

1   It is a communication document, which supports any discussion and devel-
     opment amongst those concerned with the system.
2   It is a reference document during implementation, maintenance and review.
3   It may be a legal document in that it forms part of the contract with the sup-
     plier.

Different levels of detail may be appropriate for different specifications, but the
specification is always a central document. The definition phase will lead naturally into the design phase.

....
Reflection   Explain why the systems requirements specification might be
                  useful as a reference document during implementation.
....

Design phase (detailed design and programming)

If new software is to be written, the design phase is concerned with the analysis,
flowcharting and other charting of the functions and operations that the system
must perform before the programs can be written. When an existing system or
applications software package is to be selected, such a detailed analysis is not normally necessary, although a detailed system specification is essential as a basis for
the final selection of the package, and to provide the groundwork for the implementation of the system. The detailed specification should outline all of the features required in the system, and is important in negotiations with the system
supplier. The systems requirements specification developed in the previous phase
should perform this function.

If a large system for, say, a library management system is under consideration,
an invitation to tender will be issued at this stage to a limited number (say, three
to six) of systems suppliers. These suppliers will be required to submit a quotation against the specification by a particular date. Where separate pieces of hardware and software are being acquired from different suppliers, a number of
quotations may need to be gathered. Some organizations such as local authorities
have a specific tendering procedure which must be followed, and legal assistance
may be available in drafting contracts.

When bids have been received, or with smaller systems as quotations are being
negotiated, systems should be demonstrated by their suppliers. Demonstrations
for large systems should preferably be on-site, and should certainly permit a number of the staff who will be affected by the new system to inspect the proposed
option.

Demonstrations facilitate communication, and can be used as an opportunity
for staff who will be included in the day-to-day running of the system to learn a
little about it and to ask questions. After the demonstrations, further discussions

should lead to the choice of system, including hardware and software. Subsequently, orders must be placed, contracts signed etc.

Reflection   What does a demonstration allow an information manager to learn about the applications software package? Write a checklist of some of the questions that you might seek to pose during such a demonstration.

Implementation phase

Normally, once orders have been placed there will be a lull whilst the information manager waits to see whether delivery dates will be met. This time should be spent in planning the installation and implementation of the system. Implementation can be lengthy and it is important not to underestimate the impact that the implementation of a new system may have on working practices and customer service. The installation phase starts with a review of the way in which the system will affect the existing operations of the organization. If a thorough analysis has been performed in the earlier stages of the systems-analysis exercise, many of the jobs, issues and other matters concerned with the installation of the system will have been identified and planned already. At this point it is necessary to gather a quantitative picture of the work to be done in order to achieve implementation, and to identify specific staff responsibilities.

A detailed **timetable** of training, installation and other activities needs to be agreed and finalized. The timetable should cover the various aspects of implementation as discussed below. The order of treatment is not significant. Indeed, many of these activities may be proceeding in parallel.

Preparation and planning

Various preparatory activities may be necessary. Although most of these issues should already have been thoroughly discussed, any new factors or options that were left open should be examined. The forms of records and files for various applications and databases need to be finalized. The sites for any central installation and for any workstations will need to be prepared, and appropriate telecommunication links installed.

Installing hardware

This includes both the computer itself and the various workstations, as well as other peripherals and links to telecommunication networks.

Installing software

Once the hardware has been installed, the next stage is to install the software, run it, and test it on small trial databases.

Creating databases

Once it is clear that the hardware and software are performing satisfactorily, work must begin on the construction of the full databases for the system. When moving between systems it is important to convert databases from earlier formats. The records for the databases may be derived from a variety of different sources. Procedures must be established for the creation of records for new items, including, for example, new borrowers, new books, new citations, new personnel. If a circulation-control system is being implemented for the first time, book labelling (with bar codes) can be a major task.

Staff training

The preparation of appropriate checklists, instruction and reference manuals is important for successful implementation of a system. Sessions with different objectives may be necessary for staff, depending on their role. Training may need to be phased over an extended period.

Changeover

There are a number of implementation strategies that can be adopted for moving from one system to another. The options include:

1 **Complete changeover** involves the old system being replaced by a new system on a specified day. This is risky if the system is central to the organization's operations, and should only be contemplated if all aspects of the new system have been carefully tested and the changeover has been very carefully planned.
2 **Phased approach**, in which the total system is divided into sections, each section is installed individually and sections are introduced one at a time. This approach allows staff to change gradually, but there can on occasions be difficulties associated with maintaining parts of an old system, whilst introducing a new system.
3 **Parallel running**, is where both old and new systems are operated in parallel for a period of time, until there is confidence in the new system and the old system can cease to operate. Although this is a secure approach, it is expensive and staff can easily become impatient at having to operate two systems.

4   **Pilot operation** of a system in a more controlled environment, such as a smaller department, before full introduction at all sites. Pilot running allows the system to be tested in operation in a controlled environment upon which systems staff can focus their support, as a means of testing the system before it is released system-wide.

Reflection   What parts of a college's information systems do you think might be affected by the introduction of an ID card system? What are the implications for changeover in the context of the introduction of the ID card system?

Evaluation phase (maintenance and review)

The last stage of a systems-analysis exercise is a long way from the initial establishment of requirements, but it is nevertheless important to emphasize that after successful implementation it is necessary to complete the exercise by going back to the specification and assessing the extent to which the system is meeting its stated objectives. Such an assessment may lead to improvements and refinements in the way in which a system is used.

Participation in user groups or cooperatives (for software packages and turnkey systems) may also assist in the process of formulating evaluative comments about the system, and pressing for changes from the system designer or supplier. Such groups can also be a means of maintaining a sound relationship with the system supplier.

6.4 Ergonomic considerations

Although the situation has improved, systems designers in the past have not always paid appropriate attention to ergonomic considerations when designing workstations and the environment in which they are situated. Often full consideration of ergonomic issues requires additional investment in new furniture, and other expensive adjustments to the environment. When computer workstations are being introduced into an existing working environment, it may be difficult to take full account of ergonomic considerations, since this may lead to requests for new furniture, new room layouts and assorted building works. In office and other environments, such as in educational institutions, full consideration of ergonomic issues has often awaited the refurbishment of buildings or the construction of new buildings. There are two key groups of ergonomic considerations: workstation design and the wider workplace environment.

General considerations in workstation design

There are three principles of good workstation design:

1   The workstation should fit the user, although creative and occasional users are more tolerant of poor fit than data-entry personnel, who may be engaged in repetitive work for extended periods of time. Designing the workstation to fit the user may present particular problems in the context of multi-user workstations.
2   The workstation should take into account the tasks to be performed by the user. For instance, if the task involves a lot of paper, a large desk area is necessary.
3   The workstation should support good posture. Poor posture can lead to backache, headache, pain in the neck and shoulders, and digestive and circulatory problems.

This means that it is necessary to consider the chair and desk that are to be part of the workstation. Adjustability is important since not all users are the same size or wish to position themselves at the workstation in the same way. Workstation design should not, however, be restricted to the office environment. For example, with multimedia kiosks for public use or ATM machines in banking it is important to consider access for, for example, wheelchair-bound users.

Wider workplace design considerations

In addition to the characteristics of the workstation itself, a number of other environmental considerations influence the comfort associated with the use of computer systems. Lighting, noise and heating and ventilation should all be considered.

Lighting

Especially in established buildings, there may not always be the opportunity to review lighting levels to ensure that they are appropriate for working with computer systems. When the opportunity arises it is important to conduct a lighting audit. When considering lighting it is important to take into account

*   recommended **illumination levels** for different tasks
*   **light sources**, including artificial and natural light
*   **lighting colour** (ranges form bright dazzling white to cosy yellow)
*   **glare** (caused by light reflected off highly reflective surfaces).

Noise

Noise is sound that the hearer considers to be unpleasant or disturbing. Noises
seldom occur singly, and should not be considered in isolation. The problems
caused by noise are:

*   hindrance to communication
*   stress caused by distraction from intermittent noises
*   hearing damage from high noise levels
*   lack of noise (people often need some background noise and feel uncomfort-
    able with total silence).

Noise sources include people talking, people moving, telephones ringing, printers,
air conditioning and heating, photocopiers and external traffic noise. Noise levels
are dependent upon the acoustic characteristics of a room. In particular, carpets,
soft furnishings and soft upholstery absorb noise and help to reduce reflected
noise.

Heating and ventilation

Heating and ventilation also contribute to a comfortable working environment.
There are four key factors: air temperature, radiant heat, humidity and air movement.

6.5 People and jobs in systems development

Systems development projects may be conducted in relation to systems of varying
sizes, may extend over differing time periods, and may require differing levels of
staff involvement. Nevertheless, in every situation there must be staff who are
responsible for:

*   decision making
*   getting the work done.

For large and specific projects, central control will normally be vested in a committee, often dubbed the Project Management Committee. Senior management, together with various other interested parties, must be represented on this committee. Representatives will be selected in accordance with the project being undertaken, and from different levels of the management structure. Trade union representatives may also be important if the changes in the system are likely to challenge or change people's jobs. Clearly it is also appropriate for the systems project manager to be a member of this committee. Whilst striving to maintain a compact group, the Project Management Committee also needs to be representative and to gather expertise from as wide a group as possible. The roles of the Project Management Committee are:

- to direct the project
- to monitor the progress of the project
- to facilitate communication about the progress of the project.

An organization may choose to establish a project management committee in respect of every individual project, or alternatively a committee or working group with a consultative or a decision-making role may be established to cover all projects. In the latter case it is likely that specific individuals may be invited to join the group when it considers specific projects.

The day-to-day execution of the decisions taken by a decision-making group such as the Project Management Committee is the task of the systems developer or systems team, who work together with other staff whose work will be affected by any system changes. The systems person is important as a source of expertise in computer systems and their applications, and offers advice and information to the Project Management Committee or its equivalent.

Apart from in the very smallest organizations, at least one full-time member of staff needs to be appointed to have responsibility for information systems. In a large company or a local authority, a complete department may be devoted to systems development. Consultants may be used to assist with specific projects. A number of organizations have used outsourcing extensively. **Outsourcing** is the use of an external organization that, in this instance, specializes in the maintenance and development of information systems. A contract is negotiated with an outsourcing agency for the provision and support of computer systems. This removes the need for the organization to be concerned with the systems. The only computer expertise required within the organization is that necessary to dialogue effectively with the outsourcing agency.

The tasks of a systems developer are:

- to investigate and assimilate information about the way in which a system currently operates

- to analyse its performance in the light of the system objectives which are identified by management
- to develop and evaluate ideas about how the system can be improved or reorganized
- to design in detail a new system meeting the requirements that have been identified
- to implement the new system once it has been developed.

The central role of the systems analyst is as an intermediary between the user and the computer system. In this role the systems person is required to be a catalyst and agent for change, an advisor, educator, salesperson, and communicator. In order to be successful the systems person needs an appropriate mix of personal qualities, skills and knowledge.

Consultants can be a useful way of drawing in additional expertise. They may be used to execute tasks for which the permanent staff do not have time. They are also in a better position to be impartial, and can often encourage staff to explain details that they might not wish to describe to a colleague. The one main drawback of consultants lies in their lack of ongoing commitment to an organization. They are usually employed to complete a job, and sever links with the organization when that job is finished. This can mean that:

- their expertise is only available to the organization for a short period of time
- the consultant will need to take some time to familiarize him/herself with the organization, its culture and objectives.

These potential drawbacks can be minimized, where appropriate, if an organization develops a continuing link with a consultant.

6.6   Information-systems methodologies

An information-systems methodology is a methodical approach to information-systems planning, analysis and design. A methodology involves recommendations about:

- phases, subphases and tasks
- when to use which and their sequence
- what sort of people should perform each task
- what documents, products or reports should result from each phase
- management, control, evaluation and planning of developments.

Information-system methodologies have been developed by systems developers and designers as a tool to aid in modelling information systems and designing a computer-based system which meets the requirements of the users of the information. Information-systems methodologies have not been designed to assist the user of a computer system to specify requirements, although there are good reasons why such a user might borrow some of the tools and approaches of the recognized methodologies to assist in a systematic analysis of requirements and the specification of a system.

Certainly, where a large and complex system is being considered, the adoption of a clearly defined methodology may well lead to more effective systems.

There are a number of different methodologies available on the market, each offering different features, and encompassing different aspects of the systems-analysis, design and implementation process. The use of these methods is difficult without computer support in the drawing of the necessary diagrams and in the logical design of the system. CASE tools have been developed for this purpose.

Approaches to systems analysis and design have been divided into two categories: hard and soft. Typically, **hard approaches** seek to develop a technical solution to problems through the implementation of a computer system. They assume the possibility of a clear and agreed statement, both of the current situation and its problems, and of the desired state of affairs to be achieved. The problem for systems development is then seen as that of designing a solution that will take us from where we are now to where we want to be. Users are viewed as sources of information about the system, and are viewed in terms of their information requirements and as devices for data input. The role of the analyst is that of the expert who is responsible for the design of the system.

Soft approaches recognize the impact of human beings within the area of systems analysis and design. Firstly, these methodologies deny the premise that it is easy to specify current and desired solutions, and assert that problem situations are messy. Secondly, the role of the analyst is more as a participant in a team, and the role of the participants in the existing system is integral to successful system development. With the advent of more sophisticated design tools, and in the face of the more complex design specifications required such as GUI and multimedia interfaces, methodologies which integrate analysis and design, such as prototyping and object-oriented methodologies, have become more important.

Structured information-systems methodologies

The more established systems methodologies can all be regarded as structured methodologies.

All structured methodologies hold some features in common. They all use graphical models, place emphasis on user communication, and involve repetition of the previous phase(s), step(s) and reviews. In structured analysis and design, the models represent the functions of the system rather than how to accomplish them. Emphasis is on the logical components of the system rather than its physical components. More specifically most methods have the following components:

- a set of models, usually expressed as diagrams which support specification and design
- techniques for conducting analysis and specification
- guidelines and procedures for conducting analysis and design
- procedures for managing the process of systems development.

All methodologies are distinct, but they do have some common features. They all use structured tools. A shared property of these tools is that many are graphical. Another characteristic of most of the structured tools is that they are based on the tree concept. Many of the tools are characteristic components of their respective systems-development methodologies. Some such tools are hierarchy charts, dataflow diagrams, entity relationship diagrams, entity life histories and data dictionaries. More specifically:

1   **Hierarchy charts** show the organizational structure. They record the division of responsibilities and functions within an organization.
2   **Data flow diagrams** represent systems in terms of the data flows between data stores, processes and sources or sinks.
3   **Data dictionaries** are simply dictionaries of data, or collections of data about data. A data dictionary typically holds information about stores, process flows, data elements and data structures, and in each case stores a name and further details in the dictionary entry. Figure 6.3 shows the data that might be held for a data element
4   **Entity life histories** provide a means of representing how entities change within a system with the passage of time. ELHs start with the creation of an entity, record the sequence of changes which take place during its life within the system, and end with its removal from the system.
5   **Entity relationship diagrams** are a means of representing the entities in a system and depicting the relationships between those entities.

```
Name description – of the data element
Aliases – alternative terms used for the same data element
Type – i.e. numeric, character or alphanumeric
Format
Values – the range of values that the element may take
Security – who is allowed to modify, add or delete a given data item
Editing
Comments – any special information.
```

Fig. 6.3 *Components of an entry in a data dictionary in respect of a data element.*

Reflection   Why is it helpful to use a structured methodology for systems
development?

Structured Systems Analysis and Design Method (SSADM)

In order to illustrate the nature of structured methodologies in more detail, we shall describe in outline the stages of one particular methodology. SSADM is probably the most widely used information-systems methodology in the UK because it has been adopted by the UK Government. It was originally developed by Learmouth and Burchett Management Systems for the Computer and Telecommunication Agency (CCTA). SSADM is a data-driven methodology which places emphasis on data modelling, but also advises analysis and specification of process views with data flow diagrams and behaviour using entity life histories. SSADM is structured in three phases: feasibility study, systems analysis and systems design. The first phase, feasibility study, may not be necessary for small projects. Each of these three phases is subdivided into a number of stages, which in turn are subdivided into a number of steps. SSADM comprises eight stages, fifty steps and about 230 tasks. The eight stages are, in outline:

First stage: problem definition

The aim of this stage is to obtain a precise definition of the overall problem or resolution by the system to be developed. Overviews are created of the present systems and data structure, and current problems are identified.

Second stage: project identification

This stage aims to create a number of options for dealing with the problems identified in the first stage. The options are evaluated and formalized for inclusion in the feasibility report.

Third stage: analysis of present system and problems

This stage analyses the existing system, and documents it in the form of data flow diagrams and logical data structures. In addition, the identification of the problems is refined from the second stage.

Fourth stage: specification of requirements

In this stage the user requirements determined in the previous stage are defined more closely. A data structure is defined based on the documentation created in the third stage. Audit, security and control aspects are defined. The output is the systems specification.

Fifth stage: selection from physical options

This stage involves the users and systems staff in selecting a suitable physical system. In most cases it is possible to decide on the hardware configuration and on the characteristics of the appropriate software.

Sixth stage: data design

Data structures for the proposed system are designed by combining the top-down view of the organization derived from the third stage with the bottom-up view of data groupings.

Seventh stage – process design

This stage is carried out in conjunction with the data design stage. The logical processing associated with enquiries and updating is defined. The logical design is then validated by means of a quality assurance review before proceeding to the physical design

Eighth stage: physical design

The logical design is translated into programs and the database content. The data dictionary is updated and the design tuned to meet performance objectives. Programs and systems are tested. Operating instructions are created. The implementation plan is drawn up and the manual procedures defined.

Holistic methodologies and prototyping

The conventional approach to systems development is through the types of systems-development methods outlined above, many of which require careful communication between user and developer. When communication is unsuccessful, it is often necessary to make changes to previous design features; this may lead to several versions of the design. Prototyping is a collection of techniques which make it easier to clarify requirements during both system investigation and systems design. Prototyping tools allow the developer to create a prototype system quickly so that users can experiment with the prototypes and amendments can be made. Prototypes offer an opportunity for close communication between the developer and the user, and are particularly useful in very new applications where it is difficult for the user to envisage the system and therefore difficult for them to produce an effective and full specification.

Tools for prototyping include any tools that allow prototypes to be constructed quickly. Fourth-generation languages and associated tools such as screen painters, graphics and report generators are examples of prototyping tools.

The star life-cycle, as shown in Figure 6.4, forms the basis for a methodology in which the ordering of stages and activities is inappropriate. System development may begin at any stage (indicated by the entry arrows) and may be followed by any of the other stages (indicated by double-headed arrows). The star model also recognizes the central role of evaluation. The star model is particularly appropriate to holistic methods of design, such as prototyping where there is an incremental development of the final product, otherwise known as iterative design.

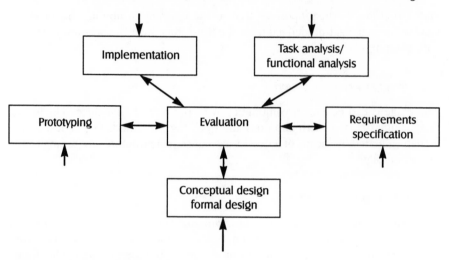

Fig. 6.4 *The star life-cycle*

Holistic approaches seek to view design as a whole. Design is a loosely structured activity with no rigorous ordering of stages. Attention focuses on the appearance and presentation of the conceptual model, and then on working with manifestations of that model using actual examples. There is a strong focus on the visual appearance of the interface and its behaviour, coupled with the need for designers to exercise their creative skills.

In many instances, holistic approaches can be effectively integrated with more structured methods. For example, information gathered from task analyses may be used. Alternatively, an initial holistic exploration of a proposed interface can form the basis for more detailed task analyses. Prototypes and sketches, for example, provide a basis for early testing with users and allow an exploration of the way that new tasks might be conducted.

Reflection   Explain how a prototype or model of a system might aid communication with potential systems users.

Understand users
List objects associated with all users and workgroups
Decide on the role of the system and identify which objects will be visible at the user interface
Describe each visible object according to the interface metaphor
Identify relationships between objects according to the interface metaphor
Decide how to view each object
Draw sketches of the interface design
Test the design with users

Fig. 6.5 *Stages in an object-oriented user interface design process*

Object-oriented methods

Object-oriented programming has demanded the development of specific object-oriented systems-analysis and design methodologies. These methodologies are relatively new, but will probably become increasingly important.

The virtue of OO methods is that the specification becomes the implementation. Analysis and design proceed by gradual addition of detail to the objects. The system is modelled as a collection of objects connected by message-passing channels. Objects pass messages to each other to request a services, such as the updating of an object's attributes or a request for a report. More detail is added to objects until the specification becomes sufficiently detailed to be programmed in an object-oriented language.

A number of object-oriented methods have been proposed. These include object-oriented analysis and object-oriented analysis and design. Both of these methods start by defining objects and classes, and then define relationships to put objects and classes together to form a system-wide view. Object detail is added successively by specifying attributes, methods and the object life history. Figure 6.5 illustrates some typical stages that might be present in an object-oriented methodology.

Designing multimedia GUI interfaces

Methodologies for the design of multimedia GUI interfaces are in their infancy. The object-oriented methodology described above is a good starting point, but it is important to remember that the design process in a multimedia context involves a whole technical team, including project manager, multimedia designers (such as graphic designers, illustrators, animators, image-processing specialists, instructional designers and interface designers), writers, video specialists, audio specialists and multimedia programmers. Vaughan (1994) offers a light-hearted checklist of actions which might be grouped to form a methodology with the stages given in Figure 6.6. Significant aspects of this methodology which have a wider relevance for public access interfaces are:

1	Market research
2	Design concept, including technical aspects
3	Identify resource, e.g. available content
4	Structure product
5	Design interface
6	Gather resources including team and content
7	Build prototype
8	User test
9	Revise design
10	Create multimedia components
11	Program and author
12	Test and fix functionality
13	Beta test
14	Create master
15	Deliver to the marketplace

Fig. 6.6 *Stages in a methodology for multimedia interface design*

1 Designers decide what they want to create on the basis of the message to be communicated or the product to be delivered.
2 A prototype is built and then tested on potential users or user representatives early in the process.
3 Storyboarding is necessary to identify how all of the different media are to be integrated.
4 There is significant design work involved in the creation of audio, video, photographs, graphics and animations.

Strategic information systems planning (SISP)

None of the methodologies described above take a strategic view of the role of the information systems within an organization. They may take as a given that business objectives are relevant. Strategic information systems planning is important for its specific focus on the use of information systems to achieve organizational objectives, possibly in relation to the provision of management information or customer services.

Innovative use of information technology in business has led to the creation of new products, improved service and dramatically reduced costs. In other words, the use of information technology has changed the way in which business is conducted and has altered the competitive position within the industry. For example, businesses traditionally pay bills by cheque on receipt of invoices. Using information technology, it is possible for the purchaser to send an electronic payment instruction to their bank when the goods are received. The payer's account is debited and the payee's account is credited. In this context, the use of IT has eliminated paperwork, and will generally lead to earlier payment, with all of the associated implications.

These types of information use can be described as strategic, and are generally managed by **strategic information systems**. Strategic information systems allow the business to achieve **competitive advantage**.

Strategic information systems are information systems that are designed to lend the business a competitive advantage. Technically, such systems may be very similar to traditional IT systems, but they differ in that their focus is on treating information as a strategic resource. Strategic information systems are business-driven and focus on the environment in which the business operates. More specifically, strategic information systems are:

- outward-looking, with a focus on the service to customers
- offering real benefit to the customers
- capable of changing the marketplace's perception of the firm.

Strategic information systems planning (SISP) is a methodology which seeks to develop strategic information systems. SISP is the process of establishing a programme for the implementation and use of information systems in such a way that it will optimize the effectiveness of the organization's information resources and use them to support the objectives of the whole enterprise as much as possible. The outcomes of an SISP are typically a short-term plan for the next 12 to 18 months, as well as a longer-term plan for the next three to five years. SISP has a dual nature. It covers both detailed planning and budgeting for information systems at one level, and strategic issues and formulation at another.

An SISP is a complex planning activity which requires a small project team, supported by input from a relatively large number of members of staff and possibly consultants. SISP is usually conducted as a project lasting from three to six months. It is important for the scope of the project to be defined at the outset. The scope may be the whole organization, or more narrowly defined with regard to a specific product. SISP provides a broad context in which to examine and plan for information product development that will lend the organization a competitive advantage. Although it is concerned primarily with information systems within the organization, it can also be used to inform the planning of those systems or products that support customer service, because it embeds consideration of marketplace factors such as critical success factors and cost benefit analysis.

Figure 6.7 lists 20 steps that might lead to the creation of an SISP. These steps can be grouped into seven phases:

- Steps 1 to 3 are associated with setting the development of SISP into action
- Steps 4 to 8 are concerned with identifying and formulating goals, objectives, missions and strategies for the organization. The process involves the identi-

fication of critical success factors, or factors that are key to organizational success.

- Steps 9 to 11 consider the existing information systems through a systems audit.
- Steps 12 to 14 identify as many information systems opportunities as possible, with an focus on the way in which systems can be used to achieve competitive advantage. These opportunities are filtered in order to identify those which offer the best return on investment.
- Step 15 leads to the production of an action plan.
- Steps 16 to 18 are concerned with the implementation and adoption of the action plan.
- Steps 19 to 20 focus on maintenance of the SISP.

Twenty steps to an SISP

1   Obtain authorization.
2   Establish a team and arrange accommodation, tolls etc.
3   Allocate responsibilities and create a timetable.
4   Determine the corporate goals, objectives, missions etc.
5   Establish the firm's corporate strategy, explicitly or implicitly.
6   Define the critical success factors
7   Establish the key performance indictators.
8   Define the critical data set.
9   Incorporate the forms Information Technology Architecture.
10 Conduct a systems audit.
11 Rank current systems condition and prioritize current systems proposals.
12 Brainstorm for new systems and create an IT opportunities list.
13 Perform cost-benefit and risk analysis.
14 Conduct filtering workshops.
15 Produce an action plan.
16 Communicate the action plan to all appropriate staff.
17 Identify and appoint project champions.
18 Arrange for top management to commit themselves publicly to SISP.
19 Create feedback mechanisms.
20 Update the SISP.

Fig.6.7 *An example of SISP*

Reflection   Under what circumstances will SISP lead to strategic information systems?

6.7 Day-to-day management

The previous sections of this chapter have focused on information systems planning, and the stages in a project which should lead to the successful implementation of a new system. The installation of a new system represents a major investment, and should have a significant impact on the organization. It is both inevitable and appropriate that planning should receive significant attention. However, a successful system also needs day-to-day management.

One person should have overall responsibility for the system. The number of people involved in system support and maintenance will depend upon the system size, the number of users and the location of workstations. Systems trigger five types of activity: documentation, maintenance, security, user support and planning. The systems manager coordinates these activities.

Systems documentation

Documentation is important throughout the process of systems design and implementation:

1   It gives a clear picture of work completed.
2   It supports good communication between everyone concerned with the system.
3   It acts as an archival reference record.

Documentation should include:

•   reports, mainly addressed to management, which should be generated during systems development, and cover aims, costs, savings and a description of the proposed system
•   instructions to users
•   specifications which describe the system functions
•   instructions to computer operating and control staff in relation to the running of jobs.

Maintenance

System maintenance is concerned with keeping the hardware and software working. This involves:

•   monitoring the quality and integrity of databases
•   dealing with any malfunctions, such as faulty workstations
•   making sure adequate back-ups of files are kept
•   troubleshooting any situations where the system does not work as it might

- implementing upgrades of software and hardware
- liaison with hardware and software suppliers.

Security

It is easy to neglect security during the implementation of a system, where the priority is to ensure that the system works. However, continued operation of the system depends on the security of its components. Loss of security occurs from accidental and deliberate threats. Accidental threats arise from poor system features such as overloaded networks or software bugs. Deliberate threats arise from human intent, and include theft, computer fraud, vandalism and other attempts to break the system. Typically such threats may lead to:

- the interruption of data preparation and data input
- the destruction or corruption of stored data
- the destruction or corruption of software
- the disclosure of personal proprietary information
- injury to personnel
- the removal of equipment or information.

In order to prevent exposure to security threats, organizations need a security policy which:

- identifies the risks to which the system is exposed
- assesses the probability of any threat being carried out and the possible consequences of any given threat
- selects the counter-measures for threats on the basis of effectiveness, cost and security demands
- outlines contingency measures to tackle situations where loss of security is unavoidable.

It is also important to ensure that all those associated with the system acknowledge their responsibility for security.

User support

User support is essentially about making sure that users know how to make the most effective and efficient use of the system. Training is a central plank of support. Some training will have been conducted during implementation, but systems change and personnel change, people forget and people become more experienced, and are ready to learn more. Training can be achieved through courses and one-to-one on-the-job training. User documentation and help-desk facilities are also important user support tools.

Future planning

Planning staff review the overall function of the system. Problem areas need to be identified, and changes in the technology and the marketplace for systems must be monitored. Once problems have been identified, proposals for improvement must be submitted to management. Once these proposals have been approved, planning for the implementation of these proposals must proceed. This may lead to modest system enhancements, or the introduction of the next generation of system.

Summary   Information systems must be managed effectively if they are to give faithful and useful service. The system life-cycle involves analysis, design, implementation, operating evolution, decay and replacement. When a new system is under consideration, a systems development project should be conducted. The phases in such a project are definition of objectives, definition of systems requirements, design, implementation and evaluation. Information-systems methodologies have been developed in order to provide a methodical approach to systems analysis and design. One such method is SSADM. Prototyping, and special methodologies that support the design of multimedia and object-based applications, are increasingly important. Strategic information systems planning seeks to ensure that information-systems planning is integral to the organization's strategic plan. Finally, a system, once implemented, requires day-to-day management. This involves consideration of documentation, maintenance, security, user support and future systems planning.

REVIEW QUESTIONS

1   Describe the stages in the systems life-cycle.
2   What is the role of a systems specification?
3   What needs to be considered during the implementation phase of a systems project?
4   Identify some of the ergonomic considerations that need to be taken into account when developing a systems project.
5   What are the characteristics of a structured systems methodology?
6   Compare prototyping as a systems design approach, with a hard systems methodology.

7   What relevance does strategic information systems planning
   (SSIP) have for information managers?
8   Outline briefly how security can be managed within an information systems environment.

References

Vaughan, T. (1994) *Multimedia: making it work*, Berkeley/London, Osborne/
   McGraw-Hill.

Bibliography

Note: Some of the texts listed at the end of Chapter 2 offer a useful simple introduction to systems analysis and design.

Avison, D. E. and Fitzgerald, G. (1988) *Information systems development: method-
   ologies, techniques and tools*, Oxford, Blackwell.
Checkland, P. (1991) *Systems thinking, systems practice*, Chichester, Wiley,
Crinnion, J. E. (1992) *Evolutionary systems development*, London, Pitman.
Cutts, G. (1991) *Structured systems analysis and design methodology*, Oxford,
   Blackwell.
Harbour, R. T. (1994) *Managing library automation*, London, Aslib.
Holloway, S. (1989) *Methodology handbook for information managers*, Aldershot,
   Gower.
Hughes, M. J. (1992) *A practical introduction to systems analysis and design: an
   active learning approach*, London, DP Publications.
Lester, G. (1992) *Business information systems volume. 2: Systems analysis and
   design*, London, Pitman.
Mandelbaum, J. (1992) *Small project automation of libraries and information cen-
   tres*, CN, Meckler.
Mason, D. and Willcocks, L. (1994) *Systems analysis, systems design*, Henley-on-
   Thames, Alfred Waller.
National Computing Centre (1990) *Systems training library*, Oxford, Blackwell.
Pachent, G. (1996) 'Network '95: choosing a third generation automated infor-
   mation system for Suffolk Libraries & Heritage', *Program*, **30** (3), 213–28.
Preece, J. (1994) *Human–computer interaction*, Wokingham, Addison-Wesley.
Remenyi, D. S. J. (1991) *Introducing strategic information systems planning*,
   Oxford, Blackwell.
Robb, A. F. (1992) *The management guide to the selection and implementation of
   computer systems*, Oxford, Blackwell.
Rowley, J. (1990) *Basics of systems analysis and design*, London, Library
   Association Publishing.

Schuyler, M. (ed.) (1991) *The systems librarian's guide to computers*, Westport, CN, Meckler.

Senn, J. A. (1989) *Analysis and design of information systems*, New York/London, McGraw-Hill.

Skidmore, S. (1994) *Introducing systems analysis*, Manchester/Oxford, NCC/Blackwell.

Skidmore, S. and Wroe, B. (1990) *Introducing systems design*, Oxford, Blackwell.

Ward, I. (et al.) (1990) *Strategic planning for information systems*, Chichester: Wiley.

Wilson, B. (1990) *Systems concepts, methodologies and applications*, Chichester, Wiley.

Part 2

Information retrieval

7

The basics of information retrieval

LEARNING OUTCOMES

This chapter introduces the basic concepts associated with information retrieval. At the end of this chapter you will

- be aware of the basic components of any information retrieval system
- have an awareness of the different roles of corporate and external information systems
- be aware of the basic characteristics of the different types of information retrieval systems
- be able to differentiate between the different types of indexing and searching languages
- understand Boolean logic and relevance ranking
- be acquainted with the retrieval facilities that are common to most information retrieval systems
- be aware of the different approaches to the development of a search strategy
- understand that different users have different needs.

7.1 The nature of information retrieval

Information retrieval systems have become almost synonymous with computers, but paper-based systems, such as card and document filing systems, do still exist, and certainly were in evidence before the advent of computers. This chapter and Chapters 8 to 12 discuss facilities for the retrieval and dissemination of information or documents, as distinct from systems which support library management activities. These systems are the central concern of Chapters 13 to 15. Cataloguing systems are considered as part of library management systems, although OPACs specifically may be regarded as a special category of information retrieval system.

All information-retrieval systems may be viewed as comprising three stages:

- indexing
- storage
- retrieval.

Indexing

Indexing is the process of allocating index terms or keys to a record or document: these index terms or keys assist in the later retrieval of the document or record. The assignment of indexing terms may be intellectual (i.e. conducted by a human) or computer-based. A computer can only select index terms in accordance with a set of instructions. Selection will depend upon word occurrence. The index terms that may be assigned will be drawn from a standard list or computer thesaurus, on the basis of word occurrence in a record or document. Alternatively, computers may also be enlisted to arrange humanly assigned index terms. Such terms will be selected and assigned by indexers on the basis of the indexer's subjective assessment of the content or the assignment of terms that are likely to be sought by a subsequent searcher; the terms may be drawn from a controlled list or may be uncontrolled. Many systems incorporate elements of both controlled and uncontrolled indexing languages. The computer acts as a reliable workhorse for arranging index entries in alphabetical order for display on the screen or for the printing of an index.

Storage

Information retrieval systems may use the computer itself to store both the document files and the index files, and to maintain databases. Database structures that are used to support these processes have been discussed in Chapter 5.

Retrieval

The key issue is that the retrieval process is very dependent upon the indexing and storage stages; to a large extent they determine the optimum strategy for searching an information retrieval system. But another factor which influences the retrieval process remains constant, irrespective of the system design. The system user and the queries that are submitted to the system do not, in general, change with the system. The user's needs do not change with the availability of specific systems, although they may become more sophisticated as the user's experience with those systems develops.

The nature of computer-produced indexes varies greatly, and searchers will have more success if they recognize some of the inherent limitations. Computers are still used to generate printed indexes, and the contribution that these make to information retrieval should not be overlooked. Nevertheless, retrieval from a computer database is usually by online interrogation of the database. Online searching introduces a flexibility of search not possible with print-based systems. Accordingly, it is more necessary for the user to become acquainted with a wide range of search facilities and their potential if the user is to optimize their use of the system.

Retrieval can be conceptualized as involving three key stages:

- accepting as input a query (as a representation of information need) formulated by the user
- carrying out a comparison of the query with each of the records (representation of document) in a database
- producing as output, for consideration by the user, a retrieval set (sometimes an empty one) of records identified on the basis of this comparison.

Many searchers will pass through these three stages several times before completing a search.

The remainder of this chapter explores the features that characterize information retrieval systems. Dialogue design styles, indexing and searching languages, search logic and search facilities all influence the effectiveness of retrieval. Later chapters consider these features in the differing environments of retrieval from the online search services, the Internet, document management and publishing systems, CD-ROM and other products. Table 7.1 summarizes some of the key features of such systems. In addition, it is important to remember that, whilst interrogation of databases is an important product of information retrieval systems, one of the fundamental characteristics of computer-based information retrieval systems is that the database at the heart of the system may also be used as the basis for a plethora of different products, ranging from CD-ROM, through access to an online search service, to printed indexes and current-awareness bulletins. This range of products is illustrated in Figure 5.3 in respect of one database and its derivatives.

7.2 Corporate and external databases and systems

All types of information database and many of the products derived from them may be maintained and produced either corporately or from an external vendor. Corporate products are generated by the information staff and possibly other staff within an organization for its own corporate internal customers. External services derive from databases that are marketed commercially, and are usually available worldwide from database producers, publishers and online search services, and other Internet servers. Information managers have a responsibility to manage access to both types of information sources, and specifically (and often more problematically) the interface between information from the two categories of source. Organizations and individual users need access to a wide range of information resources. These resources will have different originators, often different retrieval software, and will have many different characteristics. The information manager will have a central role in

- managing and coordinating the mechanisms for keeping a business team aware of market developments, and taking some responsibility for wider environmental scanning

Table 7.1 Different types of information retrieval systems

	User characteristics	Environment	Tasks	Technology
Online search services	Expert users and information managers	Office, academic library, corporate information centre	Retrieval of information, downloading information and integrating into other documents	Range of different workstations; earlier configurations with direct link to service; more state-of-the-art applications links through the Internet.
CD-ROM	Depends on database – can include children, general public library users, professional users and others	Library, airport, home, office	Retrieval of information, downloading information and integrating information into other documents	Often multimedia, GUI, mouse
Internet	Internet surfers – preponderance of academics, students and males	Study/work place, home	E-mail communication, shopping, file transfer screen and mouse	Desktop and portable PCs, with keyboard,
OPACs	Library users – profile depends on type of library	Library, office/home, other public venues	Narrowly defined – identifying book availability, searching for information	Sometimes large screens, touch screen, special-purpose keyboard, but also accessed through standard office equipment; remote and local access may use different workstations
Document management systems	Corporate users with some shared experience of the system, and shared objectives and tasks	Office-based, but may also extend to mobile operation and use in production units and in, say, trains and cars	Consultation of corporate archive in the pursuit of work-based tasks	Workstations linked to a powerful central computing resource; some applications will be state-of-the-art

- designing, implementing, when necessary monitoring and updating information systems, and exploiting information in information systems in appropriate decision-making.

In contexts such as academic institutions, where access to the existing knowledge base is central to their business of disseminating existing knowledge and creating new knowledge, these roles may be separately managed. Here the library and information service is likely to have primary responsibility for access to external databases, while management information services probably manage those systems that collate and disseminate management information, and ensure that effective communication permeates the organization. Table 7.2 summarizes some key differences between corporate information systems (and the resources to which they provide access) and external information systems, from the perspective of the information manager. In addition to these two major categories of shared information, individual users will also develop their own personal information systems. Information managers may need to understand the relationship between these systems and corporate or external systems, and should be in a position to lend training and advice that can promote good practice. The principles of information retrieval that follow apply in all three of these contexts: corporate systems, external systems, and individual personal systems.

....

Reflection   Make a list of some of the different information retrieval systems that you have used.

....

Table 7.2 *Corporate systems versus external systems*

Feature	Corporate systems	External systems
Coverage	Includes both corporately generated documents and data from transactions, and also external documents	Probably covers greater numbers of documents in published literature, yielding a wider discipline perspective
Cost	Costs are set up, including maintenance costs, which may be quite high; costs are therefore more likely to relate to the size of the databank than the extent of its use	Costs incurred are broadly on a use basis, although there is a wide range of pricing strategies from pay-as-you-go to subscriptions
Retrieval facilities	Should suit corporate requirements in terms of index terms, searchable fields and form of records	May have a similar range to corporate database, but more likely to have a greater range of more sophisticated facilities; user needs more skill in selection; training schemes are well established, but may be regarded as expensive

Training for users	Will vary depending on local environment; can be an important role for information managers	Training schemes are well established, but may be regarded as expensive
Products	Usually a more limited range of products, since user requirements may be less diverse	As full a range of products as can be marketed
Audience	Smaller, more coherent group	Larger group, often classified by discipline and employer group

Generations of information retrieval systems

Computer-based information-retrieval systems, in common with many other systems, can be viewed as having passed through a number of generations in the past 20 years. These generations have been experienced in all of the different types of information system. Table 7.3 encapsulates some of the features of these generations. Whilst the latest or third generation is of primary concern, earlier generations are important because

- a number of operational systems may be based on older technology and belong to the second generation
- they form the foundations for today's state-of-the-art systems.

Each succeeding generation is based on more advanced technology; this has implications for the way in which the systems are used. So, as one generation emerges from the last one, the types of data stored in the systems, the connectivity of systems, the user interface, and the nature of the user group, have evolved.

Table 7.3 *Generations of information retrieval systems*

First generation	Metadata	Command-based interfaces, expert and intermediary users; a limited number of online systems within organizations and available externally through online search services
Second generation	Full-text data	Menus and command-based interfaces; additional retrieval facilities, such as hypertext and full-text search facilities; DOS-based interfaces; end-user access intended but not always possible or achieved; online systems, with early CD-ROM-based systems
Third generation	Multimedia	GUI interfaces; focus on end-user access; market orientation, and emphasis on product packages; storage and distribution on CD-ROM or over high-capacity networks; multimedia; intermediary as trainer; greater use in the home and other public-access environments

7.3 Interface design

Chapter 4 reviewed the basic dialogue or interface design styles that may be adopted in computer systems. Most systems now operate with a GUI-based interface, which embraces:

- direct manipulation
- menu selection
- command languages
- form-filling
- question and answer.

There are still a few applications which use one or more of these dialogue styles in non-GUI-based interfaces. In early systems the emphasis was on command-based interfaces and menu-based interfaces. Until a few years ago all information-retrieval systems were command-based. These systems were regarded as impenetrable for the inexperienced user. The need to learn the command language was aggravated by the fact that nearly every software package used a different command language. Menu-based interfaces were introduced as a means of making systems more accessible to the new and occasional user. They first emerged in CD-ROMs and OPACs, and some specialist online applications, and were later adopted by online search services as interfaces for their services that are marketed directly to end-users. The first menu-based systems were very simple full-screen menus, but most systems now have full GUI-based interfaces. Menu-based systems sometimes embed the use of commands in a menu-based environment by offering the searcher a list of commands from which the appropriate ones can be selected. This still requires the searcher to have some appreciation of the effect that the application of a specific command may have, but eliminates the requirement for the searcher to remember the exact form of a command for a given information retrieval system. In information-retrieval applications, features of GUI interfaces which facilitate the search process include the following:

1   The facility for moving more easily between applications, so that, for example, through the one interface the user might perform a search on an external database, download some information, enter a word-processing package to reformat that data, and then, finally, communicate the reformatted data to a colleague through an e-mail system.
2   The use of windows so that a user can build a search strategy in one window whilst consulting a thesaurus or a help system in another window. Once the search has been completed, the search strategy window can remain on display whilst the records are displayed.
3   The use of direct manipulation and the opportunity to click on hypertext links in a document.

4   The use of much more visually appealing and easy-to-understand interfaces.
5   Ease of navigation through different menus and actions available within the system.
6   Opportunities for the display of multimedia documents with, for example, on-screen display of photographs and video.

In general, then, GUI interfaces have made information-retrieval systems much more user-friendly, but there are some public-access environments, particularly those where a kiosk is used for public access, in which the use of the full functionality of a GUI interface would be regarded as confusing by a significant proportion of the users.

Reflection   Make a list of those aspects of the GUI interface that you think might present difficulties to a user who is new to GUI interfaces.

7.4 Indexing and searching languages

An indexing language can be defined as the terms or codes that might be used as access points in an index. A searching language can be defined as the terms that are used by a searcher when specifying a search requirement. If the terms or codes are assigned by an indexer when a database is created, then the indexing language is used in indexing. The same terms or codes may also be used as access points to records during searching. Whilst the indexing language may be distinct from the searching language, clearly, if retrieval is to be successful, the two must be closely related. We shall return to this point later.

Indexing languages may be of three different types: controlled indexing languages or assigned-term systems, natural indexing languages or derived-term systems, and free indexing languages. Each of these is briefly discussed below.

Controlled indexing languages or assigned-term systems

With these languages a person controls the terms that are used as index terms. Controlled indexing languages may be used for names and other labels, but much emphasis is placed upon languages with terms that describe subjects. Normally an authority list identifies the terms that may be assigned. Indexing involves a person assigning terms from this list to specific documents on the basis of subjective interpretations of the concepts in the document; in this process the indexer exercises some intellectual discrimination in choosing appropriate terms.

There are two types of subject-based controlled indexing languages: alphabetical indexing languages and classification schemes. In **alphabetical indexing languages,** such as are recorded in thesauri and subject headings lists, the subject terms are the alphabetical names of subjects. Control is exercised over which terms are used, and relationships between terms are indicated, but the terms themselves are ordinary words. In **classification schemes** each subject is represented by a code or notation. Classification schemes are particularly intended to place subjects in a framework which crystallizes their relationships one to another.

Thesauri have always been a feature of the document management systems that have been designed to manage larger collections. They are increasingly featuring in OPACs and other information retrieval environments, and their applicability for Internet applications is of interest. Thesauri typically show the controlled indexing term, with related, narrower and broader terms. They may be displayed in a window during search strategy formulation, to aid a user in the selection of terms. Often terms can be selected from the thesaurus listing simply by clicking on them. Hypertext links in thesauri listings can be used to move between different occurrences of the same term in the list. Another application of thesauri is as a basis for automatic indexing. All terms in the documents that appear in the thesaurus will generate an entry in the inverted index. Related applications of thesauri are in the creation of semantic nets and semantic knowledge bases.

Natural indexing languages, or derived-term systems

These are not really a distinct or stable language in their own right, but are rather the 'natural' or ordinary language of the document being indexed. Strictly, natural-language systems are only one type of derived-term system. A derived-term system is one where all descriptors are taken from the document being indexed. Thus author indexes, title indexes and citation indexes, as well as natural-language subject indexes, are derived-term systems. Any terms that appear in the document may be candidates for index terms. Emphasis has traditionally been on the terms in titles and abstracts, but increasingly the full text of the document is used as the basis for indexing. Natural-language indexing using the full text of the document may be very detailed, and in some systems a mechanism for deciding which terms are the most important for the indexing of a given document may be appropriate. Such mechanisms are often based upon statistical analysis of the relative frequency of the occurrence of terms. Natural-language indexing can be executed by a human indexer, or automatically by the computer. The computer might index every term in the document, apart from a limited stop-list of very common terms, or may only index those terms that have been listed in a computer-held thesaurus.

Free indexing languages

A free indexing language cannot be listed. Indexing is free in the sense that there are no constraints on the terms that can be used in the indexing process. Free-language indexing is different from natural-language indexing in that the latter is constrained by the language of the document being indexed, whereas the former is not – any appropriate terms may be assigned. Free-language indexing may be executed by a human indexer, where the quality of the index will be very dependent on the indexer's knowledge of the subject and its terminology. Computerized free indexing is, for all practical purposes, the same as natural-language indexing, since the computer must have some basis upon which to assign terms. This is usually the text of the document being indexed.

Natural-language indexing and controlled-language indexing are used extensively in many information-retrieval applications. Both are used in retrieval on CD-ROM, via the online search services, in document management systems, and in online public access catalogues. The examples of searches in these environments in subsequent chapters demonstrate the use of these languages. Controlled indexing languages are claimed to be more consistent, and therefore more efficient and straightforward for the searcher, but research has failed to prove this convincingly. The dilemma facing systems designers is that to offer anything other than natural-language indexing in the context of the huge databanks available through the Internet would be prohibitively expensive. On the other hand, controlled-language indexing is seen as valuable in a supportive environment for inexperienced users because they do not need to navigate all of the variations inherent in natural language. Significant effort is being directed towards the development of system interfaces which manage this variability, either implicitly or explicitly, on behalf of the user. Many databases include terms from controlled indexing languages (often including both alphabetical indexing languages and classification schemes) and also support searching on the text of the record, thus covering all options. Table 7.4 lists the options.

Table 7.4 *Comparing uncontrolled and controlled indexing languages*

	Advantages	Disadvantages
Uncontrolled indexing languages	Low cost; simplified searching; full database contents searchable; every word has equal retrieval value; no human indexing errors; no delay in incorporating new terms	Greater burden on searcher; information implicitly but not overtly included in text may be missed; absence of specific to generic linkage; vocabulary of discipline must be known
Controlled vocabulary	Solves many semantic problems; permits generic relationships to be identified; maps areas of knowledge	High cost; possible inadequacies of coverage; human error; possibility of out-of-date vocabulary; difficulty of systematically incorporating all relevant relationships between terms

7.5   Search logic

Search logic is the means of specifying combinations of terms which must be matched for successful retrieval. Boolean search logic is employed in searching most systems. It may be used to link terms from either controlled or natural indexing languages, or both. The logic is used to link the terms that describe the concepts present in the statement of the search. As many as 20 to 30 or more search terms may be linked together by search logic in order to frame the search statement. Search logic permits the inclusion in the search statement of all syn-onyms and related terms, and also specifies acceptable and unacceptable search-term combinations. Search strategies often need to be more complex with natural-language terms in order to accommodate all the potential spelling varia-tions and near-synonyms. The Boolean logic operators are AND, OR and NOT. Figure 7.2 uses Venn diagrams to demonstrate the use of each of these operators.

In an online search the search statements are evolved one at a time, and feed-back is available at each stage. The searcher specifies a search statement and the computer responds with the number of relevant records. With this type of search facility, the search strategy can be refined to yield a satisfactory output.

Operator	Search type	Venn diagrams	Meaning
AND	Conjunctive		Logical product, symbolized by A AND B, A, B, A X B OR (A) (B). Both index terms A and B must be assigned to a document for a match, e.g. Stage X Lighting X Ballroom implies that all of the above terms must have been assigned to a document for a match
OR	Additive		Logical sum, symbolized by A OR B, or A + B. Only one of the two index terms, A or B, need be associated with a document for a match. This operator is usually intro-duced when A and B can be regarded as equivalent for the purposes of the search, e.g. Billiards + Snooker would serve to retrieve all documents with either the term 'Billiards' or the term 'Snooker' assigned.
NOT	Subtractive		Logical difference, symbolized by A NOT B, or A – B. The index term A must be assigned, and assigned in the absence of the term B for a match, e.g. Ball games – Golf requires all documents on ball games except those where 'Golf' is also assigned.

Fig. 7.2 *Boolean logic operators*

The Boolean operators AND, OR and NOT are subject to some variation. For example, some systems use AND NOT. Also, they may often be abbreviated, so that for example * can be used to represent AND and + for OR. It is common to use more than one operator in a search statement, as in for instance

SELECT BOOKSTORE? OR BOOK( )STORE AND MYSTERY

Once a string of operators has been introduced, the priority of execution needs to be considered. In the example above, it is necessary to specify whether the search should be conducted as

SELECT BOOKSTORE? OR (BOOKSTORE AND MYSTERY)

or as

SELECT (BOOKSTORE? OR BOOK( )STORE) AND MYSTERY.

Each software package (or search service) has its own priority rules (for example, AND may always be processed before OR), and successful searching depends on heeding these rules, or making appropriate use of parentheses. Parentheses force priority, and often offer a clear specification from the searcher's perspective.

Reflection   Analyse the above two search statements and explain the difference between them.

Relevancy ranking and best-match search logic

In most search statements it is possible to designate certain concepts as being more significant than their neighbours. In its role in formulating search profiles, weighted-term logic may be introduced, either as a search logic in its own right, or as a means of reducing or ranking (relevancy ranking) the search output from a search whose basic logic is Boolean.

In an application where weighted-term logic is the primary search logic, each search term in a search profile is allocated a weight. These weights can be allocated by the searcher, but more commonly are allocated automatically. Automatic allocation of weights is usually based on the inverse-frequency algorithm which weights terms in accordance with the inverse frequency of their occurrence in the database. Thus common words are not seen to be particularly valuable in uniquely identifying documents. If the weights are assigned by the searcher they are associated with a relevance rating on a document which is found containing that term as a search term. Search profiles combine terms and their weights in a simple sum, and items rated as suitable for retrieval must have weights which exceed a specified threshold weight. A simple SDI-type profile showing the use of weighted-term logic is shown below:

Search description: The use of radioactive isotopes in measuring the productivity of soil. A simple search profile (which does not explore all possible synonyms) might be:

8 Soil	4 Plants
7 Radioisotopes	3 Food
7 Isotopes	2 Environment
6 Radioactive	2 Agriculture
5 Radiation	1 Productivity
5 Agricultural chemistry	1 Water.

A threshold weight appropriate to the specificity of the searchers' enquiry must be established. For instance, a threshold weight of 12 would retrieve documents with the following combinations of terms assigned, and these documents or records would be regarded as relevant:

Soil and Plants
Soil and Radioisotopes
Soil and Agricultural chemistry
Radioisotopes and Agricultural chemistry
Soil, Food and Agriculture.

Documents with the following terms assigned would be rejected on the grounds that their combined weights from each of the terms identified in the records did not exceed the pre-selected threshold:

Productivity and Water
Food and Soil
Radioactive and Agriculture.

Alternatively, no threshold weight may be used, and then users will simply be presented with records in ranked order, and can make their own choice as to how far down the list they choose to scan.

Weighted-term search logic may also be used to supplement Boolean logic. Here weighted-term logic is a means of limiting or ranking the output from a search that has been conducted with the use of a search profile which was framed in terms of Boolean logic operators. In the search, and prior to display or printing, references or records are ranked according to the weighting that they achieve, and records with sufficiently high rankings will be deemed most relevant, and selected for display or printing. In this application, relevancy ranking is most often achieved through an analysis of the number of occurrences of search terms or hits in the document.

The inverted indexes that need to be created to support Boolean searching and relevance ranking respectively, are different. An inverted index may be stored in the form of a large matrix, with each row corresponding to an individual term, and each column to an individual record. A Boolean search simply requires that each of these cells in the matrix have a value of one or zero. A mechanism that uses some type of term-weighting scheme will require the cell of the matrix to have a value, say, n, where n is the result of a more complicated function of a number of variables. These values may be calculated on the basis of term occurrences. Each record may be considered as a vector or sequence of values.

7.6 Search facilities

Standard retrieval facilities are available in most information-retrieval applications. These facilities have been developed to cater for a text-based environment, where the user does not know what documents are available and/or does not know the terms by which records can be retrieved. In other database applications, where records can be retrieved through pre-assigned codes, many of the facilities listed below are not necessary. These facilities cater for the uncertainty in document-based systems, such as those of the external online search services, document management systems, CD-ROM applications and online public-access catalogues. The key facilities and their functions are listed in Table 7.5. In command-based systems these facilitates are accessed through the use of an appropriate command; in GUI-based interfaces the options are likely to be embedded in pull-down menus, or buttons and check boxes on dialogue boxes.

Table 7.5 *Typical search facilities*

Facility	Function
1 Set-up facilities, e.g. help, news, log-off	Sets up the environment
2 Selecting search terms	Allows the searcher to identify possible search terms by viewing index lists or thesauri
3 Entering search terms	Allows the searcher to enter search terms
4 Combining search terms	Allows the development of search strategies using search logic
5 Specifying fields	Allows the choice of the fields in which search terms appear
6 Truncation	Allows searching on text strings that are not complete words
7 Proximity, adjacency and context searching	Requires words to appear in a specified context

8 Range searching and limiting	Searches for values within a range
9 Displaying search or results sets	Shows the user how many documents and search term references were found
10 Displaying records	Displays records on the screen
11 Search management	Reviews the search
12 Advanced display options	Accommodates records in full-text databases
13 Nested or joined queries	Aggregates search results from large sets of distributed document collections
14 Displaying the thesaurus	Displays controlled indexing terms and relationships between terms
15 Hyperlinks	Allows users to navigate between occurrences of links in different records or between concepts linked by hypermedia links

Set-up facilities

These facilities set up the environment in which the search will proceed and are therefore environment-dependent. Help and news are common, as well as connection facilities, sometimes in the form of log-on and log-off facilities. Web-based interfaces often also offer access to information about the search service, its databases and customer service arrangements. The selection of database is usually a further preliminary.

Selecting search terms

The identification of search terms can be assisted by the display of search-term listings. The display may show index or search terms. and sometimes the number of postings.

Entering search terms

Once a search term has been selected it must be entered. This may merely involve clicking on the term in a search term listing, typing the term in, or using the term as a component in a more complex search statement.

Combining search terms

Search terms may be combined into search statements with the aid of a search logic as discussed in Section 7.5. Boolean search logic or relevance ranking is common.

Specifying fields

Specifying sections of documents or fields in records to be searched – i.e. the ability to search for the occurrence of terms in a specific section of a document, or in specific fields in a record – facilitates more precise searching. In order to be able to specify appropriate field labels, it is necessary to know the fields in a given database and which fields are indexed for successful field-based searching. Often it may be possible to search on a combination of fields or sections.

Truncation and search-term strings

Truncation supports searching on word stems. Through use of the truncation character at either end of a word, the system can be instructed to search for a string of characters, regardless of whether that string is a complete word. For example, if the user asks for a search on Countr* this would retrieve records including words such as Country, Countries, Countryside, and Countrywide. The use of truncation eliminates the need to specify each word variant, and thus simplifies search strategies. This is particularly useful in natural-language information retrieval systems, where word variations are uncontrolled.

The most basic truncation is **right-hand truncation** where characters to the right of the character string are ignored. **Left-hand truncation** can be useful in circumstances where a variety of prefixes might occur. This is particularly useful in searching chemical databases. For example, *chloride might retrieve records of 'chloride' with various prefixes. Truncation, or masking as it is called in this context, is sometimes also available in the middle of words. Here truncation can be useful to cater for alternative spellings. So, for example, NA$IONAL will search for records with NATIONAL and NACIONAL.

In order to control the array of word variants that might be retrieved as the result of a truncation, in some systems it is possible to specify the number of characters that are to appear after the truncated string. For example, S-EMPLOY??? might select terms with a maximum of three additional characters.

Proximity, adjacency and context searching

Often a subject is best described by a phrase of two, three or more words. Subjects such as Information Retrieval and Competitive Advantage each need two words to describe them. It is useful if a search can be performed for such phrases. One obvious option is to search for the two words ANDed together, for example:

Information AND Retrieval

This should retrieve records containing the phrase, but will also retrieve other records where these two words appear, even though they do not appear next to each other. This method, then, only allows crude phrase searching.

Another option is to store such terms as phrases, possibly by inserting hyphens to mark phrases. Then, for example, Information-Retrieval would be stored as one term in the inverted file. This method is satisfactory but is primarily applicable to controlled indexing; phrases must be marked at input, and searchers must enter the term in exactly the form in which it was originally entered.

A more flexible option is the use of **proximity operators**. There are various different kinds of proximity operators. These may require:

- that two words appear next to each other
- that two words appear within the same field or paragraph
- that two words be within a specified distance of one another, indicating the maximum number of words to come between the two words.

Range searching and limiting

Range searching is particularly useful when selecting records on the basis of numeric or date fields. It might, for instance, be used to select records according to a price field or publication date field. Fairly common range operators are

EQ	equal to	LT	less than
NE	not equal to	NL	not less than
GT	greater than	WL	within the limits
NG	not greater than	OL	outside the limits.

Displaying search or results sets

Shows the user how many documents and search terms and references were found, and thereby indicates whether it might be appropriate to refine the search further.

Displaying records

Once a successful search has been performed, it is necessary to display the records. OPACs first display one-line records and then allow the user to display the full record. Online search services offer a variety of commands for displaying records on the screen, offline printing and downloading. Default formats are the norm, but user-defined formats are becoming more common. In addition to specifying the record format, users need to be able to specify which records are to be displayed. OPACs tend to let users select records and display them one at a time. CD-ROM and online search services have commands or options that allow the set of records for display to be indicated.

Search management

Search management includes opportunities to review the search strategy that has been adopted and to permanently or temporarily save a search profile for subsequent use.

Advanced display options

Records in full-text databases are long, and a full record usually occupies several screens. In such circumstances, special display facilities can support browsing through relevant portions of the text. The ability to stop as soon as the screen is full is useful, as are facilities for moving backwards and forwards through the document. If the text is divided into numbered paragraphs, it is possible to select paragraphs for display. Another approach is to use a KWIC facility, which shows relevant index terms with bits of adjacent text in small windows. Another option that might prove useful is the ability to sort a set of records into order before displaying them. Numeric or financial data may be best displayed in reverse or descending order. Some financial databases offer statistical presentation and analysis.

Nested or joined queries and multi-file searching

In cases such as the online search services, where there are a number of databases that might generate relevant records in response to one search, multi-file search facilities are beneficial. The most user-friendly multi-file search option is when several databases can be searched without reformulating the strategy. This requires the system to make the appropriate adjustments in the search terms and fields to be searched. The most refined multi-file searching then goes on to produce an integrated set of records drawn from several databases, and with duplicate records eliminated.

Displaying the thesaurus

Where a controlled indexing language has been used to provide index terms, a thesaurus will often be available in both printed and online formats. This thesaurus displays the controlled vocabulary used and the relationships between terms, and is therefore a useful tool in narrowing or broadening searches. It is useful if the thesaurus can be displayed in a window to assist users as they attempt to develop a search strategy. Free-language thesauri which show relationships between terms may be available on some systems, but these take considerable effort to set up. GUI interfaces offer fascinating opportunities for the display of graphical thesauri, showing multiple tree structures and explode options.

Hyperlinks

Many systems, including the WWW, offer searching based on hyperlinks. True hypertext searching relies upon an indexer establishing conceptual links between documents. Creators of Web pages often do this when they indicate which terms are to be used as links to other pages. However, in a large database, this is very labour-intensive. An alternative is to rely upon the content, including the text and other objects in the record, and to use the occurrence of objects or terms as the basis for hypermedia links. Thus, if the same term or object appears in two records or documents, the user may move from one record to another by, say, clicking on the term or object and without explicitly returning to the index.

Reflection   Which of the above search facilities might be difficult for a
                  novice user to understand? Why?

7.7 Search strategies

The previous few sections have briefly reviewed the components of an information-retrieval system. The tools offered by such systems must be used by the searcher in such a way as to achieve successful searches. The set of decisions and actions taken during a search is known as a search strategy. Some searchers are more methodical in the construction of search strategies than others, but every searcher aims

* to retrieve sufficient relevant records
* to avoid retrieving irrelevant records
* to avoid retrieving too many records
* to avoid retrieving too few records.

Often it will be necessary to broaden or narrow a search on the basis of the success of the first search statement. This can be achieved by using various of the retrieval facilities reviewed in Section 7.6, or by introducing different search terms. The effective development of a search strategy requires knowledge of the subject, databases and literature being searched.

Different search strategies might be appropriate for different kinds of searches. Four types of search strategies have been proposed:

1   **Briefsearch** is a quick search using AND to retrieve a few articles only. This may be all that is required, or this record may be used as the basis for a subsequent search.
2   **Building blocks** extends the original query by taking each of the concepts in a query in turn, and introducing their synonyms and related terms using OR.

All concepts are then ANDed to produce the final set. Building blocks is thorough, but can be time-consuming.

3   **Successive fractions** is a method for reducing a large set by selecting from that set through the use of AND and NOT.

4   **Citation pearl-growing** uses a small set of records or just one record as inspiration for suitable search terms, and then performs searches under these terms.

Reflection   Give some examples of search histories which illustrate each of the four types of search strategy identified above.

7.8   Users

The previous sections in this chapter have concentrated on the systems, and specifically the software elements of information-retrieval systems. The objective of any information-retrieval system is that it should be used by the group of people for whom it has been designed. Systems designers have defined the concept of usability in order to reflect this concern with users:

'The usability of a product is the degree to which specific users can achieve specific goals within a particular environment; effectively, efficiently and comfortably, and in an acceptable manner.' [Booth 1989]

More specifically, the components of usability which were identified by Bennett (1984) and later operationalized by Shackel (1990) so that they could be tested, can be expressed in terms of:

*   **learnability** or **ease of learning** – the time and effort required to reach a specified level of use performance
*   **throughput** or **ease of use** - the tasks accomplished by experienced users, the speed of task execution and the errors made
*   **flexibility** – the extent to which the system can accommodate changes to the tasks and environments beyond those first specified
*   **attitude** – the positive attitude engendered in users by the system.

Such designers have also recognized that there are a number of different categories of users. Typical categories are: novice, expert, occasional, frequent, child, older adult and user with special needs. Many users may fall into more than one of these categories, and none of the categories is mutually exclusive. The categories are used as stereotypes for ranges of experience with public access systems. More specifically:

Novice users are users who have never used a specific system before. They need to learn how to perform information retrieval tasks quickly and easily. Simple and intuitive interfaces are preferable. It is important to remember that whenever a system is changed all users become relative novices, although they may bring a conceptual framework based on their knowledge of other systems to the new system. Similarly, novice users of a particular system who have used other similar systems will bring an underlying conceptual framework to their learning.

Expert users use the system on a regular basis, and are therefore familiar with most functions and can negotiate any problems that might arise with the system. The expert user can complete the task quickly, but may be frustrated by wizards and menus, and other features that slow down interaction with the system.

Many systems have more than one interaction mode to cater for these different categories of users. For example, a number of OPACs and CD-ROM systems allow expert users to use short-cut keys rather than menus, and also offer 'expert user modes' so that individuals can execute complex search tasks.

Occasional users can often be viewed as near-novice users, because they use the system so infrequently that whenever they use the system they need to learn how to use the system again. **Frequent users**, on the other hand, are generally assumed to be expert users, although some frequent users will continue to limit the range of functions that they use, and thus never truly become expert users.

Another important category is **users with special needs**. Such users may be vision- or hearing-impaired, or may have specific physical needs or learning disabilities. The system must be capable of supporting the user's special need. So, for example, for the user who is hearing-impaired the interface must give clear visual cues.

Information managers and intermediaries, who search systems on behalf of other users, can generally be expected to be expert users, but they may also require additional functionality so that they can easily re-format and communicate information to the ultimate end-user.

7.9   The future of information retrieval

Each of the subsequent chapters in this part of the book concludes by reviewing recent developments and identifying some possible directions for refinement. Any analysis that attempts to identify the major trends in information retrieval must take into account these developments in each of the application areas. However, many of these developments are fired by the same motivations. The researcher is concerned to develop the best retrieval system, and strives to develop new systems and evaluate these systems. System suppliers are concerned to offer a software package or a service that is superior to those of competitors, so that they can retain a commercial advantage. Both groups share a striving for better systems. However, in this endeavour one major factor needs to be taken into account. Retrieval has traditionally been concerned with fairly structured information contained in fairly well-defined databases. Current expansion of network access via the Internet is offering vast quantities of rapidly changing, ill-defined information to large numbers of users who are relatively new to information retrieval. Better retrieval systems for this environment may be achieved by:

1   **Better systems design,** where there is an attempt to improve the efficiency and effectiveness of the system, including such characteristics as the storage requirements, the retrieval speed and the effectiveness of the system. Work in this area seeks to overcome the limitations of the inverted file (see Chapter 5) by developing fast methods of scanning the contents of a database. Two lines of development have been investigated. The first of these is text-scanning algorithms to improve the speed of searching in serial files. The alternative is to seek hardware-based solutions, most of which speed of text scanning by the use of parallel processors so that several operations can be conducted simultaneously.

2   **Improved retrieval facilities and strategies,** to improve methods for matching document descriptions with query descriptions. One major line of enquiry has been the search for an alternative to Boolean search logic. Work in this area has led to more widespread use of best match searching and hypermedia links. Ultimately the user is interested in being able to interact with the system using natural language, and wants a retrieval mechanism that supplies not too many hits but a reasonable proportion of relevant hits, even in large unstructured databases. Also, each interaction response should take no more than, say, ten seconds to complete. A number of products are available that use a combination of natural-language query, content-based ranking or concept trees and expert systems techniques to achieve a search environment which depends upon automatic indexing.

3   **Better dialogue design,** and attention to the quality of the human–computer interface. Work in this area has focused on two distinct areas: GUI interfaces that are more user-friendly, and self-explanatory and front-end or intermediary computer systems that are interposed between the system and the user. More recent work has looked at front-ends that simulate best-match searching, or model the actions of a human intermediary. This research uses knowledge-based techniques from the field of artificial intelligence.

It is difficult to predict which of these lines of enquiry will prove the most successful in the long term. In forecasting future developments it is also important to recognize that existing databases and the services based on them represent a significant inertial force, and progress can be slow. Nevertheless, these three lines of development represent the major ways in which systems can be improved.

Summary   There are a number of features that are common to all information-retrieval systems, including CD-ROM, the Internet, online search services, document management systems and OPACs. Information retrieval systems find both corporate and external applications. Interface design is particularly important in applications where a large number of users, each with a different background, may search a database. An indexing language is the terms or codes that might be used as access points in an index. Options are natural, controlled and free indexing languages. Search logic is the means of specifying combinations of terms that must be matched for successful retrieval. Boolean search logic and relevance ranking are two of the main approaches. The key search facilities are those supporting: selection of search terms; entry of search terms; combination of search terms; specification of fields to be searched; truncation; use of phrases, adjacency and proximity operators; range searching and limiting; display of records; search management; advanced display options; nested or joined queries and multi-file searching; display of thesaurus; and hypermedia. Users may employ a number of different search strategies in pursuit of a relevant set of records or documents. Different users have different needs, and it is often useful to differentiate between expert and novice users. Better systems may emerge from research focused on improving the efficiency and effectiveness of systems, improved retrieval facilities and strategies, and more sophisticated dialogue design.

REVIEW QUESTIONS

1 What are the three stages in information retrieval?
2 Why do organizations need access to both corporate and external information retrieval systems?
3 What are the advantages of controlled language indexing for inexperience information retrieval system users?
4 In Boolean search logic, what is the difference between combining two sets using OR and combining to sets using AND?
5 Explain the following terms:
   • truncation,
   • proximity searching,
   • range searching, and
   • hyperlinks.

References

Bennett, J. L. (1994) 'Managing to meet usability requirements', in *Visual display terminals: usability issues and health concerns*, ed. J. L. Bennet, D. Case, J. Sandelin and M. Smith, Englewood Cliffs, NJ, Prentice-Hall.

Booth, P. (1989) *An introduction to human–computer interaction*, Hove, Lawrence Erlbaum.

Shackel, B. (1990) 'Human factors and usability' in *Human–computer interaction: selected readings*, ed. J. Preece and L. Keller, London, Prentice-Hall.

Bibliography

Aithison, J., Gilchrist, A. and Bawden, D. (1997) *Thesaurus construction and use: a practical manual*, Aslib, London.

Basch, R. (1989) 'The seven deadly sins of full text searching', *Database*, 15–23.

Basch, R. (1991) 'My most difficult search', *Database*, 65–7.

Bates, M. J. (1989) 'Re-thinking subject cataloguing in the online environment', *Library resources and technical services*, 33, 403–11.

Cleverdon, C. W. (1967) 'The Cranfield tests on index language devices', *Aslib proceedings*, 19, 173–94.

Cousins, S. A. (1992) 'Enhancing subject access to OPAC's: controlled vocabulary versus natural language', *Journal of documentation*, 48 (3), 291–309.

Ellis, D. (1992) 'The physical and cognitive paradigms in information retrieval research', *Journal of documentation*, 48, 45–64.

Ellis, D. (1996) *Progress and problems in information retrieval*, London, Library Association Publishing.

Ellis, D., Furner-Hines, J. and Willett, P. (1994) 'On the creation of hypertext links in full text documents: measurements of inter-linker consistency', *Journal of documentation*, 50, 67–98.

Fidel, R. (1992) 'Who needs controlled vocabulary?', *Special libraries*, 83 (1), 1–9.

Ingwersen, P. (1992) *Information retrieval interaction*, London, Taylor Graham.

Lancaster, F. W. (1991) *Indexing and abstracting in theory and practice*, London, Library Association Publishing.

Meadows, J. (1994) 'Text retrieval – dead or alive?: the active management of text', *Journal of document and text management*, 2 (1), 1–9.

Rowley, J. (1994) 'The controlled versus natural indexing languages debate revisited: a perspective on information retrieval practice and research', *Journal of information science*, 20 (2), 108–19.

Smeaton, A. F. (1991) 'Retrieving information from hypertext: issues and problems', *European journal of information systems*, 1, 239–47.

Srinivasan, P. (1996) 'Optimal document indexing vocabulary for MEDLINE', *Information processing and management*, 32 (5), 503–14.

8

The Internet

LEARNING OUTCOMES

The Internet offers new opportunities for international communication, and very appropriately has received a lot of attention in recent years. Many books have been written on the Internet. Here we offer a brief introduction, which is intended to explain some of the key terminology and some of the issues associated with Internet access for libraries.

At the end of this chapter, you will:

- understand the basic nature of the Internet
- be aware of the types of services and resources that are available over the Internet
- be aware of the issues associated with the location and evaluation of Internet resources
- be able to propose some uses of Internet access in libraries
- be aware of the opportunities that intranets offer in libraries.

8.1 What is the Internet?

Reflection   There has been a lot of media exposure in relation to the Internet. What do you already know about the Internet?

The Internet is a collection of interlinked computer networks, or a network of networks. Currently it connects over one million different computers and the rate of increase in use and new subscribers is growing month by month. The Internet provides global connectivity via a mesh of networks based on the TCP/IP and Open Systems Interconnection (OSI) protocols, which we introduced in an earlier chapter. Other protocols can also be sent over the Internet, including Systems Network Architecture (SNA), Decnet/IV, Appletalk and Novell IPX/SPX.

Historically, the Internet was essentially an academic network, but business use is growing, so that the Internet is no longer merely an elite network for communication between eminent research centres, but is also accessible to small colleges, small businesses and libraries throughout the world. The Internet offers a gateway to a myriad of online databases, library catalogues and collections, and software and document archives, in addition to frequently used store-and-forward services, such as UserNet News and e-mail.

How did the Internet begin? The Internet began as one single network called ARPANET. The ARPANET began as a United States government experiment in packet-switched networking in 1969. DARPA, the Department of Defence Advanced Research Project Agency, initially linked researchers with remote computer centres in the United States, allowing them to share hardware and software resources such as computer disk space and databases. Other experimental networks using packet radio and satellite were connected via the ARPANET using internetwork technology sponsored by DARPA. At first, the inter-connection of experimental and production networks was called the DARPA Internet, but this was subsequently shortened to the Internet. The most significant contribution that this project made to the future of computer networking was the research into, and the development of, a set of communication codes allowing computers on the 'net' to 'talk' to each other. These are called Internet Protocols (IP). During the 1980s IP and the UNIX operating system became synonymous. IP was being used by most of the leading vendors as the standard communication protocol between UNIX systems which were connected together on a local-area network (LAN). This led to a demand for the ability to connect computers linked to a LAN to the large computers on ARPANET and other emergent networks using the IP protocol.

Access to the ARPANET was initially limited to the United States military, defence contractors and universities doing defence research. Advances in the provision of nationwide networking systems allowed increased computer communication within the academic research community. The creation of the National Science Foundation Network (NSFNET) in 1988 linked researchers across America with 12 super computer centres. Connection to NSFNET was usually via regional centres each supporting regional networks. This solution was so successful in that not only did it allow the connection to a super computing centre, but it inadvertently achieved the connection of all of the regional centres. Thus the Internet came about as a computer network cooperative with no central agency overseeing its activities. The NSFNET began to replace the ARPANET for research networking and ARPANET was dismantled in 1990. At the time when the NSFNET was being built, the Internet began to grow significantly, showing exponential gains in the number of networks, human participants and computers. The current Internet links over 2 million computers and more than 10,000 networks, and extends to more than 50 countries. It is estimated to serve over 15 million users. The Internet is the precursor to the 'information superhighway', the National Research and Education Network which will link businesses throughout the United States, and worldwide, enabling them to share information and to hold video conferences.

Connecting to the Internet

Local-area networks can be attached to the Internet by installing TCP/IP networking software on the LAN server and obtaining a connection between the LAN and the Internet. A wide range of different types of machines that are connected to the LAN can access the Internet, including DOS- and Windows-based PCs, Macintoshes and UNIX workstations.

There are three types of Internet connection:

- **full connection**, where there is a permanent telecommunications link and the computer has a registered Internet name and address
- **dial-up connection**, via a temporary telecommunications link to a machine that has full access
- **gateway connection**, where a connection is made through another network or service supplier such as CompuServe.

8.2   Services and resources available via the Internet

The resources available via the Internet are constantly changing, so any list is liable to date. Nevertheless, in order to indicate the scope of the information available on the Internet, a brief review of some of the types of databases and other services is offered.

There are a number of different types of use of the Internet:

- e-mail – allowing users to send messages or files to each other
- news – to inform users of available information
- remote log in – allowing users to log in to remote sites
- ftp (file transfer protocol) – allowing users to access and retrieve files at remote sites.

The information and services available at remote sites include:

1   **Listservs and discussion groups** on a very wide variety of topics. Participants have the opportunity to exchange current information and conduct a dialogue. Some listservs are of particular interest to information managers.
2   **Subject databases**, particularly from academic institutions. Increasing numbers of institutions, especially academic and research institutions, are making databases in their subject specialties available. Indiana University has, for example, mounted a number of files in the area of biology.
3   **Community information**. Often through their public libraries, communities are providing access, either dial-up, or via Internet, to local data such as the catalogue of the public library, a tour of the art gallery, tourist information, weather reports and other demographic information.

4   **Government resources**. Both national and local governments are providing information. For example, the Indiana State Library has mounted a Gopher server, which provides access to the Indiana Code (the state law), and the US Federal government has opened a Website.

5   **Library catalogues**. Increasing numbers of libraries are making their catalogues available over the Internet. Although the majority of library catalogues available are those of large university libraries, public libraries are also beginning to make their catalogues available.

6   **Commercial resources**. Commercial information databases available on the Internet include: DIALOG, Lexis/Nexis, Dow Jones News/Retrieval and many others. DIALOG offers the user more than 400 databases on every possible subject, and Dow Jones News/Retrieval gives users access to more than 1300 publications and 70 databases.

7   **Bulletin boards,** or the electronic equivalent of newsletters

8   **Shopping and other commercial transactions**. There are now a number of significant shopping malls, and other Websites that have been mounted by individual retailers which offer the customers the opportunity to shop from their home. Almost any product can be purchased over the Internet, although a number of the early entrants sold primarily computer hardware and software, and other information products such as books and database access. Other significant product groups include music and CDs, gifts, toys and other commodities previously available via mail order.

9   **Document delivery**. A number of major libraries and document delivery services are also making document search and delivery services available (see Chapter 15).

Reflection   Which of the services described above do you think that you would find useful?

A number of these services offer access to database records or documents. These documents can be divided into categories or collections on the basis of the following characteristics (which also serve to demonstrate the diversity of the documents):

*   storage location – documents grouped on the basis of physical storage in a geographical area, or on a specific computer or network of computers
*   data type – a document may be made up of textual, numerical, graphical, video or audio symbols or a combination of these
*   format – - including plain ASCII, or with its physical layout specified in a PostScript or Acrobat file, or with its logical structure explicitly signalled using a scheme such as the Standard Generalized Markup Language (SGML) or the HyperText Markup Language (HTML)

- method of transfer – a document may be transferable using one of a variety of standard Internet transfer protocols, such as the File Transfer Protocol (FTP) or the HyperText Transfer Protocol (HTTP)
- size or length – ranging from a few bytes or words to many megabytes
- subject matter or topic
- depth of coverage
- frequency of update and currency
- language
- originator – from among commercial, governmental, professional and academic organization, and individual users
- audience – documents may be targeted to individuals or members of specific groups, or may be generally available.

In addition to search engines and browsers which support the user in finding their way around the Internet, there are numerous directories of Internet resources. One of the most valuable of these is BUBL (the Bulletin Board for Libraries) BUBL is an information service designed to support library and information-science professionals. Amongst a wide range of services, it includes directories of resources, users and hints, current content of LIS journals, and electronic journals and texts

8.3 Searching on the Internet

With such a vast array of databases and other services available via the Internet, it has been important to design interfaces that help users search the information sources and services available on the Internet. Retrieval is recognized to be a significant problem on the Internet, with databases in a wide variety of different formats, and numerous different search retrieval software packages mounted on the different computers and providing access via different interfaces to subsets of the databases. Various print-based similes have been used to describe the situation, one of which is that the current state of the Internet can be likened to a library in which everyone in the community has donated a book and tossed it into the middle of the library floor.

Tools that are used for searching the Internet often operate in client–server mode. Server software which allows the user to search the database in a more intuitive way has been set up on many computers on the Internet. The user's local system runs the equivalent client software which communicates with the server software and gives a homogeneous interface to the data. The user does not need to know where the data is stored or how to manage the server system's file store structure.

There are two types of tools available to support searching on the World Wide Web: browsers and search engines. Browsers support browsing on the WWW; this involves the successive retrieval of individual documents on the basis of some relationship existing between one document and another. This is achieved through hypertext systems which offer the representation of links. The most widely used hypertext system is the Web. Browsing is supported through:

- an addressing system that allows the location of any object stored on a networked computer to be uniquely identified by a Uniform Resource Locator (URL)
- a markup language (HTML) that allows the authors of a document to identify particular locations within their document as the source of links, and to specify the location of the target of those links
- a transfer protocol (HTTP) that allows copies of target documents stored on remote servers to be retrieved and displayed
- a client program or Web browser such as Netscape Navigator or Internet Explorer that provides the user with control over the retrieval process and over the links to be activated.

People and organizations create home pages to present their own information or service. A collection of home pages located on the same server is called a Website. Access to these pages is via the Uniform Resource Locator (URL) using a browser. Examples of browsers are Lynx, Mosaic and Netscape. These addresses link the user to the host computer and their individual files; these are then displayed on the user's personal workstation. With the appropriate software, users can read documents, view pictures, listen to sound and retrieve information.

In indexing terms, the hyperlinks on the WWW that form the basis of the browsing network are uncontrolled but humanly assigned index terms. There is no general control over which terms should be used as hyperlinks, but each hyperlink is individually coded by the creator of the HTML Web page that contains the hyperlink. A Web browser add-on to a Web client program is an external program that can run individually without the help of the Web client software. Many Web clients allow a link to other software in order to represent the contents of a file on which the Web client software has no built-in functionality. A plug-in to a Web client program is almost the same as an add-on, except that this plug-in cannot run on its own. Examples of add-ons are Adobe Acrobat and the Portable Document Format (PDF); this is often used to distribute documents in computer-readable form, giving a high-quality document which is very similar to the original hard copy. Microsoft PowerPoint Animation Player is another add-on, which enables the publication of Microsoft PowerPoint presentations on the WWW.

Whilst browsers encourage movement through a network of linked documents, browsing is not an effective approach to the identification of specific information; this requires a search engine.

A search engine is a retrieval mechanism which performs the basic retrieval task, the acceptance of a query, a comparison of the query with each of the records in a database, and the production of a retrieval set as output. Although the primary application of such search engines is to provide access to the resources that are available on the WWW and stored on many different servers, a related area of application that is likely to grow in the next few years is the use of search engines as retrieval mechanisms in intranet environments for retrieval of documents from one organization's collection. This application is also likely to drive the development of the functionality of search engines until that functionality replicates that which is available in document management systems.

Since search engines need to provide access to a large and distributed document collection, the retrieval process must be efficient. This efficiency is achieved by the search engines not working with the original source but with a document representation or a record. This record may contain two types of data:

- data that is equivalent to the information contained in the document that the record represents
- metadata about the document that the record represents

Records that contain both of these types of data are hybrid records; those that contain only metadata are bibliographic records. Each of the records contained in the database maintained by a global Web search service is created automatically by a program called a spider. Each time a spider is run, it is initially issued with the URLs of a small seed set of target Web pages; it retrieves and downloads copies of the targets of those links; it then activates every link contained in those pages; and so on, until it has downloaded copies of every single page that it can find. The content of each page is stored in a record which also contains other fields containing basic metadata such as the title of the document, the date on which it was last modified, its size in megabytes and its URL. The values of these attributes are determined automatically from the document. Searching on these records is facilitated by the creation of an inverted index. The nature of this index depends on whether searching is by Boolean search or best-match searching (see Chapter 7). The inverted index is stored using compression techniques which reduce to a significant extent the storage capacity that it requires.

The user interface supports the interaction between the user and the system. For query formulation, the Web page presented to the user of a Web search engine typically contains a 'form' made up of a text entry box in which the user is invited to enter search terms, possibly accompanied by check boxes or menu boxes to allow field limitations or the use of operators. Once the query has been formulated, the depression of a button labelled 'submit' or some related term triggers a standard HTTP request to GET a document of a particular URL from the search service's Web server. The data entered by the user is appended to the URL in the form of a string of characters representing certain parameters and their values, together with a specification of the search program which is to be run, and to which those values should be passed, before the GET request is fulfilled.

Most Web search services use a best match search process, which involves:

- converting the query into the form of a vector of values, each value indicating either the presence or absence or the 'weight' of a particular term in that query
- computing scores using any one of a variety of simple mathematical formulae known as similarity coefficients in order to express the degree of similarity between this query vector and the record vectors making up the inverted index to the database.
- ranking all of the records in the database by their score, and outputting them for display in ranked order, with those ranked highest appearing first.

The assumption here is that, the more similar a record is to a query, the more likely the document that it represents will be relevant to the user's information need.

Some search services such as Yahoo add value through human intervention in the assignment of subject headings to records in databases. This is a labour-intensive process, which means that the search service needs to be selective in the records that it indexes. However, such human intervention should lead to search outputs that more closely match user needs. Experiments are underway in the areas of semantic knowledge bases and the use of thesauri to improve search effectiveness. In addition, the user's ability to assess the relevance of a document depends critically upon the metadata that is displayed about the document in the displays of the retrieved set. Various attempts are underway to assess this optimum metadata element set.

Once the search has been run, the Web server responds to the GET request by sending to the user a Web page for display in place of the original search form, whose content includes the output of the search program. The display of the retrieval set typically takes the form of a list of surrogates representing the records retrieved, ranked in order of their potential relevance to the query and presented a certain number, say 10, at a time; each of these incorporates a hypertext link to the source document presented by the record, and clicking on it will call up the source document.

Search engines differ from one another in the following important respects:

1   **Coverage of the database.** Some engines only provide access to WWW resources, whereas others provide access to a wide range of Internet resources.
2   **Search facilities and process.** Search engines search different parts of HTML documents. Some search only titles and headers, and not the full text of the HTML document. The range of search facilities also varies. Some search engines offer only basic keyword searching, but others offer Boolean searching and even proximity searching.

3   **Results list**. Some engines display a simple list of resources, whilst others include the context of the hit, weighted results, and options to link to similar pages.

An awareness of the strengths and weaknesses of the different search engines is important when searching the Internet for resources. If a library is designing a Website, it is important to be aware of the search engines that users may use in accessing the Website.

....

Reflection   What is the World Wide Web and how does it work?

....

Table 8.1 *Some of the major research networks linked by the Internet*

Acronym	Name
ACSNET	Australian Computer Science Network
BITNET	Because It's Time Network
CDNNET	Canadian National Network
CSNET	Computer Science Network
DFN	Deutsche Forschung Netz
EARN	European Academic Research Network
JANET	Joint Academic Network (UK)
JUNET	Japanese UNIX Network
NSFNET	National Science Foundation network
Usenet	Largely UNIX network (US)

8.4   Evaluating Internet resources

Whether a library is concerned to use Internet resources to answer questions on behalf of users, or to offer services that direct users to specific Internet resources, it is necessary to evaluate Internet resources. Despite the concern about the potential lack of structure with electronic information, the traditional criteria used for print evaluation are equally applicable in this context. Let us first summarize some of these traditional criteria that can be used in the evaluation of Internet resources:

1   What is the intended audience? Is this academic or popular?
2   What is the frequency of update? Is there information on updating?
3   What is the affiliated institution?
4   What are the resource developer's areas of expertise? Is there an about section that describes the author/creator?
5   What is the relationship between resources and other resources on the same topic? Are there any links or references to these related resources?

6   Are there any reviews or evaluations of the site? What do these say?
7   Is any permission needed for access, and are any charges made for access?

Yip (1997) offers some additional selection criteria based on his experience at the Hong Kong University of Science and Technology. When identifying those resources to which they would offer guided access over the Internet, they found it useful to take into account the following factors:

1   **Site access type.** This may include FTP sites, gopher sites, telnet sessions and Usenet news. They preferred WWW sites because of the hypertext links and the multimedia nature of the WWW sites.
2   **Level of selection.** Should users, for example, be directed to the sites of individual newspapers, or to sites which offered access to a collection of newspapers? Here it is important to consider the match between user needs and the packaging of resources that is available, and to make individual decisions.
3   **Software requirements.** Sites that required that users have specialist software on their PCs, such as software to deal with Chinese characters, were avoided, because access to these sites would not be possible for all users.
4   **Accessibility of site.** Some sites are difficult to access, either because they are on a heavily used link, or because they are on a slow Internet link.
5   **Fee-based services** are a special case, and the relative merits of Internet access and CD-ROM access need to be evaluated. Table 8.2 summarizes what were seen to be the key issues in making this choice.
6   **Resources already held in other formats.** Is it worthwhile to encourage access to these resources? Internet resources need to be evaluated in order to assess what they can give that is not available through existing resources. Potential reasons for the use of Internet resources may be that they offer:

- more current information
- better search capabilities
- multiple and network access
- some combination of the above.

8.5   Uses of Internet access in libraries

Libraries that establish a server and a Website may offer any combination of the following to enhance their service to users:

1   **Basic library information,** such as hours of operation, contact people, addresses and policies. There is an opportunity to make such information more interesting than through other media, such as through the inclusion of pictures of staff, a short sound file, or direct e-mail links which allow users to send messages.

2   **New ways of access to library facilities**, such as:

- book-request forms that can be completed by users and then converted into catalogue data
- remote access to catalogues
- improved OPAC search interfaces
- showcase to library resources, such as library tours or a video of storytime
- new information services, such as a home page linked to a collection of electronic texts, databases and other Internet resources (such access can be designed for specific user groups, such as children or the housebound)
- access to the resources of the online hosts.

3   **Interactive home pages**, offering facilities such as:

- fill-in forms to be used for feedback and services
- requests for purchases, reservation of library material and general library suggestions
- interlibrary loan and circulation
- reference questions.

4   **Links to remote information**, and connections to information resources around the world. Library staff can identify hot-lists and bookmark files of frequently used resources for support in answering frequently asked questions.

Other uses of the Internet support some of the operations of libraries, and thereby have an indirect impact on customer service. These include:

1   **Staff development**. Offering a WWW service offers staff the opportunity to keep involved in developments in this field.
2   **Acquisitions**. The Internet can provide access to databases provided by publishers of books and journals, booksellers and journal distributors.
3   **Cataloguing and classification**. Web pages can be used to distribute and access rules, schemes and recommendations concerning cataloguing and classification.
4   **Interlibrary lending and document delivery**. The use of the networked pubic access catalogues of other libraries, document delivery services and others can support the identification of requested documents.

Equipment

Mounting a Website on the WWW does not require any very expensive or sophisticated equipment. The basic components of a configuration are:

Hardware

An appropriate computer, running under almost any operating system, to use as a server. Systems running under DOS, Windows, Macintosh and UNIX can all be used as servers for creating WWW documents.

Network access

Network access can be through either a dial-up or a direct-access line. Direct lines are dedicated, and are faster and more reliable than dial-up lines. In addition, dial-up lines are not really an option for a server. Direct lines may be leased, or accessible on a subscription basis through a commercial service provider.

Software

Several types of software are necessary:

- **server software** to operate a server, allowing client software (WWW browser or other Internet application) to interact with the information of your server
- **word-processing software** for HTML work (standard word-processors such as Word, or WordPerfect or UNIX text editors are appropriate, but software called HTML converters take a word-processed document and convert it to HTML, and editors, word-processors with special tagging facilities, can be used to create HTML documents)
- **graphics software** to create images and icons
- **scripting and programming software** that allows the extension of the interaction between the client and server beyond that of static download and transfer of HTML pages (this interaction can be achieved with the use of scripts or programs, and tools such as Java programming, Netscape's Javascript and Microsoft's Visual Basic Script).
- and, for the really ambitious, **Virtual Reality Modeling Language (VRML)** – a file format for describing interactive 3D objects.

Table 8.2 *Comparing Internet access and CD-ROM access*

Currency	Web resources are generally more current than CD-ROMs
Retrieval	CD-ROM generally has better search capabilities
Ease of access	Slow Internet access affects Web databases, but CD-ROM networks should be immune
Maintenance	Less maintenance for Internet access
Platform dependency	Web is platform-independent, but CD-ROMs run on particular platforms.

The list of problems that Yip (1997) encountered in the selection of Internet resources should also act as a cautionary list for others embarking on the same route:

- a large amount of junk
- rapid growth of resources, and therefore changes in available resources
- disappearing and shifting resources
- time involved in the identification and evaluation of resources, both initially and on an ongoing basis.

Their strategy, which may be appropriate in other contexts, was to select a limited number of high-quality sources of high potential interest to users, to make these easily available through the interface, and then to offer workshops on searching to allow users to develop their own skills in identifying, evaluating and selecting additional sources that were of specific relevance to their interests.

8.6 Managing a Website

What are the key issues in establishing and subsequently maintaining a Website if that Website is to provide a useful service for users and an appropriate shop window for the organization's services? The issues listed briefly below are a reminder that a Website needs to be managed in much the same way as any other promotional venture or service. Clear objectives need to be identified at the beginning of a project to create a Website; these will determine the content and design of the site. In a burst of enthusiasm it is easy to view a Website as a one-off project. For continued effectiveness the resources need to be available for updating, evaluation and maintenance.

Policies

The creation of a Website must start with the identification of the objectives of the Website. This will be linked to the coverage of, and services offered through, the Website.

Staff ownership

Staff should identify with, and be aware of, the site and the objectives that it is intended to achieve. This can most effectively be achieved by keeping staff involved in the development of the site.

Content

Information may need to be drawn from sources across the organization; these sources must be identified. Any new content will need to be designed. Remote content needs to be located, and evaluated prior to selection.

Presentation

Presentation is a matter of structure and style. The web-space structure is determined by the way in which pages are linked together. A common design style needs to be created and applied.

Promotion

Promotion is concerned with attracting visitors to the site. This can be achieved through workshops, posters and over the WWW.

Evaluation

This is the business of monitoring whether the Website is achieving its objectives. The level of visits to the site is one measure of success, but more searching evaluation can be achieved through user evaluation.

Maintenance

This can be a major task. Information needs to be updated, and as the information is updated, links between pages must be reviewed. A new design requires a complete overhaul of the design of all pages in the Website.

Reflection   Identify some strategies that an information manager might use in order to tackle some of the issues listed above.

8.7 Intranets

The general definition of an intranet, is: 'an organization's internal communications system using Internet technology'. Intranets use two of the key applications of the Internet: the web browsers, with their graphical user interfaces, and e-mail. They are being used to support a wide range of information services, including, for example, access to document collections in document management systems, and e-mail.

Benefits

Intranet technology is attractive to organizations because:

1   The interface is easy to use; it also encompasses access to multimedia formats such as text, video, sound and graphical images.
2   A single interface to all formats of information using the Internet open standard removes the requirement for an organization's network to provide several dedicated interfaces traditionally needed to interrogate proprietary systems such as databanks, bibliographic information retrieval systems and management information systems. Also, the user only needs to be familiar with one interface.
3   Compared to the cost of employing proprietary information systems, or groupware, intranets are very inexpensive to set up. In addition, proprietary packages also use in-house protocols, which often result in a dependency on the software distributor, and update and utilities may only be acquired from the original vendor.
4   They provide improved access in a number of respects:

    • documents may be shared across all major networking platforms
    • information is accessible regardless of the user's location
    • a workstation configured for use on an intranet is also ready for Internet use if the necessary gateways are incorporated into the network
    • access and use of groups using the intranet may be monitored, making it possible to assess the value of services and resources offered on the intranet
    • user authentication systems can be incorporated into browsers, so that access to information can be controlled.

5   They allow for maintenance of current documents, by offering access to electronic documents that will always be the latest version. This eliminates significant reprography, and time spent trying to locate lost paper-based documents.

Applications of Intranets

The applications for which intranets can be used depend upon the type of intranet. There are two main types of intranet: flat-content intranets, and interactive intranets.

In flat-file intranets, files are simply requested from a storage location or server, received by the desktop computer and viewed through the Web browser. Some applications of such intranets are:

• travel aids, maps

- telephone directories
- newsletters
- calendars
- policy manuals
- quality systems
- recruitment pointers to information available on the Internet
- document distribution and updating
- current awareness bulletins
- electronic journal delivery
- Internet subject resource listing
- library opening times and service, and other contact information
- information skills support material.

Interactive intranets offer many opportunities for two-way communication within an organization. However, the configuration is slightly more complex. When a user wishes to send, change, respond to or forward any kind of information to another location or person, a specific program or script is needed to process this information. These scripts need to be held on an internal Web server which uses TCP/IP. If an organization's network does not run under TCP/IP, then gateway or firewall software may be used as an interface between the organization's network protocol and the TCP/IP protocol. Applications with such a configuration include:

- e-mail, including messages and attached documents
- computer-based training and learning (packages can be authored and delivered in-house)
- video conferencing
- interactive services such as reservations systems, order/purchase documents, reports and surveys, facilitated by 'forms processing' and 'mailto' HTML commands
- Web boards or online conferencing areas
- support desks
- online enquiry services
- loans renewals
- access to the library catalogue from the World Wide Web.

8.8 The future

Projections of the growth in the number of Internet servers and users accessing Internet resources are available from numerous sources. These change too rapidly to be encapsulated in a book; so none of them are reproduced here. Nevertheless, the Internet has the potential to realize the final stage of the exponential curve which was embedded in the speculations of writers on the information explosion earlier in the century. This in itself will pose yet more problems for information management, but in the meantime there are a number of other problems associated with the exchange of information over the Internet that need to be addressed. Some of these are less pressing if the Internet is viewed largely as a tool for a community of IT enthusiasts and as a means for communication between individuals, but now that commercial applications are becoming significant they will need to be addressed.

The 'World Wide Wait'

One of the most annoying features of the Internet is the speed with which Web pages are delivered to a screen. The graphics which are embedded in many pages demands a lot of transmission capacity and there are a number of servers and clients that suffer from relatively slow telecommunications links. Delays can be further aggravated by high traffic on some sections of the Internet. This will get worse rather than better as the volume of traffic increases, unless higher-capacity telecommunications links become available across more elements of the networks that comprise the Internet, and/ or improved data compression algorithms allow more data to be transmitted through the same bandwidth.

Reflection   Describe situations in which you have experienced the consequences of inadequate bandwidth on the Internet. What were the characteristics of these situations?

Security and ownership

Issues of copyright and intellectual property are of particular concern to the information industry, since issues of ownership are at the heart of rights and responsibilities, and who has the authority to make commercial arrangements associated with information. These must be addressed through a mixture of legislation which is relevant across an international network (and this is a true challenge in itself), practice and licenses and agreements. Also, for people to be able to enact commerce on the Internet, the ability to keep monetary and other proprietary information (such as order information) secure as it passes across the Internet, and the need to authenticate the status and identity of the sender, is crucial for effective commercial transactions.

Structure

Users cannot locate the information or the site that they want on the Internet unless they are searching with a specific address, and even addresses change. Even the most hardened of technocrats have been heard to rehearse the wonders of Dewey and other classification schemes. As discussed above, some of the search engines offer evaluation, classification and indexing of Internet resources. The role that search engines play in providing access to Internet resources will evolve over the next few years. Search engines will be viewed as increasingly central in determining which sites users visit; as consumer guides they have potential to be very powerful. In addition, a greater number of search engines will be necessary to meet the needs of different client groups. An important element in the professional development of information managers will be the scope and features of the search engines.

Summary   The Internet is a series of linked networks, which operates on the basis of standard network protocols. The World Wide Web is an important component of the Internet. Services and resources available over the Internet include: listservs and discussion groups, subject databases, community information, government resources, library catalogues, commercial resources, bulletin boards, shopping and commercial transactions, and document delivery. With such a vast array of resources and databases available over the Internet, it has been important to design interfaces that help users search the information resources and services available. Two types of tools, browsers and search engines, are used to search the Internet. Browsers support browsing and moving between sites and pages on the basis of hyperlinks, but the identification of specific resources requires a search engine. Potential library applications of the Internet include: new ways of accessing library facilities, interactive home pages, linking to remote information, staff development, acquisitions, and cataloguing and classification. Intranets reflect the use of Internet technology for an organization's internal communications system. The types of applications depend upon whether flat-content intranets or interactive intranets are in use. Issues that need attention to support the further development of Internet technologies are the 'World Wide Wait', security and ownership, and structure.

REVIEW QUESTIONS

1   What is the difference between the Internet and the World Wide Web?
2   Explain the terms HTTP, HTML, and URL.
3   Make a list of some of the databases and services available over the Internet.

4   What is the difference between a browser and a search engine? Explain how a search engine works.
5   List some criteria for the evaluation of the databases available over the Internet.
6   Discuss how a library might use Internet technology to provide its customers with access to information.
7   What is an Intranet? Why are organization's making use of Intranet technology?

IMPLEMENTATION CASE STUDY: CAMBRIDGESHIRE LIBRARIES AND INFORMATION SERVICE

Nature of the project

The project is based on recognition that IT is integral to the management, delivery and development of the public library service. The convergence of systems, and the increasing prevalence of information in electronic formats, are factors which make IT more and more viable in public libraries.

This leads to a concern over the increasing potential for groups of 'information poor' and 'information rich'. Public libraries have an essential role to play in ensuring free access to information regardless of format.

This led to the development of the following policy:

1   The library will use IT whenever it can help improve the service, or improve efficiency.
2   The library will provide access to software to help people who have access to IT to make the most of it.
3   The library will provide access to computers for those who do not otherwise have access to them.
4   The library will provide training for those who do not have computing skills.

A comparison was made with the earliest public libraries, which provided access to books – the format of the day – and encouraged literacy to ensure maximum benefit from the library for the community. In the future, computer literacy will have as important a role to play as regular literacy.

The services introduced in response to this policy include:

*   CD-ROM network for staff and public use
*   CD-ROM for loan (through Ramesis)
*   Diskbank (shareware for sale, also through Ramesis).
*   partnership in Cambridge Online City project, to provide local information using public-access Internet terminals, of which one is located at Cambridge Central Library, another at Arbury Court Library

- Eight public-access Internet terminals providing Web access only – four located in Reference and Information, and four in the Input Output Centre.

Further services implemented include:

1   Cambridgeshire Libraries and Information Service has a home page for every library. The page for Cambridge Central Library also includes basic information on using the Internet, and hotlinks to useful sites.
2   Input Output Centre, provides computers for hire, and sells training courses.
3   The Centre's staff will provide free training on a geographical information system providing mapping of Cambridgeshire.
4   Cambridge Central Library and its staff have e-mail addresses to enable and encourage customers to contact us in this way.
5   Plescon self issue terminal was piloted in July 1997.

Public access to the Internet
Simply, the internet shows how information will be collected, managed and disseminated in the future. If the public do not have access to the networks, they may lose access to the information currently available in other formats.

The Internet is only a tool – a format. The public should have as much access to the information on the Internet as it does to any other source of information available.

Are public libraries the appropriate avenue?
Yes – simply because for most people they are the principle source of free unbiased information essential to the effective workings of democracy and a free society.

The free access to information must continue, whatever the format. Indeed, Internet and networking technology may provide a challenge for the future of libraries. Whilst the book will not become obsolete as such, it may be superseded for some purposes. The day will come when information is piped everywhere as water and electricity is now. The issue will then be access and charging.

The services that public libraries currently provide, including information, are largely building-based. Although a network may remove the need to visit a building, the access to the information itself will need to be maintained. This could – and should – be part of the future role of the public library service: the collection, management and publishing of information on the Net.

To ensure this future becomes a reality, the Internet should be embraced wholeheartedly and exploited wherever possible. In the public mind, the library should be as synonymous with electronic data as it currently is with books.

User support
Public libraries should recognize that customers need help using formats they are not familiar with. They should also recognize that most people, once familiar prefer

to serve themselves. In the same way that libraries in the last century promoted literacy, public libraries should promote computer literacy, and provide free basic training. The same should apply to the Internet, with help and support freely available to enable customers to serve themselves, and with staff on hand to help and mediate where necessary.

Martyn Wade
Cambridgeshire Libraries and Information Service

References

Yip, K. F. (1997) 'Selecting internet resources: experience at the Hong Kong University of Science an Technology (HKUST) Library', *The electronic library*, **15** (2), 91–8.

Bibliography

Note: There are a wide range of sources on the Internet and intranet, both in print and electronic form. This is a small sample of such resources that either offer practical advice or describe case-study experiences that might also offer guidance to others embarking on similar projects.

Biddiscombe, R., Knowles, K., Upton, J. and Wilson, K. (1997) 'Developing a web library guide for an academic library: problems, solutions and future possibilities', *Program*, **31** (1), 59–74.

Biddiscombe, R. and Watson, M. (1994) 'Developing a hypertext guide to an academic library: problems and progress', *Program*, **28** (1), 29–41.

Blackmore, P. (1997) 'The development of an intranet within a college of further and higher education', *Aslib proceedings*, **49** (3), 67–72.

Bradley, P. and Smith, A. (1995) *World Wide Web: how to design and construct home pages*, London, Aslib.

Cawkell, T. (1997) 'The information superhighway: a review of some determining factors', *Journal of information science*, **23** (3), 187–208.

Davenport, E., Proctor, R. and Goldenberg, A. (1997) 'Distributed expertise: remote reference service on a metropolitan area network', *The electronic library*, **15** (4), 271–8.

Dawson, A. (1997) *The Internet for library and information professionals*, London, Library Association Publishing.

Dong, X. and Su, L. T. (1997) 'Search engines on the world wide web and information retrieval from the Internet: a review and evaluation', *Online and CD-ROM review*, **21** (2), 67–81.

Falk, H. (1996) 'Working the Web', *The electronic library*, **14** (5), 453–69.

Fishenden, J. (1997) 'Managing intranets to improve business process', *Aslib proceedings*, 90–6.

Garlock, K. L. and Piontek, S. (1996) *Building the service based library Website: a step-by-step guide to design and options*, Chicago/London, ALA.

Harrison, S. (1997) 'NHSWeb: a health intranet', *Aslib proceedings*, 49 (2), 36–7.

Heery, R. (1996) 'Review of metadata formats', *Program*, 30 (4), 345–73.

Helm, P. (1997) 'Hewlett Packard and the intranet – case study and alliances', *Aslib proceedings*, 49 (2), 32–5.

Jasco, P. (1996) 'The Internet as a CD-ROM alternative', *Information today*, 13 (3), 29–31.

Jeffcoate, G. (1996) 'Gabriel: gateway to European national libraries', *Program*, 30 (3), 229–38.

Kalin, S. and Wright, C. (1994) 'Internexus: a partnership for Internet instruction', in Kinder, R. (ed.) *Libraries on the Internet: impact on reference services*, New York, Haworth Press, 29–41.

MacLeod, R. and Kerr, L. (1997) 'EEVL: past, present and future', *The electronic library*, 15 (4), 279–86.

McMahon, K. (1995) 'Using the BUBL information service as an Internet reference resource', *Managing information*, 2 (4), 33–5.

Merchant, B. and Winters, N. (1997) Small libraries on the Internet', *Library technology*, 2 (4), 78–9.

Morrel, P. (1997) 'Building intranet-based information systems for international companies etc.', *Aslib proceedings*, 49 (2), 27–31.

Pal, A., Ring, K. and Downes, V. (1996) *Intranets for business applications*, London, Ovum Reports.

Rowley, J. (1996) 'Retailing and shopping on the Internet', *Internet research: electronic networking applications and policy*, 6 (1), 81–91.

Still, J. (ed.) (1994) *The Internet library: case studies of library internet management and use*, Westport, Mecklermedia.

Storey, T. and Daryuple, T. (1996) 'On the Web with OCLC FirstSearch and NetFirst', *OCLC newsletter*, 220, 26–9.

Tedd, L. A. (1995) 'An introduction to sharing resources via the Internet in academic libraries and information centers in Europe', *Program*, 29 (1), 43–61.

Tseng, G., Poulter, A. and Sargent, G. (1998) *The library and information professional's guide to the World Wide Web*, London, Library Association Publishing.

Woodward, J. (1996) 'Cataloguing and classifying information resources on the Internet', in Williams, M. E. (ed.) *Annual review of information science and technology*, Medford, Information Today for ASIS, 189–220.

9

Online search services

LEARNING OUTCOMES

Online search services offer access to a wide range of online databases and other resources. At the end of this chapter you will:

- be aware of the nature of online search services
- know when such services might be useful
- understand the different roles of intermediaries and end-users
- appreciate the wide range of different online search services
- be aware of the criteria for the evaluation of an online search service and its databases
- understand the nature of an online search
- be aware of some of the issues in managing an online search service on behalf of end-users
- be aware of the factors that will influence the future of online search services.

9.1 Introduction

What is an online search service? The online search services that we are primarily concerned with in this chapter are what might be described as the traditional online search services. In the last few years these have been joined by consumer online services such as America Online, CompuServe and Prodigy, and a wide range of other organizations that mount databases on servers on the Internet. The online search services that we are concerned with here mount a range of databases upon a large computer system and offer users access to these databases, usually in exchange for a fee. Some search services have an international market, and encourage and support users from all over the world (or, more accurately, the developed world). Other search services, whilst they may have some users in other countries, operate essentially as national services. The early search services were established in the late 1960s and early 1970s. There are now well over 10,000 databases available via such search services and mounted on computers based at various locations throughout the world. The intending user of such an online search service must be able to access the search service computer. This may be achieved with the use of a terminal or workstation which can be linked through a telecommunications network to the search service computer. This is usually a PC with communications software and a modem, or a PC linked to a server which has appropriate communications software mounted. A wide range of different networks can be used, but increasingly the search services are accessed through the Internet. Internet access to online search services that were previously accessed through other telecommunications networks can make it difficult to differentiate between an Internet server and an online search service. Both offer access to databases. The diversification of the roles of online search services also adds to the complexity. Here we define an online search service as a special category of Internet service, that can be described thus:

An online search service seeks to mount a range of databases designed to meet the needs of a specific audience. It acts as an intermediary between the database producer and the end-user.

Table 9.1 *The three generations of online searching*

First generation (until 1981)	Dumb terminals, slow transmission speeds, bibliographic databases, intermediary searching, commercial online systems such as DIALOG
Second generation (1982–91)	PCs as workstations, medium transmission speeds, bibliographic, directory and ASCII full-text databases, specialized end-users and intermediaries
Third generation (1991–)	Multimedia PCs, higher transmission speeds, ASCII and full-text databases, consumer end-users, intermediaries and specialized end-users

Reflection   Identify and list the criteria used to differentiate between the three generations in Table 9.1.

The role of the online search service is currently under threat, and consequently undergoing transformation. Table 9.1 characterizes the three generations of online searching. The original role of the online search services was to mount databases on behalf of database producers, and to manage on behalf of those database producers access to their databases. This included dealing with technical aspects associated with access to networks, bearing the capital investment associated with the acquisition and continuing development of large computer systems, and managing billing and associated financial transactions. Database producers paid online search services to perform this service for them. Now, with much cheaper hardware, much greater standardization and more widespread access to networks, almost any individual or organization can set up in the business of selling electronic information, and provide direct access to their own databases. The survival of organizations that will continue to be successful online search services will depend upon:

- access to an established and defined customer base
- the quality and effectiveness of marketing activities (branding may be important in symbolizing quality in respect of both service and databases)
- document delivery options and the speed with which documents can be delivered
- high revenues to database producers, coupled with low prices to end-users
- accessibility, in the sense that the search services are easy to access on the Internet
- availability of search facilities to accommodate different user categories
- availability of a range of interface options, including potential for access through local library OPACs
- alliances in order to maximize the quality and range of the service that service suppliers can offer to users.

9.2 When to access an online search service

The most obvious situation where you might consider accessing an online search service is when you suspect that the information that you need has been published somewhere and you do not have direct access to the source which provides the information locally. To be a little more explicit, there are a number of main sources of information that might be consulted during a search for information:

- printed and published documents, such as journals, books, conference proceedings, and reports, which might be in your own collection or in an accessible library.
- a colleague or friend
- electronic or printed documents that are confidential to a given organization, such as reports, letters and internal files, and which may be managed through a document management system
- databases available on CD-ROM or other optical media
- databases available within an organization covering in-house information, such as might form part of a management information system
- the online public access catalogue of a convenient library
- the variety of sources available over the Internet, including other Websites.

The core source to which the online search services provide access are databases. These databases include both bibliographic and document databases. Many of the other sources listed above may offer access either to the data or to the document itself, or to locations, sources or documents in which the information may be found. Checklist 9.1 indicates some of the key factors that might be considered when selecting an information source.

....

CHECKLIST 9.1

Factors to be considered when selecting an Information source

1   *Subject and source coverage must be appropriate.*
2   *Search type.* In some searches flexibility in search strategy is useful, and it may be useful to be able to change or modify search strategy in the light of knowledge acquired during the search process. Initial search strategies may be modified as the searcher learns more about the subject, the terms which are effective in retrieval, and the literature of the subject.
3   *Search terms.* Computer-based searches may search on both controlled indexing terms and natural indexing terms, and are thus not constrained only to search on those terms which have been assigned by an indexer, but may also take advantage of other terms that occur in the text of the document.
4   *The need to formulate search phrases.* Some searches require complex search statements comprising a number of interlinked concepts in order to specify a topic adequately – for example, marketing opportunities for the financial services industry in Germany. Such search statements may not be matched in a printed index, but can easily be sought by framing a search strategy which combines terms in an online search. In addition, if the first combination of terms is unsuccessful, an alternative can be tested with little difficulty.
5   *Search output required.* Output from online searches can either be printed, often in a specified format and order, or downloaded. Once downloaded, the records can be modified and added to a local database, or merely re-formatted and printed for dispatch to others for consultation. This is particularly convenient when large numbers of records, such as in the creation of a bibliography, might need to be processed. Such downloaded records may be integrated with other records to form the basis of a personal database.
6   *Search cost.* There are a number of costs that must be considered in assessing the cost of a search. The billed cost is an element that it is difficult to ignore: someone has to pay it! Other costs may be the cost of the searcher's time, and the cost of training the searcher. In addition, it can be difficult to assess the cost of a specific search in advance. The most cost-effective route to information retrieval will depend upon the cost of the search, the cost of the searcher's time, the end-user's willingness or ability to pay, the currency of the information required, and the number of users using a service. Although cost is important, each information manager must establish broad policies and assess each search in the context of these.
7   *Access to additional resources.* All libraries have limited stock. Online searching of external databases offers access to resources in the library network that are

not held by a particular library. If the library's resources are particularly limited, online searching can be a boon to those of its users who need other documents, but the library may need to be prepared for an increase in the interlibrary loans transactions or document delivery orders.

8   *Currency and time period required.* Although the time-span covered by many databases is now quite substantial, there are still limitations, and it is important to check the time-span offered by the database. Some databases, such as bibliographic databases, specialize in long runs going back 20 or more years. In other databases, currency is paramount. In some finance and business databases the databases are updated in real time (i.e. as the information becomes available) as it is important for the user to have up-to-the-minute information.

9   *Search experience.* Users may enjoy an online search, whereas they would not be prepared to engage in the slog of a manual search.

The criteria presented in the above checklist may be applied in order to identify situations when the use of an online search service might be beneficial. Since most of the criteria listed also apply to other environments where online searching may be performed, such as on CD-ROM or on a corporate database, they may also find application in these environments. This theme will be further developed in Chapters 10 and 11 which deal with CD-ROM and document management and publishing systems.

9.3 Intermediaries or end-user searching

So far we have side-stepped the issue of who is the searcher. There are two potential categories of searcher:

1   **The end-user,** or the person who actually wants to use the information. The end-user as a searcher should have a good perception of the information that is required, and also understand the terminology of the topic which is being sought.

2   **The intermediary,** usually an information professional such as a librarian or information manager. The intermediary sometimes performs the search on behalf of the user. Ideally the intermediary should be adequately trained in the search facilities of the online search services, and keeps alert to developments in those facilities and in database availability. The intermediary is an experienced searcher and so should be able to adopt efficient and effective search strategies, and in the best circumstances should be familiar with the indexing language of those databases that he/she searches regularly.

The end-user and the intermediary, then, bring different expertise to the search situation. Both can make a contribution, and many would argue that the best searches can be performed with both present, although the dialogue that might then ensue might slow the search. Certainly the expertise of both can usually be harnessed in the search situation.

This book is addressed to information professionals, and therefore tends to emphasize their role. Consequently, there is some focus on the role of the intermediary in this chapter, although many of the decisions to be made, for example, in selecting a database or a search service must be made whoever is the searcher.

Intermediaries were accepted by end-users in the early days of online searching because the systems were so complex, and there were other hazards to negotiate, such as unreliable telecommunications links. In addition, only a relatively limited number of searches could be performed online; others called upon the skills of the information professional as a manual searcher. The information professional was often a better judge of when an online search might prove fruitful. In the 1990s, the search services have seen their market threatened by CD-ROM, which is most emphatically an end-user tool, and there has been much more attention focused on dialogue design in computer systems in general. In addition, many of the earlier databases were bibliographic and, some would say, beloved of librarians but a mystery to all others; there has since been a major growth in source databases. Online search services have significantly developed their end-user focus and services. Both Internet and GUI interfaces are user-friendly, and many online search services offer packages of service designed to meet a substantial element of the information needs of specifically targeted groups. Similarly, pricing strategies have been simplified to appeal to the end-user, with both subscription and pay-as-you-go options.

The role of the intermediary is constantly shifting, and the demand and need for intermediaries may vary depending on the users and their information needs. Some databases are notoriously difficult to search effectively; here the intermediary is always likely to have a role as a searcher. The intermediary has a role in alerting users to changes in facilities, in keeping a wide perspective and in training users in new facilities and in training new users.

Reflection   Is there a future role for the information intermediary in this context?

9.4 Online search services

Online search services, sometimes known as online systems suppliers, search services or online service spinners, are responsible for mounting databases on a computer and making the arrangements necessary for such databases to be searchable from a large number of remote user workstations. Online search services that provide access to a large number of databases convert the databases into a uniform format with some standardization in element names so that the basic commands and search techniques apply across all of the databases that are offered by a given vendor. The intending searcher needs some awareness of the range of search services that are available. Increasingly, any one database may be available from several search services. Access to that database may be considerably cheaper, especially once telecommunications charges have been taken into account, via one search service than another. Alternatively, another search service may offer search facilities which support much more effective searching for a given topic than might be possible via another search service. Search services can no longer differentiate themselves on the availability of specific databases, but must offer customers other benefits, such as ease of searching, processing speed and competitive pricing. There are a number of different types of search service:

1   **The traditional supermarket online search services** that offer a range of 50 to 300-plus databases on behalf of database producers. Examples include: DIALOG, DataStar and Questel Orbit. Although these online search services may offer many databases, and may hope to be seen to be a major presence in the information industry, continued commercial success depends on their ability to segment their market and to develop specialisms to match those segments. These are increasingly offering tailored services, such as KR ScienceBase, and Web-based services which support access to a range of services, such as DIALOG Web.

2   **Specialist online search services**, such as DBE-Link, which offers German-language and other European databases, and the search services offering access to business and financial databases, such as ICC. ICC deliver data online (with a Windows interface), offline or via CD-ROM. Alternatively, data can be delivered in bulk for integration into a company's own database or intranet, via either magnetic tape or Electronic Data Delivery (EDD). Some search services such as Information Access Company that started with a database catalogue focused on one subject have started to diversify.

3   **Publishers as search services.** A number of major publishers have entered the marketplace as search services. Some of these will have gained experience of electronic publishing through CD-ROM publishing, whilst others have formed alliances with other online service suppliers in order, to be able to offer an integrated information solution which embraces both bibliographic databases for locating information and full-text databases for document delivery. Examples are EBSCO search service, Information Access Search Bank and UMI's ProQuest Direct.

4   **Platform-independent search services**, which provide access to databases on CD-ROM, the Web, and client–server platforms, possibly through a common user interface. Ovid Technologies are a good example of this type of search service. SilverPlatter is moving in this direction.

5   **Bibliographic utilities** that offer access for specific communities to a select range of databases, often at special rates. Examples are OCLC FirstSearch and BIDS (for more details see Chapter 15).

In general online service suppliers are beginning to be able to respond to the long-standing need for common interfaces to tools, such as bibliographic databases and directories (including directories of Websites) which indicate the location of information and the full text of the document which contains information. The identification of a document and its delivery are much closer to being integrated into a seamless service. The more sophisticated offerings also offer access to other information channels, such as the databases mounted by other services, the contents of other Websites, information collections such as libraries, and people as information channels. This could be described as an integrated information solution.

Some examples of integrated information solutions

Here are four examples of services which seek to generate this integrated information solution. Such solutions need to be targeted to meet the needs of specific groups, and the service supplier must understand those needs, not only in terms of the type of database to be accessed, but also in terms of specific features of interfaces and the most acceptable pricing strategies.

KR ScienceBase for the WWW

This is a tailored product, featuring:

*   access to industry periodicals, patent documents, scientific journals, conference papers, handbooks, scientific reference and regulatory documents
*   coverage of chemistry, biochemistry, physical science, and business and industry news
*   access to databases such as BIOSIS,CAS, Derwent, Dun & Bradstreet, and the National Library of Medicine.

DIALOG Web

This is a WWW service which features:

*   a database directory that works like a Web-based search engine to support database location
*   access to over 450 DIALOG databases
*   Web Bluesheets to provide access to up-to-the-minute DIALOG content, capabilities and prices

- Electronic Redistribution and Archiving (ERA), which allows distribution by e-mail or through the local intranet
- a Web interface to Alert (a current-awareness service)
- a link to KR SourceOne, the document delivery service
- e-mail feedback for comments and suggestions.

Engineering Information Village

Ei Village is an Internet-based virtual community which is designed as a packaged solution to all engineering information needs. The services offered with Ei include:

- Ei Village Directory, which provides quick access to relevant Web sites
- Ei Tech Alert – natural-language concept searching for new developments
- Filtered News – access to bulletins on special disciplines
- Ei Corporate Gallery
- Ei Spotlights – weekly updates on topics
- Ei Annotation – guides to Web sites
- Articles on Call – ready to access, selected, prescanned articles
- EiDDS – e-mail document delivery
- Ei Connexion – an easy interface and gateway to 150 DIALOG databases
- Ei Compendex*Web – unlimited fixed-price access
- Ask a Librarian/Ask an Engineer – advice on information searching
- Ask your Peers – listservs and newsgroups selected.

Ei Village with Ei Compendex*Web can be purchased as a package or, alternatively, either may be purchased separately. Ei also publish a number of their databases on CD-ROM, and Engineering Index Monthly and Engineering Index Annual in print format.

Literature Online (Lion) from Chadwyck Healey

Lion offers access to thousands of literary texts, reference works, bibliographies and catalogues through their Website. New texts are being converted to electronic form by Chadwyck Healey, and licenses are negotiated with other publishers; texts and resources at other Websites are being identified, linked and added to the Master Index. Lion currently contains more than 210,000 texts of poems, plays and novels in fully searchable SGML format. In addition, it provides hypertext links to approximately 15,000 more literary texts located on free Websites throughout the Internet. It contains dictionaries and well-known reference works and bibliographies in the field of English and American literature, including works not previously available electronically. It provides structured access to discussion groups, electronic journals, metapages, author pages, general literary Websites and library catalogues. The Master Index is a comprehensive list of authors and works available in electronic form in Lion and on the Internet as a whole. Searching is on the basis of author or title keyword, with Boolean and proximity operators. Access is on a subscription basis and prices are based on the number of concurrent users and the specific databases to which access is required. There are substantial reductions in subscription prices for institutions which have already licensed full-text databases on CD-ROM or magnetic tape.

Reflection   What are the common features of the integrated information
                  solutions described above?

In order to be able to access the databases offered by a specific search service, for most services it is necessary to register as a user. Most searchers have registered with two, three or four main suppliers. Amongst these are likely to be one or more of the major supermarket online search services, and also possibly some specialist search services that are appropriate for the type of search that is to be performed. With the increasing tailoring of the service offered, especially in the business and financial information fields, a user may find that one online search service can meet most of their needs, and indeed support them in becoming a much more effective information user. The criteria that are appropriate in the selection of an online search service are listed in Checklist 9.2. Some searchers, after familiarizing themselves with the facilities and search techniques offered by these search services, will progress to a wider range of search services. Once a user is registered, a password is issued; this provides access to all or most of the databases offered by the search service.

Table 9.2 *The range of databases offered by some of the major online search services*

Search service	Base	Number of databases	Scope of databases
DIALOG Information Retrieval Services	Palo Alto, California	Over 450	Science and technology, bibliography, reference, business, news, social sciences and humanities
European Space Agency's Information Retrieval Service (ESA-IRS)	Frascati, Italy	Over 130	Science and technology, business and finance, corporate intelligence, health and safety, patents, news
DataStar	Switzerland	Over 350	Business and finance, chemical, engineering, news and media, medicine, food and agriculture, law and

			government, energy and the environment, science and technology, social sciences
FT Information	London	Over 400	Full-text information, business sources including major newspapers, other international news services, international business magazines, companies, industries, markets, countries
STN International		Around 200	Agriculture, bioscience and technology, chemistry, medicine, patents, physics and science in general
Questel-Orbit	France	Around 300	Business, chemical information, energy and earth science, engineering, health, safety and the environment, humanities and social sciences, materials science, news, patents, science and technology, trademarks
DIMDI	Germany		Biomedical, with some emphasis on German-language databases
BLAISE	London	22	Bibliographic records, catalogue databases
ICC	Hampton		Financial and industry analysis on all British companies
Information Access	Various	Around 30	Many full-text databases, including areas such as academic, business and industry, computer technology, and general reference
LEXIS-NEXIS	London	11,000 sources	News, Financial reports, company and market reports
Dow Jones	United States		Business, investment support
WilsonWeb	New York	36 databases	Full text, abstracts and indexes.
Ovid Technologies	London	80 databases	Health, biomedical, business, general reference, science and technology, humanities and social sciences

Table 9.2 lists some of the major search services, shows the total number of their databases that may be accessed, and gives some indication of the scope of the databases on offer. In addition to the range of databases available, many search services offer other services. Some of these are indicated in the product and ser-

vice description in Table 9.3. These include current-awareness services, access to Web resources, Web directories, document delivery and databases on CD-ROM.

Table 9.3 *The range of services available from one major online search service: DIALOG*

DIALOG	Online search service
DataStar	Online search service
KR OnDisc	CD-ROM supply service
DIALOG and DataStar Alert Services	Tailored current-awareness services
KR ProBase	End-user Windows based-online service
DataMail	E-mail service
DataMail Bulletin Boards	Bulletin board
OneSearch and StarSearch	Removes duplicates in searches on multiple databases
DIALOGLink	Communications software which also supports the viewing of images from some databases
DIALOG ERA (Electronic Redistribution and Archiving)	Covers copyright for downloading and redistribution of documents
Report	A command to facilitate the selection of data and its formatting into tables, fax and e-mail delivery of outputs
KR SourceOne/UnCover	Document delivery
DIALORDER	Document delivery
KR ScienceBase	WWW-based intelligent search guide
DIALOGWeb	WWW-based online service

9.5 Review of online databases

The array of databases available through the various online search services has expanded significantly in recent years. Chapter 5 discussed the basic types of databases and offered examples in each category. Databases may be reference or document, and the scope of their subject coverage may range from relatively specific through to interdisciplinary. Certain types of database are more common in some areas than others. For example, full-text databases are dominant in business and legal information, but less evident in science and technology. The directories of the major search services, available both online and in print form, such as DIALOG, serve as important lists of databases.

The first steps in an online search are the choice of search service and database. For most searches only a few databases might be appropriate, and once the user has identified the databases that cover the required subject area, further choice may be between only two or three databases. In general it is not sufficient simply to know the subject coverage of a database. An experienced searcher will, for example, also be familiar with the style of the indexing language, the time-span of the database, and how items are selected for inclusion in the database. Often there may be no one database that will provide an exhaustive search, and it may be necessary to consult two or more databases before a search is complete. Checklists 9.2 and 9.3 list some of the factors that the experienced searcher will weigh in the selection of a database.

CHECKLIST 9.2

The evaluation of online search services

1   The databases offered. The number of databases offered by any specific search service will vary, as can the subject coverage and language of the available databases. Also, different search services may have different time-spans with respect to any given database available for online searching.
2   Search facilities. The elements of records that can be searched may differ from one search service to another. Certainly the field formats may vary and the field names may be different. Some systems offer more extensive facilities with regard to truncation and contextual or proximity searching. For source and full-text databases various special facilities may be required. Some services such as KR ScienceBase have interfaces that require the searcher simply to type in a search term. Relevance ranking then produces an answer. The drawback of such services is that the user cannot understand the search process, and the retrieval of narrowly defined search sets may present problems.
3   Interfaces intended for expert use still feature search commands. At one time searchers needed to memorize a command language before they commenced searching. Now prompts for appropriate commands may be embedded in menus or offered as options on GUI interfaces. Although the searcher does not need to remember the commands, an understanding of the effect of their application on searching is still necessary. Different search services have different command languages depending upon their search software.
4   Formats for records. Various formats are available for viewing the details of retrieved references. Sometimes it is possible for the searcher to select the elements that he/she requires, but in searching other search services only a few standard formats are available.
5   Additional facilities. Many search services offer other facilities in addition to the basic online search facility. Often SDI or document delivery services are available (see Chapter 12 for further information).
6   Support services. Most search services offer some support and training services. Help desks, training courses, manuals, newsletters and other search aids can influence the effectiveness of a search. Good training and careful instruction can often lead to a searcher being effective with even the most complex searching systems and databases. The availability of such support services must be considered, but availability is not the only factor. Support services must be effec-

tive, accessible (e.g. providing training courses in the searcher's own locality) and reasonably cheap.

7   Cost. The cost of searching a specific database for a given search can be difficult to assess, because it is made up of a number of components. Different search services have different pricing strategies. Some services are available on a subscription basis, whilst others are priced on a transaction basis. Some services allow a mixture of these two approaches, with customers such as libraries taking out a subscription for frequently used databases, and a transaction arrangement for less frequently used databases. There will also be special rates for additional services such as SDI or document delivery. The cost of telecommunications should also be considered, and this may vary between and within countries.

8   Experience. The searcher's experience with a specific search service may be an important factor in determining his/her search effectiveness. Thus, from the searcher's point of view it is important not only to assess the specific features of the search service but also to examine his/her own skills.

....
....

CHECKLIST 9.3

Features to consider in the evaluation of databases

1   Subject coverage. Most database directories specify the subject coverage of databases; this will clearly identify the core coverage of the database, but the quality or depth of coverage in peripheral areas may be more difficult to ascertain. The selection criteria for the database may also repay examination. In reference databases all articles in a journal may be included, or only those over a specified length; letters and editorial comment may be included or may be omitted. Having established the coverage of a particular database, the next step is to compare the coverage of that database with that of others with similar coverage.

2   Type of database, and the type of information supplied. Possible data are references, full text of documents, facts, figures, images and multimedia. With the increasing use of full-text databases it is important to recognize that there are two types of full-content database: ASCII files (which include text only), and image databases (which include images, graphics and the original formatting of the article). The same service may mix both of these types of databases, or alternatively the ASCII text may be available for searching and location of documents, while the image database is delivered through a document delivery request. It is also important to recognize that electronic full texts vary, even for a single title; the full-text version may contain only major articles, or only those articles for which the author has released copyright to the publisher, or articles from a specified time period; some graphics, tables and photographs may be omitted. The most serious problem is trying to identify what has been left out.

3   Currency. What is the currency of the database and the frequency of updates? Some databases, such as those containing Stock Exchange data, are updated

continuously in real time – i.e. as the information changes so the values in the database are updated. Reference databases are often updated monthly. Some databases, such as reference databases are cumulative, but other databases only contain the most recent information.

4   Ease of use. Ease of use of the database will be influenced by a number of factors, including the interface, the indexing language and the structure of the database. Another factor will be the searcher's experience with the database.

5   Type of output. Clearly the output available from the database will be largely determined by the type of information in the database, but in addition there may be options for the format of output records and the availability of different print and download formats.

6   Indexing language. There are many features of the indexing language that might be considered. These are briefly reviewed in Section 7.4. Is the language controlled or natural language? What is the depth and exhaustivity of indexing? Are the search terms that describe the search topic available in the indexing language of the database?

7   Cost. Pricing strategies often differentiate between different types of database. For example, pricing for full-text databases may depend upon the extent of the database that is viewed or downloaded.

8   Documentation and search aids. Various aids may be available, especially to support searching of the larger databases. Tools include classification schedules, printed or on-screen thesauri and other assistance.

9   Bias. Bias, such as an undue emphasis on European or American information, needs to be assessed.

10 Time-span. The length of time the database is available online, and its starting date.

11 Search service. The search service through whom the database is available.

Table 9.4 *Some examples of databases accessible through Questel-Orbit*

Database	Subject
Duns Switzerland	Business
Derwent Biotechnology Abstracts	Chemical information
PASCAL (Science & Technology)	Energy and earth sciences
INSPEC	Engineering
RAPRA Trade Names	Materials science
Chemical Abstracts	Medicine
Predicasts Overview of Markets & Technology	News
ABI/Inform (Business & Management)	News
CLAIMS (US Patents)	Patents

Derwent World Patents Index	Patents
Weldasearch	Science and technology
UKMARK (UK Trademarks)	Trademarks

9.6 The online search

Chapter 7 introduced the basics of searching in online systems. The aim here is merely to demonstrate the typical route to searching an online search service, and to offer a few examples of features of searches. This section demonstrates the use of:

- indexing and search languages
- search logic
- search facilities
- interfaces.

Figure 9.1 shows an online search which has been executed on one of the major search services, using commands. This example illustrates the important components of a search, and indicates how to conduct a simple search. Figure 9.2 shows a search in a Web-based interface. Other texts, such as Armstrong and Large (1988) and Hartley et al. (1990) explore search strategies and the optimization of searching techniques in more depth.

Some features of the online search merit further comment. The first stage in conducting a search is to develop a clear specification of the information required. This may be conducted by the end-user alone, or by the end-user and the intermediary in cooperation. Sometimes it may not be possible to specify exactly what information is sought in advance of performing the first search, but it is always possible to strive for as precise a specification as the end-user can achieve on the basis of present knowledge. This specification may include a preliminary attempt to express the search in the indexing language of the database to be searched, and to frame a search strategy. The second stage will be the selection of the database or databases, and the selection of appropriate search services. After these preliminary planning stages have been negotiated, the searcher connects to the chosen search service, and may view any news or the information on a welcome screen or home page. Once the database or range of databases has been selected, the search proceeds as the user introduces a series of search parameters, and the system responds by indicating the number of records that match the search criteria. The user may opt to display details of these records. If the search is for a specific item of information or document, this may be read online. More usually, the user will assess the relevance of records on the basis of abstracts and bibliographic records, and then perform other operations such as downloading, or print records or view full text. A few additional comments on the use of some key facilities need to be added to the introductory comments in Chapter 7.

Search or index terms

The search or index terms are the terms used to describe subjects in the retrieval process. Depending on the databases and the search service system, a variety of fields may be searched for index terms. In some databases there are special fields in which controlled index language terms, which are usually used to represent the subject of a document, are located. Searching on such terms will tend to offer higher precision than searching on terms that appear, for instance, in the full text or the abstract of the document. On some databases the range of fields that can be searched may be wide, and may include the author field, the text of the abstract, the full text of a document, and various elements of the bibliographic citation, such as date of publication and journal title. Most search services allow the searcher to specify the field in which a search term must be located for a match.

Searching, then, may be based on a controlled indexing language or upon the natural language of the document. Many of the controlled indexing languages that are used in conjunction with a database are recorded in a published thesaurus or subject headings list. There is, for example, the INSPEC thesaurus, which lists the terms to be found as index terms in the records in the INSPEC database.

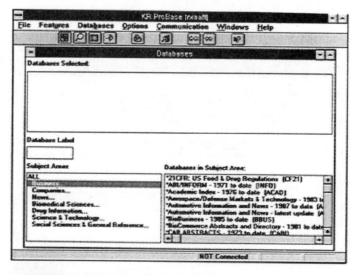

Step 1

Select databases in your chosen subject area

Fig.9.1 *An online search*

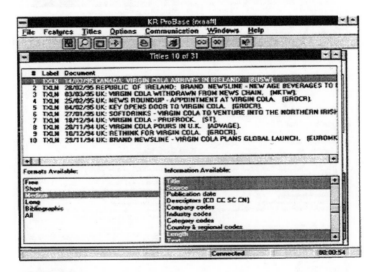

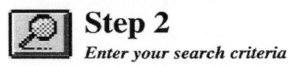

Step 2
Enter your search criteria

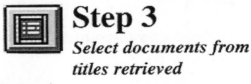

Step 3
Select documents from titles retrieved

Fig.9.1 *Continued*

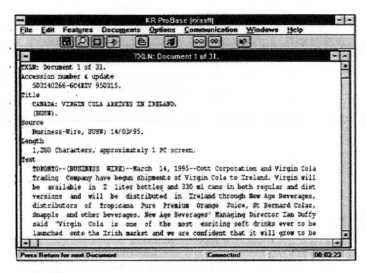

Step 4

View the documents

Fig.9.1 *Continued*

Step 1
Sign on

Fig.9.2 *Searching through a Web interface*

Step 2
Choose a
search category

Step 3
Enter a
search term

Fig.9.2 *Continued*

**Step 4
Report on
search results**

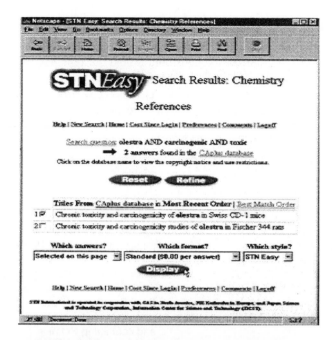

**Step 5
Display records
retrieved**

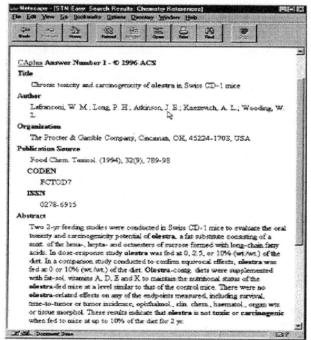

Fig.9.2 *Continued*

Similarly, SHE, or Subject Headings for Engineering, shows the subject headings used in the Ei databases. Most of these thesauri are available in printed format, and many of them can be consulted online during a search. In GUI interfaces, extracts from the thesaurus can be displayed in a window, and users can click on words in the display in order to select them. The thesaurus may offer additional related search terms, and help in the selection of appropriate search terms.

Table 9.5 *Commands in an online search service: DIALOG*

	Command	Description
1	HELP or ?	Calls help
	SET NOTICE	Previews output charges
	LOGOFF	Logs user off from system
2	E ART	Displays portion of database index in which ART appears
3	S JURY	Creates set of records that contain the term JURY
4	S MIME AND DANCE	Creates set of records containing MIME and DANCE
	S S3 AND HOME	Creates set of records based on those in set S3 and containing HOME
5	S AU=WOLFE,V	Selects records with WOLFE,V in the author field
	S CABLE/TI,DE	Selects records with CABLE in the title or descriptor field
6	S AU=WOLFE,V?	Selects records with WOLFE,V plus any number of characters in the author field
	S EMPLOY?	Selects records with EMPLOY plus any number of characters
	S WOM?N	Selects records with one character varying at ?
	S COMPUT???	Selects records with a maximum of three additional characters
7	S SOLAR(W)ENERGY	Selects records with SOLAR and ENERGY adjacent and in specified order
	S SOLAR(3W)ENERGY	Selects records with SOLAR and ENERGY within three words of each other and in specified order
	S SOLAR(S)HEAT	Selects records with SOLAR and HEAT in the same subfield
8	S DRUG(W)ADDICT?/ENG	Selects records with DRUG adjacent to ADDICT? in English-language documents
	S PY=1988:1990	Selects records with publication years 1988–1990
9	T S3/5/ALL	Displays all records in set S3 in format 5
	PR S3/9/ALL	Prints offline all records in set S3 in format 9
10	SAVE	Stores search strategy since last BEGIN command
	D S	Reviews sets created during search
11	BEGIN 28,96	Commences searching in databases 28 and 96.

Command languages and interfaces

Although GUI and menu-based interfaces are offered by many of the online search services, the command language, or a subset of it, is embedded in the interface, and continues to define the features that are available to support searching. Table 9.5 shows commands in an online search service. These command languages have become increasingly complex as the range of facilities offered by the online search services has expanded. Some while ago, Negus identified the 14 basic functions for which commands must be present in any online command language. These command functions are

CONNECT	to provide for logging-on
BASE	to identify the database to be searched
FIND	to input a search term
DISPLAY	to display a list of alphabetically linked terms
RELATE	to display logically related terms
SHOW	to print references online
PRINT	to print references online
FORMAT	to specify the format to be displayed
DELETE	to delete search terms or print requests
SAVE	to save a search formulation for later use on the same or another database on the same system
OWN	to use a system's own command language when the standardized command language does not cater for a specific function available on a particular system
STOP	to end the session and log-off
MORE	to request the system to display more information – for instance, to continue the alphabetical display of terms
HELP	to obtain guidance when in difficulty.

In addition to the basic command, many commands can be issued with different qualifiers. So, for example, in DIALOG there is the EXPAND command to support the display of appropriate sections of the inverted file. Depending upon which portion of the inverted file is required to be displayed, so the basic command may operate differently. So for E for EXPAND we might specify

E TELEVISION	to display the inverted file around the word TELE-VISION
E AU=KEEN,J	to display the author inverted file around the author KEEN,J
E (HOME COOKING)	to display the inverted file around the two words HOME COOKING

E E4   to display the related terms in a thesaurus file for the
                                        term labelled E4.

In order to use an online search service effectively, the user needs to understand
the meaning of most of the terms in the command language. The necessary learning is made all the more onerous by the fact that each search service uses its own
command language. The different command languages arise partly from history
and partly from more practical or commercial considerations. As the early search
services pioneered their systems, they developed software to support the services
that they sought to offer. The command language is a function of this software.
Command languages must also reflect the functions offered by the search service,
and whilst there are many functions that are offered by all of the search services,
there are also functions that are unique to specific search services. Commercial
considerations mean that if a search service offers a standard command language,
that search service may be able to poach another search service's customers, but
the converse will also be the case. Information searchers find it easy to search with
a command language with which they are familiar.

Search facilities

Chapter 7 briefly reviews the facilities available for searching most information
retrieval systems. Most of these facilities are offered by most of the major search
services. Figures 9.1 and 9.2 demonstrate how these search statements may be
linked to conduct a search.

Some types of database also require special search features. For example,
LEXIS-NEXIS offer the following features:

LINK   to mark citations that appear in the text of documents, with a
                view to moving directly to the full text of cases, statutes and law
                review articles
LEXSEE   to allow a search based not on a subject but rather on a citation
LEXSTAT   to search on a citation and retrieve the full text of a code or
                statute.
BROWSE   to browse through full text.

9.7 Managing an online search service

This chapter has reviewed many of the features that need to be considered when
performing an online search. This section briefly draws together some of the
issues that face the information professional who needs to run an online search
service for end-users. As discussed earlier, online searching may be performed by
the end-user or by an intermediary. In many organizations some access to online
services is centralized and operated through a library or other intermediary

agency, whilst in others the users access the online services directly. Centralization brings some benefits associated with financial control and coordination of the facilities being used within an organization. Central expertise can be developed, training can be coordinated and expertise shared.

There are a number of issues to be considered in the establishment of the service. First, it is necessary to establish which databases are best accessed online, as opposed to on CD-ROM, in printed form or through some other avenue. Once these databases have been identified, consideration can be given to the online services that offer the best access to the combination of databases required. Once two, three or four initial online search services have been selected, contracts with the service can be negotiated. A number of other issues may then need to be considered:

Location of workstations

The number of workstations and their location needs to be decided. The location needs to be quiet to aid concentration, and there needs to be space for secure storage of associated documentation.

Searchers and training

Who are the searchers – end-users or information professional staff? If intermediaries are to be used, how many staff should be trained, and who should they be? Do end-users need training? As the number of end-users has increased, so the need has become more evident for a librarian or information intermediary to act as a tutor or instructor and to guide users through the complex mix of commercial online systems, the WWW resources, databases on CD-ROM, and locally loaded databases. The organization and coordination of help and training is a significant issue.

Charging and fees

Charging practices vary. Some libraries feel that online searches should be free to users, while others succumb to the pressure to recoup costs. A charging policy must be established. Workstations with credit-card facilities are making it easier for libraries to collect charges.

Record-keeping

Records must be kept of the searches that are performed, so that these can be checked against accounts submitted by the search service supplier. Records also form the basis of management information which can be used to monitor the success of the service.

Documentation

Although directories of databases are increasingly accessed in electronic form, some print documents may often still be retained for convenience. This documentation might include loose-leaf manuals, thesauri, directories of databases and newsletters. Documentation must be organized, made available and kept up to date. An in-house procedures manual can also serve to control the way in which searching is performed. It might record:

- which search services are available
- access routes
- passwords
- current policy with regard to charging users.

Impact on other services

Searching bibliographic databases is likely to generate a demand for documents that are not available locally. An increase in interlibrary loan requests and document delivery orders should be expected.

9.8   Online futures

There has been an upsurge in the interest in electronic information sources. As part of the infrastructure of the information industry, the online search services are likely to benefit from this increased interest in information. On the other hand, new competitors have entered the marketplace, and the future of the online search services will be influenced by the competing media such as CD-ROM, DVD and the plethora of Internet resources.

Current and future developments have been, and will continue to be, focused on the following areas:

Interfaces

Users have become accustomed to easy-to-use GUI interfaces in business software and CD-ROM. Many online search services have introduced Web interfaces, and this trend is likely to continue, with users having some choice of interface. In addition, the use of Java to design online database interfaces offers the possibility of faster interfaces, which can also incorporate a number of Windows features, such as a static tool bar, tree displays, thesauri, mapping, explode/implode, search fields and context-sensitive help. For example, with the use of the Z39.50 complaint Ovid Web Gateway, every site can choose an interface, whether it be the Ovid interface or a local OPAC interface, for each group of users. Undergraduates might therefore use the OPAC interfaces, while those who require more sophisticated searching might use the Ovid interface. Others are likely to emulate the Requester interface released by LEXIS-NEXIS which allows researchers to search databases using their e-mail clients. Such interfaces will seem familiar to users who are accustomed to using e-mail. Increasingly, online search services within libraries and organizations will be achieved through OPAC interfaces. There is some concern that the interfaces of the future will lack the power that is demanded by experienced searchers, as interface designers strive to woo end-users.

Telecommunications

The digital network ISDN (Integrated Services Data Network), has offered faster and more accurate transmission of data. The network will need to continue to be enhanced and its bandwidth increased if increases in traffic caused by more users and the transmission of multimedia documents are to be sustained. Enhanced dedicated networks, such as SuperJanet for the UK academic community, will also make an important contribution to increased bandwidth. Some online search services are recognizing that they must make considerable investment in private, dedicated data connections to supply guaranteed bandwidth and avoid Internet traffic jams.

Databases

The increase in the number of full-text, statistical and other numeric databases is expected to continue. Updating of databases is much more frequent than it once was. The current split between ASCII full-text databases and image databases needs to be resolved so that online search services can deliver multimedia documents as a matter of course. Search services will seek to offer previewing and ordering of full-image articles on all platforms. Users will need high-specification PCs and modems in order to be able to exploit these services. Financial constraints mean that it takes time for libraries and users to upgrade their hardware and software configurations. Another issue for databases will be database quality. The librarian's task of selection, evaluation and pointing to authoritative and high-quality content will become all the more important. In the longer term, also, services will not merely provide access to databases and resources, but will have fact-answering interfaces to these resources.

Interface integration

This includes common interfaces to a range of information resources. Cross-file searching, where the user can transfer a search strategy across a number of databases and achieve a search output from this variety of sources, has been available for some time on some online search services. But the user needs a much more integrated service, in which information and records can be drawn from a variety of different sources and integrated into a file in a format that supports the creation of local databases or local documents. The removal of duplicate records that appear in more than one database is a start, but in general such issues have only been considered in relation to bibliographic databases, and much work remains to be done in this area. The new integrated information solutions are one approach that is likely to appeal to end-user communities.

Pricing strategies

Pricing strategies must continue to evolve. There have been some significant changes over the past two years, as services have sought at long last to tailor pricing to meet both library and end-user needs. A mixture of transaction-based pricing and subscriptions is likely to persist, but discounts and special arrangements to cover site license and parallel print subscriptions leave plenty of scope for development. Some of these changes in pricing strategies are relatively recent, and the online search services will still be evaluating the consequences for revenue. Pricing of electronic information is a notoriously difficult area, and will not become any simpler as authors, editors and publishers increasingly assert their right to returns from the use of their intellectual property.

Alliances and integration

Alliances and integration go hand in hand. In order to offer an integrated service online search services are increasingly acquiring or merging with other organizations in the information industry. Significant amongst these other partners are (and will continue to be) document delivery services, library management systems vendors and library networks. On the other hand, the traditional relationship between database producer and online search service is looking less mutually beneficial. In future, database producers will carefully assess distribution channels in order to identify those that give the best return within the communities that they serve. This evolution in the shape of the online marketplace will produce new search services, such as those recently launched by, for instance, SilverPlatter Information, and database producers. Mergers such as the recent merger between DIALOG and Maid, and also disposals, are likely to be a characteristic of an industry whose market and products are in flux.

Summary   An online search service seeks to mount a range of databases designed to meet the needs of a specific audience, and acts as an intermediary between the database producer and the end-user. There are a number of factors that need to be considered in the evaluation of online search services and the databases to which they provide access. Online searchers may be performed by intermediaries or end-users. The types of online search service include the traditional supermarket service, specialist search services, publishers and bibliographic utilities. An online search makes use of search or index terms, and command languages and interfaces. A number of issues need to be considered in managing an online search service. Future developments will be in the areas of interfaces, telecommunications, databases, integration, pricing and strategic alliances.

REVIEW QUESTIONS

1   Describe the different categories of online search service.
2   What criteria would you use in comparing the online search services?
3   Explain how indexing languages are used in performing an online search.
4   What are the key issues in managing an online search service?
5   In what ways are the roles and services of the online search services changing?

IMPLEMENTATION CASE STUDY: USING OCLC FIRSTSEARCH

Background

Oxford is the oldest university in the English-speaking world. There is no known date for its foundation, but teaching has been going on since 1096. The University is made up of 36 colleges, six permanent private halls, and a School for Management Studies.

The University has a population of around 10,000 undergraduates, 4000 post-graduates, and 6500 academic and other staff. Approximately 3000 members of the student body are drawn from a total of 110 overseas countries. Around 10,000 students are enrolled each year for courses in the Department for Continuing Education. Oxford has an extremely rich, diverse and fragmented library service provided by over 100 independently managed libraries.

Choosing FirstSearch

The Oxford University Report on Technical Strategy includes the following statement:

> A University such as Oxford which aspires to leadership in research, scholarship and the publication and dissemination of information must be at the forefront not only of using IT but also of developing its use into new areas.

The University is dispersed over a wide area of Oxford due to its collegiate structure. As a result, library provision is necessarily organized and distributed in the same manner. As the statement mentions, Oxford focuses on being a centre for scholarly research, and as a result its demands for information are high.

The libraries play a major role in this provision, and see IT development as a tool to meet the ever-increasing demands for information. Due to the dispersed structure of the University, it is essential that information should be easily accessible in a common format regardless of location and require minimum support. In addition, the implementation of a solution to these requirements would involve the least possible investment in staff time, and would coexist within the existing IT structure.

FirstSearch was evaluated during the 1993 UK pre-launch trials offered in association with CHEST (Combined Higher Education Software Team). CHEST is an organization set up in 1988 to work on behalf of the UK higher-education community to arrange with suppliers competitive pricing for software and datasets. Through CHEST a consortium pricing for certain datasets was offered via FirstSearch.

Oxford selected an option containing approximately 25 databases. The selection offered access to unique databases such as OCLCs WorldCat and ArticleFirst, along with many popular subject-specific databases. Through the pricing mechanism, once we have subscribed to a particular option there is the opportunity to 'add-on' other databases as required. Recently, we made available MLA Bibliography on FirstSearch. New files are reviewed as they become available; for example, we see an interest in OCLC's NetFirst database, an authoritative index to Internet resources.

It was decided to go ahead with FirstSearch via a subscription in Oxford for the following reasons:

1   The service is free at the point-of-use thanks to the CHEST subscription-based agreement with OCLC. This means people can use it without worrying about running up a large bill.
2   The subject areas covered are wide-ranging, suitable for a large institution such as Oxford. The mix of databases gives us access across the University to information on arts and humanities, business information, engineering and technology, life sciences, public affairs and law, medicine and health science, social sciences etc.
3   The service complements and integrates well with existing CD-ROM and online-based facilities already available within the University.

The three major strengths of FirstSearch at Oxford are seen as:

- ease-of-use for readers with tight schedules
- very up-to-date information with regular updates
- excellent online help screens.

Implementing FirstSearch

As there are over 100 libraries in Oxford, the librarians were targeted first, with mail-shots of basic information about the service, logging-on instructions and passwords. Information was also made available electronically on OLIS (Oxford Libraries Information System), the union catalogue, which is used widely by staff and students.

Two technical contacts were selected to field enquiries from librarians about the service at site level. An annual training day provided by OCLC Europe staff came free with the package, the day being organized and customized to meet our needs. Two half-day training sessions were organized in June 1994 and were very well attended. Feedback was very positive and technical enquiries have been few. These indications suggest the users are experiencing very few difficulties with the service.

After the librarians have been introduced to, and become comfortable with FirstSearch, access was expanded to the University community. Now all members of the University can have access to FirstSearch. In some libraries a terminal is dedicated to FirstSearch use, giving students easy access to the service.

Additional help is available in the form of User Guides that were mounted on OCLC's server, and downloaded and adapted to suit Oxford use.

References

Armstrong, C.. J. and Large, J. A. (eds.) (1988) *Manual of online search strategies*, Aldershot, Gower.

Hartley, R. J. et al. (1990) *On-line searching: principles and practice*, London, Bowker-Saur.

Bibliography

Amor, L. (1996) *The online manual: a practical guide to business databases*, Oxford: Learned Information.

Amor, L. (1997) *Online company information 1997: the directory of financial and corporate databases worldwide*, Oxford, Learned Information.

Armstrong, C. J. and Madawar, K. (1996) 'Investigation into the quality of databases in general use in the UK', *British Library research and innovation reports*, 11, 149.

Basch, R. (1993) 'Annual review of database development', *Database*, 16 (6), 29–41.

Bates, M. E. (1996) 'What's behind the pretty face?', *New user interfaces*, 19 (4), 24–32.

Bates, M. J. (1996) 'The Getty end-user online searching project in the humanities: report no. 6: overview and conclusions', *College and research libraries*, 57 (6), 514–23.

Bjorner, S. (1994) 'Get ready, get SET, go for more control on DIALOG', *Online*, 18 (1), 103–8.

Christi, S. H. (1993) 'CD-ROM vs online: a comparison of PsycLIT (CD-ROM) and PsycINFO (DIALOG)', *Reference librarian*, 40, 131–55.

Convey, J. (1992) *Online information retrieval: an introductory manual to principles and practice*, London, Library Association Publishing.

Foote, J. B., Harrison, M. M. and Watson, M. (1997) 'Electronic Library resources: managing the maze', *Resource sharing and information networks*, 12 (2), 5–17.

Foster, A. and Foster, P. (1990) *On-line business sourcebook*, Headland, Cleveland, Headland Press.

Foster, P. (ed.) (1990) *On-line business information*, Headland, Cleveland, Headland Press,.

Head, A. J. (1997) 'A question of interface design: how do online search service GUI's measure up?', *Online*, 21 (3), 20–9.

Jeffcoate, J. (1993) 'Multimedia in the business market: is there a multimedia market?', *Information management and technology*, 26 (5), 222–5, 228.

Online Information (1993–6) *Proceedings of the 17th–20th International On-line Information meeting, London December 1993–6*, Oxford/New Jersey, Learned Information.

Online Information (1997) *Online company information*, Oxford, Learned Information.

Parker, N. (1991) *On-line management and marketing databases*, London, Aslib. (Also others in the same series on building, construction and architecture databases, environment databases, medical databases, law databases, and business and company databases)

Poynder, R. (1996) 'Elsevier moves full text onto the Web', *Information world review*, 119, 5.

Poynder, R. (1996) 'STN International: the scientific and technical search service', *Business information review*, 13 (2), 183–90.

Rehkop, B. L. (1994) 'Cypress: a GUI interface to Dow Jones News/Retrieval', *Online*, 18 (1), 72–5.

Scott, J. (1996) 'Online access to international newspapers & wires: a status report', *Database*, 19 (4), 42–9.

Storey, T. and Dalrymple, T. (1996) 'On the Web with OCLC First Search and NetFirst', *OCLC newsletter*, 220, 34–5.

Tenopir, C. (1996) 'Generations of online searching', *Library journal*, **121** (14), 128, 130.

Tenopir, C. (1996) 'Moving to the information village', *Library journal*, **121** (4), 29–30.

Tenopir, C. and Bergland, S. (1993) 'Full text searching on major supermarket systems: DIALOG, DATA-STAR and NEXIS', *Database*, **16** (5),32–42.

Vickery, B. and Vickery, A. (1993) 'Online search interface design', *Journal of documentation*, **49** (2), 103–87.

Webber, S. et al. (1994) *UKOLUG quick guide to online commands*, London, UK Online User Group.

10

CD-ROMs

....

LEARNING OUTCOMES

This chapter reviews the types and applications of CD-ROMs. At the end of the chapter you will:

- be acquainted with the configurations for networking CD-ROMs
- be aware of the range of different types of CD-ROM producers
- be familiar with the range of databases available on CD-ROM
- be aware of some of the issues in searching a CD-ROM database
- have considered some of the key issues in the management of a CD-ROM service for end-users.
....

10.1 Introduction

Optical discs, specifically in the form of CD-ROMs, have become increasingly important as a medium for the storage and dissemination of information during the 1990s. CD-ROMs can be purchased by users and consulted at their own workstation. The price of discs is currently such that many discs users would not buy for personal use, but organizations and libraries buy discs on behalf of end-users. In this context, CD-ROMs represent a means of access to information alternative to online access to external databases via telecommunications networks, including the WWW. When the database recorded on the CD-ROM is the full text of a document such as a directory or an encyclopaedia, CD-ROMs may challenge the market position of the printed book. All three media are likely to continue to coexist, with each finding its market niche. Table 10.1 summarizes some of the applications where CD-ROM is currently an appropriate medium, and others where online and WWW access is more appropriate.

This chapter contains a brief review of CD-ROM network configurations. This is followed by a section covering the suppliers, and another which looks at the types of databases that can be accessed on optical discs. The next two sections deal with various aspects of conducting a search, and managing the CD-ROM-based information service. A final section looks at the future potential for CD-ROM.

10.2 Network configurations

Network configurations have a significant impact on the way in which CD-ROMs can be exploited, especially in a multi-user environment. The basic standalone CD-ROM workstation provides a single user with access to a single disc. Clearly this configuration is incompatible with a networked environment, where users are accustomed to access shared databases via their own workstations. The ideal CD-ROM configuration offers multi-user access to many databases in a way that allows the integration of databases on CD-ROM with other databases used by the information-seeker. First, we consider the basic standalone configuration.

CD-ROM drive linked to a standalone PC

The basic components of the stand-alone configuration are:

- a standalone PC
- a CD-ROM drive
- appropriate software
- a printer (if required).

Most PCs have an integral CD ROM drive, but if this is not available, the PC needs a spare expansion slot via which the drive can be linked. If hard-copy print-outs of the results of a CD-ROM search are required, then a printer is essential. The choice of printer depends upon the environment and the relative priorities associated with noise, print quality and price.

In the early days of CD-ROM, compatibility was a very significant problem. There is much more standardization now, but it is still wise to check that all of the hardware and software components work with one another. The software situation is a little complex. In addition to the operating system of the microcomputer it is also necessary to have:

- device driver software, which tells the microcomputer that a CD-ROM drive is connected and how to communicate with the drive
- retrieval software, which supports the searching of the CD-ROM database (this will be supplied by the producer of the CD-ROM product)
- installation software, which controls the installation of the product on the user's equipment, and supports the setting of configuration options, such as user-defined passwords, and equipment specification.

Networking internal CD-ROM drives

There are two ways to network stand alone drives:

- placing the machines with their internal drives attached on a network; users need to place the disc in their drive before they can use it
- peer-to-peer networking, where one computer acts a the host machine, with the CD-ROM drive on that machine and other PCs able to request access to the database; this approach is easily implemented through Windows for Workgroups, but may be less easy to implement on other platforms; also the performance depends on what tasks the host is performing.

Using file servers and jukeboxes

The file server on a network can be used to provide access to the discs and software, rather than installing the software on individual machines. This file server can be the standard network file server, or may be a dedicated CD-ROM server or optical file server. This can either be directly plugged into the server, or logically connected across the network to the server. A dedicated server is preferable. The load on the network server may be too great, and not all CD-ROM titles will work off the server if they are not network aware. With a CD-ROM server it is easier to have all the discs and their software in one place for updating and general maintenance, and the configuration is expandable, and offering support for higher-capacity jukebox systems.

A jukebox is a device which offers access to a large number of CD-ROM discs. Unlike CD-ROM drives, jukeboxes do not have a read head available for each individual disc. When a user wants to access a particular title it will be loaded by the jukebox and returned to its position after use in the same way as in audio jukeboxes. However, if there is simultaneous demand for more discs than there are drives, the need to swap discs can slow down system performance.

Pre-caching

Pre-caching is a relatively new approach to offering more speedy access to CD-ROM. Some publishers allow the user to copy the data from the CD-ROM disc directly onto a large magnetic hard drive. Pre-caching reduces the requirement for multiple CD-ROM drives, and more users can access the database at any one time. There are, however, a number of disadvantages:

1   Permission to pre-cache (from database producers and publishers) can be expensive.
2   Not all publishers offer pre-caching.
3   The databases have to be updated. When using CD-ROM discs this is achieved by simply replacing the old disc; with a pre-cached system the disc has to be copied across.

Internet access

Another type of pre-caching can be achieved through Internet access. Ultimately this has very little to do with CD-ROM, since the data is not being held on CD-ROM; instead it is held on a remote site, belonging either to the publisher or to one of their appointed agents. The software to access the databases is held locally, with a pointer to where on the Internet the retrieval interface should be looking. This option is being offered by only a limited number of CD-ROM publishers but is likely to become more significant. This solution has many of the same advantages as pre-caching, and in addition, the publisher's technical support department is charged with the task of keeping the system up and running on a 24-hours, seven-days a week basis. Updating of databases is the responsibility of the publisher, and can be done much quicker, and if appropriate more frequently, since the publisher can simply upload the data. The only drawback is that access to the data is subject to any Internet problems.

Reflection   Do you have access to any databases on CD-ROM? Which of the above configurations is used?

Table 10.1 *Comparing CD-ROM and online search services*

Applications where CD-ROM is best	Applications where online searching is best
Multimedia such as books, games and reference materials	Bibliographic databases that are large, frequently used and updated
Standalone titles such as single books	Directories, especially those with frequent updates
CD book collections	ASCII full text, especially large databases
Where content, interface, and search techniques are tied to one another	Image collections or static texts, such as journal articles, where only a few items in a journal collection will be used
Where learning (and not simply answering facts) is part of the experience	Large databases
When serving a relatively homogeneous population such as in a school library	Large numbers of simultaneous users
Where publishers do not publish elsewhere for reasons of security and copyright	Where sophisticated cross-file searching is required
	Where a heterogeneous population requires a great variety in types of sources, subjects or topics, such as in public and university libraries

10.3 CD-ROM publishers and publishing

SIMBA reported that in the United States total CD-ROM unit sales had increased from 2 million in 1992 to 8.5 million in 1993 to 27.8 million in 1994. Forester Research predicted that retail CD-ROM sales would nearly triple from 584 million in 1994 to 1476 million in 1996 and almost 4000 million in 1999. (Tenopir 1996). Some 95% of all new PCs come equipped with CD-ROM drives; this provides an enormous installed base of CD-ROM drives. The bulk of the retail CD-ROM sales are multimedia, with games and children's titles, followed by adult reference, being the most popular sellers. Libraries supplement this personal ownership by offering access to multiple titles. Some 70% of libraries have bibliographic databases on CD-ROM, 59 % have other reference titles, and 32 % have specialized titles. (*Library journal* 1995). For the United Kingdom, a report commissioned by Tinsley Robor predicted that disc output from UK CD manufacturers was set to increase from 272.8 million units in 1995 to 505 million units in 2000, with the proportion of CD-ROM discs increasing from 25% to 35% in the same period. Consumer and education titles make up the largest category of CD-ROM titles. The report predicts further development of CD/online hybridization, in which CD-ROM is used for data storage and online for updates, and digital versatile disc (DVD).

CD-ROM publishing is a relatively easy market to enter, and consequently there are a large number of CD-ROM publishers. Most publishers are not prolific, and many have only a single product. Publishers may be engaged in various other aspects of the information industry. CD-ROM suppliers can be broadly divided into the following categories:

1   **Supermarket CD publishers**, with a very significant catalogue of databases which are produced by other organizations. Examples are Information Technology Supply Ltd and SilverPlatter. Another group are the online service services, such as DIALOG with their KR OnDisc.
2   **Database producers**, who will probably also be making their databases available via online and WWW media. Examples are CA (Chemical Abstracts) on CD, Wilson Business Abstracts, Mintel CD and Biosis GenRef on Compact Disc.
3   **Publishers** such as Blackwell, Wiley and Chadwyck Healey, who started by publishing their own databases on CD-ROM but have added other HMSO and related documents.
4   **Document supply centres** (such as the British Library), who make serials, books and conference proceedings available on CD-ROM.

The market is still volatile, with new products entering the market as others leave. Nevertheless. the number of titles and associated publishers continues to grow.

Reflection   Will the publication of encyclopaedias on CD-ROM lead to the demise of the market for print encyclopaedias? If you think that this might happen, what are the significant advantages to the user of the CD-ROM format that might fuel such a development?

10.4 Databases on CD-ROM

Databases available on CD-ROM are drawn from most of the main categories of database that were listed in Chapter 5. More specifically, the databases currently available on CD-ROM can be grouped into the following categories:

1   **Bibliographic databases**, with or without abstracts, which offer access to the literature of a subject field or list a type of publication, such as patents.
2   **Catalogue** and **book-trade databases** are a special type of bibliographic database. Catalogue databases comprise the records in the catalogue of a major library. Book-trade databases list items published during a given period. Both kinds of databases may be used either to identify the location of specific documents or in the selection of documents during collection development.
3   **Source databases** contain the total contents of a document, including, as appropriate, computer software, images or sound, and maps and charts, as well as any text and numeric data.
4   **Quick-reference databases** are a type of source database. They offer the kinds of facts and figures that are characteristic of directories.
5   **Mixed discs** can be fitted into any of the above categories because they contain a mixture of bibliographic, full-text and quick-reference data. For example, the McGraw-Hill Scientific and Technical Reference Set has both full text and images, while the Nimbus Music Catalogue has text, graphics and sound.
6   **Multimedia databases**, including databases in the CD-I, CD-ROM XA, DVI and CDTV formats. These products offer motion-picture graphics and sound, and often the opportunity to interact with the computer.

Figure 10.1 shows further details of a limited number of databases, and identifies the key features of the databases that might be considered in the selection of databases. The critical criteria will depend to some extent on the nature of the database and the context in which it is to be used. Checklist 10.1 summarizes these criteria. These criteria have much in common with the criteria that might be applied in the selection of a database for online searching. Clearly, in both cases, the first and most crucial question is whether the databases hold the required data.

British Pharmacopoeia

MED	
Publisher:	HMSO
Subjects:	chemistry; medicine & biomedicine; pharmacology; veterinary science
Platform(s):	IBM-PC 486 or compatible with 4MB RAM Windows 3.1 or higher, networkable
Coverage:	United Kingdom
Frequency:	annually
Price:	£500
	£970 for new order

Contains full text data from the print version of British Pharmacopoeia and British Pharmacopoeia Veterinary from 1993 onward. Access to over 2,300 monographs, each of which sets out legally enforceable standards for medical substances and preparations. Runs under Windows and features hypertext links, graphics for chemical structures and infrared spectra, chemical formulae displayed as in the printed version.

British Standards on CD-ROM

ST	
Publisher:	Technical Indexes Ltd
Subjects:	standards
Platform(s):	IBM-compatible PC, MS-DOS, networkable
Frequency:	monthly
Price:	contact CD Complete

Complete British Standards on CD-ROM. Information included by special agreement with BSI. Full text with images divided into 12 sections.

Social Sciences Citation Index

LS/SS	
Publisher:	Institute for Scientific Information (ISI)
Subject(s):	social sciences
Platform(s):	IBM-compatible PC, NEC 9800 series; Apple Macintosh, MS-DOS 3.1 or higher; MS-DOS CD-ROM Extensions; NEC 9800; Apple System 6.0.2 or higher, 640K with 417K free (DOS); 1 MB (Mac), networkable
Coverage:	worldwide
Frequency:	quarterly
Price:	$5,930

Provides coverage of over 1,400 of the world's leading social science journals by title word, cited author, cited work, journal title, author name, and author address. The Related Records feature links and displays all the articles that have one or more references in common. Includes items from 3,200 technical journals.

Social Sciences Index

LS	
Publisher:	H.W. Wilson
Subject(s):	social sciences
Platform(s):	IBM-compatible PC, Macintosh 68020, 68030, 68040 or PowerPC. MS-DOS 3.1 or higher, 485K (DOS); 2MB (Mac), networkable
Coverage:	worldwide
Frequency:	monthly
Price:	$1,295 (annual subscription); $975 (elementary and secondary school rate)

Searchable indexing of 400 core periodicals, starting with February 1983, on a single disc. Specific subheadings and extensive cross-referencing covers the applied and theoretical aspects of 18 specialities, and the title enhancements clarify the content of articles or indicate special features. Complete bibliographic data for easy access.

Fig. 10.1 *CD-ROM databases: some details*

Oxford English Dictionary (Second Edition) on CD-ROM

ENCY

Publisher:	Oxford University Press, Electronic Publishing Department
Subject(s):	dictionaries; languages; linguistics
Platform(s):	Apple Macintosh, Motorola 68030 processor, Apple 6.07 and higher, 2 MB (4MB on printer), networkable, IBM compatible PC
Price:	£495 for single user

Contains the Second Edition of the Oxford English Dictionary, published in print form in 1989, with some modifications. Instant search for every occurrence of one or more specified words, abbreviations, quotations, etymology, headwords and the entire text.

Social Sciences Index

LS/SS

Publisher:	SilverPlatter Information Ltd (UK)
Subject(s):	social sciences; sociology
Platform(s):	IBM compatible PC, MS-DOS 3.1 or higher; Windows, 640K, networkable
Coverage:	USA, Europe, Australasia, Asia
Frequency:	monthly
Price:	contact CD Complete

Offers accurate and timely indexing of over 340 key English-language periodicals in the social sciences, providing up-to-date coverage of this multi-faceted, interdisciplinary field. Coverage includes anthropology, area studies, community health and medical care, economics, ethnic studies, geography, international relations, law, criminology, minority studies, planning, public administration, and more.

UK Markets - Limited Sector Editions

BC

Publisher:	Taylor Nelson AGB Publications
Subject(s):	import & export; market research; marketing; product information
Platform(s):	IBM-compatible PC
Frequency:	quarterly
Price:	contact CD Complete

Provides selections of the interactive data, divided by broad industry category, e.g. food and drink, clothing, construction, paper, packaging, glass & ceramics, basic chemicals, inorganic chemicals etc. UK Production, UK Manufacturer Sales, Exports, Imports and Net Supply to the UK market and Average Price on some 4,800 UK products.

Ultimate Frank Lloyd Wright

ARCH

Publisher:	Microsoft Corporation
Subject(s):	architecture
Platform(s):	IBM-compatible PC, Windows 3.1, Windows 95, Apple Macintosh
Price:	£29.99

This title explores the architect Frank Lloyd Wright's life and designs, both built and unbuilt. It includes illustrations, photographs, narration, music, video and 3D tour of his structures.

Fig. 10.1 *Continued*

Ultimate Human Body

MED	
Publisher:	Dorling Kindersley Multimedia
Subject(s):	anatomy
Platform(s):	Apple Macintosh, LCII, Apple, System 7.0 or higher, 4MB minimum (6MB recommended), IBM compatible PC
Price:	$79.95

An interactive journey inside the human body to discover what every part of the body is called, where it is situated, what it looks like and how it functions. Users can explore the body through three intuitive search paths, The Body Machine, The Body Organs, The Body Systems.

Fig. 10.1 *Continued*

....

CHECKLIST 10.1

Criteria for the selection of databases on CD-ROM

1   Database contents. Coverage, and whether illustrations and other details are included in a full-text database.
2   Currency. Time period covered by the database. How up-to-date is the information, and how frequently are updates issued? Online databases have the potential to be more current than the equivalent CD-ROM database, since CD-ROMs are issued at intervals of, say, a month, and cannot be updated in real time.
3   Backfiles. Backfiles of a large database may occupy a number of CD-ROM discs. Are all backfiles available? How are backfiles split between discs?
4   Retrieval software and indexing. Retrieval software must be user-friendly, efficient and effective. Retrieval software must offer a full range of retrieval facilities, and must be able to support both the novice end-user and the experienced searcher. Indexing must be appropriate and consistent, and the index terms assigned should represent the document well, in addition to being accessible to the user.
5   User interface. One aspect of the retrieval software will be the user interface that it offers. The retrieval software must be not only powerful but also easy to use. The dialogue design should assist all categories of user, and there should be an adequate help system.
6   Post-processing. Once information has been retrieved and displayed on screen, it may be desirable to transfer the information to paper on another disc. Facilities

must be available so that data can be downloaded and printed, and possibly also integrated with information from other sources.

7   Data access time. CD-ROM searching can appear to be slow, since CD-ROM players operate more slowly than hard disk drives, and in addition there may be network delays in transmitting graphical data.

8   Costs. There are two types of costs associated with CD-ROM: set-up costs arising from the acquisition of hardware; and subscription costs arising from the acquisition and updating of discs. The fixed costs associated with subscriptions can be easier to manage than the pay-as-you-go costs sometimes associated with access to online search services. Pricing strategies for CD-ROMs are designed to reflect the extent of use of the database. There are usually different prices for standalone users, single network users, other-size user groups (e.g. 208 users, 9–12 users), and site licenses.

9   Standardization. Standards for CD-ROM were initially a serious problem, and difficulties can still arise if a number of discs from different suppliers are being run on the one workstation or network. It is important to check that all hardware and software components work satisfactorily with one another.

Reflection   Explain in more detail why a subscription-based product is more attractive than a pay-as-you-go service for information managers.

10.5 Conducting a CD-ROM search

CD-ROM products have been specifically designed for ease of use and to facilitate end-user searching. Many offer both novice and expert mode interfaces.

Retrieval facilities are similar to those that might be expected in any information retrieval product. For example, Boolean logic, truncation, field-specific searching, phrase searching and other facilities are featured in most of the software used for retrieval in CD-ROM databases. Some examples are given in Figure 10.2. The unique feature of CD-ROM is the interface and dialogue design.

Some databases and user groups demand special information-retrieval facilities. For example, Disclosure's Global Researcher has features that support the searching and analysis task that a company researcher might need to perform, including those that

- identify companies by name, ticker symbol, geographic location, line of business or financial criteria
- rank companies based on financial performance
- perform instant point-and-click peer-group comparisons
- analyse financial data using an Excel add-in
- create user-defined reports and ratios
- view real-time electronic filings.

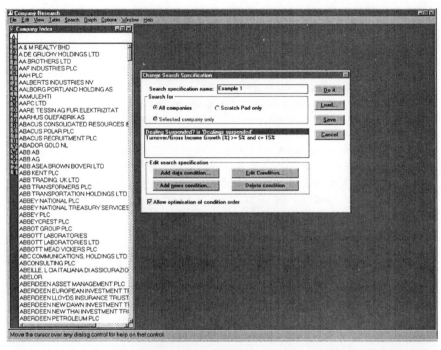

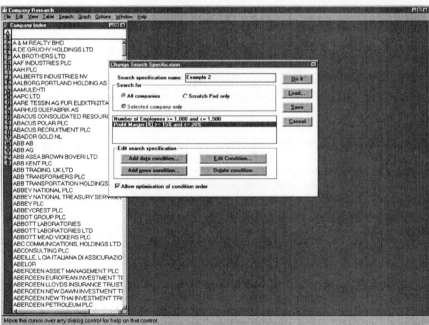

Fig. 10.2 *A CD-ROM search*

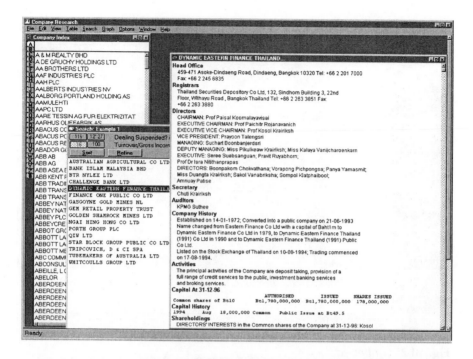

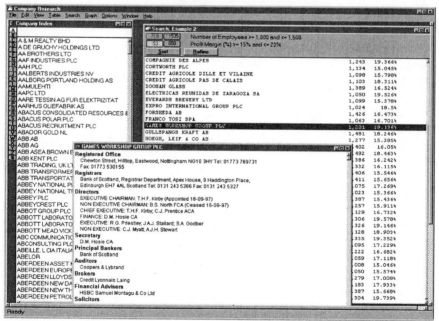

Fig. 10.2 *Continued*

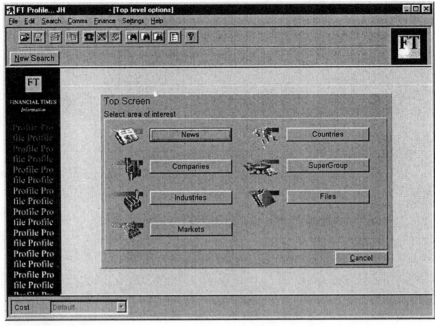

Fig. 10.2 *Continued*

....

CHECKLIST 10.2

Information-retrieval features on CD-ROM

1   Index
- browse index
- number of postings
- cross references
- thesaurus.

2   Search structure
- term selection from index
- term selection from record
- case sensitivity
- search types
- combine searches.

3   Search features
- Boolean
- truncation
- adjacency/proximity

- positional
- arithmetic.

4 *Search profile management*
- speed of performance
- save searched
- purge old searches
- search status
- set and query management
- number of search sets
- search history display
- search modification
- search selection
- statistic gathering.

CHECKLIST 10.3

Interface features on CD-ROM

1 *Operational*
- break
- escape/exit/abort
- input options (e.g. keyboard, mouse, other).

2 *Navigational*
- navigation between records
- navigation within records
- standard options.

3 *Communication*
- screen titles
- terminology
- screen layout – general appearance
- instructions/prompts
- flexible dialogue tailored according to user level
- consistency in prompts, menus and help messages
- consistency in use of colour, typography and graphics
- consistency in use of terminology.

4 *Support*
- online tutor
- online help
- error messages.

10.6 Interface/dialogue design

Earlier reference has been made to the essentially user-friendly interface design of CD-ROM. Figure 10.2 shows some screens from a search on a CD-ROM, and demonstrates the style of interface. The intention of the CD-ROM producers has been to design an interface that allows the end-user to search without the intervention of an intermediary or any previous experience. To this end most CD-ROM interfaces use:

- menus, especially pop-up menus in Windows, and often displaying several menus simultaneously
- colour
- graphics (sometimes)
- help system.

In addition, many CD-ROMs offer a GUI interface option. Unfortunately, however although most of the interfaces are menu-based, beyond this there is little standardization except among the products from a specific supplier. In addition to variability in screen display, there is a lack of standardization in keyboard functions, with different function keys being used for different purposes. It is common, but not universal, to use the F1 key to call Help. Users are likely to encounter a range of different software if they search more than one CD-ROM. These software packages will have different search facilities and different interfaces, and they may be used to search databases with varying contents (e.g. bibliographic and full text) and structure (full text can be divided into sections in different ways). There are two potential strategies for enhancing the usability of CD-ROM interfaces:

1   Design user-friendly interfaces that are so self-explanatory in the context of the task users seek to achieve that they find it very easy to learn further interfaces.
2   Seek to instil some consistency into interfaces, via standard guidelines, or via the use of a client–server configuration.

Some progress has been made with both of these options. GUI-based interfaces, in particular, display a range of menus, help and support. The Special Interest

Group on CD-ROM Applications and Technology (SIGCAT) guidelines released in 1992 were an early attempt to instil some standardization into CD-ROM interface design, and have been successful at least in identifying the 13 basic functions in user interaction with CD-ROM systems. These are shown in Figure 10.3. Intranet technology and the use of the Z39.50 protocol underpins the use of client–server configurations. This allows a library to offer a standard interface to all CD-ROMs that users access through a library, although if users are accessing services from more than one library, they may still encounter different interfaces; the networked user is then still likely to experience significant variability.

Interface design will continue to improve. Graphics and icons offer potential for more attractive and comprehensive interfaces. Eventually the user may seek to control aspects of the interface design, and the use of natural language in dialogues will affect many aspects of the interface design.

10.7 Managing a CD-ROM-based information service

A library or information service that offers information services based on a number of CD-ROM products will need to consider all of the factors listed in Checklist 10.1 in selecting appropriate databases for its clientele. The development of a CD-ROM-based service also raises a number of other issues that need to be addressed. Some of these are day-to-day practical issues that are overlooked at the information manager's peril. Others involve more strategic management

---

Top-level functions
Help (show explanatory information)
Browse index (show terms in indexes)
Search (look for information that satisfies a search statement)
Display (show information on screen)
Print (direct output to hard-copy device)
Download (direct output to electronic media)
Restart (go to beginning of application)
Choose (change discs or databases)
Quit (end the application)

Operational functions
Execute (alert application to begin processing)
Break (interrupt activity in a program)
Escape (back up one step at a time)

Navigational functions
Navigation (movement within a database or search set)

Fig. 10.3 *The functions identified by the SIGCAT Guidelines*

decisions, and require the information manager to consider how the CD-ROM service integrates with other information services available to the library's users. The issues can be grouped into the following categories:

1   **Terms of use**. Ownership of the CD-ROM should be considered. Many CD-ROMs are only leased from the suppliers. Thus, if a subscription is cancelled, a library loses not only its current file, but also any back-files. There may also be restrictions on the downloading of data.
2   **Resources**. Any CD-ROM service will cost money to maintain. The source of resources, whether it be the users or some other budget, must be identified, and any effects on the resources available for other services must be considered.
3   **Impact on staff**. The introduction of CD-ROM offers an ideal opportunity for the end-user to learn to perform his/her own computer-based searching of large databases. Increasingly the information worker will find that his/her role has shifted from that of the intermediary, or searching expert, to that of the trainer and educator. In order to fulfil this role satisfactorily, it is important that staff be well trained not only in using the hardware and software effectively but also in teaching others.
4   **User training**. As indicated above, information staff are likely to find themselves involved in training end-users to perform their own searches. The interfaces on CD-ROM are relatively user-friendly, but most end-users still benefit from some support. If many end-users can be expected to use a service, a programme for end-user training must be planned and executed.
5   **Housekeeping**. All CD-ROMs need to be acquired, catalogued and issued. Acquisition needs to cater for the receipt of regular updates. Some means of control and issue is likely to be necessary in order to avoid discs being mislaid. A booking system may be advisable if discs are very popular.
6   **Other services**. In general, the provision of a CD-ROM-based service has been seen to have positive benefits for the image of the library as a provider of information. This improved image may lead to other opportunities and additional resources, and is also likely to lead to increased demand upon library services. The bibliographic database on CD-ROM will alert users to documents whose existence they would not otherwise have suspected. This may lead to fuller exploitation of existing library resources, and more demand for documents that can be acquired via document delivery and interlibrary loan. There may be some impact on the demand for online searching, but often the two services continue in tandem, meeting differing needs.
7   **Integration**. CD-ROM is likely to be only one of a number of computer-based information services available to a user or in operation in a library. It is important that CD-ROM can be integrated into the wider environment. The user will wish to access CD-ROM via the same workstation that he/she uses for other purposes such as accessing institutional databases. The information

manager may wish to see some common interfaces for searching the different databases available to users.

Reflection   What is the best way to encourage users to evaluate the range of information sources available to them, rather than just using the most convenient?

10.8 The future for CD-ROMs

The number of publishers and products in the CD-ROM marketplace is continuing to increase. A major issue for the future of the medium is the continued development of a consumer market. Table 10.1 summarizes the strengths of competing technologies. In addition to the Internet, CD-ROM may be overtaken by other technologies, such as DVD.

Specific developments that are already under way and that can be expected to continue include:

1   Continuing growth in the number of CD-ROM titles. The most significant growth in recent years has been in the business and professional marketplace; this may continue or there may be a resurgence of emphasis on multimedia titles and a renewed development of the consumer marketplace.
2   Pricing strategies are likely to consolidate in such a way that they recognize the different market sectors for different products. This will partly be content-dependent, so that, for example, encyclopaedias and dictionaries are priced as consumer products, while bibliographic databases are priced for library and corporate purchase. Customers will demand greater transparency and simplicity of pricing strategies for networked use of CD-ROM.
3   Further integration of technologies whereby CD-ROM will be used for core information delivery, while online access, often via the Web, will be used for more current or real-time information to update the data available on the CD-ROM. Consumers will pay for the immediacy of information that is only required occasionally. Frequently required material will be already paid for and available on disc. Also, the high-capacity of DVD may be attractive for some applications.
4   Increasing sophistication of search interfaces, with tailoring to the requirements of specific user groups and types of databases. SilverPlatter's Search Advisor, which works with a GUI interface, may be a model for the future. An intelligent retrieval client, the Search Advisor offers the tools used by professional searchers to develop search strategies, and supports novice searchers in their use of these tools. CD-ROM multimedia databases should be at the leading edge of the enhancement of interface design.

5   Increased sophistication in customer support from suppliers. KR has, for instance, recently launched Crossroads, a Web-based service that provides a forum for users to share their expertise and knowledge, and Learning Center, which links visitors to a range of training options. These include web training sessions that are Web-cast live to participants, and prepared instructional modules.

6   The use of intranet technology to provide access to networked CD-ROMs. For example, KRSite offers access to the Knight Ridder collection of CD-ROMs via corporate intranets.

Summary   CD-ROM has become increasingly important as a medium for the storage and dissemination of information. CD-ROM configurations include: a CD-ROM drive linked to a standalone PC, networked file servers and jukeboxes, pre-caching and Internet access. CD-ROM publishers may be engaged in any of several areas of the information industry. CD-ROM publishers include supermarket publishers, database producers, publishers and document supply centres. The databases available on CD-ROM are equally various. They can be categorized as: bibliographic, catalogue and book-trade, source, quick-reference, mixed and multimedia databases. Facilities for searching CD-ROM may not differ significantly from facilities for searching other databases, but CD-ROM products have led the way in interface design. GUI-based interfaces are becoming common. It is important for information managers to consider key issues in the management of CD-ROM-based information services. CD-ROM is an end-user product, and users who have never successfully searched a database in the past may be expected to use a CD-ROM product with the minimum of assistance. The role of the information manager as intermediary becomes less central, with the training function taking pride of place. The future for CD-ROM will depend upon the development of other storage media, and the relative economics of the use of national and international networks compared with access to CD-ROM more locally.

REVIEW QUESTIONS

1   List the features of the applications for which CD-ROM is particularly suitable.
2   Explain the difference between pre-caching and jukeboxes as means of providing access to CD-ROM.

3   Give some examples of the different types of CD-ROM suppliers.
4   Describe the characteristics of one CD-ROM database.
5   What are the key criteria in the selection of a CD-ROM database.
6   Explain the following search features:
    • search history display
    • search modification
    • truncation
    • term selection from record.
7   Discuss the management of a CD-ROM-based information ser-
    vice.

IMPLEMENTATION CASE STUDY: IMPLEMENTING CD-ROM IN A SMALL ACADEMIC LIBRARY

An Interview with Margaret Robinson, Librarian, Crewe & Alsager Faculty, Manchester Metropolitan University

Interviewer
Could you start by briefly describing the role of the library within the Faculty?

Librarian
The Faculty library facilities comprise two libraries one on each of the Crewe and Alsager sites of the Faculty. The library was previously the library of the former Crewe and Alsager College of Higher Education. The College merged with Manchester Metropolitan University (MMU) in 1992 and became the Crewe and Alsager Faculty of MMU. The library is therefore now one of the several faculty libraries that comprise the library service of Manchester Metropolitan University. However, all other MMU faculties are discipline-based. The Crewe and Alsager Faculty is multidisciplinary, with departments responsible for courses in education, business and management, art, design and performance, humanities, social science, sports science and environmental science. A major issue for the library service is providing an appropriate stock and level of service across such a wide range of disciplines.

The library is the major information and learning resource provider in the Faculty. Priority is accorded to making such resources available to students and establishing effective relationships with staff and students.

Interviewer
What were your objectives in installing CD-ROMs?

Librarian
CD-ROM was first implemented in 1991, when the library did not have any other information-technology-based applications and resources were restricted. One workstation with a CD-ROM drive was installed. This implementation was designed to

enhance the 'i-tech' image of the library at a time when its involvement in IT in other areas was very weak. In addition, the library had at that time a reasonable level of expenditure on periodicals, and CD-ROM was seen as offering an opportunity to encourage students to make better use of the periodicals stock.

Interviewer
Which databases to you make available via CD-ROM?

Librarian
The initial choice of database was difficult. The strategy was to select some general titles that would be broadly of use to many library users. This led initially to the selection of:
- Business Periodicals Index
- General Science Index
- Sports Discus
- ERIC
- *The Guardian* and International ERIC (more recently).

Cost was a significant factor and it was necessary to choose cost-effective options. Expenditure was affected by the need to have a copy of ERIC on both sites of the College.

Interviewer
How do you cater for multiple access?

Librarian
We had moved on from our initial standalone configuration. Most CD-ROMs on the Crewe site are available through a CD-ROM network which runs as an integral part of the Faculty network. Only ERIC, International ERIC and back runs of *The Guardian* are still on standalone machines, but it is hoped to transfer these to network access in the near future. The Alsager site is (currently) less fully networked than the Crewe site, but options for further networking are being explored. Although CD-ROMs are only searchable from workstations in the library, information derived from the CD-ROMs on the Faculty network is automatically saved to the students' network space. The next stage of development is to seek to provide access over the Faculty network to CD-ROMs via workstations in staff offices. Subsequently, access may be available in student drop-in IT workshops in the libraries, and later in student workshops elsewhere on the campus. Issues associated with licensing need to be carefully investigated and resolved before wider network access is offered. Another issue that needs to be considered is user support, especially to workstations that are not located in the library.

Interviewer
What types of users use the CD-ROM?

Librarian

Everybody! CD-ROM is popular with all groups of students, including those on a range of taught programmes and research students. Staff are less well represented as users of CD-ROM, but nevertheless they are beginning to integrate the collection of information via CD-ROM into assignments. This has sometimes caused a surge in use, but this can be managed.

Interviewer

How do you conduct user training?

Librarian

User training is important. When we first launched CD-ROM, we ran a series of seminars, for about ten students, twice a week, but we have never needed to repeat this level of induction. Peer tutoring is an important learning strategy, which makes it unnecessary to specifically build the use of CD-ROM databases into courses. In addition, students are well versed in the use of the Faculty network, and are confident in saving and printing files. Library staff offer three different types of user training:

1   Students are introduced to the range of CD-ROMs available as part of their induction tours.
2   Students and staff can book one-to-one training sessions with members of library staff.
3   Literature searching services are offered to specific student groups. These always include CD-ROM demonstrations.

It is important to recognize that different user groups have different levels of confidence with IT. Staff and mature part-time students, such as those on in-service teacher education courses, may feel most vulnerable and need to be offered support sensitively. The recent availability of International ERIC has been an opportunity to offer staff seminars.

Interviewer

What benefits have the CD-ROMs bought?

Librarian

There have been a number of benefits:

1   CD-ROM has offered much greater access to a far wider range of information sources in an easy-to-use format.
2   Since CD-ROMs can be exploited directly by end-users, they therefore help to increase student/staff exposure to IT.

3   Students are much more likely to use indexes on CD-ROM than their printed equivalents. Generally, CD-ROM has improved the image of the library as a 'high-tech' resource and helped to foster links with other support services.

Interviewer
What factors determined where the workstations were sited?

Librarian
Workstations have been sited as close as is convenient to the library issue desk on each site. An important issue was the availability of security, supervision and support. Also, power supply and network points were important.

Interviewer
What problems did you encounter?

Librarian
There were few teething problems. A good relationship with Computing Services, forged partly through an IT specialist on the library staff, has meant that there have been no serious technical problems and even minor issues were rapidly addressed. The network implementations of CD-ROM 'went live' whilst the finishing touches to the refurbishment of the Crewe library were taking place. This was a busy time: initial problems with printers were quickly overcome by directing students to save the output of searches to their network space and then to print this at workstations in the drop-in facility.
    A more persistent issue is the generation of many more interlibrary loan requests. Initially this absorbed staff time, but since the automation of interlibrary loans this is less of a problem. It has, however, become evident that students may not always be appropriately discriminating in their selection of items for interlibrary loan. We are currently experimenting with tutor vetting of interlibrary loan requests.

Interviewer
Is there anything that you would do differently if you were working through this again?

Librarian
Not much – we might have anticipated the printing problems and avoided the very short-term early difficulties in this area.

Interviewer
What are your plans for future development of the service?

Librarian
Recently we have published some CD-ROM guides for users. In the near future, we expect to increase the number of slots available on the network so that it will be pos-

sible to load more CD-ROMs, and also to make access to CD-ROM available from all workstations on the Faculty network. MMU Library Service is engaged in reviewing the issue of access to CD-ROM and licensing arrangements appropriate to the institution as a whole, and further developments in the Faculty will be informed by the outcome of this review.

Interviewer
Thank you for talking about your implementation of CD-ROM. It effectively illustrates a number of issues surrounding the implementation of CD-ROM in a variety of different library environments.

Interview conducted 1994

References

Tenopir, C. (1996) 'Has online made CD-ROM obsolete?', *Library journal*, **121** (16), 33–4.

Bibliography

Adkins, S. L. (1993) 'CD-ROM: a review of the 1992 literature', *Computers in libraries*, **13** (8), 20–53.

Akeroyd, J. (1989) 'CD-ROM usage and prospects: an overview', *Program*, **23** (4), 367–76.

Armstrong, C. J. and Large, J. A. (1990) *CD-ROM information products: an evaluative guide and directory*, Aldershot, Gower.

Batterbee, C. and Nicholas, D. (1995) 'CD-ROMs in public libraries: a survey', *Aslib proceedings*, **47** (3), 63–72.

Bevan, N. (1994) 'Transient technology? The future of CD-ROM in libraries', *Program*, **28** (1), 271–81.

Biddiscombe, R. (1992) 'Networking CD-ROMs in an academic library environment', *British journal of academic librarianship*, **6** (3), 175–83.

Black, K. (1992) 'CD-ROM networking: the Leicester Polytechnic experience', *Aslib information*, **20** (7/8), 288–90.

Brackel, P. A. (1994) 'Implications of networking CD-ROM databases in a research environment', *South African journal of library and information science*, **61** (1), 26–34.

Bryant, G. (1993) 'Combining online and disc', *Online and CD-ROM review*, **17** (6), 396–8.

Budd, J. M. and Williams, K. A. (1993) 'CD-ROMs in academic libraries: a survey', *College and research libraries*, **54** (6), 529–35.

Anon (1996) 'CD-ROM indexing and authoring systems', *Digital publishing technologies*, **1** (12), 12–16.

Carlton, T. (1995) 'CD-R on the cheap?', *CD-ROM professional*, 8 (4), 20–7.

Cawkell, T. (1996) *The multimedia handbook*, London, Routledge.

Clarke, K. (1993) 'New OVID software from CD PLUS Technologies', *CD-ROM professional*, 6 (6), 230–2.

Desmarais, N. (1989) *The librarian's CD-ROM handbook*, Westport, Conn./London, Meckler.

Diamond, S. (1993) 'Creating text and image CD-ROMs: getting it right the first time', *CD-ROM professional*, 6 (6), 128, 130–1.

Falk, H. (1994) 'CD-ROM recording in every library', *The electronic library*, 12 (5), 304–7.

Hanson, T. and Day, J. (eds) (1994) *CD-ROM in libraries: management issues*, London, Bowker Saur, 25–37.

Jasco, P. (1996) 'The Internet as a CD-ROM alternative', *Information today*, 13 (3), 29–31.

Kirby, H. G. (1994) 'Public library case study: CD-ROM at Croydon Central Library', in Hanson, T. and Day, J. (eds.) *CD-ROM in libraries: management issues*, London, Bowker-Saur, 25–37.

Knight, N. H. (1997) 'Information metering: issues and implications', *Information services and use*, 17, 1–4.

Koster, D. D. (1993) 'CD-ROMs: stand alone or networked', *Library media quarterly*, 21 (2), 127–8.

Lambert, J. (1994) 'Managing CD-ROM services in academic libraries', *Journal of library and information science*, 26 (1), 23–8.

Large, J. A. (1989) 'Evaluating online and CD-ROM reference sources', *Journal of librarianship*, 21 (2), 87–108.

Large, J. A. (1991) 'The user interface to CD-ROM databases', *Journal of librarianship and information science*, 23 (4), 222–35.

Lyon, E. (1991) 'Spoilt for choice? Optical discs and online databases in the next decade', *Program*, 25 (1), 37–49.

McSeàn, T. (1992) 'CD-ROMs and beyond: buying databases sensibly', *Aslib proceedings*, 44 (6), 243–4.

McSeàn, T. and Law, D. (1990) 'Is CD-ROM a transient technology?' *Library Association record*, 92 (1), 261–3.

McBride, J. (1994) 'CD-ROM authoring and mastering: searching for the tools to bring it all together', *CD-ROM world*, 9 (1), 53–5.

Richards, T. (1995) 'Proliferation of CD-ROM retrieval software: stability at last', *Computers in libraries*, 15 (10), 61–2.

Ronen, E. (1994) 'Internet CD-ROM survey', *The electronic library*, 12 (6), 372–3.

Rowley, J. (1995) 'Issues in multiple use and network pricing for CD-ROMs', *The electronic library*, 13 (5), 483–7.

Stratton, B. (1994) 'The transiency of CD-ROM? a reappraisal for the 1990's', *Journal of librarianship and information science*, 26 (3), 157–64.

Worley, J. (1996) 'The CD-word: reflections on user behaviours and user service', *The electronic library*, **14** (5), 411–13.

Wiedemer, J. D. and Boelio, D. B. (1995) 'CD-ROM versus online: an economic analysis for publishers', *CD-ROM professional*, 8 (4), 36–42.

Yeardon, J. (1995) 'Experiences with SilverPlatter Electronic Reference Library at Imperial College', *Program*, **29** (2), 169–75.

11

Document management systems

....

LEARNING OUTCOMES

Document management systems are systems that support the creation, storage, and subsequent retrieval and dissemination, of documents and/or document represen-tations or metadata. In this sense, document management systems are complimen-tary to online search services and other avenues for access to external information. In this chapter the focus is on their basic features and their use in applications asso-ciated with document management within organizations. This is a role that library and information managers may fulfil. Information managers need to be involved in the management of both internal and external information sources. In addition, organizations will wish to share some documents with supplier and purchaser orga-nizations, and other organizations with whom they have a business relationship, so organizations need to be able to make their documents accessible but secure. This accessibility might be achieved through the use of Internet or intranet technologies or on CD-ROM. At the end of this chapter you will:

- understand the basic nature of a document management system and its range of applications
- be aware of the key dimensions of the marketplace for document management systems
- be aware of the facilities in a document management system
- be acquainted with the key aspects of the management of document manage-ment systems
- have considered in some detail some case study systems
- be able to reflect on some of the key issues for the future of document man-agement systems.

....

11.1 Introduction

Document management systems (DMS) are simply systems that support the cre-ation, storage and subsequent retrieval of documents and/or document represen-tations in electronic format. The documents that such systems manage may be in any medium, including text, graphics, sound, still or moving images, video, or any mixture of these in the form of a multimedia document. Thus such systems are applicable in a wide range of different information-retrieval applications, ranging from the access of electronic documents over the Internet and intranets, to access to CD-ROM databases and personal and organizational archives. Many of the applications discussed in other chapters of this book make use of document management systems. Here the focus is on the features and characteristics of document management systems, and their application within organizations for the management of their document collections. This is the context in which information managers are most likely to be confronted with decisions associated with the selection and management of document management systems. In other applications, the features of the document management system, such as their associated retrieval facilities, may influence the effectiveness with which an information resource can be accessed, but the choice concerning the document management system that is in use lies with the database producer.

Many document management systems have close relationships with library management systems, and have emerged from the earlier text retrieval systems that were developed in special libraries and information units. Such software was used in early systems to create abstracting and indexing services and other organizational databases.

Despite the increasing importance of multimedia approaches, many documents within such collections are largely text-based. The volume of text-based information is increasing at an alarming rate, and its diversity of form, from the relatively unstructured memo, letter or journal article, to the more formally structured report, directory or book, is continually broadening. Text-based documents were previously managed through the earlier generations of document management systems, then described as text management systems, or text-retrieval systems. Text management systems were distinguished from other database management software by a set of characteristics that supported the effective management of text-based applications. These characteristics are still applicable to document management systems:

- the ability to handle variable-length fields and the expectation that many of the fields in the records will be of variable length
- access to records usually through an inverted file of index keys or words from the text of the records on the database
- a range of retrieval facilities that support retrieval based on words in records, which are necessary to accommodate the fact that there is limited control over the form in which the search key might appear in the record
- emphasis on the management of one or more distinct databases, where the ability to draw data from a number of related databases is not central to the application
- relatively fixed applications which require limited programming or systems-development facilities.

Table 11.1 *Phases of the Internet document management and publishing process*

Phase	Description	Initiated by
Identify content	Identify a subset of documents to be indexed and made available on the Internet	Systems administrator
Database set-up	Define a database template or framework for the text database, which will store the indices of the processed documents	Systems administrator
Populate database	Perform indexing and populate database with the indices of the processed documents	Systems administrator
Internet enable/ publish	Once the documents have been processed and appropriate Internet connections have been made (i.e. TCP/IP), an MTML input form is created as an interface through which users can enter their search requests	User/client
Process search requests	When search criteria are provided to the HTML form, the text retrieval engine performs a search on the repository, which typically includes building the logic for the search and translating it (if SQL) into a native programming language	User/client
Present results	Display the search results in the form of a hit list, from which users can make selections in order to view a particular document	User/client
View/download original	When the user selects an item from the hit list, the text retrieval engine transmits the required document from its original location and presents it to the client in a viewable format; if the user wants to download the document, a request is made to the server, which assists the client Internet browser in downloading the file	User/client

Document management systems are increasingly used to achieve corporate publication, distribution and storage of documents. The stages in the process that is
associated with making documents available for searching are represented in
Table 11.1. First the systems creator will design an appropriate database environment and set up dynamic search and index support tools such as thesauri. Next
documents are entered and tagged, and converted into appropriate formats. Then
indexing, probably full text, creates a database, which will be uncompressed and
mastered for delivery in whichever format is appropriate. This may include
Internet, CD-ROM, LAN or WAN.

The key issues that a document management system needs to address are

- the integration of mixed computing platforms within an organization
- control over documents once they have been published, including issues
  associated with security and updating
- effective access and retrieval when documents are required.

Reflection   Consider a set of committee minutes prepared within an
organization known to you. What types of control needs to be
exercised over access to this document?

11.2 Applications of document management systems

Figure 11.1 lists some of the wide-ranging areas of application for document management systems. Figure 11.2 lists the applications available from a particular
document management system. Each organization is different and its need for
document management and publishing will be unique. Some organizations have
a number of individual applications, such as maintenance manuals, which need
to be updated and published across a network of maintenance centres or suppliers; others have a major corporate archive of records relating to individuals, such
as the records held by the Inland Revenue. Both types of structure are important
to the organization, but in the second the system may be more integral to the
operation and work processes of the organization. There are also small-scale applications which are used, for example, by individual researchers for creating their
own bibliographic databases. It is important to recognize that many of the data
that an organization handles are textual in nature, although not all of them may
be available in electronic format. Nevertheless, with the widespread use of elec-
tronic-based office practices such as word-processing, electronic mail and electronic data interchange (EDI), an increasing proportion of an organization's
records are in electronic format. Often the appropriate organization and retrieval
of these records can be facilitated by a document management system. It is
equally important to recognize that the document management system will not
be used in isolation within the information systems function of an organization.

Administration	Finance
Correspondence tracking	Credit history
Manual preparation	Capital budget requests
Proposals and procedures	Business plans
Legal	**Manufacturing**
Litigation support	Project control and planning
Control analysis	Process description
Brief preparation	Vendor information
Regulatory filings	Specifications
Legislative tracking	Quality-assurance procedures
Marketing	**Personnel**
Competitive analysis	Skills inventory
Customer/prospect tracking	Résumé tracking
Attitude study analysis	Employee benefit policies
Product descriptions	Self-instruction programs
Questionnaire analysis	Performance reviews
Scientific and engineering	
Technical abstracts	
Journal articles	
Research cross-reference	
Patent information	
Reaction results	

Fig. 11.1 *Some application areas for document management systems*

Compliance documentation for internal regulations
Banking procedures and regulations
Company financial information
Maintenance documentation of defence systems
Encyclopaedia for occupational health and safety
Cheque verification and signature archiving
Train maintenance and repair manuals
Stock Exchange Yearbook of company financial statistics
Internal credit policy manual
Maintenance and repair documentation for the PW 4000 series of jet engines
Surgery and general medical manual
Research testing and other general information for agricultural products

Fig. 11.2 *Applications using INSIGHT (from Enigma Information Retrieval Systems)*

It may be necessary to transfer data in and out of the document management system from and to other databases and associated systems that also operate within the organization. The document management system is merely part of the total information systems environment.

11.3 Review of document management systems

There are upwards of 200 document management packages available on the European and American markets. It is difficult to give an accurate total since, whilst some packages clearly fit into the category of a document management system, others have only some of the desirable characteristics. There is a wide range of packages, running mostly on UNIX or Windows platforms. Some are designed to support the management of the large distributed and shared database of an international organization, and possibly also offering some customer access for users outside the organization. Others are designed for individual personal use. Some have their origins in the creation of bibliographic and later full-text databases, and were previously described as text-management systems or text retrieval systems. Others have a lineage rooted in document creation and desktop publishing.

Table 11.2 lists some document management systems together with their suppliers. Price is often a good indicator of the expected market and the size of database that the software is designed to handle. Cheap single-user PC-based packages may cost a few hundred pounds. Larger multi-user systems to support huge databases may cost anything from a few thousand pounds to over 100,000 pounds. This wide range emphasizes the wide range of applications for which this software is suitable. Most of the larger systems are not sold at a fixed price. A price range can be specified, and the price for an individual configuration will depend upon the requirements of that system. With all of its inherent complexities, pricing of CD-ROM and online access is straightforward compared with pricing of DMS products. The big problem is the software developer's need to cover every different type of application for which a product with considerable connectivity might be used. Figure 11.3 shows the pricing for Personal Library Software. This shows the need to quote prices for each of several different modules, and to cover different numbers of multiple users, as well as developer's, database administrators' and searcher workstations.

Table 11.2 *Some document management systems*

System	Supplier
askSam	AskSam Systems
BASIS	Information Dimensions Inc.
CAIRS	CAIRS Text and Library Systems
DB/TextWorks	Soutron
Clearview and Clearnet Authoring and Retrieval	Clarinet Systems Ltd
Insight	Enigma-Sumitomo UK
TINlib	EOS International
AIRS	Euritis S A
FOLIO	FOLIO
OLIB	Fretwell Downing Informatics Ltd

Table 11.2 *continued*

HEADFAST	Head Software International
ODARS	Infoware Gmbh
Recall Plus	Insoft Ltd
Muscat	Muscat Ltd
PLWeb	Systematic Datasearch Ltd
ZyIMAGE	ZyLAB
WebVISION	Abacus Software Ltd
Reference Manager	Research Information Systems

PLS Pricing

Personal Librarian

1–5 users	$495 each
6–30	$175 each
31–100	$115 each
>100	$ 50 each

Additional retrieval stations
$50–$115 each, depending on number of users

Additional indexing stations
$50–$175 each, depending on number of users

PLWeb $5,000–$15,000, depending on CPU
PLWeb-CD $5,000 license, plus negotiated per title/per disc or per seat
   royalty fees
PL Sync Web add-on utility $2,000

Callable Personal Librarian

Developer's License	$20,000
additional operating system	$5,000
Required annual support	$4,000

Personal Agents
$14,000–$35,000, depending on CPU

CD-ROM Licenses
   Plan A
      £10,000 per title, as credit against royalties
      7.5% royalty on net revenue of the disc
      $1,500 annual support/upgrade fee
   Plan B
      $10,000 per title, as credit against royalties
      $25 royalty per disc, plus $5 royalty per disc per upgrade (max. of $15 per year)
      $1,500 annual support/upgrade fee

Fig. 11.3 *Pricing structures for one document management system: PLS*

Reflection   What should guide the pricing of document management
            systems?

Often it might be appropriate to purchase some modules and add others later. Many of the larger systems have been in the market for more than 15 years, and there is a level of stability about these participants. Some smaller, PC-based systems, particularly those where there are other versions running on larger machines, have also been available for a number of years. In this sector of the market, however, new systems emerge and others die.

Checklist 11.1 summarizes some of the key features of document management systems in a form that is suitable for use as a basic list of criteria when evaluating such systems. We shall go on to make a few comments on some of the more important issues.

CHECKLIST 11.1

A checklist for the evaluation of document management systems

1 *Defining the database*
   - Basic facilities
   - What parameters are specified at definition?
   - What parameters can be modified once data has been added?
   - Display of data structure
   - Modification of data structure, both before and after database has been added
   - Relational database

2 *Data entry*
   - Pre-formatted screens
   - User-definable screens
   - Word-processing and document-creation facilities
   - Easy amendment of existing records
   - Easy deletion of existing records
   - Immediate retrieval on all keys
   - Check for duplicate records
   - User-defined fields
   - Variable- and fixed-length fields
   - Flexible field lengths
   - Multimedia options
   - Use of Windows to offer help and display authority lists
   - Protected screen areas, e.g. labels
   - Data validation

3 *Indexing*
   - Constraints on indexing terms, e.g. length
   - Stop-lists

- Go-lists
- Facilities for handling personal and corporate names
- Controlled- and natural-language indexing
- Selection of fields for indexing and tagging
- Definition of field-indexing characteristics
- Authority control for subject terms, showing synonyms, homonyms, broader terms and narrower terms

4   *Information retrieval*
- Boolean search operators
- Field-limited searching
- Proximity searching
- Truncation
- Range searching
- Search history
- Save search
- Online help and documentation
- Display of index
- Display of thesaurus
- Use of related terms in searching
- Hyperlinking
- Note search
- Search modes for different types of users

5   *Output facilities*
- Pre-formatted screen display of output
- User-defined screen display for output
- CD-ROM publication option
- Web publishing option
- Printed output formats, both pre-formatted and user-defined
- Special print formats and other facilities for SDI
- Table creation and statistical analysis facilities

6   *Security*
- Passwords
- User IDs
- Read-only access
- Access restricted to certain databases, records, and/or certain fields

7   *Other facilities*
- Other facilities such as a user-friendly interface, appropriate support, and hardware compatibility, are common to all types of software package, and have been listed in Chapter 4.

Support and maintenance are important for any component of a computer system. Upgrades of software and other support are usually available in exchange for the annual maintenance fee. Reputable systems are under continual review, and an upgrade of the software can be expected every year or so. Other support that may be available includes: help desk, manuals, on-site training, off-site training, consultancy and a user group. Clearly the quality and cost of these facilities are important, as well as their availability. Most of the larger systems offer a good range of support, but users of simpler systems are often assumed to be able to manage with the manual alone.

Document capture or input must be possible in an efficient and accurate manner. A preliminary stage to document input must be document definition. Most DMS handle a number of different document types, with each type having a variety of document attributes. Document types should normally include types for both structured documents and mixed document components such as text, images and multimedia objects. Document attributes are the metadata that are used for access to the documents, such as author, title, date, category, abstract, version and security level. Normal options for document capture or input are:

- online via keyboard or other inputting device such as a scanner
- downloading data from another system, such as that of an online search service
- batch entry from external databases
- entry via word-processing package or another database package.

Editing facilities for updating records are important, and should provide opportunities for protected labels and fields, and validation of data on some fields. Some systems have restrictions on record size, the number of fields per record and other record characteristics, which may cause particular problems with full-text databases. Similar features should be available for data entry as support data entry in a catalogue maintenance system or any other database system. Duplicate record detection should be available to cater for records or documents derived from a variety of sources that might potentially have overlapping coverage.

One element of data that will be entered is indexing terms. Certain fields in the record may be reserved for the entry of terms from a controlled indexing language. These terms will be drawn from a thesaurus or similar list. Indexing is facilitated if the thesaurus is available in electronic form and can be consulted during input by, for instance, displaying an appropriate part of the thesaurus file in a window. The use of a thesaurus is a quality-control device which increases the consistency in the assignment of index terms within the database Most systems create inverted files to cater for these keywords. Automatic indexing on the text of other specified fields in the record, otherwise described as automatic population of certain attribute types, can be available on attributes such as text, author and date. Most systems use a stop-list, to which the information manager may add words, to eliminate unnecessary entries in the inverted files. Some systems use a go-list as a basis for automatic indexing. Only terms in the go-list are added to the inverted file. Any terms that do not appear in either the go-list or the stop-list will be displayed for consideration.

Reflection   Explain the difference between a go-list and a thesaurus.

Software suppliers with a history of publishing rather than structured document management are offering a full range of desktop publishing features. This may include features such as:

- visual desktops in which documents can be easily arranged for chapter ordering
- book catalogues which manage groups of document
- ease of access to certain formats, such as word-processing, tables, charts and graphics
- advanced tools to support the creation of graphics and images.

The most sophisticated of these packages have an object-oriented architecture. Group working is supported by view-only facilities, coupled with annotation. Support for multiple languages may also be available, and special features that support the creation of SGML documents. Some of these manage document objects rather than complete documents.

Other features that are becoming increasingly important in systems that manage document rather than record creation include:

- version control – to manage document versions throughout the lifecycle
- access control – to allow different types of access to documents, as well as to implement information security policies for secure document access
- tracking – to track document access and change, creating a history to support audit requirements
- templates – for defining standard document types, behaviour and establishing consistent application properties.

Once the data have been entered and indexed, they should be available for use. Online searching will account for a major component of the use of most systems. In this context the range of information-retrieval facilities is important. Nearly every search facility is present in virtually all of the larger systems, but there are occasional omissions of which an intending purchaser should beware. Some include special facilities such as support for natural-language searching and fuzzy searching. On smaller systems, although there has been a significant increase in functionality over recent years, only a selection of the possible retrieval facilities may be available. The size of the database, its subject area and the inclinations of the users must be considered when selecting the package with the appropriate subset of retrieval facilities.

Interface design is an important factor in being able to perform a search effectively. Most DMS now offer GUI-based interfaces, which lends the advantages for information retrieval listed in Chapter 7. Some systems offer different interfaces for different categories of user, such as expert or novice modes. Multilingual interfaces are a feature of a few systems.

Other outputs from a database are likely to be in printed format. Clearly the range of potential outputs depends upon the nature of the records in a database. Most printed outputs will be formatted lists of records in the database. Some systems offer a number of pre-defined formats from which the information manager may select. Other systems, in addition, allow users or information managers to design their own formats, and a few systems have a sophisticated report language, which allows a great deal of flexibility in the design of reports, and even some analysis of management data. Some systems also offer specially designed facilities to support the generation of SDI notification and printed indexes. Both of these topics are explored further in Chapter 12.

Security is important in any multi-user database environment. The first level of security is concerned with database security. Features such as automatic recovery subsequent to a system failure are important in maintaining the integrity of the database. Access to the database is another aspect of data security. The better systems offer selected access, according to user group, to specified databases, specified documents or records, or specified fields. Thus the early definition of document types and attributes is an important device in determining the document views that individual users have on the database. Some users may have read-only access, whereas others may be allowed to change the data. Important categories of use might be producer, consumer and administrator. Considering the document attributes identified above, the consumer may only have access to the author and title, the producer may have access also to date, category and abstract, and the administrator may also have access to version and security. It is important that this should be specifiable. The chief security measures offered are passwords and user identification numbers. Security log in is useful to report any attempts to breach security. Data encryption is a feature in some document management systems.

Some systems also have software that automates the workflow associated with document management, and support document scanning and capture.

Total information management is the ultimate aim. This means that a document management system supplier must either offer a range of integrated modules or ensure that data stored in the system can be handled by other software. Interfaces with various types of business software such as word-processing and spreadsheet software are extensive. Many systems also operate with electronic mail, downloading and graphics software. Some also interface to image processing, accounting, financial modelling and chemical structure software. There is a major divide between those systems that are marketed alongside library management systems and targeted to the corporate information manager, and those that are not.

11.4 Retrieval facilities

The retrieval facilities associated with a document management system are central to the effective operation of the system, and indeed serve to distinguish such systems from other database systems. These facilities were once unique to text management systems and online searching. With increasing connectivity, many more users need sophisticated search facilities as they seek to navigate their way through vast quantities of knowledge. Accordingly, more and more of the search facilities that were once unique to text management systems are now to be found in the search engines on the Internet and library public-access systems. Nevertheless, DMS have continued to refine indexing and search facilities. Some offer unique indexing facilities, including indexing on any field, and combinations of automatic indexing, tagged indexing (terms manually selected from text), manual keyword indexing and relational indexing. Thesaurus construction and maintenance facilities are important, and may, for instance, allow the automatic posting of preferred and macro (generic group) terms. The use of GUI interfaces has facilitated search strategy editing, recall of earlier search sets, browsing, and the selection and highlighting of relevant documents for later printing or downloading to a personal database.

For those DMS systems that did not previously offer hypertext searching, this has been one of the major innovations in recent years. Such a facility is important in any client search interface and in other contexts where the DMS might be used over the Internet or an intranet. Hypertext is usually achieved through clicking on the hypertext link. In a multimedia database, these hypertext links may be pictures, images, spreadsheets and word processed documents. Other new facilities include 'note search', which allows the user to collect selected terms from the output and to use these as a basis for another search if required.

Figure 11.4 demonstrates how some of the information-retrieval facilities in one document management system might be used to perform a search.

Reflection   Describe the information retrieval facilities that are used or available for use in Figure 11.4.

The phases identified in Table 11.1 are a good representation of the elements of document publishing in this context, but elements of the application of document management and publishing vary between systems. Specifically, variations exist in:

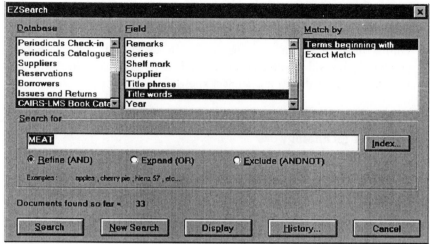

Fig. 11.4 *Searching in a document management system: CAIRS*

- the location of the document indexes, which can be placed either locally on the application server, or remotely with the data
- the way in which queries are submitted; requests must be submitted in a query format that can be interpreted by the text-retrieval engine, which may range from proprietary databases to ODBC-compliant databases accepting standard SQL queries
- the support for administrative functions, such as security, billing and logging and database administration
- presentation and document viewing; documents might be converted to HTML format and then indexed, or converted 'on the fly' during retrieval, or not converted at all but viewed with appropriate viewer technology
- the range of search features.

The really large systems need to be capable of operating on multiple servers to serve vast user communities and store vast databases. This requires VLDB (very large database) capability to allow an index to be spilt physically across several files.

11.5 Database quality

As the number of databases available expands, expectations regarding database quality are becoming more exacting. Quality must be achieved in three domains:

1 **Database production**, including the structural and compilation of the database; accuracy and consistency are important.

2   **Computer implementation**, or specifically the system that makes the data available.
3   **Online retrieval and use**, or the system by which data are selected and employed; this will be affected by the end-user's experience in the areas of technology, methodology and subject knowledge.

11.6 Document management and publishing and intranet and Internet technology

The shift in emphasis from storage to access has been accompanied by a shift of focus in document management applications towards publishing. Many of these publishing activities will take place in an Internet or intranet environment.

What is the attraction of a document management system in this environment? What is the difference between such Internet text retrieval products and Internet search engines such as Yahoo and Lycos? Yahoo and Lycos work on repositories of HTML documents. However, HTML-only indexing and retrieval tools have limitations. In the corporate environment, considerable information exists in documents that are not HTML-structured, such as word-processing documents and spreadsheets. If these repositories are large it may not be feasible to convert them to HTML documents, or if they are changing it may not be desirable to manage an ongoing conversion process. In such cases Yahoo and Lycos cannot index or search the documents. Internet text-retrieval products support the indexing of unstructured documents, and provide users of those indices with full-text searching capabilities. The original document format can be directly searched and made available on the Internet through an HTML search form. These capabilities facilitate the publishing of internally generated documents for either Internet or intranet use.

Client search software can be installed on any remote PC connected via a network to the DMS central database. Any number of clients must be able to search simultaneously on the DMS database, without interfering with updating or other activities being performed on the database. Document management systems, unlike other information-retrieval systems, such as public catalogues, or electronic documents published on CD-ROM (see below) and online search systems, need to be able to support clients that allow database administration and systems administration functions to be performed. Also, options such as user selection of colours and fonts can support variation in the search environment to suit a specific user on the PC. Figure 11.5 shows the software components in a CAIRS-WEB application. The database server manages the underlying CAIRS database, whilst the Web server manages the interface that is available to the user over the Web. The user views the HTML user screens, which are defined using HTML and Java with CGI scripts.

CAIRS-WEB

CAIRS-WEB server comprises a series of software elements which provide you with complet control over the information you provide via the Web and how that information is found by, a presented to, your users.

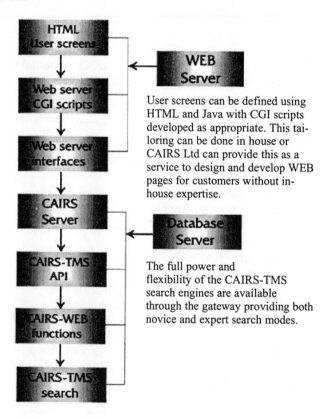

User screens can be defined using HTML and Java with CGI scripts developed as appropriate. This tailoring can be done in house or CAIRS Ltd can provide this as a service to design and develop WEB pages for customers without in-house expertise.

The full power and flexibility of the CAIRS-TMS search engines are available through the gateway providing both novice and expert search modes.

Fig. 11.5 *Interfacing CAIRS-WEB with the Internet*

11.7 CD-ROM output

CD-ROM output modules allow database producers to create a searchable version of their databases and to store it on CD-ROM. This CD-ROM product can then be marketed, and is one important route in the direction of electronic publication for a number of libraries and other organizations involved in the creation of unique data archives that might be marketable to individuals and other organizations. This product will include a version of the DMS software which allows the user to search the database. In-house CD-ROM publishing has been facilitated by the increased availability of CD-recordable drives.

There are some CD-specific factors that may affect the selection of an appropriate document management product:

1   Any software that produces working files on the PC's hard disk is not appropriate for CD publishing.
2   There is no need for features associated with ease and speed of indexing, because the end-user is not updating or indexing the database.
3   Some document management packages are bound with authoring tools. This locks the publisher in to one producer, but the integration may lead to enhanced efficiency.

....

CHECKLIST 11.2

Factors for document management systems for CD-ROM publishing

The ability to handle complex queries
Whether content may be or must be structured into files, each separately indexed
Whether the system is general-purpose or was particularly designed for CD-ROM applications
What data types may be imported, linked to the text, and published on the disc
What authoring tools are available
How easy it is to work with the technology in-house
How much the look and feel can be customized
Whether retrieval and output functions can be customized
Whether there are links to use-metering software
The ability to run create discs which will run on more than one computing platform, with a suitable runtime version for each distributable on the CD
The ability to handle HTML, and to move seamlessly between material held on CD-ROM and the Internet/intranet.

....

11.8 Managing document management applications

Document management systems undergo the same systems life-cycle phases as other computer-based information systems. As outlined in Chapter 6, these phases are:

*   analysis
*   design
*   implementation
*   operating evolution

- decay
- replacement.

The management of document management systems must take in all of these phases in the life-cycle. Analysis, design and implementation are important, but operating evolution should be the longest phase. During this phase, key issues for the information manager are likely to be monitoring, maintenance and planning. There are four components in any system:

- users
- software
- hardware
- databases.

They all need monitoring and maintenance if a system is to continue to operate effectively. There are some further specific issues that need attention:

1   Monitoring and, where necessary, improving system performance. This may involve testing to ensure that the hardware configuration is satisfactory and that the appropriate database structures have been adopted for optimum performance. As databases grow, and the number and nature of users changes, it may be necessary to make adjustments to procedures or to add extra hardware. Monitoring should identify any developing mismatches between the system management and user requirements.
2   Monitoring and adjusting database quality. Coverage and currency of the data may be important. Other considerations include accuracy and security.
3   Monitoring the use made of the system. Who uses the system and what information do they draw from it? How do they use the data? Do users of the system suggest any potential areas for further development, or any problem areas that need resolution?
4   Maintenance of users' skills in the effective use of the system. Documentation must be updated, and regular training courses should be available to new users and those who need to update their skills.
5   Maintenance of software. The twin concerns in this area are the implementation of software upgrades and the negotiation of any problems that arise as a result of the software being used in slightly different ways from tried-and-tested procedures.
6   Maintenance of hardware. Effective troubleshooting when hardware malfunctions is important in building confidence in the system.
7   Maintenance of databases. Open databases need additional data input on a regular basis. One of the main activities during the operating evolution of the system will often be the updating, editing and deletion of database records.

If any breaches of security occur or databases are corrupted, then attempts must be made to rectify the situation.

8   A preliminary phase of planning is the monitoring of developments in technology with a view to incorporating new features into the local system.

9   Planning for any major system changes as the objectives of the organization change and systems need to adapt to accommodate these changes.

Special issues that need to be considered when publishing databases over the Internet include:

1   **Access**. Ensuring that access to the database is stable, but also that users only have access to the files on the server to which they are entitled. Security must be afforded for confidential information such as staffing or financial records. Search speed is also crucial; this requires a sufficiently powerful file server.

2   **Database quality and maintenance**, including appropriate indexing, needs just as much attention in the Internet environment as in other contexts.

3   **Support**, often in the form of online help, but possibly also accompanied by printed documentation. A telephone or e-mail contact point for when things go wrong is also often necessary. Also, communication with users about new developments is important.

4   **Marketing**. Databases need to be promoted. Channels include electronic mailing lists and bulletin boards. Other channels such as press releases and receptions still remain important, as are any other contacts with key user groups, such as those at exhibitions. The databases also needs to be included in database directories and Internet resource guides. Demonstration disks are valuable.

It is difficult to make generalizations about the management of document management systems because of the wide range of application areas, encompassing both small personal systems and much larger multi-user systems serving thousands of users. Larger systems will be operating within an environment where other information systems are also in operation. They may have dedicated processors, but databases supported by document management systems are certainly likely to be accessed through an organization-wide network, through which users also access other databases and applications. In this context the management of the document management system must be integrated into, or interfaced with, the management of the information systems in the organization as a whole. Ideally, an organization should use strategic information systems planning to develop an information systems strategy that will support the objectives of the organization. Document management systems should feature in such an information systems strategy.

    In an environment where an organization has developed an information systems strategy, the management of document management systems may be subsumed into the general management of the information systems within the organization. This may affect the role of the information manager and the degree of control that can be exercised over the document management system, either for the better or otherwise. Nevertheless, the issues listed above still need to be addressed if an effective system is to be maintained.

11.9 Two examples of document management systems

CAIRS

CAIRS has for a long time offered facilities that cover both document management and library management. The product range includes:

- CAIRS- IMS – a free text-indexing and retrieval system
- CAIRS-LMS – a library management system
- CAIRS-MDS, which provides a hypertext linkage between data held in a CAIRS system and an external multimedia resource on the same computer or local network
- CAIRS-TMS and CAIRS-ARC – text and image management for archives and museum collections
- CAIRS-TLMS – a combined library management system and text management system for large industrial, academic and public libraries
- CAIRS-Retriever – client GUI-based search software
- CAIRS-CDS – CD–ROM creation and search software
- CAIRS-WEB – supporting Web publishing.

Many of the features of CAIRS are shared by several of these products. CAIRS-IMS is the document indexing and management system.

CAIRS-IMS is described as a free text-indexing and retrieval system, which is suitable for network applications, in which many users will access the same database. User-designed catalogues can be set up and indexed in a variety of different forms. In addition to author, title and ISBN, indexing can be supported on any field, including free text, phrase, automatic, tagged indexing, manual keyword and relational indexing. Multiple authors and corporate authors can be differentiated, and titles and abstracts can be indexed on every word using built-in stop lists.

A thesaurus construction and maintenance system is provided, allowing the automatic posting of preferred and macro terms. Also supported are broader and narrower relationships with search aid and related terms. Full browse and auto-search expansion are available.

Expert and novice search systems cater for all levels of user. Standard features include full Boolean, nesting, profile editing, recall, expansion, browse, selection and highlighting. Other features include bulletin and index generation, SDI, security, command and menu modes, data editing, import/export and report generation. When used with CAIRS-MDS, CAIRS-IMS can hyperlink to pictures, images, word-processed documents and spreadsheets.

CAIRS-Retriever can be used as a client companion to CAIRS-IMS. It can be installed on any remote PC connected via a network to a CAIRS database. Any number of CAIRS-Retriever clients can be running simultaneously on the same CAIRS database. Controls can be put in place by means of a password-protected set-up enabling cross-database searching, field search and output choice selection, standard output device formats, and truncation and field-descriptor options. User selection of colours and fonts is provided along with an array of controls that can vary the search environment to suit a specific user on the PC. A switchable note-search facility is available that allows the user to collect selected terms from the output. These terms are then used for another search if required. Full set-oriented searching is supported, and the sets can then be incorporated into search expressions. Retriever can use a thesaurus and index scan and select searching.

BASISPLUS

BASISPLUS has been developed and is marketed by Information Dimensions as a document management and retrieval system for an entire organization. The software is designed to manage electronic documents in a variety of different formats and created by, for example, fax machines, mainframes, PCs, photocopiers and even typewriters. As a comprehensive and integrated document management system, it can:

- easily find documents regardless of how or where they were generated
- perform instant updates
- always find the latest version
- make sure others have access to any revised documents
- secure sensitive or classified documents
- record document history
- simultaneously display graphics, images and text
- distribute documents to any number of presentation applications
- distribute processing to achieve maximum utilization of equipment.

Information Dimensions claim that 'BASISPLUS is based on the five pillars of document management and retrieval: finding, managing, controlling, distributing information, and an integrated environment. We consider each of these briefly in turn.

Finding documents

BASISPLUS offers the full range of search facilities expected in a text management system. It is possible to search for specific words and phrases within the text, and to:

- search a document's table of contents
- search on any document component, such as title, author, publication date, revision or number
- find information based on any word, phrase, topic or data value
- search by spelling words phonetically
- browse indexes to get ideas for possible search terms
- search with prefix, suffix, or embedded string wildcards
- expand search terms, whether by using the thesaurus automatically, or by selectively creating customized thesauri, or by using commercial thesauri.

Managing the document collection

BASISPLUS works as an information administrator. When a document is changed, BASISPLUS automatically places the new version of the document in the database and immediately makes the necessary changes to the index file. BASISPLUS can also monitor when changes are made and by whom. In the event of a media failure, BASISPLUS can restore the document collection to its original state by replaying the journal transactions of the database. BASISPLUS ensures that the complete document collection is intact and that retrieved documents are current and accurate. BASISPLUS can display and export the text of any document in a readable format, and also supports the Digital Document Interchange Format standard. Compound documents with attributes such as type font and references to graphics, photos, charts and images can all be successfully handled.

Security

Controlled access to a document collection makes it more shareable. BASISPLUS allows groups of documents or individual document parts to have both read and write protection. Flexible document protection can be particularly important when there are several contributors to a document. Writers need to check their sections simultaneously for modification. Readers need to know when they are looking at documents in revision, and revised portions of the document need to be immediately available once a revision is complete.

Distributed workload

Distribution can mean one of three things:

- distributing documents between unlike devices
- distributing pieces of documents to people
- processing distributing across a network.

Documents with mixed objects of text, images and graphics should be viewable whenever the desktop can support their presentation. Workstations, from unsophisticated non-programmable terminals through to highly intelligent desktops, must be able to display documents.

The second form of distribution is the extraction of formatted sections of documents to share them throughout a user population. For example, with BASIS-PLUS you could retrieve all of the documents created over the past 12 months and extract the author, title and date of each. This could then be presented in a report format and distributed via electronic mail or exported to an external file.

The third form of distribution is client–server processing, whereby machine resources are shared across a network. Client programs in BASISPLUS include user interfaces, data dictionaries, context-sensitive help and user-defined search strategies.

Integration

Integration has a number of facets. One important issue is the ability to support interfaces running on a wide range of different workstations. BASISPLUS interfaces range from powerful command interaction to graphical user interfaces.

BASISPLUS also offers a set of application development tools to support the development of specific applications. For example, BASISPLUS offers a text-retrieval-oriented 4GL, a complete application-programming interface, and search service-language precompilers for FORTRAN and COBOL.

Images also feature in the fully integrated document. Document management systems must be able to integrate with imaging systems. The document management system is the link between the image and the searcher. Using BASISPLUS you can find images by searching:

- auto-generated tags such as image numbers
- image captions
- key words that describe the image
- full text associated with the image.

BASISPLUS has been designed to be portable across a number of different platforms. A portion of its code is written specifically to exploit the native I/O services, character manipulation, and memory management for each search service platform. Thus it is possible to port BASISPLUS across platforms without sacrificing proprietary hardware capabilities.

11.10   The future

As more and more organizations recognize the value of effective management of their electronic document collections, the role for DMS will become ever more significant. It is likely that a significant number of these applications will be supported by intranet technology, because this offers the immense attraction of platform independence. Large and international organizations will always have a mixture of platforms and generations of workstations. Accordingly, the main question for suppliers of DMS is whether these applications will make use of the latest versions of established document management systems, or whether the new intranet products will absorb a significant proportion of the marketplace.

Other key focuses for development in recent years have been:

1   **Interface design.** Over less than ten years there has been a transition from extremely unfriendly command-based interfaces, with equally unbeguiling printed user manuals, to colourful, multimedia GUI-based interfaces with embedded help. Help systems may be seen in the form of a tutor that can be switched on and off as the user chooses. Different types of interface to support novice and expert searching are fairly common. Whilst existing systems are a significant improvement on earlier systems, there is still scope for more detailed investigation which will lead to improvements in design, as information is gathered about the ways in which users interact with such interfaces. In time, concepts such as Boolean logic will become familiar even to the novice users of a specific system, and users will become less patient with interfaces that do not offer the full functionality for searches which provide high precision and recall. Users will be willing to learn, and interfaces must support the learning that is necessary for all searchers to use the full functionality of the retrieval facilities. Embedded help which gauges the user's level of understanding and responds accordingly will be necessary.

2   **Open systems.** Earlier text information management systems ran on an amazing range of operating systems and hardware platforms, and it was a real challenge to the software supplier to maintain all versions of the package. Over the past few years, there has been a general trend towards the development of systems that run under standard operating systems such as UNIX and Windows. This has made software easier to maintain, and more portable from one hardware platform to another. A further element of portability is the ability to move documents between systems. Further improvements that support open systems are to be expected.

3   **Multimedia and image handling.** Data storage on CD-ROM and associated media significantly enhances the potential for integrating the storage and retrieval of text and graphics, pictures and video. Most of the larger systems have multimedia capability. Indexing of the content of multimedia docu-

ments is an area of significant research interest which should lead to innovations in systems over the next few years.

4 **Optical character recognition** (see Chapter 2) has improved significantly in recent years. Documents can now be scanned directly into databases. If the text of a document is to be recognized on a character-by-character basis, then the accuracy of the scanning is crucial. Accuracy is now good on the best machines, but scanned text may still need editing and checking for some applications. OCR is fuelling the creation of large corporate electronic document collections. Such collections require document management systems which manage not only publication and retrieval, but also archiving and weeding functions.

5 **Internet and intranet publishing**. The technology is available to support wide publication of corporate documents, not only to corporate users across global organizations, but also to international customer and supplier communities. Over the next few years organizations will make decisions about how to exploit this technology. This will necessitate the formulation or revision of information access policies, and attention to security policies and practices.

6 **Workgroup publishing**. Suppliers are beginning to revisit the document creation aspect of document management and to incorporate features that support team-based document creation. As the demand to create more documents in multimedia format grows, so the facilities for group-work publishing will need to become more sophisticated.

7 **Increased use of hybrid publication**, including the use of disc/online features necessary to support integration of access to data in different formats. This will include indexing facilities that can provide access to data stored in these different formats.

8 **Pricing strategies** for DMS are amazingly complex, reflecting both the management and the publishing applications of DMS. Other parts of the information industry are beginning to recognize that complexity in pricing strategies is not popular with customers, be they corporate customers or end-users. This issue will need to be re-visited.

9 **Increasing globalization**, with applications supporting organizations operating across several countries. The need to manage documents in multiple languages is becoming more pressing.

10 **Closer integration** of document publishing and document management facilities in order to create a seamless process of document assembly, management, retrieval, distribution and publication. For some products this will be linked to increased sophistication in their facilities for data entry and document creation.

11 **Closer integration with Webserver technology** in order to provide Web opportunities which offer seamless access to information. For example, the

BASIS WEBserver gateway is fully integrated with Microsoft Internet Server (IIS) and Netscape Enterprise Server.

Summary   Document management systems are a type of software that is designed to support the creation, maintenance and use of databases. In order to be able to support speedy retrieval from text and multimedia databases, document management systems are characterized by the ability to handle variable-length data, indexes based upon inverted files, a range of sophisticated retrieval facilities and relatively fixed applications. Systems may range from single-user microcomputer-based applications through to mainframe-based applications that serve several thousand users. Document management applications include electronic publication, corporate document archives and personal information systems. Important features of these systems are: price, support, data input facilities, data output facilities, information retrieval facilities, interfaces, and the extent to which such systems can be integrated or interfaced with other software. Special features are necessary for Internet/intranet applications and CD-ROM publication. Management issues centre upon monitoring, maintenance and planning. Stability and marketing are issue of specific concern for Internet applications. The chapter concludes with a description of two document management systems: CAIRS and BASIS.

REVIEW QUESTIONS

1   What are the defining characteristics of document management systems?
2   List the key issues in the selection of document management systems.
3   What are the two main categories of document management systems?
4   List some application areas for document management systems. Explain how a document management system might be used to provide access to the database or document that is created with the support of the document management system.
5   Discuss the issue of security in relation to a document management system.

6   Why is a document management systems necessary in Internet access to databases?
7   Identify some of the issues to be considered when publishing databases over the Internet.
8   Discuss the future development of document management systems.

IMPLEMENTATION CASE STUDY: MERCK SHARP AND DOHME

Merck, Sharp and Dohme is the UK subsidiary of American parent Merck and Co. Inc. and incorporates the Neurosciences Research Centre (NRC) in Harlow, a specialist division dedicated to the discovery and development of therapeutics for neurological diseases. The NRC is one of MSD's premier research facilities. Addressing the issue of information management, the NRC turned to Information Dimensions to implement a computerized information management system.

The system was built on BASIS. BASIS Intranet Solutions is the most recent addition to the system and gives MSD a secure internal communication network providing seamless search of its own private document collection as well as the Internet. BASIS Intranet Solutions is an integration of Information Dimensions BASIS Document Manager with Netscape Server and provides company-wide access to resources held in BASIS and IMAGE databases which store and manipulate information on text and image-based research materials. This enhancement is the latest stage in the development of the information system that began in NRC's Library and Research Information Centre.

The comprehensive on-site library serves the Chemistry, Biochemistry and Pharmacology Department, and manages the thousands of scientific publications required by readers. In addition to handling material held within the library itself, staff coordinate access to materials held in libraries and information centres outside the organization. Historically, internal records and procedures for ordering material from other sources were largely paper-based, the only database being the online catalogue of books held in the library. After initial discussion with Information Dimensions, the interlibrary loan system was fully computerized in March 1993. Information Dimensions BILLplus, the BASIS data storage and formatting tool, was customized to meet the library's needs. This application met the format requirements at NRC and those of other libraries, whilst running on the existing VAX network. This initial flexibility has made it easier to develop the system stage by stage. Since this development, BASIS has managed requests for material not available internally, and has provided library users with a simple Windows interface for ordering material from popular outside sources such as the British Library, the Royal Society of Chemistry and the British Medical Association. Staff are able to use the system to monitor the status of borrowing and orders. Critically, computerization has made evaluation of readership much easier, allowing staff to make informed decisions on which journals and books to purchase. Feedback on the BILLplus system made it possible to assess requirements, and formed the basis for the development of BASIS Desktop, which was implemented in 1995.

BASIS Desktop gave individual NRC researchers access to database information via a uniform, easy-to-use Windows-based 'find' screen, which presents them with a brief display of fields. Researchers are able to search the journal holdings list to check availability of materials in the library, and scan the 'new book' listing, updated regularly by library staff, to check the latest materials available. The system is fully interactive, allowing individuals to communicate internal and external borrowing requests to the library staff with a simple click on the title required. The most dramatic benefit of bringing the information to the end-user via BASIS Desktop is to be seen in the 'news service', a comprehensive service providing online access to the latest news from the world of medicine and science.

Response to corporate wide access to information critical to research is understandably a driver from all divisions. With information on availability of research materials readily accessible, it made sense to look into the possibility of putting more and more information of relevance to the entire organization online. BASIS Intranet Solutions was identified as the answer to MSD's needs. BASIS Intranet Solutions, already used within Merck and Co. for the Clinical Literature Information Centre's database, was implemented as a common tool. Library information features heavily as key material shared across the intranet. End-users access the information via WEBserver at their own terminals, be they PC or MAC based.

From the wider perspective, BASIS Intranet Solutions also offered Internet connection. This provided researchers with links to journals available on the World Wide Web as well as to specific external Websites, providing additional information sources. Web access to these alternative sources provides MSD with an extensive range of resources, including those outside the scientific realm, giving details on business and other information.

Another key benefit of the intranet facility is the capacity that it provides for researchers to share reports, briefs, analyses and general information of relevance to the wider MSD research community, regardless of which side of the Atlantic they reside. A security protection feature is built into the system to give some of these 'discussion groups' restricted access. Together with e-mail, BASIS provides an unrivalled method of speedy, wide-reaching communication.

In addition to text-based resources held in BASIS, images from in-house documents and research reports held in the IMAGE database can also be scanned onto the intranet for viewing by individual users.

Implementing BASIS Intranet Solutions was seen as a natural next step in the development of the corporate information system at MSD. Further developments will focus on text-retrieval facilities and the other aspects of a complete information service.

Bibliography

Anonymous (1996) 'CD-ROM indexing/authoring systems', *Digital publishing techniques*, **1** (12), 12–16.

Ashford, J. A. and Willet, P. (1989) *Text retrieval and document databases*, Bromley, Chartwell Bratt.

Cox, J. (1995) 'Publishing databases on the Internet', *Managing information*, **2** (4), 30–2.

Crane, J. A. (1991) 'Selection of a text retrieval system in two user environments', *Journal of information science*, **17** (1), 93–104.

Cunningham, S. (1995) *Electronic publishing on CD-ROM* In *International Conference on Digital Media and Electronic Publishing*, Weetwood Hall Conference Centre, Leeds, December 1994, London, British Computer Society, 56–74.

Grawick, L. (1991) 'Assuring the quality of information dissemination: responsibilities of the database producer', *Information services and use*, **11**, 117–36.

Jasco, P. (1996) 'Who's doing what in the CD-ROM publishing realm', *Computers in libraries*, **16** (9), 55–6.

Kimberley, R. (1986) *Integrating text with non-text: a picture is worth 1K words: proceedings of the Institute of Information Scientists Text Retrieval '85 Conference*, London, Taylor-Graham.

Kimberley, R. (ed.) (1990) *Text retrieval: a directory of software*, Aldershot, Gower.

Kimberley, R. et al. (eds.) (1985) *Text retrieval in context: proceedings of the Institute of Information Scientists Text Retrieval '84 Conference*, London, Taylor-Graham.

Lundeen, G. and Tenopir, C. (1988) *Managing your information: how to design and create textual databases on your microcomputer*, New York, Schuman.

Marcoux, Y. and Sevigny, M. (1997) 'Why SGML? Why Now?', *Journal of the American Society for Information Science*, **48** (7), 584–92.

Nkereuwem, E. E. (1997) 'Theory and practice of cataloguing library material by using TINLIB software', *International cataloguing and bibliographic control*, **26** (3), 66–7.

Rittberger, M. and Rittberger, W. (1997) 'Measuring quality in the production of databases', *Journal of information science*, **23** (1), 25–8.

Rowlands, I. (ed.) (1987) Text retrieval: an introduction, London, Taylor-Graham.

Tenopir, C. (1995) 'Priorities of quality', in Basch, R. (ed.) *Electronic information delivery: ensuring quality and value, part III: Quality testing*, Aldershot, Gower, 119–39.

Wainwright, J. (1997) 'An enquiries management database at the House of Commons Library using BASISPlus', *Program*, **31** (3), 211–26.

Watson, J. (1996) 'Evaluating Internet text retrieval products', *Document world*.

Willet, P. (ed.) (1988) *Document retrieval systems*, London, Taylor-Graham.

12

Printed indexes and current-awareness services

LEARNING OUTCOMES

Information technology has been used in a number of additional application areas to offer specific services. Printed indexes are an application in which information technology is used to produce a printed product. In other applications such as current awareness, the output might be in either printed or electronic form. At the end of this chapter you will:

- understand some of the ways in which information technology can be used to generate printed indexes
- be acquainted with the types of current-awareness service and the processes for their creation.

12.1 Introduction

This chapter draws together two distinct topics that can appropriately be considered in this part of the book on information retrieval. There is insufficient space in a book of this nature to devote a chapter to each topic, but the principles of each of the topics should not be overlooked. This chapter, then, deals with printed indexes and current-awareness services. Printed indexes and current-awareness services can be derived from a database that might, for example, be mounted by one of the online search services or maintained within an organization with the assistance of a document management system. They are, then, database products. Printed indexes are by definition print products. Current-awareness notifications also can be print products, but users can also opt for current-awareness notifications on diskette, CD-ROM, online or via the Internet.

12.2 Printed indexes

One of the first applications of computers in information retrieval was in the production of printed indexes. Computers were used, both for in-house indexes to reports lists, local abstracting and indexing bulletins, patents lists etc., and for the production of published indexes to many of the major abstracting journals. Particularly for the large abstracting and indexing organizations, computerization of indexes and indexing yielded considerable savings in the production and cumulation of indexes. Originally index production was an isolated operation. Now many indexes are merely one of a range of database products.

Reflection   List some types of documents in which printed indexes are used.

In spite of the growth of online searching, for some time yet there will be searches in which reference to a printed index is cheaper and simpler. Several different access points may be used in printed indexes. The most important of these are subject and author; but chemical formulae, trade names, company names and patent numbers are all possible access points.

All indexes consist of a series of lead terms, usually arranged in alphabetical order. Each lead term may be qualified and must have a link that leads the user to other lists or documents. A one-stage index has a link which gives sufficient bibliographic details to locate the original document, e.g. the full journal reference for a journal article. A link in a two-stage index merely directs to another listing, where fuller details of the original document are usually to be found.

Computer-generated indexes may rely on automatically assigned index terms or intellectually assigned terms. Each of these possibilities will now be considered.

KWIC, KWOC, KWIT and KWAC

A KWIC (keyword-in-context) index is the most basic of natural-language indexes; KWIC or KWIT (keyword-in-title) indexes are popular because they are straightforward and relatively cheap to create. In the most basic of KWIC indexes, words in a title are compared with a stop-list in order to suppress the generation of useless index entries. The stop-list or stopword-list contains words under which entries are not required, such as them, his, her, other, and. Each word in the title is compared with those in the stop-list, and if a match occurs it is rejected; but if no match is found, the term is designated a keyword. These keywords are used as entry words, with one entry relating to the document for each word. The word is printed in context with the remainder of the title (including stopwords). Entry words are arranged alphabetically and aligned in the centre or left column. A single-line entry, including title and source reference, is produced for each significant word in the title. The source reference frequently amounts to no more than a document or abstract number, but may extend to an abbreviated journal citation. Alternatively, a full bibliographic description, with or without abstract, can be located in a separate listing. Entries under one word are arranged alphabetically by title. Figure 12.1 presents an example of a KWIC index layout.

The merits of title indexes derive mainly from the low human intervention. Since a simple KWIC index is entirely computer-generated, a large number of

the professions. The effect of	language	on social mobility in	059606
of Esperanto	Language	awareness and the place	06355
fisheries periodicals literature./	Language	use patterns in the	07921
trends of international activities in	languages/	A report on the present	05555
The use of command	languages	in online information retrieval./	07341
indexing	languages:	some dilemmas./	06781
Who's who in special	libraries./		04431
	Libraries	and the MARC format./	05423
communications networks for	libraries./	Electronic mail systems:	05609
Use of systems programs in	library	applications of microcomputers./	06782
The structure and dynamics of	library	services./	04612

Fig. 12.1 *An example of a KWIC index layout*

titles can be processed quickly and cheaply. The elimination of personal interpretation enhances consistency and predictability. Indexing based on words in titles reflects current terminology, automatically evolving with the use of the terminology. Also, the creation of cumulative indexes (e.g. to say cover five-yearly annual volumes) is easier and does not demand any added intellectual effort, only an extra computer run.

However, for all their convenience, title indexes are open to criticism on the following four main counts:

1 Titles do not accurately mirror the content of a document. Titles can always be found which are misleading or eye-catching rather than informative, e.g. 'The black–white divide' (politics or graphics?).
2 Basic KWIC indexes are unattractive and uncomfortable to read, due to their physical arrangement and typeface.
3 Subarrangement at entry terms would also improve the scannability and searchability of KWIC indexes, by breaking down long sequences of entries under the same keyword.
4 The remainder of the criticisms of title indexes are concerned with the absence of terminology control. Irrelevant and redundant entries are inevitable. The mere appearance of a term in a title does not necessarily herald the treatment of a topic at any length in the body of the text. Further, even when the term assigned is relevant, with no terminology control, all the problems which a controlled language aims to counter re-emerge. Subjects will be scattered under a variety of terms with similar meanings. No directions are inserted between related subjects.

The more sophisticated KWIC-type programs attempt to negotiate these four limitations. Readability can be improved by simply altering the printed format. A KWOC (keyword-out-of-context) index, for instance, extracts the keyword from the title; the keyword is used as a separate heading, with titles and accession numbers listed beneath it. An asterisk sometimes replaces the keyword in the printed title. Indexes where the keyword appears both as heading and in the title are strictly KWAC (keyword-and-context) indexes, but this distinction is rarely made, and KWOC is the generic term used.

Subarrangement at entry terms further enhances scannability. The index user is released from the necessity of scanning every entry associated with an index term, and can select relevant entries by the alphabetical arrangement of qualifying terms. Both Permuterm and double-KWIC indexes provide a solution.

The Permuterm index (as used in Science and Social Sciences Citation Indexes) is based on pairs of significant words extracted from the title. All pairs of significant terms in a title are used as the basis of index entries; such pairs are arranged alphabetically with respect to each other. An accession number accompanies each pair but no title. Accession numbers, titles and other information are printed in a separate listing. Similar paired listings can also be used in searching the electronic database associated with Science and other Citation Indexes.

A double-KWIC index also gives subarrangement at entry terms, but is fuller than a Permuterm index in that the title is displayed as part of the entries in the index. The first significant keyword is extracted from the title, and treated as the main index term. This term's position in the title is then occupied by an asterisk, and the remaining words in the title are rotated to permit each remaining significant keyword to be displayed, using a wrap-around format, under the main term. A similar procedure for all significant words in the title generates a series of main terms with subarrangements for each title. Index entries are arranged alphabetically by main term and, within a main term, alphabetically by subterm.

More refined computer-indexing packages instil a degree of control into the selection of index terms. By widening the indexing field, terms from free or controlled vocabularies may be added to the title and treated in the same way as terms in the title. Alternatively, specific terms in the remainder of the record in, say, the abstract may be marked by the indexer to be used as terms to augment the index terms in the title. Further control may be exercised in such a way that all of the keywords under which index entries are to be found can be designated manually, prior to input. Exerting this amount of control tends to undermine most of the advantages of title indexing, but does provide for terms to be assigned in accordance with the document being indexed and its content, rather than arbitrarily assigning a term as an index term merely because it appears in a record. Also, with control, terms may be signalled as comprising more than one word, e.g. international economics, since two words can be signalled as being linked.

Indexes based on string manipulation

Controlled indexing languages (such as may be recorded in thesauri and lists of subject headings) are still preferred by many index producers, including, for example, Index Medicus, Science Abstracts, Engineering Index and the British National Bibliography. Nevertheless, the computer still has a role in the production of indexes based on intellectually assigned index terms. The computer may be entrusted with the printing and formatting of such indexes, and is particularly useful in cumulating indexes. In addition, the computer has a hand in the generation of indexes based on string manipulation. Here, the human indexer selects a string of index terms from which the computer, under appropriate instructions, prints a series of entries for the document to which the string of index terms relate.

Articulated subject indexes

In an articulated subject index, the entry consists of a subject heading and a modifying phrase; these can be combined to form a title-like phrase. Modifying phrases are arranged alphabetically under a subject heading. The words or strings of words may be machine-selected or drawn manually from a controlled vocabulary. In indexing, the words or phrases which are to appear as lead terms are indicated by the indexer. For example, the following string would cause the programs used by World Textile Abstracts to generate the type of entries given:

Indexing string
<<Soil-resistant<finishing>>of<carpets>and<wall-coverings>.

Index entries
1   Finishing
soil-resistant, of carpets and wall-coverings
2   Wall-coverings
soil-resistant finishing of
3   Carpets
soil-resistant finishing of
4   Soil-resistant, Finishing
of carpets and wall-coverings.

The structure of the phrases is analysed, and various connectives and prepositions cause the generation of different arrays of entries. Note that prepositions are retained in the index.

....

Reflection   Write out the index entries that might be created for the following title, using first KWIC indexing and then articulated subject indexing: The use of videoconferencing in health and safety training.

....

Shunted and rotated subject indexes

PRECIS and the index generation algorithm used in Abstracts in New Technologies and Engineering (ANTE) are rotated or shunted subject indexes, based on a more rigid framework of conceptual analysis than in articulated subject indexing. A series of terms from a controlled vocabulary of single-concept terms is chosen to represent a document. These terms are amalgamated into an index string, which may also include delimiters which denote the way in which each term is to be treated in index entries, e.g. whether it is to appear as a lead term.

The index for ANTE is generated by rotating the terms in the subject heading under which abstracts have been displayed in the main abstract listing. The main abstract listing is arranged under numbered subject headings, and the subject string is used as a display heading in this list. Index entries in a separate index lead back to the numbers used in this main list. The example below shows the index entries that would be generated from a subject string:

Indexing string
    Computerized production management – Scheduling – Graphical methods

Index entries and references
1   Scheduling
                Computerized production management
2   Graphical methods
                Scheduling: Computerized production management
3   Production management
                Narrower term: Computerized production management

PRECIS is a similar set of working procedures; its main use was in the indexes to the British National Bibliography, where it was used as a subject index to a classified catalogue, but the principles are well suited to other environments. It is included here to illustrate an approach that is based on in-depth analysis of concepts and their relationships. PRECIS index strings are built from a series of index terms (from a controlled vocabulary), linked together into a string by role operators. These role operators define the role of the concept represented by the term to which they are applied in the index string. Role operators are often represented in a string in brackets. The role operators are used to order concepts in the string. The main numerical operators are arranged in numerical order. To illustrate this approach with an example, the indexing string and the index entries for a work on 'The use of boats in fly fishing for trout in still waters' are shown below:

Indexing string
    (0) Still waters (1) Trout (2) Fly fishing (3) Boats.

Index entries

1	Still waters			
		Trout	Fly fishing	Boats
2	Trout		Still waters	
		Fly fishing	Boats	
3	Fly fishing		Trout	Still waters
		Boats		
4	Boats		Fly fishing	Trout	Still waters

Note: This example has been coded with role operators relatively simply. The use of differencing operators would have permitted more entries to be generated, and allowed, for instance, words such as 'Fishing' to take the lead position. Nevertheless this coding demonstrates the basic principles of PRECIS indexing.

There are three positions in an index entry – Lead, Qualifier and Display – and the terms are shunted through these positions to create the series of index entries. Note that each entry shows the lead term in context and is in effect a PRECIS of the subject of the document.

In both PRECIS and ANTE, 'see' and 'see also' references between individual terms and related terms can be input as a distinct operation. If such relationships are noted on the first use of an index term, then thereafter the presence of that term will trigger the printing of appropriate references. For example:

Prejudice see also Sexism
Press see also Journalism
Philately see Postage stamps.

PRECIS indexing represents a significant contribution to the theory of subject indexing. However, indexes based on PRECIS were very labour-intensive. In January 1991, PRECIS was replaced in the British National Bibliography by COMPASS. COMPASS is based on PRECIS, but uses only its basic components as a subject authority system. Most of the complex coding has been jettisoned.

Other indexes

There are various other rotational indexing systems. We will demonstrate three of these by using A, B and C to represent three indexing terms. Selective Listing in Combination (SLIC) indexing involves the combination of elements in one direction only. In other words the index entries from an index string ABC would be ABC, AC, BC, and C. Cyclic indexing is based on the shunting of the lead term into the last position until each element has occupied the lead position. The entries would be: ABC, BCA, CAB. Rotational indexing is achieved by retaining the same citation order, but underlining the elements acting as the lead term. For example: $\underline{A}BC$, $A\underline{B}C$, $AB\underline{C}$.

Citation indexing is a means of producing an effective index by exploiting the computer's capacity for arranging and re-formatting entries. Input to the indexing system comprises the references of recent articles in relatively few core journals and, for each article, the list of works that it refers to. A citation index then lists 'cited' documents together with a list of those items that have cited them (citing articles). This is an effective way of covering a fairly wide subject field with almost no human intervention. The prime examples of citation indexes are those produced by the Institute for Scientific Information (ISI), i.e. Social Sciences, Arts and Humanities and Science Citation Indexes. Thus, given one document in a field, the searcher should be able to trace other related documents. However, the many inconsistencies in citation standards cause problems, and the reasons for citing a document are not always to do with shared subject content. Whilst citation indexes started life as printed products, most users now encounter citation in databases, (such as those produced by ISI), that include citation links. In this context, citation links can provide a valuable additional approach to the identification of related documents.

Reflection   Why would citation links be useful in searching an online
database?

12.3 Current-awareness services

Current-awareness services are those information services whose primary intent is to keep information users alert to advances in their field. Appropriate current awareness is central for businesses in maintaining their competitive advantage, and for public-sector organizations in responding effectively to environmental change. Although much useful news information is available in newsletters, journals, electronic bulletin boards and newspapers, it can be very time-consuming for individual information users to scan all of the appropriate sources. In order to support their employees in keeping up to date, organizations have traditionally provided current-awareness services.

The scale of the operation may vary both in terms of the number of users served and the volume of literature or data handled. At one extreme, large services such as BIOSIS and INSPEC are selling services to an international audience across a broad discipline, whilst at the other, small company information units may be serving only a few hundred users in a relatively narrow and well-defined subject.

Components of a current-awareness service

The components of a current-awareness service are as shown in Figure 12.2. Any current-awareness system requires a mechanism for creating and maintaining user interest profiles and the database against which user-interest profiles will be run. If the current-awareness service is individualized, each user will have a personal profile. Alternatively, notification may be grouped into bulletins, which serve the needs of a number of users, and a broader profile may be maintained. Once notifications have been reviewed by users, the service provider needs feedback on the value or relevance of the service, in order that the coverage of the database and the user-interest profiles can be modified to accommodate changes in user interests. Users require delivery of the full text of documents, or access to other information sources, once they have identified those notifications which they wish to pursue further.

Although the basic components and process remains stable, the past five years has witnessed a number of changes in the character of current-awareness services. These will be illustrated more fully in subsequent sections of this chapter. Here they are summarized in terms of the components of the current-awareness service:

Database

The range of databases that may be scanned during a current-awareness search now includes bibliographic databases, databases of the contents pages of journals and other documents, full-text databases, Websites and multimedia databases. Many current-awareness services search more than one database or source, and make use of cross-file searching. Where the sources searched are likely to yield records that can be identified as duplicates, such as in bibliographic databases, duplicates can be eliminated.

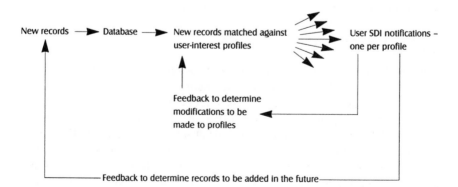

Fig. 12.2 *Refining user-interest profiles in a current-awareness system*

User-interest profiles

These were traditionally based on Boolean searching, and may have employed other search facilities such as truncation and proximity searching. Relevancy ranking based on complex statistical algorithms, which are based on the frequency of occurrence of terms in documents or records, are used by some current-awareness services. In addition, when full-text databases or Websites are being searched, information-retrieval features that support searching in these environments may be employed. Enhanced search facilities should allow more effective targeting in response to user interests.

Notifications

These are more commonly given in electronic format, often to an e-mail box, rather than in print format. This facilitates the use of the notifications to create local personal databases, which may subsequently be used in the creation of other electronic documents, and specifically may contribute to the creation of bibliographies of documents and sources. Electronic notification can easily be used to order a document from a document delivery service, or may be forwarded to colleagues to support group working.

Feedback

Provided that the provider of the current-awareness service is aware of the document delivery requests that are triggered by the alerting service, document ordering can be a useful feedback mechanism. However, there are a number of other actions which may result from an alert, and these may be much more difficult for a service supplier to monitor. Online evaluation forms are a relatively straightforward means of gathering feedback information on an occasional basis.

Document delivery

Document delivery is the area in which there has been the most significant change. Effecting fast and responsive document delivery was always a challenge for earlier current-awareness services. Document delivery used to be by post, or at best fax, and the supply chain between the current-awareness service, user and document delivery service was often somewhat piecemeal, while its effectiveness varied depending upon the particular document that was requested. Digitization of documents permits very much more speedy and effective delivery, although post and fax remain as options. In addition, the major current-awareness service providers have forged links or strategic alliances with document delivery services. These links are evident in services such as BIOSIS Document Express, and ISI's the Genuine Article. Other document delivery services include the British Library Document Supply Centre, INDIVIDUAL Inc., UMI InfoStore and UnCover.

Evaluating current-awareness services

The characteristics that make any current-awareness service valuable will vary from one user to another. Key characteristics of any current-awareness service are cost, currency and coverage. Most users will consider these alongside other criteria when evaluating current-awareness services. A typical example is provided by Checklist 12.1. The final criterion – relevance of outputs to user's requirements – is the bottom line. If all other criteria are met, then this one should also be satisfied, but it is still worth specifying it as a separate criterion.

Current-awareness services can be divided broadly into those managed by an organization on behalf of its user community, or corporate current awareness, and external services that may be acquired with a view to meeting the needs of specific end-users. Typically, corporate current-awareness services may be more tailored to the needs of the organization, and may embrace both documents and sources internal and external to the organization, possibly including sources that are available through both the organization's intranet and the Internet. Another attraction of corporate current-awareness services is confidentiality and security. In the use of external services a profile of the organization's interests needs to be published outside the organization. The cost of providing appropriate services to a large user community will be a further consideration. Many organizations make some use of both external current-awareness services and corporate services.

Reflection   What do you understand by the concepts 'news' and 'up-to-date'?

CHECKLIST 12.1

Evaluating current-awareness services

- Database coverage, i.e. subject and (for bibliographic databases) literature coverage of the service.
- Timeliness or currency of the information provided.
- Cost of the service.
- Mechanisms for creating and maintaining profiles including any constraints and the user-friendliness of the interfaces that support these activities.
- Range of formats in which records are available.
- Document delivery service, especially to support current awareness associated with bibliographic databases.

*   Relevance of outputs to users' requirements.

Corporate current-awareness services

Printed current-awareness notifications, in the context of either SDI or bulletins covering, say, contents pages and newspaper cuttings, are becoming less significant as it is becoming possible to place more reliance on machine-based scanning and to use this as a substitute for costly personal scanning. However, basic services, such as the circulation of journals and in-house newsletters, may continue to meet some current-awareness needs (and desktop publishing software may be used in their creation). Increasingly, newsletters are likely to be posted via electronic bulletin boards.

Personal Agent, from Personal Library Software, is a good example of the type of software that is available to support effective current-awareness services, based on profiles that users can create and customize easily. Personal Agent works with PL Web, PLS's Internet searching and publishing system, to create a Web-based current-awareness service. Personal Agent allows users to submit, via the WWW, persistent 'intelligent queries' called agents. These agents search full-text databases, such as news feeds and posted texts, at periodic intervals. Personal Agent then automatically sends an e-mail notification. The e-mail contains a URL where a list of links to the new documents can be found. Users use their Web browser to visit the URL and view the search results. Information can then be shared internally on an organization's intranet, and externally with customers, thereby encouraging them to visit the organization's Website for updated and possibly personalized information.

PLS also features natural-language query and advanced search features. Other parameters that can be specified include how much information is required, how often the user wants to be updated, and the time criticality of information need.

13 Daily Briefing and 13 Live Alert are two comparable products which provide current-awareness within corporate intranets. Available from Autonomy Systems, they monitor and deliver relevant information from the numerous sources accessible on a company's intranet, including the Web, news feeds, e-mail, corporate memoranda, archives and document stores. 13 Daily Briefing uses concept agents, defined by users, to monitor specific internal or external information sources. On a large company intranet this might be used to collect and distribute internal information, such as memos, health-and-safety policies, regulatory issues, personnel notices and updates on a company's competitive situation. 13 Live Alert monitors live news feeds such as Reuters and Bloomberg, and alerts users via e-mail or a mobile phone as soon as a news story of interest appears.

Many recent releases of library management systems which feature Web access also incorporate features that will support alerting services. For example, in Inheritance from Heritage Library Management Systems, users searching the OPAC can save previous searches to be used again.

BNB on CD-ROM is issued monthly and can be a useful basis for the identification of new book titles. A New Record search can be performed to identify recent publications, for perusal by users or by library staff in stock selection. Searches can be saved in order to provide regular updates on a topic, for users or library staff.

Reflection   Using an organization known to you, what types of new information might users benefit from having drawn to their attention?

External current-awareness services

External current-awareness services are available from a number of different sources. These include:

- contents page services, available from the British Library (Inside) and Blackwell (Uncover)
- services available from the online search services
- services available from the database producers.

Contents page services

In 1994, new current-awareness services entered the marketplace. These services used the large serials databases that their providers were already generating for other purposes. Inside, from the British Library Document Supply Centre, provides a short listing of the key features of each article in the world's principal scholarly periodicals. Swetscan, from Swets Subscription Service is based on the database that Swets maintain to support their library subscription services. Uncover is a collaborative venture between Blackwell and CARL, and offers access to a multidisciplinary database, based on the serial holdings of the participating libraries, with additional titles for which Blackwell acts as subscription agent. UnCover Reveal is the alerting service based on the UnCover database. For a small annual fee, users receive the tables of contents of up to 50 journals and the results of up to 25 search strategies automatically e-mailed to them on a regular basis. Access to the UnCover database itself is free, but charges are made for documents ordered. In this context, UnCover could be viewed as free alerting which is used to market or promote the resources available through a document delivery service. One of the important aspects of these services is that announcement is linked to a fast document delivery service. Swetscan, for example, uses document delivery from the British Library Document Supply Centre. These services are available in a variety of options. Swetscan, for example, is available on diskette, paper, FTP and (via DataSwets) an online service, and can be formatted to suit the client organization.

Database producers

A number of database producers market current-awareness services directly to the end-user. Whilst print-based current-awareness services, such as current contents listings or key topics, have been available from some of the main database producers for many years, experience with end-user markets for electronic information in the form of CD-ROM has given a number of database producers a stronger base from which to launch end-user services. The large number of such services means that it is difficult to generalize, but services will typically embrace both basic bulletin-type products and SDI. Typical products are:

1   Abstracting and indexing journals, in both print and electronic forms, and available online (either through a host or directly from the database producer over the WWW) and on CD-ROM.
2   Standard SDI services covering a set of topics. Examples are Food Science Alerts from IFIS, INSPEC Topics from the Institution of Electrical Engineers. Broader bulletins are available from some database producers, such as INSPEC's Key Abstracts, CAS Selects Plus (a series of 17 weekly bulletins), and CAS BioTech Updates.
3   SDI services are also available. Corporate Alert from the Institute of Scientific Information is one such service. Corporate Alert delivers notifications over the Internet. An information specialist sets up a master profile containing all of the journals that their users wish to monitor. As the journals are processed for inclusion in the multidisciplinary databases, the tables of content matching users' individual profiles are retrieved and forwarded to them via the Internet. Users can scan the tables of contents, read abstracts and place any orders for articles with their local library, a document supplier or via ISI's document delivery service. ISI also offers Keyword Plus, which is an SDI service that uses title words, authors and author keywords in advanced profiling and cited reference searching.
4   Current Contents services, which offer the contents lists of recent journal issues, are produced and marketed by the Institute for Scientific Information. Current Contents are available in various subject areas, and can be acquired in various formats.

Table 12.1 lists the current-awareness services available from CAS, a typical database producer.

Reflection   Would you prefer a bulletin type current-awareness service in a
broad area which allowed some browsing, or a more targeted
service based on your individual profile?

Table 12.1 *Current-awareness services from one major database producer:
CAS*

Service	Description
CA Selects	A bi-weekly group profile service that generates a range of 231 printed publications
CA Select Plus	A bi-weekly group profile on a limited range of topics which features express coverage of 1300 journals
CA BioTech Updates	A bi-weekly bulletin on selected topics
CASurveyor	CD-ROM-based topic databases covering subjects such as magnetic resonance, and polymer synthesis; updated monthly
CA Section Groupings	CA Abstracts in five subsets (printed)
Chemical Industry Notes	Weekly issues on industry topics
Chemical Titles	Article titles from 800 chemical journals
Corporate Updates	Customized printed bulletins
Individual Search Service (ISS)	Individual SDI, with bi-weekly outputs

Engineering Index have recently launched an interesting integrated product
called the Engineering Village, which provides access within the village metaphor
to a range of engineering databases, other information sources and Websites.
Amongst the services included in the Engineering Village are Ei Spotlights and Ei
Page One. Ei Spotlights offers weekly updated summaries with bibliographic references on any new developments in the topics chosen through the user profile.
Results are delivered to the user's e-mail address. Ei Page One reports from the
tables of contents of over 5000 journals, individual conference proceedings, and
technical reports and trade publications. Available on CD-ROM, or for site licensing, Ei Page One can form the basis of an internal current-awareness service.

Online search services

The third category of producers of SDI are the traditional online search services,
such as DIALOG, Data-Star and Questel-Orbit. An SDI facility is a feature
offered by most of the major hosts. As with a local database, SDI can obviously be
gleaned by a diligent user by re-running a search profile at intervals in order to
check whether any new items have been retrieved. Most hosts offer a command

which permits profiles to be saved, and some offer a special facility for SDI which ensures that, if a profile is saved as an SDI profile, then the profile will be run every time that the database is updated (say, monthly). This type of facility is available for many of the databases which are searchable through the online hosts, but usually not all of the databases of any given host. The DIALOG and Data-Star Alert services, for example, provide current information based on specified databases, and in accordance with a specified profile. Alerts are delivered directly to an internal electronic mailbox or by post. A similar service is also offered by Questel-Orbit. Electronic delivery of results is available through both the Questel and Orbit systems, and also via e-mail. Profiles in such environments can make use of multifile searching and features for chemical structure searching. Document delivery is through the normal channels associated with the online service, such as the ORBDOC feature on Orbit, or the ORDER feature on Questel.

Online search services also often offer access to newspapers and newswires. For example, the *New York Times*, the *Financial Times*, *Fortune*, *Asiaweek* and *PR Newswire* can all be accessed through DIALOG. FT Profile, a more specialized financial information host, offers access to a wide range of newspapers and newswires. Many of these sources are updated daily or in real time. Another kind of alerting service is available from company information hosts such as Dun & Bradstreet. Their monitoring services alert users to changes in the business's status as and when they occur. Dow Jones, which offers access to a number of exclusive newswires, and a wide range of other industry and business sources, offers CustomClips. CustomClips is an SDI service based on keywords. The service is continuously updated, and stories may be read online or via e-mail. Dow Jones also have a bulletin-type service, Current News This Just In, which shows the top stories of the day on business and world events.

The future for current-awareness services

Current-awareness services will develop as an integral part of the services offered by any online service provider. The information to which that provider offers access will be the latest available. Alerting services will fall into two categories: those to support browsing (electronic bulletins), and those to support specific searching (electronic SDI). These services will cover all of the sources to which the online service provider offers access. Users will be able to modify their profiles online, and choose the style and time period for delivery of the alerting service. Libraries and information services may provide corporate access to such services through interfaces on their library management system. They will select from a range of such services to meet the needs of their various client groups. Typically, a significant incentive to end-users to work through the library, rather than working independently with the online service supplier, will be the library's ability to negotiate more competitive rates for the service, and to ensure seamless delivery of a range of information services (including print-based documents) to the end-user.

That is one scenario! The other is already embedded in the service offered by UnCover and Inside. Alerting services may become the promotional front-end of publishers and document delivery services, and may be offered for free. A large and powerful publisher or document delivery service will understand the needs of its various client groups, and be able to tailor services to their specific needs. The free added value embedded in an alerting service may perhaps eliminate the need for intermediary services, such as libraries.

Summary   Printed indexes were one of the early products from computer-based systems. Printed indexes are used in printed abstracting and indexing services, books, periodicals and a range of other contexts. There are two main categories of printed indexes: those based on manipulation of terms in titles, and those based on manipulation of intellectually assigned index strings. Such index strings are also used in Internet search engines. Citation indexes are a special type of printed index.

Current-awareness services are important for establishing competitive intelligence. The basic components of a current-awareness service are: the databases, user-interest profiles, notifications, feedback, and document delivery. Current-awareness services can be broadly divided into corporate current-awareness services and those from external suppliers. External current-awareness service suppliers include: contents page services, database producers, and online search services. The future for alerting services is as part of an integrated information solution

REVIEW QUESTIONS

1   Identify three different types of printed indexes. Explain the differences between these indexes.
2   What is a citation index? How might citation links be useful in online search environments?
3   What are the basic components of a current-awareness service?
4   What is a corporate current-awareness service? Discuss how such a service might be used to satisfy the needs of corporate information users.
5   Identify the different types of external current-awareness service.
6   What is the purpose of alerting services in a Web-based environment? How might such a service be integrated with access to information resources?

Bibliography

Printed indexes

Note: Most of the significant works that describe the concepts associated with printed indexes were written some years ago. The principles still apply.

American National Standards Institute (1984) *American standard for library and information sciences and related publishing practices: basic criteria for indexes*, New York, ANSI (ANSI Z39.4–1984).

Anderson, J. D. and Radford, G. (1988) 'Back of the book indexing with the nested phrase indexing system (NEPHIS)', *Indexer*, 16 (2), 79–84.

Armitage, J. E. and Lynch, M. F. (1967) 'Articulation in the generation of subject indexes by computer', *Journal of chemical documentation*, 7 (3), 170–8.

Austin, D. and Digger, J. A. (1977) 'PRECIS: the PREserved Context Index System', *Library resources and technical services*, (1), 13–30.

Austin, D. and Dykstra, M. (1984) *PRECIS: a manual of concept analysis and subject indexing*, London, British Library.

Bawden, D. (1988) 'Citation indexing' in *Manual of online search strategies*, Boston, MS, G. K. Hall, 44–83.

Craven, T. C. (1986) *String indexing*, Orlando, FL., Academic Press.

Farradane, J. (1980) 'Relational indexing', *Journal of information science*, 1, 267–76, 313–24.

Garfield, E. (1979) *Citation indexing, its theory and application in science, technology and humanities*, New York, Wiley.

Garfield, E. (1964) 'Science Citation Index: a new dimension in indexing', *Science*, 144 (3619), 649–54.

Martyn, J. (1975) 'Citation analysis', *Journal of documentation*, 31 (4), 290–7.

Weintraub, D. K. (1979) 'An extended review of PRECIS', *Library resources and technical services*, 23 (2), 101–15.

Current-awareness services

Beeson, A. (1991) 'Text reformatting and current-awareness services in a medical library using Reform', *Library micromation news*, 34, 12–14.

Cropley, J. (1991) 'The practice of intelligence: adding value', *The intelligent enterprise*, 1 (1), 25.

Ellis, E. (1991) 'Bulletin production using CAIRS', *Library micromation news*, 34, 9–12.

Hall, A. (1990) 'The Social Work Information Bulletin: current awareness for social scientists', *ASSIGnation: Aslib Social Sciences Information Group newsletter*, 7 (2), 30–1.

Kemp, A. (1979) Current-awareness services, London, Bingley.

Richards, D. (1992) 'Dissemination of information' in *Handbook of special librarianship and information work*, London, Aslib.

Rowley, J. (1985) 'Bibliographic current-awareness services', Aslib proceedings, 37 (9), Sept., 345–53.

Rowley, J. (1992) 'Current-awareness services and the online hosts' in *Online Information 92*, 8–10 December 1992. London, Learned Information, 251–62.

Rowley, J. (1992) 'Current awareness or competitive intelligence: a review of the options', *Aslib proceedings*, 44 (11/12), 367–72.

Rowley, J. (1994) 'Revolution in current-awareness services', *Journal of librarianship and information science*, 26 (1), 7–13.

Whitehall, T. (1986) *Practical current-awareness services for libraries*, Aldershot, Gower.

Wiggins, T. and Miller, N. (1990) 'Reference Update and Current Contents on Diskette: a review of two new current-awareness services', *Medical reference services quarterly*, 9 (1), 1–12.

Part 3

Library management systems

13

Functions of library management systems

LEARNING OUTCOMES

This chapter identifies the basic functions that might be expected in any library management system, and discusses the nature of the information and control that a library management system might offer. The following chapter, Chapter 14, reviews the marketplace for library management systems and looks in more detail at some examples of systems. At the end of this chapter you will be acquainted with the range of functions in library management systems in each of the following areas:

- ordering and acquisitions
- cataloguing
- OPAC and other catalogue forms
- circulation control
- serials control
- management information
- interlibrary loans
- community information
- Internet access.

13.1 Introduction

Library management systems are now established as an essential tool in the support of effective customer service, stock management and, in general, management of the services offered by libraries and other agencies engaged in the provision of access to collections of documents. The focus of such systems is on maintenance, development and control of the documents in the collection. Systems support selection, ordering, acquisitions, labelling, cataloguing and circulation control of library stock. Checklist 13.1 is a useful indication of some of the functions that need to be available in a library management system. In many functions the system acts primarily as an information source on the state of the stock, and hence must hold records which describe the stock and its whereabouts. This information makes it possible to answer questions such as 'What is in stock?' or 'What is on loan to whom?' Occasionally, the system may actually control the stock – for example, by using a trapping store, which triggers a light or a 'buzz' when a reserved book is returned to the circulation desk. The more current the information is, the more effective is the control of the operation. Most systems embrace the majority of the library collection. Serials, however, because of their ongoing nature, pose special problems, especially in the area of acquisitions and subscription control.

Early systems development was piecemeal, with some libraries developing cataloguing systems first, and others focusing instead on, say, circulation control systems. Current systems are integrated systems, based on relational database architecture. In such systems the files are interlinked so that deletions, additions and other changes in one file automatically activate appropriate changes in related files.

This chapter, then, describes what would be regarded as standard features in a library management system at this stage of development. Some systems also offer additional features, as will be evident from the descriptions in Chapter 14.

CHECKLIST 13.1
BASIC FUNCTIONS OF A LIBRARY MANAGEMENT SYSTEM

Ordering and acquisitions

- Ordering
- Receipting
- Claiming
- Fund accounting
- Enquiries (about the status of orders)
- Reports and statistics (about orders)

Cataloguing

- Data entry
- Authority control
- Downloading (of records from other databases)

OPAC and other catalogue forms

- Online access
- Public access interface
- Other catalogue forms
- Internet access
- Access from remote users over the Internet

Circulation control

- Setting parameters (to reflect loans policies, opening times etc.)

- Issue
- Return
- Renewal
- Fines
- Reservations
- Short-term loans
- Borrower file maintenance
- Enquiries (concerning borrowers or the status of items)
- Notices
- Reports and statistics (about the utilization of the stock)

Serials control

- Ordering (placing and renewing subscriptions)
- Receipting (of individual issues)
- Claiming
- Binding (control of items in binding)
- Fund accounting
- Cataloguing (of new titles)
- Circulation control (if items are issued or circulated)
- Enquiries (relating to the serials)
- Reports and statistics

Management information

- Various reports and statistics
- Tools for the analysis of statistical information

Interlibrary loans

(similar to circulation control, but usually with fewer options)
- Data entry
- Issue
- Return
- Fines
- Borrower file maintenance (may use circulation control main file)
- Enquiries
- Reports and statistics

Community information

- Data entry
- Online access
- Public access interface

13.2 Ordering and acquisitions systems

The ordering process has particularly benefited from computerization, as it is a relatively simple clerical process, where similar operations are applicable to all categories of library. Most ordering systems concentrate on monographs and other once-and-for-all purchases.

The functions of an ordering or acquisitions system can be specified basically as:

- to receive records of items to be acquired
- to establish whether items requested are already in stock or on order
- to print orders or dispatch electronic orders to suppliers and otherwise order items
- to check when orders are overdue and follow up overdue orders
- to maintain a file of records of items on order
- to note the arrival of ordered items and prepare for payment
- to maintain book-fund statistics and accounts.

Some libraries also like an ordering system to notify individuals of the receipt of items either electronically or on paper, and to produce various listings or announcements of books on order or recently acquired.

Input to an ordering system which is to satisfy the above functions must include:

- details of new orders
- amendments or corrections to existing orders
- booksellers' reports
- details of received books.

All requests for an order must be checked, to ensure that the item is not already in stock or on order, and to guarantee that the bibliographic record of the item is accurate. Some of this checking can be performed by matching of items requested against computer files of existing stock or other bibliographic records. This is only likely to be successful where the citation given by the requester is at least partially accurate; ISBNs are particularly important in this respect. With the aid of the computer, bibliographic records for new orders may be drawn from a file of MARC records, from a file of existing items in the library, from a union file of records, from a file created by a book supplier, or from local inputting. Order records of each item typically include: book number (e.g. ISBN), short bibliographic details, number of copies ordered, estimated price, currency, bookseller, book fund. Such bibliographic records comprise the main file of current orders. A second file must contain names and addresses of booksellers used by the library, and this file must also be open to alterations. The order file must be amended as books arrive, or as booksellers notify non-availability, etc. There may be a facility for the library to define order types, such as firm orders, approvals, standing orders, subscriptions, gifts, exchanges and desiderata. Control may also be offered over the ordering of multiple copies for multiple locations across multiple funds.

The process is initiated by adding orders to the order file; this prompts the dispatch of orders to the supplier, in either print or electronic form. When the item is received, the order records become the basis of catalogue records. In an integrated ordering and cataloguing system, order records may be examined and upgraded to cataloguing standards. At this stage, book cards may also be generated for use in the circulation system. At regular intervals the computer checks for the orders that remain unfulfilled. In summary then, the outputs from an ordering system are typically:

- printed and electronic listings of the order file
- an accessions register (of recent items acquired)
- accounts
- chasers
- recommendations for future acquisitions
- statistics
- book cards
- processing slips.

Fund accounting must control expenditure. The system should check fund balances at order creation. The library may have the option to allow the fund to be overspent. Full financial reports are necessary, and a full audit trail desirable.

In ordering systems, batch-processed operations are generally satisfactory for some activities. The initiative for online operation of ordering systems generally developed within integrated online systems. It is quite satisfactory to add to the order file in batches, and to check the progress of orders and finances at intervals, provided the gap between the processing of adjacent batches is reasonably short. Order creation is online, and EDI has facilitated online ordering of documents from library suppliers.

Reflection   Are there any differences between library stock ordering systems and ordering systems in other environments?

13.3 Cataloguing systems

The objective of any computerized cataloguing system is to create appropriate catalogues. To this end, records may be drawn from any of the following sources:

- commercially available files of MARC records

- a union file of the stock of several libraries, or another shared database
- a file of records held by the library (i.e. the records that comprise the existing library catalogue)
- the library's ordering and acquisitions system
- local cataloguing.

Relevant and appropriate records, after modification to match local requirements (e.g. indication of added entries, references) and the addition of local data (e.g. class numbers, location) are added to the main or master file of catalogue records of the library's holdings.

Key features in a cataloguing module are:

- data entry
- downloading
- authority control.

Easy data entry for local creation of records is important. It is usual for systems to use the same record for the ordering and acquisitions function as is used in the cataloguing module. Entry is via formatted screens with word-processing-type facilities. Field labels and other areas of the screen should be protected, and data entry in some fields, such as the ISBN field, should be validated to ensure that the data entered are in the correct format.

As regards the record format, the MARC record format is a central consideration. External records from the bibliographic utilities are generally in one of the MARC record formats. Local systems must at least be able to handle the MARC record format. Some systems are totally MARC-based, others can accept records in the MARC format and convert them into an internal format. Where alternative formats are available, systems usually allow libraries to define fields for the bibliographic record. Most systems automatically update index files as soon as the record has been added to the file, so that retrieval is possible immediately. A wide range of different types of indexing may be possible.

Records from external databases may be added from tape, or by downloading direct from the files of the bibliographic utilities. A further option is to acquire records on CD-ROM and to download records from CD-ROM databases.

Authority control is important where the form of index terms or headings, such as author headings, or subject index terms need to be controlled. Libraries maintain an authority file in order to improve consistency in indexing. Records in this file may be created locally or drawn from externally available files such as the Name and Subject Authority files of the Library of Congress. The authority file can usually be consulted during indexing and cataloguing, possibly by display in a separate window, and new headings are immediately added to the authority file, with an opportunity to review or authorize recently added headings at a later date. Sometimes it is also possible to add cross-references or related terms to the authority file, and these may be displayed in the OPAC. The subject authority file may take the form of a thesaurus that displays the full range of uses for related, narrower and broader terms.

Historical perspective

Over the past 20 years, databases and online public-access catalogues have gradually replaced card, sheaf and microfiche catalogues. The effect of this evolution has been a significant change in the nature and role of the catalogue record. The impact of these changes is worth rehearsing, since they illustrate the general impact of computerization on the management of library processes:

1   The catalogue records have become the central bibliographic record for the library management system. These records are used in the cataloguing sub-system, circulation control, and ordering and acquisitions control. Conversely, this has made it necessary to consider the requirements of these systems when designing the form of the catalogue record.

2   The interchange of catalogue records has led to greater standardization in catalogue records. The tools which are used to support the creation of catalogue records, such as the Anglo-American Cataloguing Rules, the Dewey Decimal Classification Scheme, the Library of Congress Classification Scheme, and the International Standard Bibliographic Descriptions (ISBDs), have all been much more widely and much more literally adopted than was the case for their predecessors prior to the advent of computers. Further, these tools have become more important in the creation of effective catalogue records, and have themselves, in turn, been more closely refined than was necessary for their antecedents.

3   The availability of union catalogues in a more complete form has made for more effective interlibrary lending, cooperative acquisitions policies and cooperative storage ventures, while other cooperative activities concerning library resources and their exploitation on a regional or national basis have become much more effective. A union catalogue record is an important prerequisite for the enhancement of document delivery systems.

4   No filing or other routine catalogue maintenance is required of cataloguers, except where it is necessary to alter stock records as the stock itself changes.

5   Different catalogue formats can be chosen for different catalogue locations, allowing different record formats, access to different subsets of the database and differing physical forms of catalogues.

6   The cataloguing procedure has become more structured, with a significant proportion of stock being processed quickly. The extent of shared cataloguing records has meant both shared expertise in cataloguing, a reduction in cataloguing effort and a consequent reduction in the library resources that need to be devoted to cataloguing.

Reflection   What features of computer-based processing of catalogue and other records are central to the changes described above in the relation to the role of the catalogue record?

13.4 OPACs and other catalogue forms

The OPAC module usually comes with some default OPAC that can be used as a starter. Most libraries will prefer to take the opportunity to tailor the OPAC to their specific library, and there is usually provision for individual library OPAC design. The library can identify and design specific menus for staff and public use; dialogues and messages can be defined, as can any information and help texts. Help is normally context-specific so that an appropriate message can be displayed in accordance with the stage that has been reached in the search. Some systems also allow the library to define which fields are to be indexed for staff and public. Often staff can use commands to bypass menus and to display information not available to the public.

Most systems offer both phrase and keyword searching. With phrase searching there is usually implicit right-hand truncation; for keyword searching a truncation symbol is normally input if required. Keyword searching may be available across all fields, or may be limited to certain fields. Other search facilities offered are various, and differ considerably between systems. Boolean operators can be offered for use in handling phrases and two- or three-word search terms. Sometimes these are applied implicitly – in other words, the searcher does not need to key them in. If the searcher enters a two- or three-word phrase, the system performs an AND search automatically. Truncation symbols and qualifiers to identify the field in which a search term is to be found are becoming more common. With the advent of GUI-based interfaces it has become possible to include a range of information retrieval facilities in menus or as options on buttons or check boxes.

Once records have been identified there are a number of ways in which they may be displayed. Some systems display the index or a listing of brief records before a full record is displayed; others, if there is only one match, will show the record directly. Usually the full record display includes holdings information relating to individual copies, as well as the basic bibliographic data. Where such data are available to the public, it is often necessary to consult another window to discover the loan status of the document. Record displays may be library-defined. Security procedures may mask confidential information. For non-matches, some systems show the index. Since non-match will be relatively frequent, browsing of the index and/or a list of brief records is common.

Significant recent innovations in OPACs are concerned with public-access terminals in a kiosk format, and links to the Internet. Public-access terminals are often based on touch screens. These interfaces are generally heavily reliant on menus in which the user selects an option by touching the screen. The range of search facilities is more limited than with terminals that include keyboard access.

Kiosks are designed for use in any location in which there is significant foot fall, including public libraries, shopping centres and railway stations.

A number of OPAC interfaces also offer an option which allows access to the Internet, through the same interface as is used for searching the library catalogue.

In addition to the online access to catalogue databases, most systems still support the generation of hard-copy catalogues, which can be used as a back-up for security or at busy times, and which are useful in locations such as small branches or special remote collections that are not connected to any online system. Hard copy can typically be produced in the form of cards, printed catalogues, indexes and other listings, possibly selective, and COM (computer output on microform). It is important that for hard-copy listings the system is able to support the generation of a variety of different catalogue or index sequences, such as author, title and subject. Clearly these hard-copy versions also need to be formatted, or laid out on the page or card. A range of options so that the library can define its own format is valuable. An additional facility available on some systems is the option to create a catalogue on CD-ROM. This may be useful for libraries that might like to make their catalogue widely available, or which find CD-ROM more cost-effective than the extensive use of telecommunication links.

Reflection   OPACs have been described as the shop window of a library. If OPACs are to take on such a role, what are the implications for the design of OPACs?

13.5 Circulation-control systems

All circulation-control systems impinge upon one of the primary functions of a library: document availability. Library materials, including books and non-book materials, should be made available to all customers immediately or as soon after the demand arises as is practicable.

Principles of circulation control

In order to achieve maximum availability of material, all libraries must control circulation by keeping, at the very least, records to specify

- what material is in the library stock or readily accessible through other channels
- which material is on loan, and from whom or where it can be retrieved
- when material on loan will next be available in the library for other customers.

Libraries differ in the priorities that they accord to each of these functions, depending to some extent on the level of demand that they experience and the urgency of the requests that they handle. Also, some groups of material and users may be differentiated; academic libraries, for instance, often operate short-term loan collections for student texts in great demand, and offer differential loan periods to students and staff.

In addition to these three basic functions, most libraries also like their circulation-control system to:

- recognize and possibly trap reserved books on their return from loan
- prepare (including print and dispatch, or dispatch electronically) overdue and recall notices
- keep records of the number of books on loan to individual borrowers, and notify overborrowing and dubious borrowers
- facilitate renewals
- facilitate the calculation and collection of fines
- collect issue statistics
- be reliable.

Refinements on the basic functions of issue, renewal, return, fines and reservations that will support a busy multisite library include:

- multi-site provision, with each site having its own stock, borrowers and associated circulation parameters
- definition of loan periods
- location definition of patron records
- recalls or holds on items, editions or titles
- printing of check-in receipts
- a variety of categories of stock and borrowers, each with its own library-defined circulation parameters
- fine payment, accompanied by a record of the details of payment, such as date, workstation and operator, supplemented by printed receipts.

Reflection   Take three of the above facilities and explain why they might be necessary in a large public library system with a number of geographically scattered branches.

When considering the most suitable circulation-control system the following factors are important:

- the number of items available for loan

- the number of items issued and returned every day, and the distribution of loans over time
- the number of reservations made daily
- the number of borrowers
- the number of branches and service points.

It is also important to attempt to anticipate any changes in the above parameters over the next few years. For a somewhat more embracing system it is also necessary to specify parameters relating to:

- charging, renewals and overdues
- the number of charges and renewals daily
- the number of overdues
- the length of overdue notices, requests for return, notices of availability, etc.

Taken together, these parameters will decide the basic charactenstics of the computerized system, such as:

- the size of the processor
- the number of workstations
- the number of staff needed to operate the system
- the nature of telecommunications links.

Differing values of the above parameters lead to the wide variety of circulation-control systems, so it is unlikely that one type of system will always be equally appropriate.

Components of a computerized circulation-control system

Databases

The core of the circulation-control system is the transactions or loans database. This database comprises a series of records, one for each transaction. Each record must, at the very least, specify

- details of the document, e.g. document number
- details of the user, e.g. user number
- the date of the transaction (either the issue or return date).

It is common to keep bibliographic details in a separate bibliographic or document database; typically this database is the catalogue database. This database provides the information on titles, authors and publishing details that are used in notifying users of overdues. However, when the catalogue database is not entirely comprehensive and covers only recent stock, another alternative is to create a sub-file of the catalogue or minicatalogue which includes for each document, say, author and title only.

A third database must contain more details of users. When printing overdues and making other contacts with users it is essential to have the user's name and address. Additional management information concerning the user profile, such as position, sex, educational background and age, can also be useful. Such details may often be transferred from another source, such as university student records or staff records.

Document and user numbers

It has already been made clear that document and user numbers are an important component of the databases and the input to the databases of a circulation-control system. Both document and user numbers must be assigned in such a way that they identify the book and the borrower uniquely. Document numbers used in computerized circulation systems may adopt one of the following styles:

1   An accession number derived, usually, from an existing system of assigning accession numbers.
2   An alphabetic code or random number, which may often be assigned at random on the basis of pre-printed labels with numbers ready printed; such labels can easily be attached to books with little other preparation.
3   An ISBN-based book number. All ISBNs must be supplemented by a copy number, as ISBNs only uniquely identify a title and not the copy. The resulting number is rather needlessly lengthy. Also, some titles do not have ISBNs and it will be necessary to use a library equivalent to the ISBN for these titles.
4   A structured number which includes extra information about the copy. Many public libraries use non-ISBN systems based on nine- or ten-digit book numbers which specify accession number, copy number and location. Often such numbers can be linked to ISBNs used heavily in catalogue systems.

The options for user numbers are similar, except that the ISBN or non-ISBN dilemma no longer pertains. User numbers can take one of the following forms:

1   An already-assigned number used throughout the organization, e.g. student number or employee code. The use of such a number contributes to the integration of all databases on staff and/or students across an organization.
2   A unique random number, which can be easy to assign.
3   A structured number which carries information such as the branch at which the user is registered, and the user's status (e.g. resident, non-resident, student etc.).

Reflection   Examine the user number on your library registration card, and the document numbers on some books or other items that you have borrowed. Which of the above types of numbers have been used?

Online systems offer good control of stock. Issues can be recorded via a terminal and databases immediately updated. Subsequent consultation of the databases can be immediate and the databases will communicate the current situation. Thus overborrowing and problem borrowers can be identified at the circulation desk. Fines can be calculated on demand, and reservations and other modifications to book records can be made instantly or when time permits. Online systems usually have some back-up system to cover telecommunications or computer system failure. This back-up system will offer terminal recording showing various issue data etc. in an offline mode.

Data-capture devices

Data-capture devices that allow document and user numbers to be easily read, so that loans and other transactions can be completed, are important in circulation-control systems. Data-capture is generally based on bar codes, which are used to encode both user numbers and document numbers. These can be read with a flat-bed scanner set into the surface of a circulation control service station, or by using a portable light scanning device or light pen.

Reflection   Why are fast loans transactions important in managing customer services in libraries?

13.6 Serials control

A serial, as defined by the International Serials Data System (ISDS), Paris, is 'a publication issued in successive parts and intended to be continued indefinitely.' The definition continues: 'Serials include periodicals, newspapers, annuals, journals, memoirs, proceedings, transactions etc. of societies and mono graphic series. A serial can be in print or near print form and its parts usually have numerical or chronological designations.' Most libraries subscribe, at least in part, to such a definition, but the term 'serial' is certainly not always used by all information workers to mean precisely the same categories of publications.

Serials are distinguished from monographs by their ongoing nature. Any serials-control system usually has fewer titles to handle, but must record more detail for each title and can expect a greater number of transactions per title. For this reason, amongst others, serials-control systems are often distinct from monograph systems, and address themselves uniquely to the problems posed by serials. An integrated serials-control system, nevertheless, features all three of the subsystems already encountered for monographs, namely:

- an ordering and acquisitions system - to control the selection, ordering and checking-in of serials, payment, and chasers when indexes or issues fail to arrive
- cataloguing - or keeping records of stock
- circulation control - or keeping records of the availability of serials, to include circulation and binding.

It is also important to generate management statistics. Figure 13.1 presents a brief overview of serials-control system functions.

Problems unique to serials

In broad outline the ordering and cataloguing systems for serials have much in common with those for monographs. However, the following points summarize some of the features unique in serials control:

1 Successive issues are received at regular or irregular intervals, and it is important to ensure that successive issues arrive when they have been published (checking publication can cause difficulties).
2 Subscriptions must be renewed recurrently.
3 Catalogue data describe both the serial and the library's holdings of the serial, and hence must be relatively extensive.
4 Serials change their titles, are published under variant titles (e.g. translated titles) and may change their frequency of publication. References must be inserted between associated periodical titles.
5 The system should help with binding by holding and printing instructions for binding at the appropriate moment.
6 Serials may change their publisher.
7 Indexes, special issues and supplements must be controlled.
8 Some serials arrive, not by subscription but (especially in special libraries and special collections) by gift or exchange.

A large amount of data must be held for each serial, and frequent, repetitive record addition or amendment is necessary. For this reason alone, computerization is an attractive proposition for serials control. However, serials-control systems have been less influenced by cooperative and centralized practices, partly due to their academic and special-library context.

Development of computerized serials-control systems lagged behind similar systems for monographs. This slower progress was in part due to the essential complexity of a complete serials-control system, but also derived from the lower priority associated with serials control as compared with monographs control. Development of serials-control systems has more of a priority in academic and special libraries, where serials represent a larger proportion of the stock than in, say, public lending libraries.

Reflection   How many transactions will be necessary each year to ensure delivery of all issues of a journal that is published monthly in parts, with an annual index, and then to ensure that it is bound by the library in annual volumes?

Serials-control subsystems

Ordering and acquisitions systems

The initial ordering of a serial is akin to ordering a book. Ordering must encompass processes for requesting, approving, checking, ordering and accounting, in respect of each new serial title. The chief difficulties arise with the continuing nature of the subscriptions to serials. Renewals must be created and dispatched at the appropriate time. Hence, the ordering must contain records of renewal dates and subscription levels, and processing must include the capacity for scanning records to check for renewal dates. Further, sufficient data to facilitate the identification of the vendor or society from whom the serial is to be ordered must be included.

As issues appear regularly, acquisitions is one of the major functions in any serials-control system. The acquisitions function may be divided into receiving and claiming. Receiving involves a large volume of checking. When an issue arrives it must be checked to ensure that it is the correct item and then the master records must be amended to reflect new receipts. The claiming function is a smaller, but possibly more complex, activity. The point at which claiming procedures are to be initiated must be a matter for the professional judgement of the information manager. The computer can help by providing lists of the information that the information manager needs in order to exercise this judgement.

A further function also linked to the accessions function is subscriptions control. In order to fulfil this function, the master record must include details of when the subscriptions are to be renewed. At regular intervals, a list of subscriptions ripe for renewal is prepared for the librarian's perusal. After a decision on renewal has been made, printed or electronic renewal notices may be generated. The other function of the system in this context is the keeping of accounts and appropriate print-outs.

Cataloguing systems

Catalogue formats, orders, processes etc. for serials are fundamentally similar to those for monographs. From the master file, listings can be generated in several orders, e.g. title, subject, location, supplier. Serials catalogues may be printed in book form or microform, or may be accessible via an OPAC. The update frequency of such listings varies, but is usually monthly, annual or somewhere between the two. The content and format of the serial bibliographic record varies considerably between systems. Some catalogues are based on ISBD(S) and others on ISDS formats, whilst other systems use local formats. One problem which all cataloguers must address is that of changed and variant titles. References must be provided between linked titles.

Circulation control and binding

Circulation with respect to serials frequently adopts different patterns from that obtain for books. If serials are available for ordinary loan, then the same circulation-control system will suffice as for monographs. Often, however, serials are reserved for reference use only. In special libraries special circulation systems are common, and if these are large enough they may be computerized. Specific journals are circulated to those readers who have expressed an interest in that title. A computerized system to control this activity must have a list of serials taken, a list of users and their addresses, and some indication of the serials to be directed towards specific users. The computer can then be expected to print a list of readers that can be appended to each issue of each title.

Databases

In order to perform the above functions, the serials-control system must have a number of core databases. The entire system hinges on the master records database. This database includes master serials data records; which may be held in a series of linked files; each record in an all-embracing serials system will include:

Management information
Selection for purchase
Ordering (including renewals of subscriptions)
Receiving issues and claiming for issues not received
Recording current holdings and allowing access to lists of such
Circulation of issues and borrowing
Binding

Fig.13.1 *Functions to be covered by a serials-control system*

- cataloguing data (the records may be MARC-based or in another, probably more simple format)
- ordering data, including renewal dates, names and addresses of publishers, codes for vendors, costs
- receiving data, such as frequency of publication, irregularities, claiming criteria
- binding data, such as colour and style of binding, number of issues per binding volume bound, type of binding
- holdings data
- circulation data, i.e. names and addresses of locations for circulation.

Such data may form the basis of a set of lists, to aid in the control of the various functions. Such lists might cover receiving records, invoice control, bindery control, error list, claims and renewal requests, new accessions list, holdings list and statistical summaries.

13.7 Management information

Library management systems contain much data which, if appropriately extracted, summarized and analysed, may support management decision-making. Most library management systems offer three different kinds of facilities that can present management information:

- facilities for handling ad-hoc enquiries
- facilities for standard report generation
- report generators, or better, management information modules for the creation of ad-hoc and user-defined reports.

Enquiries may be submitted against any of the files in the system. For example, it may be useful to conduct an online enquiry of the order file by author, title or order number in search of detailed order information. On the circulation-control file, access to user records by name or number for details of items on loan, renewed or overdue, and fines and reservation details, is usually available.

Most systems offer a set of standard reports relating to transactions in various modules in the system. The extent of the standard reports available may be influenced by the availability and quality of any report generator. If this is easy to use, it may be argued that it is less necessary to offer standard reports. Nevertheless, even with a user-friendly report generator, standard reports remain useful. These model reports demonstrate the types of reports that are common. Examples might be:

- supplier reports showing delivery time, performance, price changes, average item cost, and budget analysis at intervals

- circulation reports giving circulation statistics, showing circulation analysed by item, branch, category and borrower.

Report generators are necessary tools if the library manager wishes to generate ad-hoc reports or to design personal reports for regular use. The sophistication of report generators available varies significantly between systems. Important characteristics to consider in the evaluation of report generators are:

- user-friendliness
- query language
- facilities for statistical analysis of data.

....

Reflection   How might a library manager make use of a circulation report that gives circulation statistics, analysed by item, branch, category and user respectively? Which summary statistics might help to inform decision-making?

....

13.8 Interlibrary loan systems

Interlibrary loan systems handle the processing associated with the borrowing of items from collections beyond that of the local library. This includes generating initial requests to other libraries, notifying users of the availability of items, keeping records of items requested, keeping records of items on loan, controlling returns, and generally monitoring users and requests.

Development of interlibrary loans systems has been relatively slow. The interlibrary loans function is suitable for running alone, and does not need to be integrated with the library's main databases. However, integration does bring some benefits. It is possible to use the circulation-control module of an integrated system, and thus use the same borrower file, with its basic data and information about the status and reliability of borrowers. It may also be possible to use an OPAC to request an interlibrary loan. One of the reasons why library management systems vendors were slow to become involved with ILL systems may be that the systems are driven by BLDSC requirements in the United Kingdom, and different practices may pertain in other countries.

Most users are in special and academic libraries, and ILL systems often assume centralized handling of ILL. A few systems have multi-site facilities.

Typically, interlibrary loans systems offer the following functions:

1   Requesting, from BLDSC and usually also from other libraries.
2   Transmission of requests, and providing a communications package for transmission of requests.

3   Receipt and loan. This may include the calculation of the due date, the printing of arrival notifications for the requester of the loan, and logs of which items are collected.
4   Returns - logging of returns and the display of special instructions.
5   Overdues and recalls. Appropriate letters are generated.
6   Renewals - handling renewal requests to supplying libraries.
7   Chasers to libraries that fail to supply.
8   Cancellations - the logging of cancellations, and the generation of cancellation letters or messages.
9   Enquiries, via request number, author, title or requester.

Most systems also offer management information and some may deal with loans to other libraries.

Clearly an efficient ILL system is a central component in any resource-sharing activities, and as networks become better established, ILL systems are likely to become more central to the operation of a library network. Integration with other functions such as the OPAC is becoming more important, and the use of telecommunications networks in transmitting requests is increasingly replacing the dispatch of letters.

Reflection   With easier access to external databases on CD-ROM, over the Internet and through the online hosts, the volume of ILL requests handled by many academic libraries has escalated. What are the wider implications of such a change?

13.9 Other facilities

In addition to the standard modules that characterize a library management system, as the marketplace has become more competitive, so extra facilities have been added to many systems. These can be divided into three main categories: community information, bulletins and electronic office facilities.

Some systems include a community information module, which is often similar to the OPAC module with regard to the searching and display of records. There must be some flexibility in the format of the record, so that different kinds of information may be accommodated. Searching may be on various fields in the entry. For example, access to local information may be by name of organization, keyword within name, or subject category.

Some systems, especially those with a special library lineage, offer special facilities for the creation of bulletins, such as current-awareness bulletins or new accessions lists, in either paper or electronic format. Facilities to assist with the production of printed indexes and the generation of electronic or printed SDI notifications may also be available. These facilities are discussed in more detail in Chapter 12.

Some systems offer electronic office facilities, including word-processing and electronic mail, in order to facilitate the fulfilment of the basic processes.

Summary   Library management systems comprise a number of modules. The functions that these modules fulfil are primarily:

- ordering and acquisitions
- cataloguing
- OPAC and other catalogue forms
- circulation control
- serials control
- interlibrary loans
- management information
- community information.

The first five of these represent the core activities.

REVIEW QUESTIONS

1   What are the advantages of integrated library management systems?
2   What are the essential functions of an ordering system?
3   What effect has the computerization of the last 20 years had on the role of catalogue records?
4   What approaches are used to ensure that searching in OPACs is user-friendly?
5   Why are document and user numbers useful in circulation control?
6   What are the components of a serials-control system? What are the unique problems associated with the effective management of the stock of a serials collection?
7   What are the functions in a typical interlibrary loan system?
8   List some of the factors that need to be considered when libraries provide access to the Internet.

Bibliography

Appropriate references are listed at the end of Chapter 14.

14

Overview of the market for library management systems

....

LEARNING OUTCOMES

This chapter reviews the nature of the library management systems marketplace. Current and future trends are identified, and case studies are used to exemplify these trends and the functions listed in Chapter 13. At the end of the chapter you will:

- be aware of the characteristics of the different generations of library management systems
- be able to identify new developments and trends in library management systems
- appreciate some of the issues associated with managing a library management system
- have examined in more detail examples of specific library management systems.

....

14.1 Introduction

Chapter 13 reviewed the functions that can be expected in library management systems. This chapter, then, considers the systems that are available in the marketplace and the nature of current and future developments. There is also a short section that reviews some of the areas of major concern for the management of library management systems. The chapter includes some case studies, which demonstrate how some of the functions and issues discussed elsewhere in this chapter and in Chapter 13 are addressed. This chapter focuses on the commercially available library management systems. There remain a few libraries that develop their own in-house systems. These libraries have the resources to develop a system, and may potentially develop a system tailored specifically to their own requirements. Commercially available systems are always a compromise, but are nevertheless a compromise that has served many libraries well. As these systems become more and more sophisticated, and offer more options which allow the library to tailor the system to its own requirements, the in-house development option has become appropriate only for those with very unusual requirements. This chapter, then, does not consider these systems further.

14.2 The marketplace

The marketplace for library management systems is now a mature market, with high market saturation for larger systems. Almost all larger academic libraries have adopted a computer-based system. Most public libraries have also been computerized, although a number of smaller authorities have been slower to take the plunge. In the large-systems market there is an increasing concentration on vendors maintaining existing customers, and continuing to upgrade their product so that existing customers do not switch systems. Library managers certainly do switch systems and are likely to continue to do so, but they will only switch systems with good reason. Clearly any library may review systems and choose to upgrade them by switching to another supplier from time to time. The mid-range and smaller-systems market is the area in which there is still growth. Smaller colleges, and special libraries in various sectors, are still entering the marketplace, and there is more volatility in systems vendors. However, even here the established players are consolidating both their product and their market position.

Reflection   Why do you think that the systems market for small systems is more volatile?

Table 14.1 *Some library management systems*

	Supplier	System
Larger systems	Automated Library Systems Ltd	Meritus
	BLCMP	TALIS
	DS Ltd	Galaxy 2000
	DYNIX Library Systems UK Ltd	DYNIX, Horizon
	GEAC	PLUS, ADVANCE
	Information Dimensions	TECHLIBplus
	SLS (Information Systems) Ltd	LIBERTAS
Mid-range systems	CAIRS	CAIRS-IMS, LMS, TMS
	Inheritance Systems	Heritage Library Management System
	Soutron	Sydney PLUS
	DS Ltd	CALM 2000
	MISYS Education and Library Systems Ltd	Genesis
	Fretwell-Downing Informatics Ltd	Olib
	DDE (Great Britain) Ltd	SUPERMAX Library Solution
	SIRSI	UNICORN
	Soutron	C2, Soutron Library System
Smaller systems	DS Ltd	CLASS 2000
	Dolphin Computer Services	Lexicon
	Eurotec Consultants	Librarian

Head Software International	ELROND
Floyd Ratcliffe	LICON
Micro-Librarian Systems	MICRO LIBRARIAN
Softlink Europe Ltd	Alice
Micoll Computing Ltd	LIMES

Table 14.1 lists examples of the main contenders in the large systems, mid-range and smaller-systems marketplaces. A number of the smaller systems are specifically marketed in the school library sector. Originally, systems could be divided into mainframe- and minicomputer-based systems, and microcomputer-based systems. With increasing emphasis on UNIX systems, this categorization is less valid. It is still, however, possible to categorize systems roughly in relation to the market sectors in which they chiefly operate and the sets of functions that are offered. Systems suppliers are becoming more familiar with their marketplace and are targeting system functionality more tightly towards specific market sectors. Indeed, a number of systems suppliers offer different products to match the requirements of different market sectors.

....

Reflection How might the functions required in an LMS for a school library differ from those required in a medium-sized public library?

....

14.3 The four generations of library systems

All systems suppliers continue to upgrade their systems. Table 14.2 gives a useful summary of the differences between the four generations of library systems. The latest releases of systems generally fall somewhere between the third- and fourth-generation systems, depending on the sophistication of their facilities for integration and interconnectiviy. To some extent the fourth generation has yet to be realized. This profile of the four generations of LMS provides a useful summary of the ways in which systems have developed over the past 20 years.

The first generation of library management systems were developed on a module-by-module basis. There was very limited integration between modules, with systems developing either circulation control or cataloguing as a priority. Thus the first edition of this text was able to divide systems according to their major function. Gradually the suppliers each developed a set of modules, and as they did so, started to recognize the benefits of linking these modules. Systems grew from an initial focus on, say, circulation control. Database structures differed, and might be described as proprietary. It was difficult to make any generalizations about database structure. Third- and fourth-generation systems are integrated systems based upon relational database structures.

In other respects too, first-generation systems demonstrated their lineage. They were developed to run on specific hardware platforms, and used proprietary software languages and operating systems. Some systems were specifically designed to be sold as part of an integrated hardware and software package as a turnkey system. Second-generation systems ran on a wider range of hardware platforms, but it took the introduction of UNIX- and DOS-based systems for systems to become much more portable between platforms. Fourth-generation systems are generally UNIX- or Windows-based.

Communication between systems was also generally non-existent in earlier systems. Links between systems for specific functions were a feature of second-generation systems. It was possible to import or export data to specific systems, but not generally. Third generation systems embodied a range of standards which were a significant step towards open system interconnection, but a number of issues associated with end-user access and interfaces required resolution. Also, implementation of systems that employed all of the appropriate standards was only gradual. Fourth-generation systems feature client–server architecture and modules which facilitate access to other servers over the Internet.

The user's interaction with the system has also become more fruitful and straightforward as systems have moved through the generations. For library managers, reports from early systems were very limited, and there was little opportunity for users to define their own reports. The range of standard reports available in third-generation systems is wide, and users may, in addition, define their own reports. The latest Executive Information System (EIS) modules will allow managers to manipulate data and investigate various scenarios, and thus they have the potential to be a full decision support tool.

The user interface has also improved beyond recognition. Colour became standard in third-generation systems. GUI features, such as windows, icons, menus and direct manipulation, have become the norm. This is in stark contrast to the crude command-based interfaces of the early online systems, where users needed to wrestle with batch processing and printed reports. Fourth-generation systems allow access to multiple sources from one multimedia interface. This greatly enhanced user interface is symbolic of the change in user or customer focus in systems over the generations. Early systems were designed primarily for staff access. OPACs started to emerge in second-generation systems. Third-generations systems saw much more sophisticated GUI-based user interfaces. The fourth-generation OPAC can be accessed through a range of interfaces depending upon the client workstation and the user. This range embraces both public-access terminals with limited functionality and sophisticated GUI interfaces with a powerful range of search facilities.

Table 14.2 *Library management systems by generation*

Feature	First generation	Second generation	Third generation	Fourth generation
Programming language	Proprietary	C, Assembler	Fourth-generation languages	Object-oriented languages
Operating system	Proprietary	Vendor-specific	UNIX, DOS	UNIX, Windows
Database management systems	Proprietary	Proprietary	Entity-relational	Object-oriented
Communication	Limited	Some interfaces	Standards and increased interface opportunities	Full connectivity across the Internet
Import/export	None	Limited	On-board	Fully integrated; records added with one click
Hardware platforms	Locked	Vendor family	Multi-vendor	Multi-vendor
Reports	Fixed format	Fixed format	User-defined	User-defined; also EIS facilities
Colour	None	None	Yes	Full multimedia
Capacity	Limited	Improved	Unlimited	Seamless
Module integration	None	Bridges	Seamless	Seamless
Architecture	Shared	Shared	Distributed	Client–server
Interface	Command-based	Menu-based	GUI-based	Choice of interface, including Web, and GUI incorporating multimedia.

....
Reflection Which generation of system is the LMS that you use in the libraries whose resources you use?
....

14.4 Some topical issues

Chapter 13 summarized the major functions of LMS. Despite the length of the chapter, the review was still essentially a summary of features, and it was not possible to focus on recent developments in the functions that are offered by systems. Any generalizations are subject to exceptions, as some systems have implemented the facilities described below some time ago, while others are still wrestling with the introduction of appropriate facilities. Nevertheless, topical areas can be grouped into:

• issues associated with enhancing the efficiency and effectiveness of library operations
• issues associated with enhanced customer service.

Each of these will be described briefly.

Improvements in library operations

Online ordering

Section 15.6 explains the value of EDI for the book world. Libraries are part of that book world, and can benefit from EDI in several ways. The interface between library management systems and the systems of individual book suppliers had to become more effective before orders could be placed on a supplier's computer through the library management system, and before records of the state of the order could be maintained in both systems, so that the library staff and users as well as the book supplier can be aware of items on order and completed orders. Many libraries use more than one supplier, so it is important that libraries are able to communicate with as many suppliers as possible.

EDI has benefited libraries by offering:

• easy access to bibliographic records
• better control over orders based on access to the supplier's database
• (in general) a faster processing cycle.

Faster catalogue creation

Improved connectivity and interfaces support faster execution of library management operations in a number of functions. For catalogue creation this leads to improved capture of MARC records. For example, a database of such records on

CD-ROM may be accessed. On the entry of an ISBN, either through scanning a bar code or through keying, the MARC record is instantly displayed for any necessary editing. It is then automatically added to the database. The streamlining of this process is a particular asset for any library and resource collection that has yet to convert their catalogue records into a MARC format.

Improved authority control

Amidst the continuing debate as to whether, with the availability of natural-language searching, it is necessary to control index terms and headings, a number of systems have enhanced their facilities for the control of index terms or headings. Authority control may be exercised in relation to subject index terms or headings, titles and author headings, or access points. Authority control systems have been added by some vendors and enhanced by others. For example, some now allow a greater range of relationships to be used in the thesaurus. Where thesauri are available, and this is mainly in the systems marketed to the special-library sector, these are often now displayed in sections via windows, and may thus be consulted much more easily than previously during either indexing or searching. More sophisticated authority control allows for (as in the most advanced systems), multiple authority files, and validation of a range of different types of heading on entry. Thesauri may also be used to provide SEE and SEE ALSO cross references.

Circulation control

In GUI interfaces it is possible to have more direct access to specific functions, with click-only functionality that avoids the need to work through sequential menus. In addition, self-service workstations allow self-renewal and self-reservation.

Interlibrary loans

Some systems have introduced interlibrary loan (ILL) modules. These offer all or a subset of the facilities outlined in Section 13.8. The DYNIX case study in Section 14.5, also illustrated in Figure 14.1, provides more details of the functionality of such modules.

Management information

In general, as transaction-processing systems have reached a plateau, attention has started to move towards the management information that such systems can generate. Some library management systems have introduced separate management information modules. In other systems, management information and reports are associated with each of the modules, so that, for example, there is a set

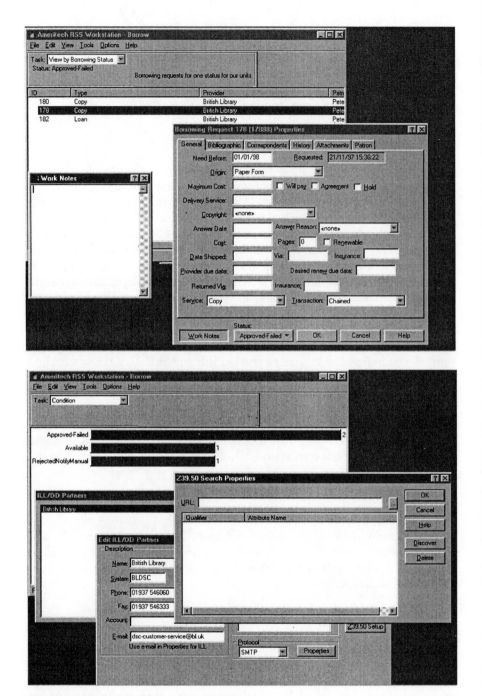

Fig. 14.1 *Dynix interlibrary loan screens*

Fig. 14.1 *Continued*

of standard reports that can be generated in association with the circulation-control module. Systems have always offered some standard reports, but increasingly the range of reports is being enhanced, and report generators have been upgraded to a more sophisticated management information system. Report generation once required an in-depth knowledge of a command-based query language. Systems increasingly offer a menu-based management information system which is easy to use and may be based upon a graphical user interface. This MIS is also likely to offer a range of statistical facilities for the analysis of data to identify trends and correlations between variables.

Customer service issues

OPACs, GUIs and connectivity

OPACs have been available in some systems – notably GEAC – for approximately ten years now. During that period OPACs have passed through three generations. First-generation OPACs were derived from traditional catalogues or computerized circulation systems. Access was via author, or title (as a phrase), classmark and possibly subject heading (as a phrase), and acronym key such as author-title acronyms. First-generation OPACs expected exact matching of terms and were intolerant of user mistakes. These OPACs were acceptable for known-item searching and offered menu-based access, but this access was based on limited search facilities.

Second-generation OPACs began to rectify some of the limitations of the first systems. Systems designers started to incorporate some of the facilities to be found in other text information management systems and the software used by the online search services. Second-generation OPACs offered much better search facilities based upon keyword searching and post-coordination of keywords. Usually these OPACs could be operated with a command language as well as through a menu-based interface. Although second-generation OPACs were a great improvement, two problems still needed to be addressed. Browsing through records remained difficult and it was necessary to work through different menu screens, while the large size and wide coverage of catalogue databases often led to many false drops.

Third-generation OPACs use a natural-language interface, so that the users may input their search strategy as a natural-language phrase. Interfaces and search facilities began to improve with the entry of the early GUI-based OPACs. The latest OPACs offer both touch screen for public access and full GUI for full functionality for more experienced users who wish to pursue complex search strategies across a number of different sources. A wide range of search facilities such as truncation and proximity searching is becoming common; access to and prompts for the use of these are embedded in the interface.

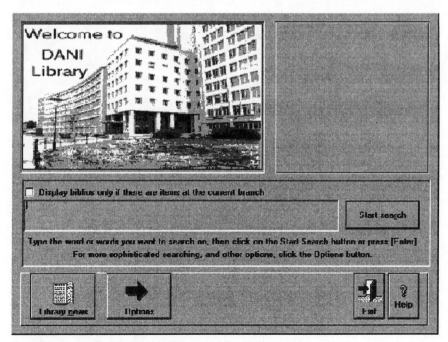

Fig.14.2 *Some OPAC screens from C2-Soutron*

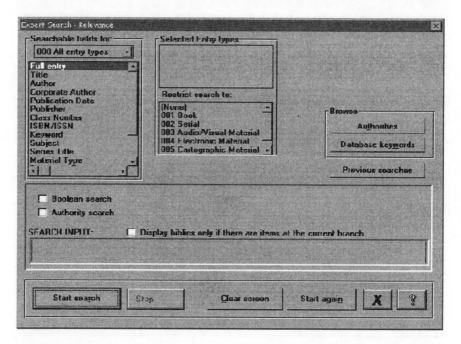

Fig.14.2 *Continued*

GUIs offer point and click, icons, pull-down menus, cut, copy and paste, and multitasking. So, as explained in Chapter 4, users can develop a search strategy in one window, call up a thesaurus display in another window, and consult help, or view the results of their search, in yet a further window. When a successful search has been completed, components of documents may be integrated into other documents via a word-processing package, or alternatively documents may be ordered through a document ordering service.

OPACs can be further enhanced by offering multimedia interfaces and access to multimedia information. This can be achieved through multimedia objects linked to bibliographic citations in such a way that the multimedia objects can be called by clicking on a button in this citation.

Multiple-client options, which mean that the client can be anything from a dumb terminal, a lower-specification PC or network computer, as to a fully configured high-specification PC with client software, will facilitate access from a greater range of networked workstations. The interface will display differently on each client, but on the other hand the client may access a number of applications through the same interface, thus making it easier for the user to develop familiarity with the interface that is available through their specific client. On the other hand, where users move between workstations to obtain access to the same database, this variation may be confusing.

Community information

Many libraries, but particularly public libraries, have offered a community information service. The core of this service is often lists of names and addresses of contacts such as local organizations. Such files may extend to many types of other information, including information about local leisure facilities, employment opportunities, children's activities and citizens' information. A community information module allows a library to develop its own database of whatever information it might like to offer its public. This module is merely a database management module which supports one or several library-defined databases and offers an interface to those databases which is similar to that used in the library's OPAC. Access to community information is often offered through the same interface as the OPAC. For those libraries that are serious in offering community information, this module has many potential uses. This type of information may be one of the first categories of information that libraries wish to make accessible over the Internet, or via public-access kiosks.

Self-service

Improved user interfaces to library management systems, coupled with the much more direct use of information resources that is possible with electronic documents, contributes to the trend towards do-it-yourself document and information retrieval. In libraries, open access to much of the library collection is already a major step in the direction of self-service, but the introduction of self-service workstations or kiosks, at which users can interact with the library management system, has advanced self-service one stage further. Such kiosks enable users to perform functions such as issue and return without an intermediary. Ideally, users should also be able to search for documents not available in the library and to order those documents without changing the interface.

Typically, self-service can only be successful if the social, economic and technical environments are suitable. Customers need to be acclimatized to open access. Economic factors such as high labour costs and a higher level of demand make self-service more attractive from the perspective of the service provider. Data and telecommunications facilitates are technical requirements of effective self-service operations.

Lagerborg (1997) investigated self service workstations. He identified the following positives and negatives:

Positives

- high acceptance by users, with few 'how-to-use-it' problems
- reduced queues and waiting times for most users
- reduced staff workloads
- location independence, so that service point can be more logical and closer to the location of associated activities
- self-service particularly appreciated by deaf users.

Negatives

The current stage of development, a number of system issues remain that need to be addressed, including:

- the limited choice of systems on the marketplace
- the poor design of user workstations, which often poses problems for the disabled and the visually impaired
- vulnerability to theft
- lack of privacy for users if their name is displayed on the screen.

The shift to greater self-service operation poses a number of issues, which, in different guises recur in many electronic information environments.

Management issues

These are associated particularly with the management of change. Specifically, with self-service both the staff and the user roles change, and there is need for training development for both of these groups. In addition, self-service may have consequences for staffing structures. On the matter of management information and customer service, self-service reduces users' familiarity with the human service agents. They may thus be more reluctant to use them when necessary. Also the staff lose the opportunity for information-gathering about customer needs.

Security issues

These cover everything, from the security of items in the library's collections, to privacy concerning user information. Some of the most important issues are:

- authentication of the user, so that users can only access their own accounts
- security of hardware, to avoid theft or vandalism
- prevention of people hacking into networks, and thereby gaining access to other databases that should not be public access
- data privacy, concerning user information
- item identifiers, and ensuring that these are unique.
- buildings design, to increase hardware and user security.

Reflection   How would you respond to self-service issue as a user? What effect do you think it might have on your perceptions of the library service?

Increased functionality in mid-range systems

When describing the functionality to be found in large state-of-the-art systems, it is easy to give the impression that the same functionality exists in all systems. This is clearly not the case, although one of the significant developments of recent years has been the development of small and mid-range systems. Many of these now offer cataloguing based on the MARC record format and facilities for downloading MARC records. They include a full range of modules, including ordering and circulation control, and possibly management information. OPAC interfaces are frequently GUI-based, and there is often a Web option, and other facilities to allow connectivity. The Heritage case study below illustrates functionality in a mid-range system.

Reflection   Compare the Heritage IV case study with the BLCMP case study. What are the common features? In what respects do the systems differ?

14.5 Case studies

BLCMP

BLCMP was founded in 1969 as a cooperative venture between three major Birmingham libraries, those of the Universities of Aston and Birmingham, and Birmingham Public Libraries. BLCMP now offers services to a large number of libraries of all types and sizes. Public, academic, college and special libraries are all represented amongst the membership. BLCMP offers a full range of computerized applications, and maintains an extensive database and telecommunications network to support the electronic library.

TALIS is BLCMP's UNIX library system. This is fully integrated with the BLCMP database of over 17 million records. All customers have unlimited access to the BLCMP databases via the Internet or a dedicated network link, and records can be downloaded into the local system at a single key stroke.

Expandable systems

There is a clear upgrade path, which allows a phased implementation with the minimum of hardware redundancy. With the fast pace of new hardware development, hardware is becoming increasingly cost-effective.

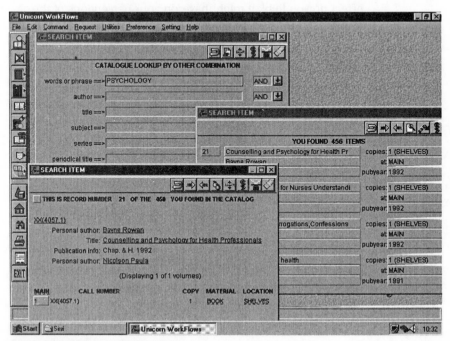

Fig. 14.3 *Features of UNICORN*

Online database

BLCMP maintains an extensive database of 17 million MARC records. All British Library BNB cataloguing since 1950 is online, together with Library of Congress files from 1975, and all extra MARC cataloguing from BLCMP members. This last category includes a significant number of records, and embraces many records for audiovisual items, music and serials. Whitakers Books in Print is also included in the BLCMP database.

The database is searchable via a number of author/title and numeric keys. Optionally, the entire database may be searched or individual files may be searched. The database may be accessed from any PC or terminal connected to TALIS, and is used as a reference tool as well as a tool in acquisitions and cataloguing.

Retrospective conversion of catalogues

The BLCMP database can be used to assist in conversion in either offline or online mode. In offline mode, data may be collected using PC-compatible microcomputers. BLCMP can also offer data-preparation facilities to assist with the conversion of card catalogues or input of forms.

Integrated and comprehensive set of modules

TALIS is an integrated set of modules covering acquisitions, cataloguing, online access, circulation control, and serials. There is also an interlibrary loans system, and the fund accounting serves various modules and thereby offers an integrated approach to budgetary control. A flexible management information system allows managers to extract management data. In addition, BLCMP offers a community information system, known as TALIS Inform.

Customer support

BLCMP has a customer support section which provides support to each new member for initial planning and training in the use of the various systems, through to full aftercare service once the system is live. Support is available outside normal working hours. Methods for remote access of each system for diagnostic and fault-finding purposes are also employed.

BLCMP's documentation is produced using modern techniques and is regularly updated. Training is offered covering all aspects of the BLCMP systems. Review meetings are held with individual customers, and user groups cater for more general matters.

Functionality

It is difficult to review all of the functions offered by all of the modules in TALIS, but the following list of some of the key features, drawn from BLCMP's literature, should help to give a flavour of the nature of the system. A full account of all modules would take more space than we have available here.

1   Acquisitions
   • fast pre-order searching of potential requirements files
   • online order entry
   • printed and electronic orders
   • ntegration with cataloguing, OPAC and circulation online currency
   • conversion
   • automatic fund accounting
   • standing orders and subscriptions
   • supplier name/address file
   • invoice processing
   • electronic data interchange (EDI)
   • clearing house facility.

2   Cataloguing
   • online cataloguing with full-screen editing
   • extensive database for online searching including music and non-book materials
   • tailored formatting
   • integration with circulation and acquisitions
   • authority control
   • cataloguing services
   • retrospective conversion.

3   Circulation
   • fully online circulation system
   • light-pen data capture
   • real-time updating of files
   • extensive enquiry facilities
   • automatic overdue and recall generation
   • comprehensive short-loan maintenance function
   • function key control
   • microcomputer back-up and mobile system
   • self-issue options.

4   Public access
   • choice of user interface, including the Web

- MARC-based bibliographic file
- Z39.50
- self-service facilities, including reservations and renewal
- subject searching, including keyword and Boolean facilities as well as author, title etc.
- borrower enquiry and public reservations
- related work searching
- advanced OPAC facilities, including relevance ranking and set manipulation.

5   Serials
- fast and flexible check-in
- powerful claiming module
- prediction of forthcoming issues
- full OPAC searching of serials
- subscriptions control for serials and standing orders
- versatile routing function
- invoice processing
- local printing of claims.

6   Management information
- flexible-report generator with access to all TALIS files
- tailor-made reports for all applications
- automatic generation of standard reports
- powerful query language
- elect-and-retrieve facilities for MARC-based files
- formatting of printed output according to library requirements.

7   Community information (TALIS Inform)
- Web-based
- full-text searching with relevance ranking
- online editing of records by information providers
- records dated and reminder letters generated.

Heritage IV

This case study on Heritage is included in order to illustrate the level of functionality that can be expected from mid-range systems.

Heritage is developed and marketed by Inheritance Systems. Inheritance Systems began life as Logical Choice in 1982, with involvement in the development of Bookshelf. Over the intervening period, they have developed and marketed the product Bookshelf PC. In 1991, Heritage was released as the successor to Bookshelf PC. Heritage is a mid-range product, designed for libraries that need strong functionality at affordable prices. Modules include:

- cataloguing
- OPAC
- circulation control
- management information
- acquisitions.

Cataloguing

A large variety of media types can be catalogued in as much detail as required. Other time-saving devices include authority files, a thesaurus which will allow the user to look up alternative terms, a calendar facility, and a calculator facility for adding up figures and making VAT adjustments. Quickcat is a CD-ROM disc containing over a million British Library records, which are retrieved by entering the ISBN. Addition and adjustments to the catalogue record can then be made using the authority files, and records transferred to the library system.

The serials cataloguing facility provides the means of entering serial catalogue details at three distinct levels: titles, issue and article. Keywording can also be performed at the article level. The serial management module also provides the means to control ordering, receipting, chasing and circulation of items. Standing orders for serials can be handled by the acquisitions facility, which can also hold e-mail addresses and suppliers' URLs that can be used within order screens to send messages or to look at Websites.

VISTA allows images to be linked to catalogue or reader records for the purposes of enhancing a search or increasing security. Photographs, maps and old examination papers can be added to catalogue records. Heritage can then automatically open the appropriate viewing device in the OPAC, such as Netscape for a URL, Word for a document, and Excel for a spreadsheet.

OPAC

The Heritage OPAC has a simple screen design, but also relatively sophisticated searching functions. These include phrase searching, proximity searching, truncation and wild cards. Other features of the OPAC include links to other systems, and other facilities to support user access including:

- a library map to enable the user to find where items are located, without reference to the classification scheme
- user-profile-based alerts to new items of stock
- user access via a PIN to information such as current and past loans and messages from the librarians

- access through the VISTA module to associated items
- access to the Internet; users can activate Netscape or other browsers from the OPAC screen, and visit sites.

A special Internet OPAC module allows libraries to offer their catalogues to library users on the Internet or intranet. Registered users are able to perform searches, print results and reserve items via e-mail.

Circulation control

All aspects of circulation, including issues, returns, reservations, booking, charges, fines, borrower history etc., are available from a single screen, which can be controlled by a bar-code scanner. The same technology can be used to operate a self-issue system with no keyboard, and enhanced security. Additional security is offered by the opportunity to hold user photographs on the database; these can be viewed at the point of issue, which removes the embarrassment associated with checking identity.

The advanced booking module enables Heritage to provide advanced reservations. Standard reservation facilities hold the item for the reader as soon as the item next becomes available. This module, additionally, allows a reader to specify a date from which an item is required and the period over which the item is to be used.

Management information.

A range of statistics can be generated. Heritage contains an enormous number of pre-defined reports. In addition, there are facilities for ad hoc report writing, user surveys and stocktaking.

DYNIX

This is a limited case study that is intended to focus primarily on the interlibrary loans module available as part of the DYNIX integrated system. DYNIX is marketed by Ameritech Library Services, who also market Horizon and other products.

The relatively new interlibrary loans (ILL) module supports DYNIX, Horizon and other supplier systems. The system automates the borrowing and lending activity within a library by linking to local systems, remote library catalogues, messaging utilities and commercial document suppliers, using a seamless interface. It allows libraries using different ILL systems to communicate regardless of the ILL software or hardware used. Users can initiate their own requests, which avoids re-keying by staff. Users can initiate requests from any of WEBPAC (DYNIX's Web OPAC), locally developed WWW forms, Horizon, DYNIX and other suppliers' systems, OCLC ILL, Docline and standard Internet e-mail. Requests are transmitted to the lending partner in the format required by that lending institution. The system supports many electronic transmission formats, including standard Internet, e-mail, fax, Z39.50, ftp and ISO 10161 (ILL protocol for communications).

GEAC

This case study is included in order to illustrate the functionality available in OPACs in large state-of-the-art systems. GEAC Computers Ltd produce two library systems products: ADVANCE designed for academic libraries, and PLUS for public libraries.

ADVANCE has the following modules:

- OPAC
- acquisitions and financial control
- circulation and interlibrary loans
- cataloguing and authority control
- serial control
- report writer.

PLUS has the following modules:

- circulation and borrower accounting
- cataloguing and authority control
- OPAC and community information
- serials control
- acquisitions and fund accounting
- management information.

GEAC has three linked cataloguing modules: GeoPac, GeoCat and GeoWeb.

GeoPac is a GUI-based OPAC, which provides the ability to search any number of local or remote databases in parallel, using a single interface. This may include the local OPAC, other libraries' catalogues and online or CD-ROM-based bibliographic databases and full-text resources. Multimedia capabilities allow the integration of electronic resources, such as sound clips, still images, video clips and full text, regardless of their location. GeoPac can also be used to search and retrieve records from major bibliographic utilities, such as OCLC, RLIN and SLS. Downloaded records can be edited or immediately transferred to the local ADVANCE or PLUS server.

GeoCat is a catalogue record creation and editing module, which makes full use of GUI facilities such as cut and paste, drag and drop, multi-lingual spell-check, and the ability to define, store and insert repetitive data using strings and macro options. Security features include forced authority file checking when a heading is created, MARC error checking and consistency checks. Full authority control allows headings to be edited at the point of use or independently, and gives full access to all works associated with any selected heading, so that correct usage can be established. Records can be retrieved directly from the local database, from any ISO 2709 (MARC) file, and from any Z39-50 server, such as any of the major bibliographic utilities.

GeoWeb provides full OPAC facilities to users accessing the ADVANCE or PLUS system via the World Wide Web. Links may easily be created directly from the institution or the library home page. The user only needs a form-based Web browser, such as Netscape or Internet Explorer. GeoWeb provides the translation between the HTML-based pages of the Web and the Z39-50 environment. GeoWeb can also be used to reach out from the library system, and acts as a gateway to other Z39.50-based catalogues and services. In this way, libraries can create virtual catalogues – a collection of Z39.50-based services which can be searched effectively with a single search. This offers significant potential to open up the library catalogue as a source of information rather than as just a referral tool.

UNICORN

UNICORN is marketed by SIRSI. It is an integrated UNIX-based collection management system in which all modules function seamlessly on a common bibliographic database, which can be accessed via a common operator interface. SIRSI has a number of client options, so that clients can be terminals personal computers with Windows or Web browsers. Specific modules include:

Bibliographic catalogue control

In addition to full MARC import and export facilities, UNICORN includes sophisticated techniques for addressing special collections, uncatalogued items and bound-with titles.

Authority control

This module establishes a single form for headings. Support for multiple authority files is standard, and any type of bibliographic heading may be controlled, with validation occurring immediately upon entry. To aid catalogue searching, a full ANSI thesaurus is also generated to provide SEE and SEE ALSO cross references.

Smartport

Smartport is fully integrated with the bibliographic catalogue and authority file. It uses the Z39-50 protocol to facilitate the capture of MARC records for acquisitions and cataloguing.

Enhanced public access

The public-access catalogue is designed to meet the needs of both novice and expert users. Separate choices are available for browsing and keyword searching. A full-text index is available. Search facilities include truncation, Boolean, relational, adjacency and proximity operators. The module also includes an information desk, a request desk and a user service desk.

Circulation

Circulation control covers check-out, check-in, renewals, holds and payments, and each of these functions is immediately available.

14.6 Managing a library management system

Systems management may be influenced by a number of factors. Here some of the issues that are perhaps peculiar to the management of these systems are briefly listed.

The environment

Libraries exist in differing kinds of organizations. The constraints imposed by policy-makers in those organizations may influence the options for computer systems, and the procedures that must be followed during systems development and evolution. Most environments in which larger libraries operate, such as local authorities and academic institutions, now have extensive experience with computer-based systems and will set standards in a number of areas.

The library

A library may be defined by its stock and its users. The users and the stock of a library may influence the optimum system for a given library. Users may, for example, determine the type of OPAC interface that is appropriate, or whether a homebound module is necessary. The nature of the stock may determine the priority that is accorded to access to other Internet resources and the types of support that might be offered to users in this context.

The systems manager

Most libraries find it necessary to identify a systems manager. In larger libraries systems management may merit a team of staff. These staff will play a central role in any planning for new or evolving systems, and will maintain existing systems. Maintenance will not only involve technical maintenance, but will also encompass user support. User support should take the form of a help desk or help line for problem-solving, training, documentation and anything else that is necessary to keep the system running. A feature of library management systems that makes them more demanding to support than some other systems is that the system records circulation transactions and must be available to do so whenever the library is open. Procedures such as the use of standalone units are necessary to cater for infrequent (!) but inevitable downtimes.

User education and training

Users of library systems fall into two categories: staff and library users. User training for staff can proceed as with many other systems, although, owing to the exigencies of the service points, much training may need to be conducted on a one-by-one basis. Training for library users is much more difficult to achieve in many libraries. The position is better in academic and organizational libraries than in public libraries, but there is always some fluidity of clientele, and generally a lack of interest in systematic training. The focus for library users is on the OPAC and associated CD-ROM products. If users are to use these products successfully, then the interface design, including the help system, is crucial.

Upgrades

Most libraries now have computer-based systems. Any further system enhancements will be based primarily on upgrades of existing systems. Providing appropriate licensing or maintenance agreements are in place, systems suppliers are increasingly supplying upgrades to all customers as a matter of routine. The systems manager must then decide how and when to implement upgrades and consider necessary changes in documentation and training.

Multiple sites

Many libraries extend over a number of different sites, and for public libraries these sites may be geographically scattered. In some instances, networks may not be appropriate to each site, and other standalone solutions such as CD-ROM OPACs may be more cost-effective. Public libraries also need to accommodate mobile libraries, special collections, and other special services such as school library services. Operating a system that serves all service points and lending support in system use may present a range of operational dilemmas.

Networks

Increasingly, as explored in the next chapter, libraries participate in networking activities. These activities generally involve communication between the local computer and an external computer, such as that of the book supplier, or bibliographic utilities or online search services. Effective communication of this kind implies the adoption of various standards.

Participation in systems development

Library management systems have developed with the assistance of library managers. Clearly, cooperative ventures have taken their direction from participants, but also most commercial systems have a user group and most systems developers listen to the proposals of the user group concerning systems developments. In addition, many systems allow library managers to configure their system to their own requirements. In both contexts, library managers do not merely acquire an off-the-shelf product and just use it. They also contribute to the development of the product, and through that to the future of library management systems.

....

Reflection   In what sense is the management of a LMS distinct from, or
integrated within, the management of the library service?
....

14.7 Futures for library management systems

Over the past few years the marketplace for library management systems has grown and matured. Most of the larger systems suppliers have been offering systems for some years, and more recently have been concentrating on enhancements to their systems, in an attempt to extend and consolidate their customer base. There is more change at the smaller end of the market, and a number of new systems have entered the scene in the past few years. Improvements in existing systems have focused on a number of areas, and these are establishing trends that can be expected to continue. Indeed, practical implementation in libraries of these developments will take some time as libraries gradually upgrade their systems. The latest releases of systems offer connectivity and user access that were no more than elements in a vision a few years ago. There is much work for library managers to do in identifying strategies for the optimum exploitation of the new technologies, without additional systems refinements. Chapter 1 reflects on some of the implications of such technological developments for the future of libraries and other organizations engaged in the information industry. These scenarios also have many implications for the future development of library management systems. Indeed, the very nature of such systems may change, as libraries and organizations select modules to fulfil specific purposes, and focus more significantly than at present on regular annual purchases and upgrades of hardware and software, rather than on the major project upgrades that have taken place every five to ten years over the past few years. Libraries are increasingly likely to tailor their own solutions using task-specific software tools, possibly with significant participation from users. These systems will handle many of the existing functions such as acquisitions and cataloguing, but will need to perform these functions in slightly different ways depending upon the additional functionality that is also made available.

Extra functions

Access to commercial resources

Systems must facilitate user access to commercial databases, other library resources, and document collections. The systems must tackle issues concerning liability, control of copyright, licensing and collecting of appropriate payments. Asset trading agreements must be forged across the information chain. Such systems may also need to accommodate the assessment and evaluation of resources by those seeking to acquire them. Systems will need to be able to manage who is allowed access to what, when, for how long or to what maximum charge, payment strategy, and associated rights. They will need to manage copyright issues as an integral function, and will need to be linked to the systems of publishers, editors, indexers, picture libraries and authors.

Meta-information about WWW sources

This needs to be easily accessible, possibly through the click of a mouse button; someone will need to maintain this information, and systems will need capabilities to support maintenance by the originators of the information.

Tailored user registration

Current systems tend to allocate users to groups linked to circulation rights. User registration will need to be more sophisticated, and users will need to be able to be members of several groups, as indeed they already are, but those groups tend to be associated with distinct systems. Typical groups might be:

- a member of staff
- a subscriber to the Internet
- a member of a local club publishing Web pages on the library's server.

Group working

Most current systems assume individual users. It will be necessary to develop tools for group working, as, for example, when a group might be performing a complex Internet search.

Enhancing existing operations

Libraries will continue to be concerned with acquisitions, cataloguing and circulation or access control, but in a multimedia environment which embraces both print and electronic sources, there are a number of potential refinements.

Acquisitions

There is plenty of scope for streamlining acquisitions. Users could submit requests electronically, including in their order reference to appropriate sources such as Internet bookshops, or publishers' alerting services. Orders will be validated on receipt, and users immediately informed of any unacceptable or unavailable documents, or any missing information. EDI will facilitate asset trading, including order processing, invoicing and delivery handling. Check-in will need to accommodate electronic as well as print documents. Profiles will allow notification of new items to users. The physical aspects of the ordering processes can be enhanced by the use of EDI to synchronize information at both ends of a supply link, so that each can understand the barcodes correctly.

Cataloguing

Cataloguing consistency can be improved further through spell checkers, style checkers and de-duplication tools. If records are to be shared it will be necessary to know which spell checker has been used. Catalogue tidying and global amendment software will improve the quality of catalogue databases. The cataloguing of electronic documents still presents a number of challenges, but also opportunities. Free text searching on the text of electronic documents offers access routes not traditionally available in catalogue records of print documents. Also, there is scope for further enhancement of links between citation records and multimedia document types, and for further work on indexing of, for example, images or video clips.

Systems evolution

Systems should be capable of evolution, and there should no longer be a need to replace complete systems every few years. Indeed, as systems become more complex, more interlinked and more integral to operations, this may be asking for trouble.

'Cybrarians'

The librarian of the future is beginning to emerge, but the future for librarians in cyberspace will only be secured through considerable adaptation and development. This will require a commitment to continuing professional development both on the part of the individual and on the part of their employing organizations.

Enhancing user access

Libraries will be able to encourage the use of electronic resources by large numbers of remote users for payment, or will be able to limit access to specific users. External users must be able to access the library's OPAC, but in addition, library users may use the OPAC to access a wide range of other Internet resources. The OPAC can act as a window on the world of information resources. Each user will have one or more personal log ins, allowing preferences, rights and activities to be stored for re-use. Search statements might be shared amongst users. Web-browser concepts such as structured bookmarks and backtracking will become widespread. Users will use the OPAC as one of a number of methods to maintain personal files without re-keying data. Users need to be able to store and re-use search statements and results. Personal documents can be linked to library citations or e-documents directly, and can be submitted as a potential library acquisition or supplied in response to a library document request. Client–server computing will allow users to select a search interface for a task, rather than accept a standard set of options.

OPAC interfaces need to be designed for different types of users. DYNIX's Kids Catalogue is an early example. Facilities for disabled people, and particularly the visually impaired, need to be incorporated into library OPACs. In all of this, users need the ability to choose their OPAC interface.

Most libraries now provide community information on Web pages rather than via a library management system. Increasingly this may involve the publication of Web documents, and even Web journals. This may necessitate converting documents to HTML format, or the use of a document management system. The same machine must be able to access these pages and the LMS, other applications on the local area network, such as CD-ROMs, the intranet, and the Internet. It is important that the look and feel and functionality of interfaces to these different resources should be consistent.

The other side of access is security. Security must be built in, and must be based on a comprehensive system of access rights, permissions, rules and parameters. Security also includes comprehensive, efficient and fast system back-up and restoration of lost data. Security will increasingly be linked to charging. Providing access to the wealth of Internet resources is expensive. Smartcards that record customers transactions are likely to be increasingly used to support charging, and may also be used as the security device for access to a range of organizational and external information resources. They could also be used with self-issue kiosks.

In summary, the future offers a number of options, but there are unlikely to be generic solutions that will accommodate every library and information management function and task. Users will continue to choose information sources on the basis of convenience, access and cost. Although future systems may offer users many opportunities to participate in systems design and to tailor interfaces and the collection of resources to which they have access, locating good, reliable and validated information is in some senses becoming more time consuming and difficult, not easier, and there will remain a role for an information manager. Library management systems will be an important tool in the armory of the information manager.

Summary   There is a range of large, mid-range and smaller library management systems. These can be grouped into four generations, with the latest releases of major systems moving towards fourth-generation systems. Recent systems enhancements can generally be grouped into the areas of: online ordering, faster catalogue creation, improved authority control, circulation control, interlibrary loans, management information, OPACs and community information. Self-service issue is an interesting new option. The management of LMS is influenced by a number of factors. These include: the environment, library resources and users, the role of the systems manager, multiple sites, upgrades and systems development, and the need for staff and user education and training. One future for LMS is that through the OPAC they may support access to a wide range of information resources and documents across the Internet. This will require attention to: metainformation, tailored registration, group working, and security and charging. We are witnessing the birth of the 'cybrarian', but development into adulthood will be contingent on appropriate continuing professional development.

REVIEW QUESTIONS

1   Describe the difference between the four generations of library management systems.
2   How can an LMS enhance customer service?
3   Discuss the applicability and consequences of self-service issue in libraries.
4   Describe the features of an OPAC of the future.
5   Identify the issues that need to be addressed for the effective management of LMS.

References

Lageborg, H. (1997) 'Self service in libraries: an overview', *Vine*, 105.

Bibliography

Adams, R. J. (1997) 'Minstrel: management information software tool for European libraries', *Program*, **31** (1), 33–45.
Alper, H. (1993) 'Selecting Heritage/Bookshelf-PC for the District Library, Queen Mary's University Hospital, Roehampton', *Program*, **27** (2), 173–82.
Anonymous (1996) 'Electronic public information/one-stop shops/kiosks', *Vine*, **102**.
Anonymous (1997) 'Self service in libraries', *Vine*, **105**.
Batt, C. (1994) *Information technology in public libraries*, London, Library Association Publishing.
Batt, C. (1995) 'The last migration', *Public library journal*, **10** (6), 159–61.
Cibbarelli, P. (1996) 'Library automation alternatives in 1996 and user satisfaction ratings of library users by operating system', *Computers in libraries*, **16** (2), 26–35.
Cortez, E. M. and Smorch, T. (1993) *Planning second generation automated library systems*, Westport, Greenwood Press.
Cousins, S. (1997) 'COPAC: new research library union catalogue', *The electronic library*, **15** (30), 185–8.
Dempsey, L., Russell, R. and Kirriemuir, J. (1996) 'Towards distributed library systems: Z39.50 in a European context', *Program*, **30** (1), 1–22.
Fisher, S. and Rowley, J. (1994) 'Management information and library management systems: an overview', *The electronic library*, **12** (2), 109–17.
Fletcher, M. (1996) 'The CATRIONA project: feasibility study and outcomes', *Program*, **30** (2), 99–107.
Furness, K. L. and Graham, M. E. (1996) 'The use of information technology in special libraries in the UK', *Program*, **30** (1), 23–37.

Griffiths, J-M. and Kertis, K. (1994) 'Automated system marketplace', *Library journal*, **119** (6).

Grosch, A. N. (1995) *Library information technologies and networks*, New York, Marcel Dekker.

Harbour, R. T. (1994) *Managing library automation*, London, Aslib.

Heseltine, R. (1994) 'Library automation', *Information UK outlooks*, 9.

Heseltine, R. (1994) 'New perspectives on library management systems', *Program*, 28 (2), 53–61.

Leeves, J. (1995) 'Library systems then and now', *Vine*, 100, 19–23.

Leeves, J. and Russell, R. (1995) *Libsys.uk: a directory of library systems in the United Kingdom*, London, LITC, South Bank University.

Mandelbaum, J. B. (1992) *Small project automation for library and information centers*, Westport/London, Meckler.

Matthews, J. (1995) 'Moving to the next generation: Aston University's selection and implementation of Galaxy 2000', *Vine*, 101, 42–9.

Muirhead, G. (1994) *The systems librarian*, London, Library Association Publishing.

Murray, I. R. (1997) 'Assessing the effect of new generation library management systems', *Program*, 31 (1-4), 313–27.

Rowley, J. and Fisher, S. M. (1992) *BOOKSHELF: a guide for librarians and systems managers*, Aldershot, Ashgate.

Saffady, W. (1994) *Introduction to automation for librarians*, Chicago, American Library Association.

Stafford, J. (1996) 'Self issue the management implications. The introduction of self service at the University of Sunderland', *Program*, 30 (4), 375–83.

Tedd, L. A. (1995) 'An introduction to sharing resources via the Internet in academic library and information centres in Europe', *Program*, 29 (1), 43–61.

Wilson, M. (1994) 'TALIS at Nene: an experience in migration in a college library', *Program*, 28 (3), 239–51.

Wood, J. (ed.) (1993) *European directory of software for libraries and information centres*, Aldershot, Ashgate.

Wright, K. C. (1995) *Computer related technologies in library operations*, Aldershot, Gower.

Yeates, R. (1996) 'Library automation: the way forward?', *Program*, 30 (3), 239–53.

15

Document delivery

LEARNING OUTCOMES

Document delivery has always been at the heart of the services offered by libraries, publishers and others in the information industry. Document delivery needs to embrace the delivery of both print and electronic documents. Although mechanisms for print delivery are well established, these have been made more efficient through the introduction of electronic ordering. There has been rapid development in recent years in electronic document delivery, particularly in relation to electronic journals. By the end of this chapter you will understand the roles of the following agents in document delivery:

- library networks and consortia
- document delivery on CD-ROM
- commercial document delivery services
- library suppliers, subscription agents and EDI
- electronic journal suppliers and publishers.

15.1 Introduction

Document delivery is a key element in access to information. Document delivery involves the integration of document discovery, the location of a supplier, request and delivery. Electronic document delivery can be defined more narrowly in terms of the delivery of documents in digitized form, or more widely to include any of these stages in electronic form. Both print and electronic document delivery are important, and form aspects of this chapter. Indeed, many of the agencies that are involved in electronic document delivery are major players in print document delivery. Important also is that the dividing line between print and electronic document delivery is often not clearly defined. Document delivery is a complex process which spans time and distance between customer and supplier. It takes many forms, can involve documents in a variety of different forms and involves a number of intermediaries. Table 15.1 summarizes some of the different routes to document delivery. This shows that document delivery can involve all of: authors, publishers, subscriptions agents, document delivery services, book suppliers and librarians. Since information is produced in a number of different formats, and this production involves different agencies, it is not surprising that there are many options for document delivery. Many of these agencies are involved in both electronic and print-based document delivery. Librarians, publishers and other document delivery services need to wrestle with the complexities of document delivery in a hybrid environment in which conventional document delivery is coupled with electronic document delivery. It is, for example, a salutary reminder of the relative infancy of electronic documents that the British Library Document Supply Centre, the UK's national document delivery service, responds to 95% of the requests that it receives for loans by sending a printed copy of the document.

The other challenge that underlies any discussion of electronic document delivery is the fact that the concept of 'document' has its origins in a print-based context. A book or an issue of a journal is clearly an identifiable unit, but how should and will the boundaries of electronic documents be defined? This can be illustrated by reflecting on the contents of the previous few chapters. Online search services, CD-ROM and document management and publishing systems are all concerned with information, and arguably document delivery. An extreme definition of a document would view an abstract as a document, although normally an abstract would be seen as a document surrogate on the basis of which a user would choose to access other resources. On the other hand, when full-text databases are delivered through these media, document delivery is certainly being achieved.

Document delivery, and specifically electronic journal delivery, has generated significant attention in recent years. Work in this area has focused on the major academic and research libraries, and has to some extent been seen as one possible solution to being able to maintain adequate access to journals for researchers and students in an era of reducing public funds and increasing journal subscriptions. Many of these projects are experimental, but some are so significant that it is likely that they will evolve into commercial ventures, provided that issues concerning charging and the management of large consortia can be resolved.

Table 15.1 *Agents in document delivery*

Creation of document	Alerting to document existence	Provision of document
Author	Library	Library
Editor	Publisher	Library consortium
Publisher	Subscription agent	Subscription agent
	Current awareness service	Publisher
	Bibliographic database producer	Current-awareness service
	Online search service	Commercial document delivery service

15.2 Options for document delivery systems

Table 15.1 shows a range of different options for document delivery channels. Document delivery channels may be categorized on the basis of the agents involved, or on the basis of other criteria, including:

1 Whether the document is delivered directly to the end-user at his/her desktop or to the library as intermediary.
2 The format of the document. The issues may be different for books, journals, journal articles, and reference works such as directories.
3 The media in which or through which the document is distributed. This might include CD-ROM, fax or online/Web. Delivery in print form might also be a consequence of a request or order that is submitted electronically.
4 The nature of the delivery contract. Delivery may be considered as tantamount to purchase (such as when a book is purchased by a user), or loan (such as when a book is borrowed by a user from a library or via an interlibrary loan network). Many electronic document delivery contracts are licenses to use the document under certain circumstances. Copyright and licensing are key issues in any electronic document delivery system.

....

Reflection   Which document delivery channels have you used? What are the criteria which determine your use of channel?

....

Here, we identify five different categories of document delivery services:

1 Library networks and consortia, which often create union catalogue databases as a means of accessing and sharing the resources of a group of libraries. Any types of document may be exchanged, but the emphasis has been on printed books. In principle, other short documents can be digitized and delivered electronically.
2 CD-ROM suppliers of full-text and multimedia databases, such as directories and encyclopaedias.
3 Document delivery services, including commercial services and the British Library, may provide access to documents announced through the database available from the online search services or other sources. The emphasis is on journal articles, conference papers and research reports, but also includes books.
4 Library suppliers and subscription agents offer electronic ordering of both print and electronic documents. Generally there is a divide between serials subscription agents and book suppliers with regard to the documents covered, and accordingly with regard to the nature of the services offered.

5   Electronic journal suppliers, including a number of publishers. Journals may be supplied on CD-ROM or for online access. Access is acquired either to the complete journal as published or on an article basis, on request.

15.3 Library networks and consortia

Librarians have engaged in cooperative ventures, or networks and consortia, for many years. The early objectives of these networks were associated with exchange of catalogue records and print-based document delivery or interlibrary loan. These functions still remain important, but they are now facilitated by electronic exchange of records, and record keeping. Often, print document delivery has been supplemented by electronic document delivery.

Groups of libraries have maintained union catalogues for many years. The earliest union catalogues were great card catalogues, whose creation was a labour of love and which were very difficult to keep up to date. Similarly, interlibrary loan arrangements existed between libraries long before the latest computer-based systems and data networks. However, under these arrangements, interlibrary loan was often a slow process. Cooperation is generally seen as a means of sharing resources or containing cataloguing costs. In recent years networks have increasingly become dependent upon telecommunications networks and computer systems. The first computer-based cooperative ventures, whilst being ambitious for their time, would seem very basic now. Batch systems, with too much paper, little connectivity between processors, and limited online access, predated the much more streamlined systems that it is easy to take for granted today. Systems have undergone major development since the late 1960s and early 1970s. Nevertheless, the central objectives of networking remain constant. These are

- to reveal the contents of a large number of libraries or a large number of publications, especially through accessibility of catalogue databases, using OPAC interfaces
- to make the resources shown in these catalogue databases available to individual libraries and users when and where they need them
- to share the expense and work involved in creating catalogue databases through the exchange of records and associated activities.

Ancillary functions that might also be fulfilled by networks include

- distribution and publication of electronic journals and other electronic documents
- end-user access to other databases, such as those available on the online hosts and CD-ROM
- value-added services such as electronic mail, directory services and file transfer
- exchange of bibliographic and authority records, usually in MARC format.

In the beginning, networks were established with limited and well-defined objectives. As the use of networking has become more pervasive, and as the infrastructure has become available which makes data transfer more common, consortia and participants in consortia are linked to other consortia or members in consortia. The end-user can choose more than one route through the maze of networks in order to locate a given document. Barriers are already less defined by the physical limitations of networks than by licensing and access arrangements. Technology imposes few constraints, but politics and economics are beginning to define the boundaries.

The key agencies in library networking fall into two main categories:

1 Large national libraries or centralized cataloguing services which create large bibliographic databases and in some instances provide leadership in document delivery.
2 Cooperatives set up by groups of libraries who feel that they and their users can profit by resource-sharing, such as might be associated with interlibrary loans, and sharing in the creation of a union catalogue database.

The United States is internationally significant in library networking, so we will review developments there first. Amongst the front-runners in United States networking, and responsible for much of the success of networking, is the Library of Congress. The Library of Congress first contributed to networking by acting as a centralized cataloguing service, and distributing printed catalogue cards, commencing in 1901. Experimentation with computer-based systems started in the 1960s with the MARC Project and led to the MARC Distribution Service. The LCMARC database is central to the Library of Congress's cataloguing services. The database is based on the Library of Congress's cataloguing of its own collections, with additional records from cooperating libraries. The database can be accessed online via a number of online search services. The Library of Congress has also played a major part in coordinating networking, and has been involved in a number of projects which demonstrate its commitment to cooperation. Two major projects that merit mention are CONSER and the Linked Systems Project. CONSER (Cooperative Online Serials) was a cooperative venture which sought to build a machine-readable database of serials cataloguing information. The Linked Systems Project (LSP), started in 1980, aimed to establish a national network of services and utilities linked by a standard interface.

Another agency in United States networking which has made a very major contribution is OCLC. OCLC was founded in 1971 by a group of Ohio college libraries. OCLC has played a major role both in the United States and beyond in record supply, research and the sharing of experience. Currently over 10,000 libraries in 26 countries make use of OCLC's services. The OCLC database is the largest catalogue records database in the world. Various services are related to the database; these are summarized in Figure 15.1.

OCLC Online Union Catalog

PRISM Cataloguing, including record supply, authority control, export format, passport software, CD-ROM cataloguing, PromptCat (a copy cataloguing service), and PromptSelect (an acquisitions service linked to Prism and FirstSearch)

Resource sharing, including PRISM ILL (interlibrary loans based on the OCLC Online Union Catalog) and access to document supply centres

Reference services, including FirstSearch and EPIC (an online search service for professional searchers)

Document delivery, including direct links from the databases in FirstSearch, and Prism ILL

Fig. 15.1 *OCLC services*

Other networks in the United States and Canada are:

- WLN, known previously as the Western Library Network, and earlier as the Washington Library Network
- RLG, or the Research Libraries Group
- UTLAS International, formerly University of Toronto Library Automation System – an important Canadian initiative.

An important recent initiative from RLG is the Ariel software. Ariel is an implementation of FTP for document delivery. It is a scanning and transmission system. The software resides on a PC running TCP/IP networking protocol and Windows GUI. It controls a locally attached scanner and printer and can sense and receive scanned documents via FTP. Records for interlending and document request are not dealt with by the system, and need to be managed separately. Ariel has been widely used between libraries within consortia. In the United Kingdom it was used in the LAMDA project, which involved four libraries from the M25 Consortium and five from the CALIM consortium. Version 2 of the software, released in 1997, included the option of transmitting documents as MIME (Multimedia Internet Mail Extensions) attachments to Internet mail. This, together with other approaches, has been an element in project JEDDS. Work from JEDDS has input into EDDIS.

EDDIS is a project that is attempting to integrate the whole process of information access, from discovery to delivery. This project will complete in 1998, and is expected to deliver an operational system in which users log into a local server, and the server manages access to remote databases and suppliers. Remote systems could be other EDDIS systems or any system which is EDDIS-compliant in the sense that it is implementing the same standards. EDDIS is designed as an end-user service which integrates document discovery, location, request and receipt available through a WWW interface. In addition it allows the librarian to control end-user activities transparently by configuring the system with library business policy decisions and by offering varying levels of mediation as part of the service. The local OPAC remains external to the server, along with remote OPACs and other bibliographic databases. The system might provide access to books and periodical articles in print and digitized form. These projects have demonstrated that electronic document delivery is possible, but implementation depends upon an acceptance of standards and a critical mass of users.

As in the United States, the first networking activities in the United Kingdom were associated with the centralized cataloguing service. The British National Bibliography, which is now the responsibility of the British Library Bibliographic Services Division, was established in 1950. Initially BNB was a printed product which listed books received on legal deposit; since 1991, the main classified section contains two sections: a list of forthcoming titles and a list of titles recently received on legal deposit. A MARC distribution service began in 1969, initially based on machine-readable versions of the records in BNB, and referred to as the BNBMARC database. Now BLMARC records are used for local cataloguing and associated purposes. The BLMARC database now includes many other records generated by other sections of the British Library. BLAISE, the British Library Automated Information Service, is a major avenue through which BLMARC records may be accessed. Alongside these developments, the British Library Document Supply Centre has established itself as one of the leading document delivery agents. The BLDSC supplies 4 million documents a year. Requests are carried out electronically through the BLDSC'S proprietary ART system, although requests by e-mail are increasing. Requests by every route are stored in the Automated Request Processing, which streams them to the relevant document storage area. Journal articles are then picked from the shelves to be copied or scanned, or selected from ADONIS (more details below). Although 94 % of documents are supplied by photocopy, fax technology is being further developed. The British Library's Digital Library Programme has given priority to article alerting and improved request and delivery from digital store.

Inside Science Plus and Inside Social Sciences and Humanities Plus jointly offer access to the contents of 20,000 journals. Electronic ordering of any articles retrieved from the database is possible. Delivery options include two-hour fax, courier and post.

BLDSC has also contributed to the EDIL (Electronic Document Interchange between Libraries) project, with partners in France, the Netherlands and Germany, working on a mechanism for fast interchange of electronic documents between libraries. This project led to EDDIS, and an experimental X400 service to use electronic mail for document delivery. EDIL identified the available mechanism for electronic document delivery, and informed the growing view that

Internet standards and electronic mail are the most appropriate approaches to electronic document delivery.

BLAISE is the British Library Automated Information Service, which provides access to over 22 databases containing over 17.5 million bibliographic records. As an online search service it can be accessed using either a command language or a GUI on the WWW. A direct link to the British Library Document Supply Centre means that customers can place orders for documents very easily. Figure 15.2 shows the bibliographic files that are available through BLAISE. These can be used for subject searching, bibliographic checking, acquisition, compiling book-lists or record supply. BLAISE also offers access to a number of specialist data-bases, and the catalogues of the British Library collections.

Reflection   Summarize the contribution that the British Library has made to document delivery. How does this compare with the role played by the Library of Congress in the United States?

British National Bibliography 1950–
Library of Congress 1968–
British Books in Print 1965–
The Stationery Office 1976–
ISSN UK Centre for Serials, 1974–

Fig. 15.2 *BLAISE bibliographic files*

There are also a number of library networks in the United Kingdom. Two long-standing organizations are: BLCMP and LASER:

BLCMP, formerly known as Birmingham Libraries Cooperative Mechanization Project, is a cooperative venture that embraces a range of services that are used by a large number of libraries. BLCMP maintains extensive MARC databases, which include records for books, audiovisual items, music and serials. An extensive authority file is also maintained. TALIS is BLMCP's library man-agement system (see Chapter 14).

LASER, or the London and South Eastern Region, started life with a focus on interlending and resource sharing rather than on cataloguing. Nevertheless, in order to achieve its objectives it built a large union catalogue, and later a biblio-graphic database. This is at the heart of LASER's V3.Online service, which pro-vides access to this database and an electronic interlending system. A significant recent development led by LASER has been EARL (Electronic Access to Resources in Libraries). The EARL consortium of UK public libraries was estab-lished in 1995 to develop the role of public libraries in providing library and infor-mation services over the network. Its membership includes more than 50% of UK public libraries. Examples of EARL initiatives include EARLWeb, a network of public library information resources, and a consortium purchase deal to OCLC's Firstsearch service.

Exchange of expertise and plans for further UK networking have also been fostered by a number of other groups, agencies and activities. CURL, the Consortium of University Research Libraries, for example, succeeded in creating a major machine-readable catalogue database, covering the catalogue records of the UK's seven largest university libraries. The records are available for shared cataloguing and are distributed on tape, using file transfer and capturing session logs. The database is available to other libraries via JANET, and via the more recently developed COPAC interface.

JANET, or the Joint Academic Network, is not a library network, but a telecommunications network that provides communication links between users of computing facilities in over 100 universities, research establishments and other institutions. JANET has been widely exploited by libraries for mutual access to library OPACs, and for file transfer and electronic mail. Gateways are available to other networks such as EARN (European Academic Research Network), the Internet and public data networks.

BIDS is a service offered by the UK Office for Library Networking, which was established in 1989 with funding from the British Library; it is based at the University of Bath. The function of the Office is to support the development of networking activities amongst UK libraries, by representing the needs of libraries to the computing and telecommunications industry, and by promoting effective use of existing and developing networking infrastructures in the UK and abroad. BIDS has played an important role in making electronic databases available at competitive rates within the UK academic community. Key databases are: BIDS ISI Service, BIDS EMBASE Service, BIDS COMPENDEX service, BIDS UnCover service and BIDS Inside Information Service. BIDS was unique in being one of the first national services to offer access to bibliographic databases free at the point of delivery.

Other consortia have been drawn together to develop projects associated with electronic journals. Amongst these are:

The **UK Pilot Site License Initiative**, instigated by the Joint Information Systems Committee (JISC) of the Higher Education Funding Councils. Publishers make their journals available, through their own servers to all universities and colleges throughout the UK. Access to the servers is provided by the JournalsOnLine service hosted by BIDS. JournalsOnLine provides Web access to a search form on which the user selects the publisher and enters the search strategy. The search is made against a headings file at BIDS, which is compiled from publishers' data. On discovering useful documents, the user has the option of requesting them online and taking delivery online. The publishers store their electronic journals in portable document format (PDF), which preserves the look of the printed counterpart when delivered to the desktop. This project finishes in

1998; if it continues as a self supporting scheme, it will have a significant impact on the document delivery services, most notable of which is the British Library.

15.4 Document delivery on CD-ROM

Chapter 10 describes CD-ROM as an information delivery medium. Databases that might be supplied on CD-ROM include both bibliographic and source databases. Typically, documents such as directories, encyclopaedias, dictionaries, collections of annual reports, collections of literary works may be recorded on CD-ROM and are available either for the consumer or in the library marketplace. Where the library acquires a document on CD-ROM, they may provide networked access to the document, under appropriate networking licenses. The details of such routes to document delivery have already been explored in Chapter 10. In this context, however, it is worthwhile to make mention of the ADONIS system.

ADONIS is a CD-ROM-based article delivery system. Articles are from over 680 titles and more than 70 publishers in the biomedical fields. It may be seen as an alternative to ILL in the context of a large research library. The documents in ADONIS are images; this means that the actual text of the article is not searchable. Items included in the index alone have currency as search terms. More recently, SGML files have been included that cover tables of contents, bibliographic searching and text searching, based at least on abstracts. This index is searchable using Boolean searching, comparative and proximity searching, and wildcard searching. Printing an article incurs the Publishers Copyrights Charges (PCC) This is set by each publisher. Update CD-ROMs are produced as soon as ADONIS has processed the journal issues; these are received at the rate of 100–120 per week.

In the latest release publishers will submit and documents will be stored in PDF files; this improves the image quality. The client software will allow individual readers to prepare and store current-awareness profiles, which store a list of titles, and retrieve the table of contents of the chosen titles at each update. Subscribing sites can select a core set of journals to which to subscribe, and site licenses are arranged accordingly. The system can be accessed through multi-platform client software or through Web browsers. This should facilitate the integration of information from the systems into the serials management systems used by the subscribing libraries.

15.5 Commercial document delivery services

The dividing line between searching databases through the online search services and obtaining documents, which began to blur when the mainstream online services began to load full-text records, is now barely evident. Many of the new commercial document delivery services are directed towards end-users. Most involve partnerships or strategic alliances between document providers and online services. They often rely on a combination of technologies, or on alternative technologies, like fax, the Internet, or a dedicated electronic bulletin board system. Although none of these arrangements are as streamlined as electronic full document delivery, most accept document requests as an integral part of the search process, and the experience is one of searching and retrieving.

OCLC FirstSearch, for example, is an online search service that is widely used in the academic community (see Figure 15.3). It provides access to a wide range of general purpose databases, with an easy-to-use menu interface with cost controls through end-use pricing. Document delivery for articles identified through access to OCLC FirstSearch's bibliographic databases can be through a number of different modes:

- ASCII full-text online
- printed document images, delivered by fax, with a one-hour delivery option available
- electronic document images in respect of a set of 1000 general-interest, health and business journals, which are available for on-screen viewing and desktop printing via the WWW

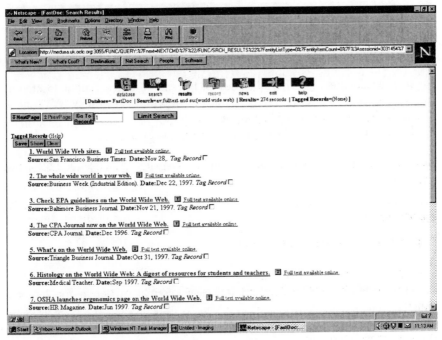

Fig. 15.3 *Document delivery through OCLC FirstSearch*

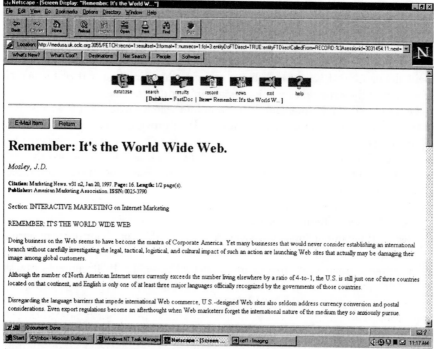

Fig. 15.3 *Continued*

- Internet documents: URL addresses for Internet resources can be located in records from OCLC's NetFirst database; hyperlinks on the WWW allow immediate linking to highlighted documents
- Prism ILL – links to 5500 libraries worldwide for ILL.

Checklist 15.1 lists document supply centres accessible through OCLC online search services.

CHECKLIST 15.1

Document supply centres used by OCLC

British Library Document Supply Centre
Canadian Institute for Scientific and Technical Information Centre for Research Libraries
Danish Loan Centre
Dynamic Information Corp
ERIC Document Reproduction Service

Facts Online
The Information Store
Information on Demand
ISI 'The Genuine Article'
National Agriculture Library
National Library of Canada
National Technical Information Service
National Translation Centre
University Microfilms International

Another example of a commercial service linked to a search service is KRSourceOne, the document delivery service offered as part of the DIALOG portfolio of products. Documents can be ordered through DIALORDER, on DIA-LOG, or through e-mail, phone, fax or the WWW. Documents are delivered by fax, Internet and e-mail, mail or express mail. The UnCover Reveal current awareness service allows users to receive tables of contents of specific journals direct to their e-mail box, in order to support alerting. Alternatively, documents can be automatically delivered on the basis of a DIALOG Alert (current-awareness) profile. In order to offer this service SourceOne has significant holdings of patents and business articles, as well as a comprehensive pharmaceutical/biomedical collection and computer/engineering collection. In addition a large number of libraries (mostly academic libraries in the United States) are used as contributing sources.

UnCover is a sister service to KRSourceOne. The current-awareness aspects of this service have already been noted in Chapter 12. Document delivery is from a periodicals database that indexes 17,000 multidisciplinary titles. This database can be searched through a Web interface (see Figure 15.4) by topic, author name, or periodical title.

Reflection   Examine Figure 15.4. What can you learn from it about the
              nature of document delivery services?

15.6 Library suppliers, subscription agents and EDI

The relationship between the library and the book supplier and subscription agent has evolved significantly in recent years. Clearly book suppliers also need to maintain up-to-date records of recent publications, so that they can indicate the stock that they have for purchase. For example, Whitaker's Books in Print and British Books in Print have long been used by libraries as collection development tools. They are now available on CD-ROM as Bookbank, and records can be more readily consulted and downloaded.

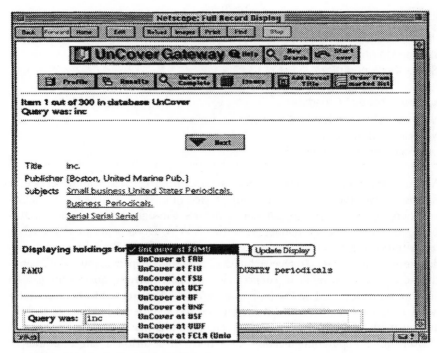

Fig. 15.4 *The Web interface to UnCover*

In recent years, many book suppliers have established electronic ordering systems. These allow the library to consult a book supplier's database online for book selection purposes. Some systems then allow librarians to download records into their own database, to form the basis of acquisitions records.

A more long-standing scheme is Cataloguing-in-Publication. CIP is the cataloguing of documents prior to their publication so that cataloguing data can be printed with the document itself. These data are also used in databases such as those of the book trade, which librarians and others may consult during collection development. CIP has been coordinated in the United States by the Library of Congress and in the United Kingdom by the British Library. From 1992, the British Library ceased to create its own CIP entries; these are now generated by Whitaker.

In the electronic ordering of books, links can be made from author to retailer via publisher, wholesaler and library. The author starts the process by preparing a manuscript on a word-processor. When the publisher receives the manuscript, details are entered into the in-house bibliographic database in a standard format. This information is then transmitted electronically to the bibliographic agencies in MARC format, for onward transmission to libraries, library suppliers and retailers. The publisher uses these data to generate catalogues, fliers and advertisements, and passes the information to the company's distribution system. These data are used by the wholesaler as a basis of stock records. The retailer identifies required titles on CD-ROM, places an order, and at the same time checks availability with the wholesaler or publisher's computer. When the order is received by a supplier, a picking instruction, order acknowledgement and electronic delivery note can be generated. When the book arrives at a bookshop, the bookseller uses a bar-code reader to check delivery against the order and enters the book into the shop's own stock-control system. When sales are made, the electronic point-of-sale system updates the stock-control system, generating a new order if required.

Not all of these stages are relevant to libraries, but clearly libraries interface with suppliers or wholesalers, and then make items available, recording transactions through their circulation-control system.

One of the challenges is to integrate EDI with library management systems, and specifically acquisitions functions. EDILIBE Project (Electronic Data Interchange for Libraries and Booksellers) is a recent European project that has investigated these issues.

Many of the serials subscriptions agents such as Swets, Ebsco and Blackwell have developed a range of other services based on the databases of journals and links with publishers and libraries that have been necessary for serials subscription services. It is important to note, however, that one component of their services relates to the management of subscriptions for print serials. Most agents, like Swets, provide documents such as invoices, checklists, packing lists and financial analysis reports in machine-readable form, and EDI is a central feature of transactions with both publishers and libraries. This data can be provided on diskette, magnetic tape, or via Internet e-mail or FTP, in formats to match library management systems. In addition, services like DataSwets, which give electronic access to the subscriptions database, enable users to search for bibliographic and price information, and to look up subscription details. Users can check invoice data, process orders and claims, and view claim replies.

Serials subscriptions agents have diversified their activities significantly. EBSCO is a good example of this diversification. EBSCO offers four services:

- EBSCO Subscription Services, to manage serials subscriptions
- EBSCO Publishing, which publishes electronic indexing, abstracting and full-text databases, both online and on CD-ROM
- EBSCOdoc, a document delivery service providing article delivery of print documents (EBSCOdoc ALERT is the associated current-awareness service)
- EBSCOhost, an online client–server system providing search and retrieval of abstracts and full-text articles from multiple databases.

15.7 Electronic journal publishers and suppliers

Electronic journals take two different forms:

- journals that are otherwise published in print form, available in digital form

- electronic-only journals, which do not necessarily need a publisher, and which can be managed by an editor and a scholarly community.

Both of these types of journals are discussed in this section.

The BLEND Project (1980–85) identified the factors that are necessary for successful electronic journals. Some of these remain unresolved, and although many exclusively e-journals have been launched, only a very few have been successful. The BLEND Project successfully archived articles in four types of journal: a referred journal, a poster journal, a software reviews journal and a bibliographic journal. Project Quartet designed and built a hypertext electronic journal. Other projects include ADONIS and ELVYN. ELVYN delivered a new start-up journal via the Internet for immediate user access via campus networks. A number of journals have more recently been created on the WWW, either with funding from various sources to support their creation, or as non-profit-making ventures. Each of these may be viewed as an experiment in its own right; the role for e-journals will become more evident as more cases of successful and established e-journals can be identified.

Much of the current interest in electronic journals has been fuelled by the commercial need for journal publishers to be at the cutting edge of developments. This has led to a number of experiments with the digitization of print journals in recent years. Some of these concern on-request delivery of articles, whilst others handle the journal as a unit. The first electronic journal projects were led by publishers, but more recently there has been a recognition of the need for collaboration, and the most successful projects are those such as the UK Pilot Site License Initiative, which is mediated by BIDS and involves major academic libraries and licensing arrangements with publishers.

Academic Press launched APPEAL, a three-year development project under which libraries or a consortium of libraries can opt for access to one of more of the 175 AP journals. APPEAL permits unlimited viewing, searching, copying, downloading and printing for personal research or company internal business purposes and for intra-library loan within the consortium. Access to the IDEAL database of journal tables of contents can be achieved with any standard Web browser. Authorized users at sites within licensed library networks of the project will be able to view, print and download compete articles in Adobe's Acrobat format.

LINK is an electronic journal service available from Springer. It provides access to a few hundred journals. Most of these are electronic versions of print journals, but there are also an increasing number of electronic-only versions of journals; books are also included. The advantages of this format are seen to be:

- proven quality, through the editorial and peer reviewing system
- rapid publication – Springer aims to make the electronic version available before the print version, and possibly as soon as the final version is approved by the author

- sophisticated or simple searching – searching results in the display of a list of hits, arranged in order by relevance raking
- multimedia supplements, including colour images, sound, video, datasets and software.

The basic services of LINK, such as searching, metainformation, tables of contents and abstracts, are free. Access to the journal collection is subscription-based, although access is initially free to subscribers to the print version. Most of the articles are available in different file formats. The format type differs from journal to journal. The most widely used format is the portable document format (.PDF). In PDF format, articles on the monitor look exactly the same as printed article. Other formats for delivery are Postscript, TeX and HTML. The user can easily choose the file format.

A number of journal publishers are making journals available in print and electronic form, yet they are worried about any significant shift to electronic journals, and away from print journals, because they cannot predict what effect this will have on their revenues. Optimum pricing strategies, both in terms of basic issues such as whether journals are made available on a subscription basis or on a pay-as-you-go basis, and in terms of price levels, are not obvious. The Internet provides an unparalleled opportunity for self-publishing, and for the exchange of information within the scientific, academic and professional communities that could entirely side-step traditional intermediaries such as publishers and librarians. If publishers are to survive in this environment, it is important to recognize the contribution that publishers offer in disseminating and adding value to scholarship and research, and to separate this from the printed artefact that has traditionally been viewed as the publishers' medium of output.

In this context, publishing can be seen as involving the preparation and packaging of information into a form that is easily accessible to the user:

1   A journal is created as an imprint or brand. The journal's scope, authority and content depends upon the editorial board.
2   A journal paper passes through a number of processes: preparation and submission, peer review, editorial preparation, copy editing and proof reading, publication (including marketing and distribution), and archiving and indexing.
3   Authors must submit new work that does not overlap significantly with previous submissions, and must link their contributions to related contributions.
4   Through this process, journals and authors acquire standing and prestige, and publishers accumulate profits.

The transition to electronic journals poses challenges in a number of areas of journal production:

1   Publishers need to develop new skills in multimedia material, and in facilitating interaction between scholars.
2   Publishers will need to acquire a much more in-depth knowledge of copyright and licensing opportunities, especially in relation to the international arena.
3   The process of peer review needs to be re-evaluated in order to accommodate methodologies for reviewing and authenticating multimedia material.
4   Academic staff, and authors in particular, need to relinquish the traditions of research publishing associated with print journals, which are intimately involved with tenure, promotion and grant, of research moneys.
5   Institutions need to be convinced that electronic journals are cost-effective and can be networked for multiple-user access at a price that is acceptable to them. In particular, at the present time, electronic journals are often in a trial phase and libraries have maintained the print subscription for archival purposes.

There is also still some scope for technological developments:

1   The printed word is still the best medium for reading narrative text. Most research papers are predominately text; they are difficult to read on screen.
2   Colour illustrations in print are of a better quality.
3   Mathematic symbols and diacritics are accommodated better in print.
4   Printed documents are portable and do not require any special equipment.
5   Print-based journals have a 'fixity' which facilitates the structuring of knowledge associated with retrieval, citation, archiving and, ultimately, scholarship.

The challenges posed by electronic journals for all of the stakeholders involved in the validation and dissemination of knowledge are significant in terms of their future roles, but they are also central to the way in which the information society will manage and understand its knowledge base.

In addition, the transition from print to electronic journals for libraries poses a number of critical questions. These are summarized by Barnes (1997):

1   Will the electronic version of the journal cost more or less than the paper version?
2   What will be the licensing terms and who will negotiate them?
3   How quickly should I transition to electronic journals?
4   Should I discontinue my print subscription?
5   Which electronic journals services will provide me with a critical mass of journals relevant to my users?
6   Will I have to link to several different e-journal services?
7   Will I be able to select the journals I want in my collection or will they be bundled by the publisher or vendor?

8   How will the electronic journal be integrated with my local catalogue and other reference services, such as bibliographic databases, table-of-contents services and document delivery?

Services such as Blackwell's Electronic Journal Navigator addresses some of these issues, by seeking to offer a single point of access, reference, control and financial management for all of a library's electronic journal subscriptions. This service includes:

- management of electronic journal subscriptions, including centralized ordering, consolidated invoicing and a central point of claims and administration (also tackles the issue of the multiplicity of pricing and licensing models offered by different publishers)
- comprehensive management reports to facilitate the tracking of usage
- an electronic archive (Blackwell are negotiating with publishers and archiving stores concerning permanent electronic archives)
- both subscription access and pay-per-view access for articles in electronic journals to which libraries do not subscribe
- a single access and authentication point for all electronic journals, on multiple servers, including simplified password and access management
- a single interface to support browsing and searching (the different viewer software used by journals, including HTML, PDF and RealPage, are all supported)
- alerting service and delivery of full-text electronic articles direct to a user's PC.

A comparable service is Microinfo's Electronic Media Service. Microinfo provides and manages access to the services of a number of publishers. It offers access to publications in various electronic media, including CD-ROM. Microinfo offers advanced subscriptions management, electronic media news mail, electronic media directory, and network licence negotiation.

Reflection   To what extent does Blackwell's Electronic Navigator address the concerns that libraries might have about the substitution of electronic journals for print journals?

15.8 The future for document delivery

Documents will continue to be delivered in a range of different electronic as well as print formats for many years to come. Different formats are appropriate for different purposes. However, there may be a shift between the size of the demand for documents in different formats, and an increasingly more sophisticated evaluation of the role of electronic documents. Similarly, there are likely to be changes in the means of access to documents and the agencies involved in providing that access. This chapter has described a range of different services, many of which are new, and some of which are still undergoing initial technical or market evaluation. The situation is extremely volatile. Worse, the nature of documents, and their role in access to information and avenues for access to documents, are fundamental to many of the services and systems described earlier in this text. Evolution rather than revolution is to be anticipated, but for some, or possibly many, resource constraints will limit appropriate development in keeping with technological and marketplace opportunities. For these the evolution may be so fast that it will be experienced as revolution. Some of the forces at work in this evolution, that are likely to impact directly on document delivery include:

1   **Increases in information available.** Quite apart from new information becoming available on Websites daily, recent years have witnessed significant increases in the number of journal titles, and the number of articles published by each journal; this has led in turn to price rises, which have posed libraries with limited-resources challenges in terms of subscriptions. Cooperative acquisitions policies within groups of libraries have become increasingly popular, but the long-term future of such arrangements must pose interesting dilemmas.

2   Recognition of the **international nature of document delivery** will have greater impact. All of the agencies mentioned in this chapter function as international organizations. As the number of countries to which services are delivered increases, so the complexity of operating across cultural boundaries, languages, legal systems and currencies will become a more significant business reality for a greater number of players in the document delivery business.

3   **Technological developments** which accommodate the retrieval and delivery of documents in image formats such as .PDF files, rather than the use of ASCII files as intermediaries and as the basis for searching and retrieval, will represent important changes.

4   **The shift from holdings- to access-based policies** has to some extent been fuelled by the changes in the economics of journal acquisitions. This has led to a greater demand for channels for accessing information, including electronic document delivery services, electronic journals, and other Internet-based services that have been described in this chapter.

5   Fundamental questions associated with the **roles of authors**, and in particular academic authors, and publishers remain to be answered. For example, if academic authors can receive recognition by circulation of their contributions through an 'invisible college' without formal publication, authors may cease to submit their articles to publishers. Publishers are concerned about their future role, and are currently engaged in a number of experiments with electronic journals and other ways of adding value to the information or doc-

uments created by authors. There is a significant and useful role for publishers here, but they may be challenged in some aspects of this role by agents that are accustomed to working with a number of publishers, such as serials subscription agents, and whose strengths lie in a more diverse collection of documents than simply journals.

6 **Each network or consortium is unique,** offering different services to participating libraries with different requirements and clientele. It is therefore difficult to identify likely future trends for networking. There are a number of national and international utilities offering different services, some of which overlap one another in the services that they provide and the markets for which they are provided. Some of these utilities are interdependent and rely upon the products of other networks or centralized cataloguing agencies. The potential for networking is great. The nature, role and evolution of the networks and consortia will not be constrained by technological factors, but rather by social and political issues..

7 **Integrated and wider catalogue access amongst libraries.** Already, library users can access the OPACs of other libraries, but the overall process has many discontinuities. Full access implies libraries acting as a group, with both OPACs and document delivery appearing seamless to the user; the user should not need to think about the location of the document.

8 Much of the debate around electronic documents has focused on journals. Delivery of some categories of books, such as encyclopaedias, dictionaries and directories, has already migrated to CD-ROM. Many of these products attract a consumer market, and the pricing and access issues that are important in that marketplace will determine the future mode of delivery for such documents. Libraries will need to accommodate appropriate electronic access to these documents alongside, say, access to bibliographic databases and electronic journals.

9 **Current-awareness services** are already a feature of many electronic journal publishers and subscriptions agents. Current-awareness services are increasingly likely to be viewed as an added-value service that is offered free in order to encourage access to specific databases or collections. They are a marketing window or opportunity. The services offered by the subscription agents are quite powerful in that they cover a range of publishers. But possibly there is a need for a meta-service that scans the content of several such services and offers a more integrated current-awareness service for individual users; it may be that this might be subject-based, offering, for example, SDI profiles in the areas of biochemistry or psychology.

10 Finally, elsewhere in this book there has been occasional reference to the need to revisit our understanding of a document. **What is an electronic document?**

Reflection In what sense is this book one document, rather than a collection of separate documents identified by the separate chapters?

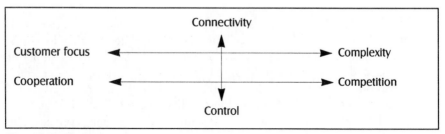

Fig. 15.5 *The six Cs*

In conclusion

The channels and avenues for document delivery described in this chapter embrace both electronic and print document delivery. Document delivery is at the heart of the hybrid library or, in the library without walls, hybrid information management at individual, systems, organizational and societal levels. The challenges for information management in this environment are summarized in Figure 15.5.

There is the tension between connectivity and control. Connectivity provides wider access to information, but such widened access must be accompanied by decisions about who and how individuals can access specific information or documents This implies attention to security, permission and pricing structures.

The drive towards customer focus, and the opportunities that technology offers for more user-friendly products which are targeted to meet the requirements of a specific group, is continuously challenged by the complexity inherent in the information marketplace. Individual products have become more user-friendly though improved interfaces, appropriate support and simplified pricing structures. Individual products may be user-friendly, but the increasing plethora of products in a variety of electronic forms, and in print form, all with different access routes and pricing strategies, must make for complexity in access to information.

Organizations that are involved in the creation of information products and services, often need to resolve the tension between cooperation and competition. They may be exhorted by government initiatives to cooperate, and indeed cooperation and strategic alliances may make commercial sense in relation to vertical partnerships or, for example, the exchange of bibliographic records. On the other hand, these organizations must be in competition for the market associated with the delivery of documents and other information services to users. The tensions that this creates may be all the more difficult to manage in a rapidly changing environment, where technological innovation may eliminate the need for certain roles in the supply chain, or merge some of those roles into a new role.

Summary   Document delivery has always been at the heart of the services offered by libraries, publishers and others in the information industry to their users. Document delivery needs to embrace the delivery of both print and electronic documents. Although mechanisms for print delivery are well established, these have been made more efficient through the introduction of electronic ordering. There has been rapid development in recent years in electronic document delivery, particularly in relation to electronic journals. There are a number of different agents in document delivery. These include:

- library networks and consortia, including national libraries and document delivery services, the central focus of these networks being resource sharing and the creation of shared bibliographic and catalogue databases, though they also offer a range of other added-value services such as library management systems and online search services
- document delivery on CD-ROM, which is particularly appropriate in the context of books, encyclopaedias and other lengthy documents
- commercial document delivery services, which often operate in alliances with online search services, and draw on the resources of a number of other libraries
- library suppliers and serials subscription agents, who have used networks and EDI to improve the document ordering process and associated processes such as alerting, invoicing and book processing
- electronic journal suppliers and publishers; there is currently a limited number of e-journals, but significant interest in the digitization of journals that have been previously distributed in printed form.

REVIEW QUESTIONS

1   Explain the difference between print-based document delivery and electronic document delivery

2   List the criteria that might differentiate between different types of document delivery service.
3   Explain the role of national libraries and document delivery services in document delivery.
4   Describe some of the features that you would expect to find in an electronic ordering service based on EDI that might be available from a library book supplier.
5   Review the role of the commercial document delivery services.
6   Discuss the key questions for libraries associated with the transition from print based journals to electronic journals.

Reference

Barnes, J. (1997) 'Electronic archives: an essential element in complete electronic journals solution', *Information services and use*, **17**, 37–7.

Bibliography

Adams, R. (1991) *Communication and delivery systems for librarians*, Aldershot, Gower,.
Anonymous (1988) 'ADONIS: a new era in document delivery', *Interlending and document supply*, **16** (2), 65–9.
Anonymous (1997) *Report on Phase 1 of the evaluation of the UK Pilot Site License Initiative*, Bristol, Commonwealth Higher Education Management Service.
Barwick, M. (1997) 'Interlending and document supply: a review of recent literature – XXXII', *Interlending and document supply*, **25** (3), 126–32.
Basch, R. (1995) *Electronic information delivering: ensuing quality and value*, Aldershot, Gower.
Blunden-Ellis, J. (1997) 'LAMDA: a project investigating new opportunities in document delivery', *Program*, **30**, 385–90.
Boss, R. W. (1990) 'Linked systems and the online catalog: the role of OSI', *Library resources and technical services*, **34** (2), 217–28.
Boyd, N. (1997) 'Towards access services: supply times, quality control and performance related services', *Interlending and document supply*, **25** (3), 118–23.
Braid, A. (1996) 'Standardisation in electronic document delivery: a practical example', *Interlending and document supply*, **24** (2), 12–18.
Brown, D. J. (1996) Electronic publishing and libraries: panning for the impact and growth to 2003, London, Bowker-Saur.
Buckland, M. K. and Lynch, C. A. (1988) 'National and international implications of the Linked Systems Protocol for online bibliographic systems', *Cataloging and classification quarterly*, **8** (3/4), 15–33.
Campbell, R. M. and Stern, B. (1987) 'ADONIS: a new approach to document delivery', *Microcomputers for information management*, **4** (2), 87–107.

Cawkell, A. E. (1991) 'Electronic document supply systems', *Journal of documentation*, **47** (1), 41–73.

Compier, H. and Campbell, R. (1995) 'ADONIS gathers momentum and faces some problems', *Interlending and document supply*, **23** (3), 22–5.

Cousins, S. A. (1997) 'COPAC: the new national OPAC service based on the CURL database', *Program*, **31** (1), 1–21.

Greenaway, J. (1997) 'Interlending and document supply in Australia: the way forward', *Interlending and document supply*, **25** (3), 103–7.

Dempsey, L. (1991) *Libraries networks and OSI: a review with a report on North American developments*, Bath, UK Office for Library Networking.

Harnard, S. (1995) 'Implementing per review on the net' in Peek, R. and Newby, G. (eds.) *Academia and electronic publishing : confronting the year 2000*, ASIS Monograph, Cambridge, MA, MIT Press, 121–32.

Hyams, E. and Green, B. (1992) 'Bringing systems to book: EDI in the book world', *Library and information briefings*, **31**.

Kelly, P. (1996) 'IRIS: study in cooperation, collaboration and funding in the information field', *Serials*, **9** (3), 227–81.

Ker, M. (1997) 'NewsAgent for libraries', *Vine*, **104**, 51–3.

Kidd, T. (1997) 'Electronic journals management: some problems and solutions', *Managing information*, **4** (10) 25–6.

Landes, S. (1997) 'ARIEL document delivery : A cost effective alternative to fax', *Interlending and document supply*, **25** (3), 113–7.

Larbey, D. (1997) 'Project EDDIS: an approach to integrating document discovery, location, request and supply', *Interlending and document supply*, **25** (3), 96–102.

Larbey, D. (1997) *Electronic document delivery* (Library and Information Briefing 77/78), London, Library and information Technology Centre.

Morrow, T. (1997) 'BIDS and electronic publishing', *Information services use*, **17**, 53–60.

Moulto, R. and Tuck, B. (1994) 'Document delivery using X.400 electronic mail', *Journal of information networking*, **1** (3), 191–203.

Pilling, S. (1994) 'The ADONIS experience: some views', Serials, 7 (3), 249–52.

Pullinger, D. (1994) 'Journals published on the Net', *Serials*, 7 (3), 243–8.

Pullinger, D. (1994) *The SuperJournal Project: electronic journals on SuperJANET*, (London Report no 6126) London, Institute of Physics Publishing.

Pullinger, D. and Howey, K. (1984) 'The development of the References, Abstracts and Annotations Journal on the BLEND system', *Journal of librarianship*, **16** (1), 19–33.

Rowland, F., McKnight, C. and Meadows, J. (eds.) (1995) *Project EVLYN*, London, Bowker Saur.

Shackel, B. (1991) *BLEND-9: Overview and appraisal (British Library research paper 82)*, London, British Library.

Stone, P. (1990) *JANET: a report on its use for libraries,* (British Library research paper 77), London, British Library Research and Development Department.

Tuck, B. (1997) 'Document delivery in an electronic world', *Interlending and document supply,* **25** (1), 11–17.

Tuck, W., McKnight, C., Hayet, M. and Archer, D. (1990) *Project quartet. (Library and information research report 76),* London, British Library.

Turner, F. (1995) 'Document ordering standards: the ILL protocol and Z39.50 item order', *Library hi-tech,* **13** (3), 25–38.

Wiesner, M. (1997) 'EDI between libraries and their suppliers: requirements and first experience based on the EDILIBE project', *Program,* **31** (2), 115–29.

Wusteman, J. (1996) 'Electronic journal formats', *Program,* **30** (4), 319–43.

Index

Note: All significant concepts are indexed, but names are only indexed where they refer to case studies, figures or other significant content. Where names of online search services and databases etc. are cited as examples only, their occurrence in the text is not indexed.